North of the DMZ

North of the DMZ

Essays on Daily Life in North Korea

ANDREI LANKOV

McFarland & Company, Inc., Publishers
Jefferson, North Carolina, and London

All essays were originally published by the *Korea Times,* except for "On Cheeses and Other Matters," "North Korea's Missionary Position," "On Disappearing Maidens and Fisherfolk," "To Market, To Market" and "Women on Top," which were originally published by the *Asia Times.* The essays are reprinted here by permission of the *Korea Times* and the *Asia Times.*

LIBRARY OF CONGRESS CATALOGUING-IN-PUBLICATION DATA

Lan',kov, A. N. (Andrei Nikolaevich)
    North of the DMZ : essays on daily life in North Korea / Andrei Lankov.
        p.   cm.
    Includes bibliographical references and index.

    ISBN-13: 978-0-7864-2839-7
    (softcover : 50# alkaline paper) ∞

    1. Korea (North)—Social conditions.   2. Korea (North)— Politics and government.   I. Title.
    HN730.6.A8L35   2007
    951.9304'3 — dc22   2007004634

British Library cataloguing data are available

On the cover: *foreground* Military Demarcation Line sign; *background* The next generation *(photo by Bernard Seiler)*

Manufactured in the United States of America

McFarland & Company, Inc., Publishers
    Box 611, Jefferson, North Carolina 28640
    www.mcfarlandpub.com

To my mother,
Valentina Lankova (Algazina)

Contents

Part 18. The Unnoticed Death of North Korean Stalinism

Preface

WHEN I ARRIVED IN NORTH KOREA for the first time on a sunny day in September 1984, I felt perplexed. I came to study at the Kim Il Sung University, as a participant in an exchange program between the then–USSR and North Korea. It was the first overseas trip of my life, and I was thrilled, but I also had some preconceived ideas — and in the first hours and days it became clear that the situation did not feel like I thought it should.

At that time I was fully aware that I was in what in 1984 was arguably the world's most brutal dictatorship. The Soviet Union was not exactly a democracy itself, but even for us, the people from Moscow and Leningrad, North Korea stood for the embodiment of inefficiency, brutality and, above all, repressive dictatorship. Even the official Soviet media sometimes allowed some subtle hints at what was going on there.

However, in those bright September days I did not see many traces of terror and repression. It definitely did not look like an Orwellian nightmare coming alive. Pretty women, dressed in modest but often cute and tasteful attire, smiled and chatted. Self-important clerks and minor bureaucrats proceeded to their offices. Old ladies walked the streets accompanied by their grandchildren. Students rushed to classes. Kids played. In short, everything looked perfectly normal — with the probable exception of the militant marches and nearly hysterical slogans which erupted from the loudspeakers placed almost everywhere, and omnipresent soldiers with Kalashnikov assault rifles. But otherwise, it seemed as if normal life was going on around me — contrary to my earlier expectations.

Indeed, it was. I was naïve, so I failed to understand one simple truth: even under the most repressive of social and political conditions, the vast majority of people still attempt to live normal lives and generally succeed at it. These lives include work and leisure, love and friendship — with not that

1

much space left for politics. There was a lot of political repression going on in 1984 North Korea, to be sure, but this repression constituted only a relatively small part of this country's daily life.

Most people's lives remain nearly untouched by high politics, and in the case of North Korea these "non-political" aspects of human existence are much underreported and underestimated. One cannot complain that North Korea in general does not receive enough attention. In recent decades, North Korea is much talked about in the international media. Actually, it is probably talked about much more than it should be: after all, North Korea is nothing but a small and grossly underdeveloped dictatorship, whose population size and major economic indicators are roughly similar to those of Mozambique.

There are two reasons which make North Korea that strangely prominent: the game of nuclear blackmail which the Pyongyang diplomats are playing with uncanny skill, and the fact of North Korea's survival against all odds as the world's last die-hard Communist (some would say Stalinist) regime.

The survival of the Kims' communist monarchy indeed can be seen as nearly miraculous, but it has deep roots in how the North Korean society is structured and how it has functioned for decades. For many decades, North Korea has been the world's most perfect specimen of a Stalinist society. Stalin remained in full control of Russia for merely 25 years, interrupted by a major war, and he had about a decade to perfect his system. The Kims' dynasty has ruled North Korea for over 60 years, of which at least the 35–40 years between 1955 and 1994 were a time of "mature Stalinism." Only a fraction of North Koreans have any memory of any other life, and at least two generations have grown up in the fully Stalinist society.

Things have changed greatly over the last decade, and nowadays North Korea cannot be really described as a "Stalinist country," but the inertia of police surveillance and the general fear of terror helped the regime to carry on even under the most adverse circumstances. Of course, a lot of other factors have contributed to North Korean survival, not least the dramatic changes in position of Seoul, whose elite, terrified by the lessons of German unification, seemingly chose to keep North Korea afloat for Seoul's own sake — and often on Seoul's money. However, the internal structure of North Korean society was also important in preventing any kind of reforms and revolutions.

North Korea fascinated me from the time of my first trip there, so I have been studying it for nearly two decades, starting from the times when the world paid this country scarcely more attention than it did (and still does) to Mozambique. Apart from purely academic publications on North Korea's early history, I also wrote columns for the *Korea Times*, the major English-language daily in Seoul, and these columns became the basis of the book you see now. In most cases columns have been seriously re-written and updated, and a few pieces in a similar vein but initially written for different publications (mostly the *Asia Times*) are also included in this book.

Perhaps, to give my readers a better understanding of what to expect from this volume, I should start by making clear what this book is *not* about. It is not about international politics, since there are so many accounts — good, bad and mediocre — on how the North Koreans conduct negotiations and what are the supposed targets of their foreign policy. It is not about North Korea's Dear Leader Marshall Kim Jong Il, the Benevolent Sun of the 21st Century — we have had enough of both professional profiling and amateur psychology, and people interested in such issues can easily find material to their liking. It is not about speculations on how and when the two Koreas will unite — the present author does have some strong opinions on this issue, but definitely lacks a crystal ball of suitable quality. Most emphatically, this book is not about the nuclear issue, which has been discussed in countless publications, easily available in our wired days.

First and foremost, this book is about the world the North Koreans themselves have created and have to live in. Some of the features of this world are truly bizarre and unique, while some others are familiar from the experience of other countries and some are just, well, "normal." To not a small extent, this world is of their own creation, and reflects their own ideals and values with which we do not necessarily agree. But to a large extent, the world was forced on them by the system which might have been quite popular initially, but eventually became nearly independent of people's wishes and hopes. At any rate, this is the only world they know, and the experiences and assumptions inherent to this world influence everything, including the way the North Korean diplomats conduct negotiations and reasons why Pyongyang chose to acquire nuclear weapons.

As will be clear from this book, the North Koreans' world is remarkably political and politicized. However, North Korea is not a country inhabited by goose-stepping fighting machines, even if this is the image its own leaders seemingly try to project to overseas audiences. Neither is it a paradise full of smiling workers, happy peasant girls and joyful children, even if the North Koreans do smile — like everybody does. This is a poor country run by a repressive regime, but this is also a place where 23 million people live their lives, and these lives, while constantly influenced and permeated by politics, still include much more than politics.

Hence, this book tells about North Korean society, about its mores and norms and about the historic changes which have taken place over recent decades. I will dwell on small things, from train tickets to radio programs, and also on things not so small, like the distribution of foodstuffs in North Korean cities. The book will show how the North Korean system is seen from inside, and how it normally functions. It will also tell about foreigners whose lives came to be influenced by North Korean affairs, be they privileged and closely watched diplomats in Pyongyang, kidnapped South Korean civilians, or Japanese revolutionary idealists who flew themselves to the supposed workers' paradise in a hijacked plane. Finally, it will treat at some length the deep and important changes which have happened in North Korea over the last decade. These changes were indeed of great significance since they amounted to the quiet — and generally unnoticed — collapse of Juche Stalinism.

So far, there has been only one book in English which familiarized Western readers with the daily life and problems of North Koreans — *Kim Il Song's North Korea* by Helen-Louise Hunter. However, this book was written nearly 15 years ago, and reflects the situation of the 1980s. Since then many things have changed, not least our access to the internal information about the country.

Nowadays we know much more. The presence of a small but significant defectors' community in South Korea, crowds of easily accessible refugees in China, the growth of Pyongyang's international contacts, the activity of foreign NGOs and aid agencies inside the North, including the country's remote countryside areas — all mean that North Korea, while still remarkably secretive, cannot be seen as a "black box" any more. The present book is based on a study of all these newly available sources, including, first of all, interviews with defectors, which are now very easy to arrange.

North Korea is changing, even though these changes are not that highly visible to outsiders. However, there is a major difference between North Korea and other once Communist countries, like China or Russia. From what we know, it seems that North Korea is not changing because a reform policy has been initiated by some farsighted leaders. Its system is now slowly disintegrating from below. But the result is all the same: North Korean Stalinism is dying.

It seems that the cruel social experiment which was forced on the North Koreans in the 1940s is coming to an end. But over the decades, countless millions of lives have been spent in this unusual society, and this book tells how these lives were lived — and, to some extent, are still lived.

I would like to express my gratitude to Dr. Brian Myers, Dr. Kim Sŏk-hyang, and Dr. Pak Sŭng-je who found time to look through the manuscript and provided me with numerous suggestions. My very special thanks are reserved for Mr. Han Yŏng-jin, a North Korean defector and journalist, with whom I went through most of the text and verified numerous queries. I also would like to thank the personnel of the *DailyNK* newspaper (both South Koreans and former defectors) who answered many queries. I am also very thankful to a few defector friends and colleagues who prefer not to be named.

My special thanks are for Darrell Dorrington and James Greenbaum, who edited the newspaper texts and then had a look through the book manuscript. I express my sincere gratitude to my friends, colleagues and supporters of the project who provided me with photo materials: Christopher Morris, Andrew Graham, Paul Bekker, Ng Han Guan, Bernd Seiler, Martin Williams, Peter Crowcroft, Anna Fifield.

PART 1

Leaders Dear and Great...

The Sacral Badges

IN THE LATE 1970S AND 1980S North Korean students could occasionally be seen on the streets of my native Leningrad. It was never difficult to tell them from, say, Chinese or Vietnamese students. The Kim Il Sung badge was the telltale sign, even if a majority of Russians were sure that those strange Asians were Chinese (the guy on the badge must be Mao, who else?).

However, even in the crazy days of Mao's mad cult, the Chinese were not required to wear the Great Helmsman's badges. Once again, North Korea was exceptional in its zeal for the personality cult — perhaps because Kim stayed in power far longer than Mao or Stalin, and also because he controlled a much smaller country.

At any rate, the Kim Il Sung badge tradition is unique. It was introduced in the 1970s, when the cult of the Great Leader reached its height. In 1972 North Korea was staging a pompous celebration of Kim Il Sung's sixtieth birthday. Around that time, one of the top officials came up with a bright idea: he suggested the introduction of badges with Kim's portrait on them, and made them obligatory for everyone. From November 1970, the mass production of these badges began, and by the great day, April 15, 1972, every adult North Korean was proudly displaying the likeness of Kim Il Sung on his or her chest.

The badge is handed to its bearer when he or she turns 12, to be placed above their Children's Union badge. From that age, North Koreans are required to wear the Kim Il Sung badge whenever they leave home (fortunately, in the privacy of one's own home it is not considered necessary — Kim Il Sung's portrait hangs in every room, and this suffices). If a person dares to venture out

The Kim Il Sung badges should be worn always, everywhere, by everybody. Photograph by Christopher Morris.

without the obligatory badge, the transgression is discussed at the next mutual criticism session — not really a pleasant option as criticism sessions can be quite an unpleasant affair, even now in the generally relaxed atmosphere of the early 2000s.

Badges come in a number of shapes, there being some twenty different types. Each type speaks volumes about its bearer. The most precious and rare type depicts Kim Il Sung and Kim Jong Il against the background of a large red banner. This is the only badge which has images of both the Dear and Great leaders, and it is extremely rare. These badges are assigned to top-level party functionaries, and the very sight of someone wearing such a badge can send many a minor North Korean bureaucrat into a stupor. Another type of badge which depicts Kim Jong Il (alone, without his father) is worn by the cadres in the security system. With the exception of these two badges, both quite rare, all others sport Kim Il Sung alone.

There are different types for military personnel, for *Saroch'ŏng* (Party Youth) members, and so on. For example, lower-level party cadres sport the so-called "large round badge," while lesser beings, North Korean commoners, are only eligible to wear the "small round badges."

Of course, relying solely on a badge to identify the position of the wearer could be fraught with difficulty, since a typical North Korean might have a number of different badges. A top bureaucrat today may once have been first a student, then a soldier, and so on. Nonetheless, in many cases the badges can be seen as an insignia of a sort which can demonstrate the social status of the bearer to everyone who is knowledgeable enough (as most North Koreans are).

The badges are designed and produced by the Mansudae creative group. This is a unique institution whose sole task is to manufacture the likenesses of Kim Il Sung, Kim Jong Il, and their family members.

Many foreigners who do not comprehend the near mystic importance attached to the badge by the North Korean official ideology, try to purchase the badge from their North Korean acquaintances. Naturally such outrageous proposals are usually rejected. After all, the badge is a symbol of loyalty, an icon in its own right. Even if, in the depth of their hearts, North Koreans do not worship the Leader as a deity, they are not supposed to let on to foreigners — this would be far too risky! What is more, the loss of the badge is seen as an almost criminal act, an act which could inflict serious damage on the culprit's career opportunities.

This does not mean, however, that the badges cannot be bought and sold — they occasionally appear on the international collectors' market, obviously smuggled via China or some other tortuous route. There were rumors that some Chinese workshops even began to produce imitations, targeting the foreign visitors of the borderland areas.

In recent days, with the de facto victory of the market economy, the badges can be purchased within North Korea as well. As one can easily guess, the "party banner badges" with portraits of Kim Il Sung and Kim Jong Il are by far the most expensive. In the early 2000s such a badge could command at least 5,000 won or $25–$30 at the then exchange rate — in other words, between six and twelve monthly salaries. Some other "special" badges can be sold at a high price, too. But this is understandable; a person with such a badge will be treated with the utmost deference by his or her fellow countrymen! The "better" types of badges recently became the target of petty thieves whose numbers grossly increased during the famine of 1996–1999.

Some younger North Koreans use the badges as a fashion statement. I remember that in the 1980s it was fashionable among Korean youth to clip the badge to the very edge of their dress. And we know from the tales of defectors that the badges are frequently an integral part of the latest fashion craze.

With the advent of famine and the gradual decline of the government's ability to control the population, a small but increasing number of Koreans have begun to venture outside without their badges or, at least, without displaying their badges prominently. This relaxed attitude was finally confirmed in 2004 when some sources reported that North Koreans were now allowed *not* to wear badges. But it seems that most still prefer to cling to the old routine. It's safer: who knows what will happen in the future, after all? So it does not hurt to continue to display one's unbending loyalty and affection.

Sooner or later, the badges will indeed become a collectors' item, but hardly an expensive one (the few special types being the exception). Too many of them have been produced....

Names for the Earthly God

IN JULY 1997, THE FIVE MOST important government agencies of North Korea — including the Central Committee and Cabinet of Ministers — published a joint declaration which informed North Korea and the entire world that the country was introducing a new calendar. The year 1912 became the First Year of *Juche*. The reason? This was the year when Kim Il Sung was born.

The decision allowed the occasional use of Christian era years, but this four-digit number had to accompany the new official date only if it was deemed necessary. Thus 2005 A.D. is the Year 94 of the *Juche* Era. In other words, Kim Il Sung's birthday replaced that of Christ in the official North Korean calendar. Indeed, this is how the dates are written now in North Korean publications, although in everyday discourse people still use Western (or Christian) era dates.

The world has seen other attempts to break with old calendar traditions. In France of the 1790s, the revolutionaries began to count years from the proclamation of the French Republic. In South Korea of the 1950s, the government tried to implement the so-called Tangun Era. None of these attempts succeeded for more than a few decades — and there are few doubts that the same fate awaits the *Juche* Era.

However, the decision to introduce the *Juche* Era was just one of several manifestations of Kim Il Sung's posthumous "personality cult." Indeed, the memory of North Korea's founding father is treated in Pyongyang with utmost respect. Perhaps this is what he intended when he appointed his elder son as the heir designate. One of the reasons behind the unusual decision to introduce a Communist monarchy might have been Kim Senior's fear that the next generation of leaders would treat his memory in the same way as the memory of Stalin was treated in the Soviet Union in the 1960s. Being his son, Kim Jong Il has a vested interest in upholding his father's image — and this is what he is actually doing with the greatest enthusiasm.

First of all, Kim Il Sung is to remain the country's only president, under the title of Chusŏk ("chairman," first introduced in 1972). After his death, the President's office was left vacant — and is meant to remain vacant forever. Kim Jong Il runs the country not as President, but merely as the "Chairman" of the National Defense Committee."

Of course, portraits of Kim Il Sung are everywhere, albeit often accompanied by the images of Kim Jong Il and his mother Kim Jong Suk. From the late 1960s, the North Korean bureaucracy has developed intricate rules which determine where and how Kim Il Sung's likeness has to be displayed. I'll tell about these rules later. For now it is sufficient to say that every living room,

Yŏngsaengt'ap or "Tower of eternal life" in Pyongyang. It states that "Kim Il Sung will live with us forever." Photograph by Andrei Lankov.

↓ creepy

every office, and the entrance to every official building as well as every railway carriage has been adorned with the portrait of the Leader from the 1970s. After 1980, it was complemented by the portrait of his son as well.

An important part of Kim Il Sung's posthumous glorification are the numerous Yŏngsaengt'ap, or "Towers of Eternal Life." Their name reflects the official slogan: "Kim Il Sung will live with us forever!" (Obviously, there

Cult!

is an influence from one of the most popular Soviet-era slogans in Russia, which said: "Lenin lived, Lenin lives, Lenin will live with us!") These towers have a shape slightly reminiscent of Ancient Egypt's obelisks and they are decorated with this slogan about Kim's alleged "eternal presence" in his realm.

As of 1997, there were 3,150 Towers of Eternal Life nationwide. Such towers were to be erected in every city, every province, every county and every shire, so there must be some 5,000 of them by now. The towers are normally placed on the crossroads in the most central locations. The structures are usually relatively cheap and easy to build, but some of them are quite expensive. The largest of all towers is, of course, located in Pyongyang. It has a height of 92.5 meters — just a bit lower than the *Juche* Tower, one of the city's major architectural monuments.

The Towers of Eternal Life are objects of regular and well-organized pilgrimage. They are to be visited on official holidays and on the anniversary of the Great Leader's death, to serve as a place of vows of loyalty to the regime and its founder.

Kim Il Sung's body has been embalmed and left on public display in a special glass-covered coffin. Actually, in this regard, Korea follows an established — if bizarre — Communist tradition. Like many other Communist traditions, this one originated from the USSR.

In 1924, the body of Vladimir Lenin, the founding father of the Soviet Union, was laid in a specially constructed mausoleum where it was kept in a glass-covered coffin. This mausoleum became a place of mass pilgrimage. Initially most visitors may have been driven by sincere devotion, but in later decades the major impulse bringing visitors was, more likely than not, just bizarre curiosity. Nonetheless, passions sometimes ran high. In the Soviet times, there were two known attempts to damage Lenin's mummy in an act of symbolic resistance against the regime. On the other hand, the post–Communist Russian government has not dared to close the mausoleum, being aware that such an act is certain to spark large-scale protests and riots of the Russian Left.

In the Soviet times, a special and highly secretive research institute with a generous budget was responsible for the maintenance of Lenin's body. Over the decades, its research staff gained unique expertise. In due time this expertise was in demand for new generations of the venerable dead.

In 1949, the Bulgarian Communist leader Dmitrov became the first person to be embalmed by the personnel of Lenin's mausoleum. After Stalin's death in 1953 the body of the Soviet dictator was also treated with this proven technique and put alongside Lenin's mummy. However, in 1961 Stalin's corpse was hastily removed from the mausoleum, to be buried below the Kremlin wall.

Meanwhile, Soviet experts were sent to take care of a number of politically important corpses across the world. They embalmed the bodies of a number of other Communist rulers: Choibalsan of Mongolia, Gottwald of Czechoslovakia, Ho Chi Minh of Vietnam, Netto of Angola (Mao's body was treated by the Chinese themselves).

Thus, when in 1994 Kim Il Sung died, few people doubted that his body would be put on display as well. The Russians confirmed that they had taken part in treating Kim Il Sung's body. According to unconfirmed reports a group of Russian biologists and chemists worked in Pyongyang for almost a year.

In the 1950s and 1960s Moscow did not charge its clients and allies for treating the bodies of their deceased rulers. But this is not the case any more. After the collapse of the Communist system in Russia, the research center has had to survive on a very tight budget, and it is not willing to provide its unique know-how for free. Incidentally, these laboratories' major income source is now the bodies of Mafia bosses or new Russian capitalists (it was not really easy to distinguish between the former and the latter in the Russia of the 1990s).

The fees for treating the earthly remains of the Great Leader, the Sun of the Nation, were never disclosed, but the Russians reportedly charged North Korea one million dollars. Frankly, this was a steal: Kim Il Sung died at the time when the former USSR was in the middle of its severest crisis, and ex–Soviet scientists were ready to accept meager rewards for their work. Nonetheless, this deal was made at the time when North Korea was on the eve of the worst famine in Korea's history. The final result of the scientists' efforts was the mummy of Kim Il Sung which, incidentally, cannot be referred to as a "mummy" but only "the eternal image of the Great Leader."

However, the million-dollar fee is only a fraction of the ongoing cost of keeping Kim Il Sung's body well preserved. A few years ago a high-level North Korean bureaucrat mentioned to visiting Indonesians that North Korea paid about 800,000 dollars annually for these expenses. On might surmise that at least a part of this money goes to the budget of the same Soviet research centre which once did the embalming.

In one respect the North Koreans did not emulate other Communist countries. The bodies of Lenin, Mao, and Ho Chi Minh were laid in mausoleums specially constructed for that purpose. The North Koreans did not erect a new structure but renovated a pre-existing building, the Kŭmsusan Palace. This large structure was erected on the outskirts of Pyongyang in the mid–1970s. In subsequent decades it served as the residence and office of Kim Il Sung. Now this building's huge central hall became the Great Leader's resting place.

Unlike the USSR, where visits to Lenin's tomb are essentially voluntary acts, the North Koreans are picked by their party secretaries to visit the Kŭmsusan Palace. Most of them, admittedly, do not mind going — partially out of curiosity and partially out of sincere reverence to the deceased strongman.

For the past few years, crowds of North Koreans have passed by the body of the Great Leader who, for better or worse, ran their country for almost half a century. The visitors are required to stop for a while and bow to the glass-covered coffin containing the embalmed body. The dim lights and quiet music emphasize the quasi-religious nature of the entire scene. The visitors pay their tribute to a person who once started the worst war in Korean history, killed at least a quarter of a million people in prisons and ran what even in the Communist world was seen as an exceptionally repressive state.

Indeed, many (I would say, most) North Koreans more or less believed in what the official propaganda told them about the Great Man. All Koreans younger than 70 have spent their entire life listening to stories about Kim Il Sung's greatness. He is supposed to be the person who defeated the Japanese in 1945, then repelled U.S. aggression in 1950 and, by keeping the cunning imperialists at bay for decades, saved North Koreans from the sorry fate of their enslaved Southern brethren. Of course, outside the North it is common knowledge that Kim Il Sung did not fire a single shot during the liberation of Korea, that the Korean war was started by him and nearly lost due to his miscalculations, that South Korea had one of the fastest growing economies of the 20th century while the North became an international basket case. But these things remain largely or completely unknown inside the North, where many people still believe in the deceased Great Fatherly Leader.

The downward spiral which the country's economy entered soon after Kim Il Sung's death has also helped to boost the posthumous standing of the Great Leader. After all, rations were coming when he was alive, and everybody enjoyed his or her 600 or 700g of rice a day. This might not sound luxurious to us, but few North Koreans knew any other life. What they know is that after 1994 things changed for the worse, and this is probably seen as a good reason to pay tribute to the dead Leader.

Carved in Rock

IMAGINE YOURSELF CLIMBING A scenic mountain somewhere in North Korea. You are surrounded by the breathtaking magnificence of peaks covered with white clouds and the lush greenness of mountain forests. And then you notice

The stones carved with odes to commemorate the "three great generals of the Paektu mountain"—Kim Il Sung, Kim Jong Il and Kim Jong-suk (Kim Jong Il's mother). Photograph by Andrei Lankov.

that one of the peaks is adorned with huge scarlet characters which are clearly visible from miles away. The inscription reads: "Long live the Great Leader" or "Hasten to battle!" or "Long live the Korean Workers' Party" or some other equally poetic statement!

Indeed, even the picturesque Korean mountains are not spared from being used as a propaganda medium. Slogans are carved out in huge letters in the most beautiful parts of the Korean mountains. There is perhaps no peak left in the Kŭmgangsan and Myohyangsan gorges which does not sport such a stimulating inscription as "Let's transform ideology, technology and culture according to *Juche*!"

The North Korean authorities have developed a sophisticated technology to further beautify the country's famous scenery. The slogans are not simply painted on the slopes. They are actually first carved deep into the rocks by teams of stonemasons. These stonemasons are selected from among model workers, and their job is seen as prestigious and full of perks — even if occasionally dangerous! The selfless devotion of these stonemasons has even been reflected in some North Korean movies. The carved slogans are then painted bright red, ensuring that they are visible from afar.

This frantic stone-cutting activity began in 1972 when North Korea celebrated Kim Il Sung's 60th birthday with hitherto unprecedented pomp. Now this activity is explained as yet another brilliant invention of General Kim Jong Il, but in the earlier stages the credit for the idea used to go to Kim Il Sung himself. Indeed, Kim Il Sung once remarked: "It would be nice to carve out some good inscriptions on the rocks for future generations!"

This is not to deny Kim Jong Il's involvement. In August 1973 he visited the Kŭmgangsan mountains and personally supervised the carving of the first inscriptions which honored his father's "immortal achievements."

A North Korean historian describes this campaign in the following terms (the quotation affords a glimpse into the modern North Korean academic style):

"Having wholeheartedly perceived the wise instructions of the Great Leader and the Dear Leader, party members and all working people rose to struggle to carve out inscriptions which would last for ten thousand generations. To this end, a 'youth shock detachment' was formed from Party Youth members and other young people who were helped by voluntary groups of workers. The members of the rapid combat detachment and helpers from the local population, inspired by a feeling of fiery devotion to the Great Leader, by February 1982 had created in Kŭmgangsan 61 carvings (3690 characters). In their scale and their deep ideological content they are not paralleled anywhere in the world [indeed!—A.L.]. Thus, the inscription '*Juche*' on Ch'on'yŏn rock is 27 meters high, 8 meters wide, while its characters are 1.2 meters deep."

In the early 1990s, this inscription was surpassed by yet another one, also located in the Kŭmgangsan mountains. In Korean, Kim Il Sung's name is depicted by three characters, and each of the three was carved in stone 20 meters long and 16 meters wide, with strokes up to 2 meters broad. What makes things worse is the depth of the carving, which is 0.9 meters. Even if the paint is scrubbed off, such a huge inscription cannot be removed without a trace — it is now probably there forever!

The entire activity is supervised by the Institute of Party History, which is subordinated to the Central Committee. The Institute officials choose the sites for new inscriptions as well as their content. Nobody knows for sure how many stunningly beautiful rocks have been "adorned" by this Institute, but recently North Korean officials boasted that they had inscribed some 20,000 characters nationwide!

One must admit that the North Korean penchant for "beautifying the scenery" has some historic roots. It is in line with East Asian tradition, since carving out poetry on a suitable rock has long been the norm for rich travellers (i.e., those who could afford to hire stonemasons to do the job!). However, these old inscriptions were quite small, and blended in with the environment, especially since they were essentially unofficial in nature. They are a far cry from Kim Il Sung's modern propaganda art.

The carved inscriptions are both conspicuous and virtually indestructible. Nothing short of dynamiting the mountains will erase them, and plastering them over is also unlikely to be completely successful. Thus, perhaps, these inscriptions will become the longest-lasting monument to Kim Il Sung's era and his ambitions. For many decades, they will cause outrage and irritation (perhaps mixed with admiration), but sooner or later they will become the amusing reminder of times long past, like those equally megalomaniac inscriptions of ancient Babylonian and Assyrian kings.

Written in Stone

IN 1987 THE WORLD (OR RATHER the very small section of it that cared about North Korea in those pre–nuclear times) learned that the North Korean bureaucrats had invented yet another way to extol the Great Leader, Sun of the Nation, Ever-victorious Marshal Kim Il Sung. They began erecting massive commemorative stones bearing enlarged facsimile reproductions of the Great Leader's own handwriting.

Actually, the idea to put the Great Leader's pronouncements in stone is not that new. From the early 1970s, the picturesque North Korean mountains have been carved with huge inscriptions conveying to the masses slogans or sayings of Kim Il Sung. But the *ch'inp'ilbi*, as the stones carrying the facsimile reproductions are known, were somewhat different. First of all, they were much larger, and second, they bore an exact copy of the sacral handwriting. Nor was this a new idea for East Asia. The art of calligraphy has been appreciated there for millennia, and it was common for a Korean king or Chinese emperor to present an especially illustrious subject or some institution with a specimen of royal handwriting.

The first *ch'inp'ilbi* was unveiled in Pyongyang on the Morangbong Hill in October 1987. This monument was of great scale: its length was 75 meters, height 10.4 meters, and total weight was said to be 650 tons. On it workers carved a facsimile copy of the entire speech which Kim Il Sung delivered on October 14, 1945, upon his arrival in Korea. This was the first public speech by the would-be Great Leader after his return to Korea. As a matter of fact,

The masses and the Leader. The obligatory tribute paid to the mammoth statue
of Kim Il Sung on top of Mansudae Hill. Photograph by Christopher Morris.

the speech was written by the propaganda officers of the Soviet 25th Army,
which was responsible for the occupation of Korea, but this fact was never
admitted in the North, needless to say.

It was followed by a new monument, erected in April 1992, to commemorate Kim Il Sung's eightieth birthday. This one was constructed in the
Myohyang Mountains, at a place where Kim Il Sung once conducted one of
his numerous "on-the-spot-guidance" homilies. This monument was smaller
and weighed merely 250 tons, being made of granite. It conveyed the following wisdom: "Water is rice. Rice is Communism. The irrigation-based socialist agriculture of our country will have a great harvest every year. Kim Il Sung,
April 15, 1992." With the wisdom of hindsight this sounds a bit ironic, especially since Kim Il Sung's incompetent advice on agricultural methods contributed to the disaster of 1996–1999. The terraced fields much promoted by
the Great Leader proved to be vulnerable to floods and were virtually washed
away. The irrigation system based on the wide use of power-driven pumps did
not survive the energy crisis of the 1990s and the heavy reliance on such a system is often mentioned among the reasons that led to the disastrous famine.

However, the most important monument was erected in the truce village
of Panmunjom. It is very short and contains only Kim Il Sung's own signature

The most famous of all ch'inp'ilbi, located in Panmunjom. The facsimile copy
of Kim Il Sung's own signature. Photograph by Andrei Lankov.

and date: 1994.7.7 (July 7, 1994). This is a facsimile of Kim's signature on
one of the documents related to the "reunification" issue. He allegedly signed
this document shortly before his sudden death on July 8. Probably this really
was the case: Kim Il Sung died amidst the preparations for the first intra–
Korean summit, which was scheduled to take place in late July 1994. The stone
was symbolically located in Panmunjom, a "truce village," which in popular
imagination has long become the symbol of Korea's division. The stone cannot be seen from the southern territory, but it is a must for all foreigners visiting Panmunjon from the North. Even Kim Jong Il once made a very public
pilgrimage to this stone.

The personality cult of Kim Jong Il is deliberately made to mirror the
cult of his father. The much-adored "Kim Il Sung flower" is paired with the
"Kim Jong Il flower." The "Song of General Kim Il Sung" nearly replaced the
national anthem, but after the promotion of Kim Jong Il the North Koreans
were made to sing "Song of General Kim Jong Il" as well. Everything now
comes in such pairs, with the exception of statues: for some reason, there are
no Kim Jong Il statues in the North.

Thus, it is only logical that Kim Jong Il's *ch'inp'ilbi* are present as well.

In August 1993 one such commemorative stone was unveiled at a school once attended by Yi In-mo, a former North Korean officer and Communist guerrilla who was taken prisoner in the South, and then spent 34 years in prison since he refused to sign a repentance declaration. The stone contains a sentence from a letter sent by Kim Jong Il to Yi In-mo's daughter: "Our Party will not forget Comrade Yi In-mo's confidence and willpower." Later this monument was augmented by some other specimens of Kim Jong Il's *ch'in-p'ilbi*. The most visible is located in the privileged Pyongyang Maternity Hospital. It says something mundane: "I wish you success in serving the people." As one can easily guess, this is a quotation from Kim Jong Il's congratulatory letter to the hospital staff.

In addition to these stones, facsimile copies of Kim Jong Il and Kim Il Sung's handwriting are carved on rocky slopes in the mountains, and sometimes even reproduced as mosaics made of colored glass. One such "decoration," for example, adorns a slope of Paektu Mountain and is reported to be 216 meters long.

I keep wondering what is going to happen to these monuments in the future. They are difficult to demolish, unlike statues that can easily be toppled. And what will grandchildren of present-day North Koreans feel while gazing on the traces of the Kims' well-calculated megalomania? Disgust? Irony? Nostalgia? Admiration?

Taking a Leaf
from His Father's Book

IN 1964, AN INDONESIAN BOTANIST called Bunt bred a new type of orchid. One year later, the then Indonesian President Sukarno decided to use the new flower to please a foreign guest — the North Korean leader Kim Il Sung. Sukarno presented the flower to Kim Il Sung and suggested naming the orchid after his guest. Kim Il Sung loved the idea.

Thus North Korea acquired its very own special flower, and it became a sort of botanical symbol of the regime. Its name — Kim-il-sŏng-*hwa* or "flower of Kim Il Sung" in Korean — is translated into English in a number of ways, *kimilsungia* being, perhaps, the most suitable.

It could not have come at a better time: in the late 1960s the North had worldwide ambitions, and the Indonesia-originated flower seemed to confirm the love that the world's peoples felt for their only true leader, Comrade Kim

Il Sung, the Creator of the Immortal *Juche* Idea. This was confirmation of the ambitions of the North Korean leaders who tried to present their tiny country as another center of the worldwide Communist movement, an alternative to, and superior to, both Moscow and Beijing.

For the next few years, until 1975, North Korean botanists diligently worked with the presented orchid. The original breed flowered in September, but the efforts of the scientists bore fruit and the improved *kimilsungia* was in full bloom every April, just in time for the North's lavish celebrations for Kim Il Sung's birthday.

The *kimilsungia* was called "the flower of loyalty" and its breeding became an important political task, yet another test of political reliability. By the late 1970s the *kimilsungia* craze had taken over the North.

Of course, this craze was heavily subsidized by the government: the Korean Peninsula is not the most suitable natural environment for a tropical orchid. In 1979 the Central Botanic Gardens in Pyongyang constructed a special "*Kimilsungia* greenhouse" which was to breed the vulnerable flowers. Initially the greenhouse area was 600 square meters, but in the 1980s it was enlarged to 1,500 square meters. Similar greenhouses were built throughout the country; every major city and every province has one.

Thus, the North Koreans now have a reliable supply of *kimilsungia*. It was difficult to breed the capricious flowers at home, so the job was entrusted to teams of professional botanists who take care of the seedlings in the greenhouses. These ecological bubbles did not come cheap, but who cared?

However, in the 1980s it became clear that the *kimilsungia* craze lacked its politically symmetrical counterpart. Every single propaganda campaign aimed at eulogizing Kim Senior had to be augmented by a similar gimmick extolling the virtues of his son and heir, soon to become a new Great Leader. Thus, in 1988 Kim Jong Il got a flower of his own. It was called kim-jŏng-il-*hwa* or *kimjongilia*.

The story of the *kimjongilia* was deliberately constructed to contain a parallel with that of *kimilsungia*. This time the flower originated in Japan, where a local botanist named Kamo Motoderu spent some twenty years breeding it from a South American begonia. He then presented the flower on the 46th birthday of the Dear Leader as a token of "friendship and goodwill between Korea and Japan." Soon afterwards, this particular begonia was bred throughout North Korea, requiring even more greenhouses, even though it is said to be easier to grow than *kimilsungia*. The first such greenhouse was erected in 1989, with a total area of 730 square meters.

Meanwhile, the North Korean composers wrote a song called "*Kimjongilia*," soon to be performed across the country. The lyrics read:

The statue on top of Mansudae Hill, 1972 vintage Stalinist realism, North Korean version. Photograph by Anna Fifield.

The red flowers that are blossoming over our land
Are like our hearts: full of love for the leader.
Our hearts follow the young buds of *kimjongilia*;
Oh! The flower of our loyalty!

Lavish exhibitions of these flowers were held in cities throughout the 1990s. In recent years a particularly extravagant and expensive exhibition of *kimjongilia* became a standard feature of the annual birthday celebrations of Kim Jong Il. The best specimens, reared by some local institutions or presented from overseas, are exhibited there. The foreign businessmen who cooperate with the North are pressured to "donate" some money and/or flowers for such an exhibition. The press runs stories about selfless Koreans who were keeping the flowers warm throughout the winter even when their houses were freezing during the disastrous years of the Great Famine.

The economic difficulties seemingly did not influence the spread of *kimjongilia* and *kimilsungia* even though tropical flowers are unlikely to prosper in a starving temperate-zone country. Indeed, the greenhouses breeding *kimjongilia* and *kimilsungia* are deemed so important that even in the midst of famine, amidst the nearly complete collapse of the energy supply, the greenhouses were still allocated generous quotas of hot water and electricity. People might have died in large numbers, but Indonesian orchids and Japanese begonias survived.

Museums of Merit

WHAT WOULD YOU EXPECT to see in a subway museum? You are probably going to say that in such a place there must be some photos documenting the subway construction, and perhaps models of the carriages and other equipment used by the subway services. Yes — but not if your museum is located in Pyongyang.

North Korean museums are very specific institutions. Basically, there are two types of museum in North Korea: museums in the normal sense of the word, and the so-called museums of merit (*sajŏkkwan* in Korean). The real museums form only a minority. There are just half a dozen of them in Pyongyang and a handful in the countryside.

Meanwhile, "museums of merit" are virtually everywhere. In the 1990s, there were some 60 museums of this type nationwide. I've seen three such museums, affiliated with a university, a railway, and a subway, as well as two local "museums of merit" in Wonsan and Ch'ŏnsanli. And, I dare to say, this was an unforgettable, if bizarre, experience!

The full official name of these institutions is "Museum of the Revolutionary Merit of the Great Leader and the Dear Leader" (that is, of Kim Il Sung and Kim Jong Il). In fact, they are museums of Kim Il Sung and Kim Jong Il but with some local or specialized touches. These establishments use the backdrop of a university, railway, subway or locality to illustrate the acts or thoughts of the Leaders.

Thus, in the subway museum, the first few halls deal with the childhood of Kim Il Sung, followed by his guerrilla activities in Manchuria, his return to the country and, of course, his wise leadership during the Korean War. The heroic deeds of Kim Jong Il are treated with equal respect, but none of the exhibits in the first halls is related to the subway in any meaningful manner. Only in later halls do materials related to the subway itself begin to appear.

Nonetheless, even these materials are, first and foremost, related to the Kims and their constant care for the development of the Pyongyang subway system. Of course, there are photos of the subway construction and of workers, and there are leaflets and newspapers that were issued during the subway construction. However, the exhibition is centered around such moving items as, say, a fountain pen that Kim Il Sung once used to sign the decree about the subway construction, or a chair in which Kim Il Sung sat while inspecting the construction site, or a microphone into which Kim Il Sung uttered a few words about the subway, or even an entire vehicle in which Kim Il Sung once traveled between two underground stations.

The walls are decorated with photos and pictures treating the same subject of "Kim Il Sung, Kim Jong Il and the subway" from all imaginable perspectives. A huge diorama equipped with numerous special effects is devoted to that great historic event: the inspection of the subway construction by Kim Il Sung.

In the railway "museum of merit" one picture was especially memorable. It depicts a girl in railway uniform holding a signal flashlight and standing near a railway line while looking with tearful eyes somewhere into the darkness. The caption explains everything: "Where are you going so late at night, our Great Leader?"

Once upon a time the "museums of merit" dealt with Kim Il Sung alone, but after Kim Jong Il was officially declared his heir in 1980, they were re-organized to relate the heroic deeds of the younger Kim as well. I was particularly moved by the hall "Kim Jong Il at a Military Camp" in the Kim Il Sung University's "museum of merit." Like all other university students in the early 1960s, the would-be heir designate was required to undertake a short course of reserve officers' training (somewhat similar to the American ROTC system, but obligatory). Among other exhibits, there is a rifle (allegedly Kim's), his shovel and even a ladle Kim Jong Il used while working a shift in the camp kitchen. Another huge picture is devoted to this historical event of great significance — Kim Jong Il working a shift in the kitchen. He is depicted giving instructions to his fellow students — attentive and admiring, needless to say!

In the late 1980s, the village of Ŏŭndong, within the administrative borders of Pyongyang, where Kim's training camp was once located, became a huge memorial complex. Even a stone on which Kim Jong Il rested after a tiring run has been specially fenced and now is carefully protected there. After all, only six months of Marshal Kim Jong Il's life were spent in the barracks, and throughout all this not-so-long time of his "military service" Kim Jong Il was in Ŏŭndong. So, the place warrants special attention indeed!

The Big Picture

IN AUGUST 2003, SOUTH KOREANS were excited about some very special and unusual guests. The North Korean athletes who came to take part in the

Such socialist realism paintings of Kim Il Sung adorn countless crossroads in the country. They should be kept in good order. Photograph by Andrei Lankov.

Taegu Universiade were accompanied by a large team of beautiful cheerleaders. The girls were stunners, indeed, and the power of the mysterious and the exotic made them an instant success.

On August 28 the girls were returning to their boarding facilities after they had cheered for North Korean archers. It was raining, and through the windows of their buses they saw portraits of Kim Jong Il pictured together with the South Korean President Kim Dae Jung. The banner was an enlarged copy of a photo taken during the summit in 2000. Obviously, it was put up by some South Korean leftist-nationalist groups (and what wonderful cheerleaders for the Dear Leader and his system these groups are!).

However, the picture had an unintended effect. Once the beauties saw it, they were outraged. The banner was wet, since it had not been duly protected against the rain! The raindrops were damaging the sacral likeness of the Dear Leader! The girls demanded the bus drivers to stop and rushed to rescue the icons. They also had an additional complaint: the banner was placed inappropriately low! The journalists were eager to take pictures of this colorful scene: a crowd of the outraged beauties running to save the likeness of the incumbent monarch, loudly screaming all the way.

North Korea is a country of portraits — portraits of Kim Il Sung and Kim Jong Il, that is. The portraits are ubiquitous. They are to be placed in every living room, in every office, in every railway (and, by extension, subway) carriage but, for some reason, not on the buses or trolleybuses. The portraits adorn the entrances of all major public buildings, railways stations and schools. Reportedly, in the late 1990s, the largest portrait of Kim Il Sung within the city limits of Pyongyang graced the First Department Store in the very center of the North Korean capital. The portrait was 15 meters high and 11 meters wide.

North Koreans have been living under the permanent gaze of the Great Leader for more than three decades. In the late 1960s North Koreans were ordered to place these icons in their homes and offices. By 1972, when Kim's 60th birthday was lavishly celebrated, North Korea had a much greater density of portraits than could ever be found in Stalin's Russia or Mao's China — the two countries that bestowed this peculiar fondness for the Leader's portraits on Korea.

In the late 1970s, the North Koreans received another set of instructions. They were ordered to display portraits of Kim Jong Il, the heir designate. This had to be done unofficially. The propaganda insisted that there was a widespread movement of North Koreans who, purely out of love for the son of their ruler, began to adorn their dwellings with his portraits. Only in the late 1980s did Kim Jong Il's portraits appear in public spaces, and from the early 1990s on they have been the same size as those of his father and they are put together in rooms and offices in pairs.

All portraits are produced by the Mansudae workshops that specialize in making images of Kim Il Sung, Kim Jong Il, and their relatives. They are framed and glazed (and only the best glass and timber will do!).

In different eras the Kims were depicted in diverse manners, and these changes tell a lot about changes in ideology and policy. In the 1960s and 1970s Kim Il Sung wore a Mao suit, stressing the austerity and quasi-military character of the regime. In the mid–1980s these portraits were replaced with new ones, depicting Kim Il Sung in a Western-type suit. This signaled the relative openness of the regime in the late 1980s. After Kim Il Sung's death in 1994, the new portraits also showed him in suits (incidentally, these portraits were called a "depiction of the Sun" since in his lifetime Kim was "the Sun of the Nation"). However, from early 2001 Kim Il Sung has appeared in newly issued portraits in the military uniform of a generalissimo, the rank he bestowed on himself in the last years of his long life.

Kim Jong Il's portrait underwent similar changes. Initially Kim Jong Il was also depicted in the dark-colored Mao suit, once his favorite. However, the 2001 version showed him in the grandeur of a marshal's uniform. This once again confirmed the importance of the "army-first policy" proclaimed by Kim Jong Il, North Korea's "Glorious Marshal" who — unlike the vast majority of North Korean males — never served in the military himself.

Nowadays, in 2004–2005, there are two sets of the portraits in North Korean houses. The households of party cadres, military officers and security officials sport three portraits: one depicts Kim Il Sung, another Kim Jong Il, and yet another Kim Il Sung's wife and Kim Jong Il's mother, Kim Jong Suk. Such sets are distributed to them by the state authorities and are supposed to be put on display.

Lesser beings have not been ordered so far to have the portraits of Kim Jong Suk, but their humbler dwellings still sport three pictures — a portrait of the Dear Leader, a portrait of the Great Leader, and a photo depicting the two great men talking together.

But this is the situation in late 2004. By the time you read this, it will probably change: the "portrait policy" has been remarkable for its constant fluidity.

North Korea is run as if it is a cult, and portraits of the Kim family are icons of this religion. The special care of these icons is prescribed by the so-called ten rules of the unified ideological system, a sort of North Korean "Ten commandments" (taking into consideration the Christian background of Kim Il Sung and many other early Communist activists, this is not necessarily a coincidence).

The portraits are put on one of the walls, and that wall cannot be used for any other images or pinups. When a North Korean family moves to another place, they must start by hanging the Kims' portraits on the wall. Random checks are conducted to make sure that proper care of the portraits is taken.

Of course, the portraits have to be kept in good order. Thus, every set comes with a special box which is used to keep tools for maintaining the portraits. Inside such a box there are two pieces of soft cloth for cleaning the portraits and a brush. The cleaning should be done daily. In offices and schools, the local cadres are responsible for organizing proper cleaning, and the quality of the job is checked by random inspections by more senior cadres. It is a major sin to have portraits undusted, and even unintentional damage to the portraits is a serious problem.

In the military, the portraits are hung in all rooms in permanent barracks. When a unit departs for a field exercise (as North Korean units do often), the portraits are taken with them. Once the platoon prepares its tent or, more commonly, its dugout, the portraits are placed there, and only after this ritual is the provisional shelter deemed suitable for life.

Often the portraits become an important part of ritual. In schools, students are required to bow to the portraits and express their gratitude to the

Dear Leader who, in his wisdom and kindness, bestowed such a wonderful life on his subjects. The portraits feature very prominently in marriage ceremonies as well. The couple has to make deep bows to the portraits of the Great Leaders. This tribute is very public and serves as a culmination of the wedding ritual. It does not matter whether the wedding ceremony is held in a public wedding hall or at home.

The portraits are jealously protected. Even incidental damage of the portrait might spell disaster for the culprit. It was recently learned that Kim Yŏng-jun, a prominent Korean leftist scholar who had defected to the North, committed suicide in the 1960s. The reason? He accidentally damaged Kim Il Sung's portrait. This suicide was an indication of neither his excessive political zeal nor his paranoia. He made a rational choice, preferring a swift death in the relative comfort of his privileged apartment block to a slow death in prison. Thus it comes as no surprise that in 2003 the North Korean cheerleaders reacted to the improper treatment of the portraits in such a violent manner. Nonetheless, it is a great unknown if the girls were sincere in their rush. Perhaps, they simply wanted to demonstrate their loyalty and score some additional points in their files or just followed the crowd with full knowledge that insufficient zeal would be dangerous.

Learning to Be a Loyal Soldier of the Dear Leader

EDUCATION IN NORTH KOREA IS POLITICAL. This is a truism, since the same can be said about education in any other country. Schools are entrusted with the task of imbuing future citizens with the values considered "correct" in any given society.

So, what is so special about North Korea? First of all, the sheer volume of propaganda which is heaped on the children is exceptional. Another peculiarity is the prominence given to the country's ruling family — the world's only Communist dynasty.

This is not really unique. Most other Communist countries have emphasized the importance and superiority of their systems over that of their adversaries. Needless to say, Stalin and Mao also received more than their fair share of adulation in the Russian and Chinese textbooks of their era. However, the scale of such propaganda in North Korea surpasses everything which has been seen before.

The emphasis is, first and foremost, on the Kim family. The North Korean system is good because it was created by the Kims, and it remains good as long as it is managed by them — or so the mantra goes.

Therefore, every North Korean student must study the biographies of Kim Il Sung and Kim Jong Il. Not real biographies, of course, but rather a collection of fairy tales where the Great and Dear Leaders are presented as the embodiment of wisdom, courage, benevolence and all other virtues.

Back in the 1980s, I had the opportunity to visit a couple of showcase North Korean kindergartens. Both boasted a special room for these "biographical" studies, with a large relief model of Mangyŏngdae, the native village of Kim Il Sung, placed in the center. Before the lesson started, all the children along with their teacher made three full bows to Kim Il Sung's portrait chanting the words: "Thank you, Marshal-Father!" And with this charming ritual, the lesson commenced. Nowadays, it is Kim Jong Il rather than Kim Il Sung who is in the center of the ritual.

One after another, the children were summoned by the teacher to approach the model. In childish voices, but doing their best to affect an "adult" intonation, they would recite various episodes from the Great Leader's childhood: "Here the Father-Leader played war games preparing himself for combat against the Japanese imperialists," or "Here the Father-Leader trained himself by playing sports." The unfortunate children are required to speak with the aggressive pathos which is common in North Korean radio broadcasts, using "adult" expressions and idiom.

The children are reminded that it is only thanks to the Kim dynasty that they are able to enjoy their "happy childhood." Even the food they eat is proof of the benevolence of the Great Leader, so after every meal all children have to thank the Leader for his care for them, chanting: "Great Leader, thank you very much, we ate well!"

As children attend primary school, they begin to study the "history of the Great Leader." Then, in secondary school, there is another round, followed by a final dose at university. Since the 1980s, the "Revolutionary history of the Great Leader" has been supplemented by the "revolutionary history of the Dear Leader" (Kim Jong Il). Now the younger Kim has supplanted the dynasty's founding father as the primary object of official veneration. Finally, Kim Jong Suk, the first wife of Kim Il Sung and mother of Kim Jong Il, has also joined the group and nowadays students are supposed to study her great deeds as well.

However, political education does not end with these indoctrination classes. Even such seemingly apolitical subjects as mathematics are awash with political messages. Take, for example, a quiz from a North Korean math textbook: "3 soldiers from the Korean People's Army killed 30 American soldiers. How many American soldiers were killed by each of them, if they all killed an equal number of enemy soldiers?" Then a child may be offered more food for thought: "The Great Leader-Father Kim Il Sung was, as a child, once given 9 apples. He gave 3 to his grandfather, 2 to his grandmother, 1 to his father and 1 to his mother. How many apples did he give away and how many did he keep for himself?"

North Korean books on social subjects are permeated with statements about the Leaders' wisdom: "The Great Leader Kim Il Sung was the great father of the people who during the 82 years of his life kept working for the people and did not allow himself a day of rest!"

One should wonder how it is possible to connect young Kim to the anti-guerrilla resistance. After all, the would-be heir designate was merely three years old when the struggle was over. However, this does not seem to be an issue: the North Korean children are taught that their nation's leader was born in a secret guerrilla base in mountain forests of Paektusan and took part in the liberation struggle in spite of being a toddler!

To what extent does such an education influence the North Koreans? If my Soviet experience is a guide, its impact should be neither overestimated nor underestimated. Some details will disappear soon, but underlying assumptions are likely to last. The North Koreans might lose their belief in the super-human qualities of the Kim family overnight, but it will probably take much longer for them to learn not to expect too much from the state and take their own lives in their own hands.

What's in a Name?

IN 1979 A BOOK WAS PUBLISHED in North Korea. It was called *On the Honorific Words Applicable to the Great Leader Comrade Kim Il Sung, and the Proper Use of Respectful Expressions in Reference to the Great Leader*. I suspect that the book was welcomed by many Koreans who had been forced to navigate the treacherous shoals of political linguistics without proper charts. By the late 1970s Kim Il Sung's personality cult had reached a near hysterical pitch, and he had to be mentioned and thanked everywhere. However, the use of an improper expression could easily land a person in a prison camp. Thus, clear instructions were badly needed. They probably existed since the 1960s but were not published openly — a major inconvenience in an era when every North Korean had to pay tribute to the Great Man.

Of all Kim Il Sung's titles, "Great Leader" was the most popular. It nearly became Kim Il Sung's second name. The English "Leader" is used here to translate Korean "*suryŏng*," which consists of two Chinese characters, the first meaning "head" and the second "lead" or "leader."

The term was introduced in the late 1940s, and initially it was applied only to Stalin and Lenin, the two "great leaders" of Communism. In 1952 Kim Il Sung was promoted to the rank of *suryŏng* as well. Nonetheless, in those early years he was usually called "*susang*" ("prime-minister"), or "*changgun*" ("general"). Suryŏng was still too lofty a designation for general use and was reserved for special occasions.

It became a standard term of reference only in the 1960s, usually combined with *widaehan,* "great," or with *ŏbŏi,* "fatherly." From around 1960 it was only Kim who could be addressed in that fashion.

"Great Leader" or "Fatherly Leader" became the two most frequently used sobriquets of the North Korean dictator. There were others — some dozens of them, and they were sometimes very picturesque. The most common were "Sun of the Nation" and "Ever-Victorious General." "Sun of Mankind" was also widely used.

In 1972 Kim Il Sung promoted himself to the newly established post of state president. It was called *chusŏk,* the Korean pronunciation of the title that was used for Mao as well. However, in Chinese the title is usually rendered in English as "Chairman," while in Korea for some reason it came to be translated as "President."

In the 1970s Kim Jong Il began to consolidate his power. For a while the rising son was enigmatically called the "Party Center," but eventually he acquired a title of his own. This was *ch'inaehanŭn chidoja* or "Dear Leader." One has to note that for father and son they use two *different* Korean words, which both are usually rendered into English as "leader." Kim Senior was "*suryŏng*" while Kim Junior was merely "*chidoja.*" It is hardly possible to render this difference in English correctly; alas, the language of Shakespeare is somewhat lacking when it comes to discriminating the subtleties of that vocabulary.

When President Kim died in 1994 his son assumed power. After the three years of mourning passed, North Koreans were informed that henceforth the designation *suryŏng* would never be employed for anyone else. This title, even posthumously, could be applied to the late Kim Il Sung alone. The position of the President was also reserved for him forever. Kim Il Sung's son became the head of state, not its president. He holds the position of Chairman of the National Defense Committee — and thus the title "Chairman Kim" can occasionally be seen in the Western press.

And what happened to the "Dear Leader" after his father's death? He changed the first part of his official appellation, becoming "great" instead of "dear." However, the second part remains the same: Kim Jong Il is "*chidoja*" or "*ryŏngdoja*." Kim Junior can occasionally be called "*suryŏng*" as well, but in general this somewhat superior title is still reserved for his late father.

Perhaps, sooner or later, Kim Jong Il will also be upgraded to *suryŏng*. After all, some titles which once were reserved for Kim Il Sung have become standard for Kim Jong Il as well. For decades, the North Koreans knew that only Kim Il Sung should be referred to as "the sun of the nation" (*minjŏkŭi t'aeyang* '), but nowadays this is one of the most common titles of Kim Jong Il.

This elaborate system creates a lot of problems for English translators. The standard titles of "Great Leader" and "Dear Leader" have long become the standard sobriquets of Kim Il Sung and Kim Jong Il in English texts. These translations give some flavor of the original, but they are not quite correct now in the 2000s when the most common titles of *both* Kim Jong Il and Kim Il Sung can be rendered as "Great Leader," with the original having the same Korean word for "great" but different words for "leader."

There are other honorific titles reserved for the Dear (or, sorry, now Great) Leader. Some of these simply reflect his official positions: he is the Supreme Commander-in-Chief, the General Secretary and the like. The titles of "Beloved General" (*kyŏngaehanŭn changgun*) and "Commander-in-Chief" (*kycngaehanŭn ch'oego saryŏnggwang*) are also quite popular. Some other titles are more inventive, like the Bright Star of Paektu Mountain (*Paektu kwangmyŏngsŏng*) or Guiding Star (*hyangdo-ui pyŏl*, a literal translation of a Western idiom, once very popular among the Russian propaganda-mongers of Stalin's era).

It appears that, when compared to his late father, Kim Jong Il is somewhat less enthusiastic about flowery titles: the rules governing the use of these terms have become less strict after his ascent to power. Indeed, Kim Jong Il knows what has happened to the numerous "little Stalins" across the world, and perhaps is not very happy about the situation in which he finds himself. But what can be done? The Soviet experience clearly demonstrated that reforms can easily lead to a revolution, and if such a revolution happens, neither the "Beloved General" nor his entourage have any place to go....

PART 2

In Times of Propaganda

In the Land of Meetings

NORTH KOREA IN THE 1970S OFTEN described itself as a "*Juche* nation" or a "nation of exemplary socialism," but many North Koreans would describe their native land as a "nation of ideological education."

Kim Il Sung once remarked that a North Korean was expected to spend "eight hours working, eight hours resting and eight hours studying." By "study" he meant, first and foremost, ideological study, and the most typical form of this study occurs in regularly scheduled meetings and indoctrination sessions of all kinds.

All Communist regimes have had a penchant for obligatory "study sessions": the party members or employees of a particular unit are herded to spend an hour or so listening to boring speeches by their ideological supervisors. The masses are enlightened about the cruel and perfidious nature of the capitalist world, the horrors of the pre-revolutionary past and the glories of the Communist present.

However, even in the worst of times, the average inhabitant of an Eastern European Communist country would spend probably a couple of hours per week at such meetings and probably even less. In North Korea from the early 1960s it was not unusual for the average worker to spend some three or four hours *per day* on ideological indoctrination!

These meetings were arranged by one's "organization." In North Korea every adult belongs to some "organization," and this means that attendance is obligatory for everyone, from the primary school student to the retired farmer's wife.

The structure of the meetings has changed over time. In the late 1950s

33

and early 1960s, when the authorities were busy purging the last vestiges of opposition, ferocious struggle sessions were common. They closely resembled the notorious Red Guard meetings of the Chinese Cultural Revolution period, with victims dragged to the podium and verbally abused for hours on end. In some cases, the interrogators did not limit themselves to verbal attacks and would beat the hapless and unrepentant counter-revolutionary in front of his former co-workers. In later eras, the sessions became less heated and more formal affairs.

In all North Korean agencies, workers started their working day with a "newspaper reading" session. It began some 45 minutes before the official start of the working day, and attendance was obligatory. For 30 minutes an appointed representative read extracts from the official North Korean newspapers, thus ensuring that every North Korean learned what was considered politically correct on a given day. Then, for the next 10–15 minutes, a low-level cadre would discuss the "tasks of the day;" this discussion largely consisted of a repetition of the currently accepted slogans. The working day was crowned with a "work analysis" meeting where workers were supposed to discuss the results of their work.

There were also political study sessions where their major task was to learn (often through rote memorization) the dictums of the Great Leader and, from the early 1980s, the Dear Leader. They also studied the official versions of Kim Il Sung's and Kim Jong Il's biography or listened to presentations on selected international and domestic issues.

There were four major areas of this education: "class education" (stories about exploitation and suffering at the hands of the class enemies); "revolutionary education" (stories about great deeds of the anti–Japanese guerrillas and other revolutionary fighters); "loyalty education" (stories about the benevolence and wisdom of the Great and Dear Leaders); and "socialist patriotism education" (stories about North Korea's prosperity and its superiority to all other countries as well as the innate virtues of the Korean nation). Party agencies distributed printed materials which were to be carefully studied and memorized by the millions of North Koreans who had to attend the sessions.

Even music was not forgotten. Koreans love singing, and even more so in Kim Il Sung's North Korea, where both TV sets and tape recorders remained a rarity until the late 1980s. Thus, the officially approved songs all carried wholesome political messages. The lyrics *had to* contain references to the infinite wisdom of the Leader(s) or the great prosperity of the country or the sufferings of the South Korea brethren under the American yoke. Thus, the songs were studied at special "song study sessions" as a part of a "song popularization activity."

But why do we use the past tense? Because things have changed a lot since the mid–1990s. Sessions are still common, and songs' lyrics still deal with lofty political subjects, but it is clear that the average length of these sessions has dramatically decreased, especially among the working class. Common North Koreans do not see much sense in attending sessions these days. Many factories are closed and their employees collect only nominal wages, earning their income rather through private trade or handicrafts. The authorities do not have many incentives to influence the reluctant commoners, and they cannot brand every absentee as a "counter-revolutionary." Finally, it appears that the new generation of officials has lost much of their fathers' revolutionary zeal.

The most dreaded type of session was the "self-criticism meeting," but this will be our next topic.

Self-Criticism

FROM THE EARLY 1960S TO THE EARLY 1990s, meetings and study sessions constituted a large part of the daily routine of every North Korean. Such sessions typically occupied between two and four hours every day! These days North Koreans spend less time listening to eulogies of the "Great Leader," but these sessions still loom large in their lives.

The most important and dreaded of these sessions are known as "self-criticism meetings." Actually, in Korean they have a different name which is quite difficult to render into English —*saenghwal ch'onghwa* (something like "Meetings on drawing the results of life"). Nevertheless, I'd rather call them self-criticism sessions, since this descriptive name reflects their nature quite well.

As with many other institutions, North Koreans insist that they, or rather the "Dear Leader" Kim Jong Il (whom else?), invented the self-criticism meetings. Once again, this is not quite correct, since these meetings were once commonplace in Mao's China, whence they were obviously borrowed in the early 1960s.

However, it is true that in the early 1970s, the then 30-year-old Kim Jong Il developed a new model for these meetings and it has been followed ever since. Since that time in most work units the self-criticism sessions have taken place once every week. For some reason farmers hold them every ten days, and people in some sensitive positions are required to deliver public self-criticism with greater frequency. Aside from the weekly sessions, there are also "self-criticism" meetings of a higher level that are held once a month or once a year.

The work unit to which a particular person belongs organizes the weekly sessions. By definition, every North Korean is a member of some organization. There are about four million members of the KWP — the North Korean version of the Communist Party (the exact number of KWP members is kept secret). Youngsters aged from 14 to 30 are members of the Party Youth. All other adults are members of the Trade Unions. Those farmers who are not KWP members, are supposed to attend sessions arranged by the Farmers' Union. Even housewives are not left without ideological guidance and spiritual care: unemployed females are members of the Women's Union. These bodies are charged with responsibility for the self-criticism sessions.

Everybody must prepare for a self-criticism session in advance. One is required to write down all his or her sins and transgressions in a special notebook. When the time comes, one has to report all the transgressions of the preceding week. But what does one confess? Soldiers confess that they did not clean their rifle properly or missed targets during a shooting practice, students express their penitence about badly done homework, housewives admit that they cleaned the neighborhood's streets without proper zeal. However, mere admission of mistakes is not enough, one has also to suggest measures for correction of the admitted mistakes.

After everybody has completed their repentance speeches with obligatory quotes from Kim Il Sung and Kim Jong Il, the time is ripe for a bout of "mutual criticism." This means that each participant must denounce some actions of his or her colleagues. Nobody can avoid participating in those dreaded rituals.

The average group, be it a Party cell or a Women's Union team or a Trade Union group, consists of 7–10 members, and the average length of a session is about 1.5 hours. In other words, there is about 10 minutes to disclose and condemn the sins of every member. This is more than enough, since every single North Korean is supposed to undergo this ideological treatment once every week, month after month, year after year, decade after decade.

As a rule, family problems are not discussed during these sessions — unless something really serious has happened, domestic matters remain in the confines of the family. Most people prudently report only minor transgressions and hope that nothing serious surfaced during a session.

The weekly public repentance has long become a habit for most North Koreans. Often people transform them into carefully arranged public performances. It is very common to pre-arrange the exchange of criticisms with one's friends and then follow the planned scenario. However, such a scenario may be broken easily if someone else draws attention to a more serious transgression (of course, in such a case the protagonist would risk retaliation). In other words, there is always a real threat that some wrongdoing will be exposed in such a session.

"Self-criticism sessions," in spite of their usual formalism, cannot be taken lightly. Indeed, for most North Koreans they are a dreaded institution. They cause everyone to be mindful of their words and deeds and, from the authorities' viewpoint, they impose a strong social cohesion. They also break mutual trust, providing co-workers with opportunities for back-stabbing which would be undreamed of in the world of "normal" office politics. A defector once observed that "self-criticism" sessions had made the greatest contribution toward political stability in North Korea.

Maybe he is right. After all, as every criminologist knows, the certainty of punishment is as good a deterrent as its severity, and peer pressure works wonders. The "self-criticism sessions" are very good in uncovering minor deviations from the prescribed code of behavior. And this is a reliable way to ensure the obedience and docility of the people. Those who are afraid to create minor disturbances are far less likely to be involved with something more serious.

National Symbols

EVERY STATE MUST HAVE ITS ANTHEM, flag and coat of arms — or must it? This package, now taken for granted, became the worldwide standard only about a century ago, when the European habits and traditions began to spread across the globe — and not all countries have all these symbols (South Korea, for example, is doing very well without an official coat of arms).

Nonetheless, the Democratic People's Republic of Korea has all three. When, in 1948, a separate North Korean state came into existence, it produced its own flag, anthem and coat of arms — all designed according to the then already established Communist tradition.

The North Korean flag is red, edged at top and bottom with thin white and wider blue bands. In the middle of the red band there is a large white circle with a red five-pointed star. The inclusion of a such a star had long been an established tradition of Communist heraldry by 1948, but the colors — red, blue and white — hint at the colors of an older *t'aegŭkki* flag, invented in the 1880s as Korea's first national flag and still used in South Korea.

Until 1948 *t'aegŭkki* was widely used in the North as well. I have seen pictures of government-sponsored rallies where the participants carried portraits of Kim Il Sung, Lenin and Stalin alongside *t'aegŭkki*! Just few years later this became unthinkable, and during the Korean War people who were found to have *t'aegŭkki* at their homes could easily be shot.

I would not say that the North Koreans treat their flag with great respect. But they are not unusual in this regard: U.S.-style flag worshipping is an exception rather than the rule worldwide. Private houses seldom have flags. It is left to the authorities to ensure that a number of flags are on display during special events or on official holidays.

Following the Communist tradition, North Korea uses its coat of arms perhaps more frequently than is normally done by Western countries. The coat of arms was also designed according to Communist traditions and essentially followed the pattern first suggested in 1918 for the Soviet coat of arms. It is oval in shape, and is surrounded by ears of rice, with the name of the state written on a red ribbon at the bottom.

Nowadays, the North Korean Constitution (Article 168) describes the coat of arms: "The national emblem of the Democratic People's Republic of Korea bears the design of a grand hydroelectric power plant under Mount Paektu, the sacred mountain of the revolution, and bearing the beaming light of a five-pointed red star, with ears of rice forming an oval frame, bound with a red ribbon bearing the inscription "The Democratic People's Republic of Korea."

This sounds right. But one cannot find anything resembling the distinctive shape of Mount Paektu in the coat of arms. It depicts a rather unremarkable and generic mountain chain instead. Indeed, this reference to Paektu was introduced only in the 1990s when this mountain, allegedly Kim Jong Il's birthplace, became the focus of a powerful propaganda campaign. This nondescript mountain in the coat of arms was claimed to be Paektu while keeping its previous unremarkable shape. The power station is a reminder of the time when the North was the industrial stronghold of all Korea; this ceased to be the case long ago.

The North Korean anthem was composed in late 1947. However, its role is somewhat ambiguous. Many North Koreans do not even know its text. This is not surprising: the anthem is seldom played in North Korea. For all practical purposes the official anthem has long been replaced by the "Song of General Kim Il Sung" and its recent imitation, "Song of General Kim Jong Il" (the latter generally follows the former). These songs are performed at most official functions, while the anthem can be heard only when a foreign dignitary visits Pyongyang or when it is played for a North Korean athlete who has won some international competition. The anthem is a symbol of the state and the nation, but it is deemed less important than the two songs which extol the leaders' personalities.

Like the South, the North has its own officially approved "state flower." This is "mokran," a kind of magnolia which was allegedly discovered and named by Kim Il Sung himself. I am not going to discuss whether Kim Il

Sung, a recent high school graduate, had enough specialized botanical knowledge to discover a new species, nor whether a guerrilla commander could easily find the requisite reference books in the Manchurian wilderness. After all, North Korean propaganda has never been particularly plausible.

The "mokran" played the role of national symbol from the late 1960s, and in 1991 it finally received state endorsement. However, in its symbolic capacity the magnolia has to compete with the *kimilsungia* and *kimjongilia*. These two flowers are far more popular, since these are symbols of the Great Leader and Dear Leader, rather than nation. And leaders are supposed to be more important, of course....

The Kim Family Tree

IN ALL SOCIETIES, THE RULING ELITE always tries to control history. This is applicable not only to dictatorships: after all, in Hollywood-produced historical movies, the presentation of supposedly real events of the past is manipulated to conform to the current U.S. political and cultural agenda. The gladiators, cowboys and nomad chieftains express ideas which they could not possibly have had in their time, but which resonate well with the interests, habits and assumptions of the present-day American public.

However, these falsifications of history are much more blatant in dictatorships. As a rule, the harsher a particular regime, the more willing it is to manipulate the past — and the more barefaced these manipulations are.

Like all other Stalinist regimes, Pyongyang is busy rewriting and re-inventing history to adjust it to the current political demands. It comes naturally, since the North Korean political culture is based on two powerful traditions, Confucian and Leninist, and both these traditions take history very seriously.

In North Korean books one can read about great battles and important meetings that never took place. However, Pyongyang out–Stalined Stalin himself. To be consistent with the latest version of the country's history it does not hesitate to manufacture hard evidence. The first enterprise of this kind was the discovery of the "slogan trees."

The early 1960s witnessed a deep schism between Pyongyang and its one-time sponsors in Moscow. Kim Il Sung, who had arrived in the North as a Red Army captain, was desperate to prove his nationalist credentials and market himself as, first and foremost, a national leader. From this the myth of Paektu was born.

Paektu, Korea's highest mountain, is located on the border with China. The mountain has long been one of the most sacred national sites, related to the centuries-old shamanist tradition. So it comes as no surprise to learn that in the early 1960s North Korean history was rewritten to include claims that in the 1930s and 1940s Kim Il Sung was leading a large-scale military operation from a secret camp allegedly located deep in the forests of Paektu (in real life, he spent most of this period in exile in Russia).

Thus, the "slogan trees" were discovered. According to the official version, the guerrillas carved or painted revolutionary slogans on the trees near their camps. In 1958 (not in 1961, as most publications have suggested so far), the official media informed North Koreans that nineteen trees with inscribed revolutionary slogans were found near Paektu. Needless to say, the slogans confirmed that this was indeed the major area of operation of Kim Il Sung's guerrillas! The trees were put into protective glass boxes, and restored inscriptions became the objects of organized pilgrimage.

And what was written on the trees? "General Kim Il Sung is the Sun of the Nation!" "20 million compatriots! We'll make General Kim Il Sung the great leader of our nation after liberation!" (It is worth remembering that these inscriptions were supposedly referring to a commander of a small guerrilla band.) Some of the inscriptions even refer, in an utterly blatant anachronism, to the *Juche* idea. But *Juche* was only first mentioned in Kim's speech in December 1955 and was not advanced as North Korean official ideology until the early 1960s.

Such astounding discoveries subsequently followed every major turn in North Korean policies. When Kim Jong Il was promoted to become the heir apparent in the 1970s, eyebrows were raised. Apart from being the Great Leader's son, the young man had no political credentials. Therefore, North Korean propaganda began to insist that Kim Jong Il had been ... an active participant in the guerrilla movement. The professional myth-makers were not at all embarrassed by the fact that the boy was a mere three years old when the war ended!

Therefore, the old weapon of slogan trees was used once again. The newly discovered slogan trees contained direct references to the newborn would-be leader and his mother. The guerrillas were obviously overcome with joy about this epiphany-to-come, for North Korean researchers located some 200 trees with eulogies to the baby (with text such as: "Korea, Rejoice! The Great Sun has been born!"). Needless to say, these trees began to be discovered when Kim Jong Il was designated as heir.

These discoveries continued into the 1990s. North Korea presently claims that an astonishing 13,000 slogan trees have been found nationwide. Indeed, it appears as if writing slogans on trees was the favorite pastime of all anti–Japanese guerrillas. The authorities even decided to discover such trees within the city of Pyongyang, where no guerrillas ever operated (obviously, to confirm the special standing of the city).

The experience garnered by the falsification of the recent past was later extended to the much more distant past. There are good reasons to believe that some archaeological discoveries made in North Korea are of a similar veracity to the slogan trees — Tangun Tomb being the best known example of such a freshly produced archaeological monument. But that will be our topic for another essay....

Great Song and Dance

EVERY NORTH KOREAN KNOWS ONLY too well what the "five revolutionary operas" are. Indeed, for three decades these plays have been officially described as the pinnacle of North Korean performance arts.

Older readers may remember that in the 1960s Jiang Qing, a former Shanghai actress and Mao Ze-dong's wife, developed new "revolutionary" operas in China. Her experiments had a large impact on North Korea. However, North Korea seldom — if ever — admits any foreign influence, thus the Chinese roots of the "revolutionary operas" remain hidden from the average North Korean. The common people believe that these operas are a unique cultural phenomenon, developed under the wise leadership of Kim Jong Il.

Indeed, Kim Jong Il made a substantial contribution to the development of these "revolutionary operas." In 1971, the 29-year-old Kim was appointed head of the Culture and Arts Department in the Party's Central Committee. This was one of the first signs that the young man was being groomed to inherit supreme power in the nation. Obviously, the field of propaganda and arts was seen as safe enough to serve as his training ground.

Having acquired a new job, Kim Jong Il busied himself with the creation of the "revolutionary operas," which soon formed the core of the North Korean theatrical repertoire. For many years in the 1970s and 1980s, the *entire* repertoire of all North Korean theatres consisted of these lavish musicals, augmented by the so-called "five revolutionary plays."

Those plays seem to be less popular — perhaps, because the boredom of the plot is not even partially compensated for by the lavishness of the music and set. At any rate, the most prominent of them is *Songhwadang*, a crude piece of anti-religious propaganda, allegedly penned by Kim Il Sung himself in the late 1920s and then revived in 1978 amidst great pomp.

It was stated that Kim Jong Il revived plays which were once staged by the anti–Japanese guerrillas in Manchuria in the 1930s. Revolutionary operas are supposedly based on the same plots. This claim is not completely improbable: the guerrillas did write and stage some simple propaganda plays to "revolutionize" the peasants. Perhaps some of their storylines, still vaguely remembered by veterans in the late 1960s, were indeed used for these operas and plays, but we cannot know for sure.

The "revolutionary opera" is surprisingly akin to an American musical. Like a Broadway production, it combines dance and song with dialogue. The story line is narrated by an off-stage chorus. The stories of the "revolutionary operas" are very simple, highly sentimental and have a clear-cut political message. The simplicity of the storyline is partially compensated for by the lavishness of the entire performance — abundant special effects, a large number of extras, and a splendid set.

The music of the North Korean "revolutionary operas" is drastically different from their Chinese prototypes: while in China Jiang Qing used traditional Chinese tunes, the music of the North Korean revolutionary operas is essentially Western in origin, although the orchestra, specially assembled for these performances, includes both Western and Korean musical instruments. The official line is that "the music of the revolutionary operas combines the best features of the Western and Eastern traditions." To a Russian ear it is reminiscent of the Soviet pop songs of the 1950s, lightly spiced with some Korean melodies — but needless to say, such references cannot be found in North Korean publications: everything in the operas is supposed to be uniquely and genuinely Korean.

The storylines of these musicals are overtly political. *Sea of Blood*, for example, is the story of a peasant woman whose son joined the Communist guerrillas in the 1930s. The woman herself ends up as a Communist fighter (those who know Soviet literature would not fail to recognize the plot: anyone read Gorky's *Mother*?).

Loyal Daughter of the Party tells of a heroic army nurse who fights the "U.S. imperialists" during the Korean War. The brave girl has a single dream: she longs to see Kim Il Sung one day! However, she is unable to realize her dream: the evil Yankees kill her. Her dying words are: "I want to see the General...."

Flower Girl recounts the suffering of a servant girl who is mistreated by a cruel landlord. The girl eventually joins the resistance forces. In the end, the evil landlord is punished and revolutionary good triumphs over feudal-capitalist evil.

Flower Girl is arguably the best known of all these productions. In the early 1990s, *Flower Girl* even became the center of the North-South controversy. In 1991, during the talks between the North and the South, the North Korean side stated that as a part of the cultural exchange program it was going to stage *Flower Girl* in Seoul. The South rejected the idea. The Northern delegation refused to continue the talks unless *Flower Girl* was performed in Seoul. The talks came to a standstill over the issue.

The performances are really extravagant, with numerous extras, elaborate scenic effects and well-designed lighting. The stage is huge: Mansudae Theater, home to the original productions, has a stage which is 100 meters deep and 150 meters broad, and the Grand Theater, another popular venue, is not much smaller.

As you have noticed, I did not say a word about the quality of the music. Being ignorant in this area, I am not in a position to make any comments, positive or otherwise. Nonetheless, my friend, a musician of some renown, who happened to visit North Korea in the late 1980s, was harsh. So harsh, indeed, that I would not cite his comments here — for the sake of public decency. He might be wrong, of course, but he is now playing violin in one of America's best symphony orchestras, and I assume that he knew what he was talking about....

Making History

COMMUNISM IN POWER PROVED TO BE surprisingly nationalist. The early Communist revolutionaries were sincere in their professions of internationalist spirit, but the ruling Communist regimes were, if anything, more given to nationalist fever than their capitalist counterparts. And they shared another peculiarity: they took history very politically. The writing of history was seen as, first and foremost, a particular kind of propaganda whose main task was to serve the current political agenda. This was true in most Communist countries, although in the North this politicization of history reached stupendous proportions — as the North Korean "Koguryŏ cult" testifies.

In order to understand the political significance of this cult, one has to remember how the unified Korean state of Silla was established in the late seventh century AD. Before that, for several centuries, the Korean Peninsula was largely divided between the Three Kingdoms: Silla in the southeast, Paekje in the southwest, and Koguryŏ in the north. The Koguryŏ territory also stretched far into what is now northeastern China, but it is significant for our story that inside the Korean peninsula its southern border was roughly similar to the present-day border of North Korea. These kingdoms fought one another in a struggle for supremacy, as well as being engaged in conflicts with China, which at that time was not a unified empire, but a group of rival kingdoms as well.

In the late sixth century, the recently unified China invaded Koguryŏ, the most powerful of all the proto–Korean kingdoms, but suffered a humiliating defeat. Then China joined forces with Silla, and between them they made Koguryŏ fight on two fronts. Koguryŏ eventually collapsed under the military pressure, and Silla emerged as the victor (though in order to survive it had to repel the Chinese once again). Thus, a unified Korean state was born.

Can you sense what is wrong in this story from the North Korean point of view? At least three things: first, Korea was unified by a *southern* kingdom; second, in order to do so, this kingdom allied itself with a powerful foreign country; third, this powerful foreign country played a major role in the wars of unification.

None of this was lost on the North Korean official historians. The analogies were simple: Silla, located in the south, could be seen as a predecessor of the ROK, while Koguryŏ, which during the latter stages of its history had its capital in Pyongyang, was, of course, perceived as a direct forerunner of the DPRK. China, a super-power of the era, was the USA of the 7th century AD. History needed to be rewritten and, when necessary, re-invented, to stress the supremacy of Koguryŏ and diminish the southerners' role in the nation's history.

Thus, in the early 1960s, the North Korean official "historians" began compiling a new, politically correct version of events that took place some fifteen centuries earlier. They declared that Koguryŏ was the most advanced of all of the Korean kingdoms, the embodiment of all possible virtues and, especially, of martial spirit. The achievements of the Koguryŏ kingdom were glorified while equally important achievements of the two other proto–Korean kingdoms were belittled. Kim Il Sung himself pronounced Koguryŏ to be the greatest era of Korea's past.

According to the new version of history, Silla did not really unify Korea since the larger part of the former Koguryŏ land remained outside its control. Thus, this nasty *southern* kingdom did not deserve the title of the first Korean unified empire! Were justice to be done, that title should go to Koryŏ, a dynasty that replaced Silla in the 10th century AD, and indeed recovered most of the former Koguryŏ area. From Pyongyang's point of view Koryŏ was preferable to its predecessor Silla because Koryŏ was based in the north (with its capital at Kaesŏng, in what is now North Korea) and often emphasized its connection with long-vanished Koguryŏ.

In the early 1970s, Kim Jong Il pointed to a major shortcoming of North

Korean archaeology: archaeologists had failed to locate the tomb of King Tongmyŏng, one of Koguryŏ's most remarkable leaders. According to Kim Jong Il, his tomb was moved to the vicinity of Pyongyang some fifteen centuries ago and then lost. Encouraged by the wise instructions of the Dear Leader, archaeologists immediately produced the required tomb which was duly "restored" and became a tourist attraction and an additional shrine of the Koguryŏ cult. There is little doubt that the tomb was, indeed, an authentic burial of the Koguryŏ period, but its relation to King Tongmyŏng is, to put it very mildly, dubious. However, North Korean "historians" are renowned for their well-proven ability not only to study ancient artifacts, but also to produce them whenever a political need arises.

As a matter of fact, they are equally adept at destroying authentic artifacts that are not supposed to exist within the current officially approved version of history: at least this is what they did to the remains of the early Chinese commandaries, which existed in Korea about two thousand years ago. The Chinese occupation actually laid the foundation for Korean culture and statehood in its present form — pretty much as the nearly simultaneous Roman rule over Britannia and Gallia created the base for the eventual emergence of the modern British and French states. But in the North Korean version of history the country is not supposed to be occupied by anybody. Hence, all evidence of these commandaries was destroyed as a part of an archaeological cleansing, *Juche* style....

The American Dream (North Korean Edition)

A GROUP OF FAT AMERICAN SOLDIERS with long Pinocchio-style noses are grinning while slicing the breasts off a screaming Korean girl. Another group of evil Yankees are busy using their bayonets to push terrified women and children into a ditch where they will, presumably, be buried alive. These are pictures one can see in countless museums across North Korea. This is how Americans have been depicted there: "two-legged wolves, imperialist bastards, people from the country of scoundrels," sadistic killers and scheming exploiters of the enslaved South Korea.

The anti–American message is an important part of official propaganda. Even though Pyongyang's upper crust have long been ardent admirers of Hollywood movies, the plebeians are fed an altogether different story. The

The propaganda poster at a Pyongyang middle school. The pictures below depict the suffering of South Koreans under the imperialist yoke: a Christian missionary is torturing a Korean child (a story known to every North Korean); innocent people are arrested; aggressive war games are conducted; unemployed people dream about jobs. Photograph by Andrew Graham.

Americans are depicted as enemies worse than even the Japanese. After all, the Japanese have been defeated and driven away from Korea by the Glorious General Kim Il Sung and his ever-victorious guerrillas, haven't they? But Americans are still there, torturing and exploiting the impoverished South, land of despair and famine, whose people dream of being liberated from their yoke.

North Koreans are bombarded by an anti–American propaganda whose hysterical pitch has reached heights undreamed of even in the Soviet Union of Stalin's times. It has been going on for many decades.

According to the North Korean version of history, the evil Americans have been planning the enslavement of the Korean people since at least the 1860s. The entire modern history of Korea is, in essence, a history of resistance to the encroachment of the perfidious Yankees.

Of course, all American missionaries are evil spies whose greatest pleasure is to occasionally kill a Korean child, preferably in some sadistic way. The U.S. diplomats are bloodthirsty maniacs who spend 24 hours a day scheming how to wipe the Korean people out of existence. The Korean War was a well-planned U.S. aggression. According to the official North Korean version of events, unchanged from June 1950, the war was launched by the South Koreans on American orders, but brave North Korean units repelled an invasion and within a few hours staged a powerful counteroffensive. This explanation goes against all the rules of warfare (one cannot instantly change a battle within such an improbably short time), but in North Korea it remains unquestioned by an overwhelming majority.

Anti-Americanism is an integral part of school curricula, including even in such seemingly innocent subjects as math. From Year One, North Korean primary school students have to study math with an anti–American twist, as is clear from the following quiz: "The brave uncles from the Korean People's Army destroyed six tanks of the wolf-like American bastards. Then they destroyed two more. How many tanks did they destroy altogether?" When kids grow older, they can operate with larger numbers: "The uncles of the Korean People's Army, in one combat, destroyed 87 American wolf-bastards. They killed 51 of the bastards, and took the remainder as prisoner. How many prisoners did they take?" (This is, as you probably guess, from a Year Two schoolbook, since the math is a little more sophisticated). And of course, one should not forget the sufferings of the South Koreans: "In a South Korean city occupied by the wolf-like U.S. Army, 2884 school-age children cannot attend school. Of them, 1561 are polishing shoes, while others are begging for food. How many children are begging for food in the Yankee-occupied city?"

North Koreans are required to attend regular meetings which are the closest real-life analogues to Orwellian nightmares: sessions in which the participants read horror-inducing — and usually very graphic and gory — stories about American (or Japanese) crimes and then profess their willingness to revenge the sufferings of the innocent Koreans. Attendance used to be obligatory, but in the recent years of relative relaxation, authorities often turn a blind eye to somebody's unwillingness to participate.

Against such a background, it comes as no surprise that a recent defector from the North shared with a South Korean academic a brilliant idea about how Kyŏngbokkung Palace should be used. This royal palace, located in downtown Seoul, was partially demolished by the Japanese in the 1910s to build the massive headquarters of the colonial government, and it was also the site of some of the more ugly scenes of imperialist scheming, including the brutal assassination of the Korean queen by Japanese agents and their Korean allies. After learning about those events, a defector instantly realized how this relic of the past should be properly used: "When I was watching the history museum and Kyŏngbokkung Palace, I thought of the [Japanese] Governors General and all those bastard Japs [...] Why not to use it as a place to pledge revenge during Rallies of Revenge against the aggressive nature of Japanese imperialism?"

We can regard all this as yet another bizarre peculiarity of what is arguably the world's most bizarre society. But let's face it: sooner or later the North Koreans will become citizens of a unified Korea, and their virulent nationalism will flow into mainstream Korean culture. The first generation of Northerners will have few if any opportunities to re-educate themselves: low incomes and their inability to understand foreign languages will ensure that their contacts with the non–Korean world will remain limited.

Psychologically, they are likely to have serious problems: after they get used to having enough rice to eat every day (still a novelty), they are nearly certain to discover that in a unified Korea the former Northerners will remain second-class citizens, due both to their insufficient skills and to discrimination of all kinds. Thus, they will need scapegoats, and nothing can rival nationalism in its ability to fabricate scapegoats. More likely, their views will infiltrate Korean society, making it more xenophobic. Or perhaps, catering to their superstitions and hunting for their votes, the politicians would add some xenophobic touch to their rhetoric and politics? Either way, not a cheerful prospect — and harmful, first of all, to Korea itself....

PART 3

The Arts and the Media

Radio Days

NORTH KOREAN PROPAGANDISTS HAVE IT EASY— for decades they have been able to operate in an environment of which no other Communist propagandist has even dreamed. Most propaganda mongers have had to contend with other visions of reality which were created and disseminated by political rivals, foreign media and even some private citizens. In most Communist countries, it was radio which served as the most natural source of unwanted information. Radio is easy to use, relatively cheap and portable. It is also capable of being received over long distances — i.e., from foreign stations. Western Russian-language programs had a big impact on the worldview of the Soviet citizen. *Voice of America*, BBC and *Radio Liberty* were listened to widely throughout the USSR of the 1970s–'80s and made a considerable contribution towards its eventual collapse.

Thus, it comes as no surprise that radio has always been a focus of special attention by the North Korean authorities. The Soviet authorities tried to jam those foreign radio stations which targeted a Soviet audience. Meanwhile, North Korea found a solution which was both cheaper and more reliable than jamming. They simply banned the domestic sale and use of free-tuning radio receivers. I could not find out when this ban was first introduced, but it is clear that it was already enforced in the 1960s.

All receivers which can be bought in North Korean shops are fixed on the wave-lengths of the official broadcasting stations. Thus, when a North Korean family gather around their large "Taedonggang" set (a locally produced valve radio using 1960s technology), they can listen only to officially approved and ideologically wholesome information.

Certainly, a person with some technical knowledge can easily make the necessary adjustments and transform such a receiver into a real radio. To prevent this from happening, the police undertake periodic random inspections of all registered receivers. Controlling the correct use of radio receivers is also an important duty of the heads of the so-called people's groups or *inminban*. The head of an *inminban* can break into any house at any time (even in the dead of night) to check for the possible presence of a non-registered receiver.

If a North Korean has access to foreign currency, he or she can buy a foreign-made radio set in one of the numerous hard-currency shops. However, after purchase the radio set was subjected to minor surgery in a police workshop — its tuning had to be fixed, so it could only receive official Pyongyang broadcasts (it appears that this practice is declining in recent years).

The control was never perfect. In the mid–1980s, at least one of my North Korean acquaintances had access to a normal radio with free tuning and listened to foreign programs with his family. Military communication specialists can also use their equipment to listen to foreign (and, above all, Seoul) broadcasts — and often do this. This is, no doubt, a risky business. A North Korean who is caught listening to a South Korean broadcast may be sent to prison camp. For example, the movie writer Chŏng Sŏng-san was sentenced to 12 years imprisonment in 1995. And his crime? When doing his military training, he was caught listening to a South Korean broadcast (Chŏng was lucky: he managed to escape and eventually defected to the South).

Thus, good North Koreans are expected and, indeed, required to listen to the local broadcast only. And what can they listen to if they switch on their politically correct radios without free tuning? To North Korean radio, of course!

The history of North Korean broadcasting began in October 1945, with what was, from 1946, called Radio Pyongyang. In 1948 it was renamed the Korean Central Broadcasting Station or KCBS. Up to this day the station remains a mainstay of the North Korean domestic broadcasting media.

North Korean broadcasting produces a rather bizarre impression on a foreigner (or, for that matter, on a South Korean). In the North Korean broadcast, music alternates with short information blocks. Every hour begins with the news, largely identical to that published in the newspaper *Nodong sinmun*. Then there are several minutes of marches or songs about Kim Il Sung, Kim Jong Il, or other lofty political subjects. Those songs are followed by a short 5–10 minute talk — either a commentary on the brilliant internal situation of the North, or on the misery of South Korean life, or on the wisdom of the philosophy of *Juche*. Often, articles from *Nodong sinmun* are also broadcast on the radio.

South Korean scholars often make a painstaking analysis of the content of North Korean programming. According to a recent estimate, in 2000 the KCBS programming spent 34.2 percent of its time praising Kim Jong Il or Kim Il Sung, 28.8 percent encouraging the workers to toil even harder, 17.4 percent explaining and promoting the *Juche* ideology, and 12.0 percent telling stories about the suffering of the South Korean "masses" and schemes of the "Seoul puppets."

Most programs are as boring as articles from *Nodong sinmun*, even for the North Koreans, who are deprived of better food for thought. However, there are some programs that target specific audiences, like "Soldiers' Hour" or "Young Pioneers' Hour," and they enjoy some popularity within their target audience.

KCBS also broadcasts programs in foreign languages — Russian, Chinese, Japanese, Arabic, and Spanish. Their content is, once again, poorly presented propaganda. Unfortunately (or, perhaps, fortunately), the North Koreans have been remarkably inept in their PR activity in the West. The problem is not the message: after all, we have seen how very unpleasant regimes have managed to win the heartfelt support of the Western public (or at least its Right or Left-inclined sectors).

The problem is the presentation, and the concomitant blatant inability to understand the mindset of foreign audiences. Most of the texts are merely translations from the Korean originals, and they often contain allusions and idioms which are either incomprehensible or strange for a non–Korean.

Quite often the inflated tributes to the Great Leader and to the Dear Leader, delivered in a badly edited foreign version, produce the opposite of the intended effect on the audience, making the North into a laughingstock. I still remember how in the 1970s, when I was a teenager in the then Soviet Union in my native Leningrad, many barbershops stocked copies of *Korea* magazine, a lavishly illustrated North Korean propaganda monthly. What was such a publication doing in the barbershops? The answer, I suspect, would be quite embarrassing for its editors: it was subscribed to in order to amuse the patrons who were waiting for a haircut. The North Korean propaganda appeared very weird to the Russians — not least because it looked like a grossly exaggerated version of their own official propaganda. The grotesquely bad Russian translation of the texts also provided unintended comical effects.

However, KCBS is not the only battleship in North Korea's broadcast system fleet. There are a number of others, but these target largely or exclusively the South.

First of all, I should mention Radio Pyongyang (not to be mixed up with the earlier version of Radio Pyongyang which existed in the 1940s). It was established in 1967 as the "Second KCBS" and acquired its present name in 1972. It broadcasts programs that are somehow adjusted to the tastes of the

South Korean audience, as well as to overseas Koreans. It also has an FM branch, whose transmitters target the northern part of South Korea. The "FM Radio Pyongyang" broadcasts musical programs, with an emphasis on classical music. It mixes that with radio dramas and book readings that eulogize the North and criticize the South, to whose population it is intended, at least partially.

Radio Pyongyang does not make a secret of whom it represents. However, the North was engaged in "black propaganda" as well. For decades the North-based "Voice of National Salvation" declared itself to be a clandestine station secretly broadcasting from somewhere in South Korean territory, and managed by the local leftist underground. This statement can even be found in the North Korean encyclopedias. I do not know whether anybody was silly enough to believe this improbable statement, but it was how the "Voice of National Salvation" described itself until 2003 when its programs were discontinued. Its transmitters were actually located in a few North Korean cities along the border, and the station which went on air in 1970 employed a number of South Korean announcers and editors who had defected to the North, or who had been kidnapped by the North Koreans (the difference in some instances between abduction and defection is hardly clear-cut).

Meanwhile, recent years have brought profound changes to North Korea. The number of radio sets with free tuning has increased considerably. Most of them have been smuggled from China during the last decade — and, of course, these radios are widely used for listening to South Korean broadcasts. Once upon a time, North Korean authorities managed to cut their people off from the outside world. But one cannot keep a country sealed forever — at least, not in the 21st century....

Cable Radio

EVERY MORNING AT 5:00 A.M. THE SOUND of the DPRK national anthem begins the new day in countless North Korean homes. The Third Radio, a nationwide network of cable radio, starts its programming.

One sometimes comes across statements claiming that the North Korean "cable radio" system is unique and has no analogues elsewhere in the world. This is not really the case: like many other North Korean institutions, the third radio came from the Soviet Union. Indeed, since the 1950s every Soviet flat was officially required to have a cable radio outlet. The "cable radio" did not only belong to the Communist world: in the 1950s and 1960s, similar networks were quite popular in South Korea. Only the spread of transistor radios pushed them out of existence in the 1970s.

In North Korea, the development of "cable radio" began in the 1940s, and by 1975 it was declared that the network had reached all cities and villages.

What is good about "cable radio?" First of all, it is very cheap. The laying of the network costs some money, but the cable sets are extremely primitive and are therefore much cheaper than wireless. Essentially, the set consists of a loudspeaker with a single knob for volume control. There is only one channel. Thus, people who would never be able to afford a relatively expensive wireless can easily buy such a simple contraption.

There are also political reasons driving North Korea's penchant for cable radio. First, wireless sets can be tuned to foreign broadcasts — and this is quite dangerous for the regime. Even though they sell radio sets without tuning in North Korea, there is still the danger that a technically savvy person could modify the radio and then learn something improper from a foreign broadcast.

Cable radio also has another advantage: it cannot be intercepted. Therefore, one can safely broadcast news not meant for foreign ears. In the 1980s, when relations with the USSR went sour and Soviet Communism was heading towards its collapse, the North Korean authorities still did not criticize their erstwhile sponsor openly. However, critical material was frequently broadcast through the third radio — and listened to with great interest!

Another important advantage of "cable radio" is its ability to target only the population of a selected area. This is widely used by the North Korean civil defense system during mock air raid drills. The "third radio" also plays a major role in staging various mass events. Through the cable radio speakers, the inhabitants of a particular district are given orders: when and where they should go to welcome a foreign delegation, how they should dress, and what they should do. When there were chances to expect that foreign guests would have an opportunity to talk to the locals, the North Koreans were provided with clear instructions how they should answer the most likely questions of the foreigners.

From the 1980s, "cable radio" outlets became obligatory in new apartment complexes, while in older buildings the wires simply go into the flats through small holes in the windows. The speakers are present not only in homes but also in offices. Quite often "cable radio" is connected to large loudspeakers installed in public places. When I think about my life in North Korea in the 1980s, I still vividly remember this ever-present background sound — the unremitting military marches, occasionally interrupted by news broadcasts.

The entire cable network is run by the Ministry of Communication, and the post offices ensure that the network and speakers are kept in good order. In better times, they were required to inspect the system once a year — but now this rule, like many others, is generally ignored.

The programming of the "third radio" is a usual mixture of music, news, and educational programs, all heavily spiced with propaganda. The morning begins with stories about the alleged heroic exploits of the Kim family, while during the day there is an abundance of short news bulletins and music. Once upon a time the music consisted only of military-style marches, but nowadays, the North Korean version of pop music is also often broadcast. In the evening one can listen to serialized "radio dramas" and readings from novels.

In spite of the rather heavy dose of ideology, North Koreans love their "third radio." It is cheap and reliable, and some of its programs enjoy great popularity. Even though some families have TV sets, in many homes the "third radio" is the only source of entertainment.

The Face Value of Nodong Sinmun

IN OCTOBER 1997 RELATIONS BETWEEN the two Koreas ran into another crisis. This crisis was so serious that North Korea temporarily halted the construction of the light water reactors, despite the immense importance the project had for the country's economy. Pyongyang explained that this was the only possible answer to the outrageous discovery that was made in the dormitory of the South Korean specialists (the latter took part in the reactor construction).

What actually happened? A recent issue of the *Nodong sinmun* was found in the waste bin — torn and crumpled! Its first page was seriously damaged! So what? — might ask a Western or South Korean reader, quite accustomed to the unceremonious treatment of old newspapers. Foolish them, for the attitude to newspapers in the North, and in particular to *Nodong sinmun*, is very different. The newspapers' front pages nearly always bear the sacred portraits of Kim Il Sung and Kim Jong Il, and this alone entitles them to special treatment. And, apart from this, *Nodong sinmun* is, well, *Nodong sinmun....*

Nodong Sinmun is published by the Korean Workers' Party's Central Committee, a body that in everything but name is the supreme ruling institution in the country. It is the mouthpiece of the Party, and every single issue of *Nodong sinmun* is, by definition, approved by the Party and Leader. The *Nodong Sinmun* is eerily reminiscent of the Soviet *Pravda* — not the mild, even occasionally entertaining *Pravda* of the 1970s, but of the venom-spitting *Pravda* of the late Stalin era.

This comes as no surprise. *Nodong sinmun* was established in 1946 and for the first years of its history was run by a group of Soviet journalists of Korean extraction. Ki Sŏk-pok, a Soviet-Korean journalist, was instrumental in establishing the *Nodong sinmun* tradition. Ki was eventually purged and fled back to the USSR — with the complete eradication of his name from North Korean history books being the predictable result. They imported not only a general style, but also a number of particular features borrowed whole-sale from the then contemporary Soviet media culture. For me, the similarity between *Nodong Sinmun* of 2000 and, say, *Pravda* of 1950 is striking: not only in the underlying ideology, but also in the layout of the paper, its structure and style.

One of those borrowed Soviet traditions was the special role of unsigned editorials. In principle, everything published in *Nodong sinmun* has supreme approval, but the editorials are seen as the voice of the Party in its purest form. Indeed, the topics and major ideas of the *Nodong sinmun* editorials are approved in the highest echelons of government, sometimes by Kim Jong Il himself.

Westerners have always considered official Communist newspapers bor-ing. They are quite correct (the inhabitants of the Communist countries are of the same opinion). Nonetheless, few Communist newspapers were ever as boring as *Nodong sinmun*. This is largely a deliberate strategy. The *Nodong sinmun* editors keep reminding their staff that their mission is to educate, not to entertain. Human interest stories of the sort that managed to find their way even onto the pages of *Pravda* and *People's Daily* are exceptional in *Nodong sinmun*.

This solemn approach was somewhat relaxed recently, and articles about sport or popular actors began to appear occasionally in the newspaper, albeit even these articles were not free from the obligatory quotations from Kim Jong Il's wise works and eulogies to the Dear Leader's wisdom and greatness.

Nodong sinmun typically has six pages, and until recently the structure of the newspaper was very orderly. Nowadays, the old system is not always followed, but the general layout still remains the same.

The first four pages of the newspaper contain official material, lengthy editorials and reports about the heroic deeds of North Korean workers, farm-ers, and soldiers. There might be some articles about the greatness and wis-dom of the Leaders as well. The fifth page occupies itself with the living hell of South Korean life, and the sufferings of the poor Southerners under U.S. occupation (GIs are shooting them at will, children are begging for food, and students sell their blood to pay tuition fees). The sixth page is taken up with international news.

Not all of the articles in *Nodong sinmun* notify the reader about achievements and heroic deeds. Now and then the newspaper also informs its readers that in a particular part of the country there are still some problems. Some local officials are not treating the masses' complaints quickly enough. Some small factory cannot meet the allocated quotas of production. Some party organization does not work hard enough to educate the students in the right spirit. These critical materials are invariably approved at a very high bureaucratic level, and for the people mentioned in such articles the critique in *Nodong sinmun* spells at least broken careers, if not worse.

What happened to the unlucky South Korean engineers whose actions triggered the scandal in October 1997? They eventually resumed work — on the condition that they would treat *Nodong sinmun* properly....

Bringing Home the ... Television

WHEN A NORTH KOREAN PROPAGANDA magazine wants to depict a supposedly typical living room in a Pyongyang house, one feature is nearly always suspiciously prominent: a large TV set somewhere in a corner. By placing such emphasis on the TV, the North Korean propagandists unwittingly reveal that TV sets are still seen as something special and as a symbol of prosperity.

Indeed, in the North a TV set remains beyond the reach of poorer families. No reliable statistics are available, but according to the most optimistic estimates there are some 2 million TV sets in the country. This means that slightly less than half of all North Korean families have access to television at home, and TV sets at home are still a sign of relative prosperity in the countryside or in small towns where only some 25 percent of households own one.

Until the recent crisis in the command economy, most TV sets were distributed through work units, a practice that applied not only to TVs but to all consumer durables, even wristwatches. Once a North Korean applied for permission to purchase a TV set through his work unit, his or her name was recorded on a waiting list. When a particular plant, workshop, or school was allocated its quota of TV sets, these were distributed among the people on the list. Strictly speaking, people were given not TVs but special permission which granted them the right to buy a TV from a state-run shop. No shop would sell a TV (or, for that matter, a wristwatch or a radio) to a person who had enough money but could not produce the required permission.

The waiting period was usually years. Its duration depended, among other things, on the type of work unit where a would-be buyer was employed:

The TV sets are going to customers. Photograph by Anna Fifield.

politically more powerful factories or plants were allocated larger quotas of consumer durables. In this regard, heavy industry enjoyed a number of important privileges, while the armament factories fared the best.

Of course, there were ways to get around all these restrictions and regulations. First of all, TVs could be bought privately even in the 1980s when the black market operated strictly underground. In those days TVs and other consumer durables were the major items sold on the market. The prices were exorbitant, however: the average black-and-white TV could easily cost the equivalent of five average annual salaries.

In the 1980s, when many Koreans tried to secure a job at the huge logging projects in the Russian Far East, the opportunity to buy a TV set was a major incentive. After one year of hard and often dangerous work, a thrifty worker could save enough money to buy a Soviet TV set, which was brought back home as a sign of prosperity and a source of joy for the family (or, alternatively, was sold on the black market at a huge profit).

Another source of TV sets was Japan. The families who had relatives there went to great lengths to persuade their uncles and aunties to present them with TVs. In some cases, the TVs received from these Japanese relatives were then sold or used to bribe officials in order to procure something extraordinarily special (I know of an instance when such a TV presented to an official was exchanged for permission to dwell in a more prestigious city).

And, of course, TV sets, together with other consumer durables, were widely sold at the hard currency shops where one could buy them for a hefty sum of "imperialist money."

In recent years, since the state-managed distribution networks came to a complete halt, the only way to get a TV has been to buy it through the market or at a currency shop. It seems that they still compile the waiting lists, but no goods are forthcoming.

A large proportion of the TV sets used in North Korea are imported. Most of these are old Russian-made black-and-white TVs, while Chinese and Romanian sets are also widely used. There were, of course, locally produced TVs as well. In the late 1970s North Korea, with Romanian technical assistance, built a factory which could produce up to 100,000 black-and-white sets a year. However, local customers strongly preferred imported items — if they could afford them, of course.

North Korea began to broadcast TV programs in color on April 15, 1974, on Kim Il Sung's 62nd birthday. By that time, color TV had long ceased to be a novelty in the developed world. Nonetheless, South Korea switched to color only in December 1980! Thus the North was six years ahead of its arch-rival — just another reminder that once upon a time the North could compete with the South on equal terms. However, nowadays the North's backwardness is all too obvious in many fields, and its TV broadcast system is no exception.

Unlike South Korea, which uses the NTSC standard first developed in the USA, the North opted for the "European" PAL standard, which is also used in China.

Special measures are taken to isolate the North Korean viewers from foreign broadcasts. This is especially important in northern border areas where Chinese programs (including Korean-language ones) can be easily received. To prevent this, in the old days the police subjected *all* private TVs in borderland areas to minor surgery. In one instance, the TV sets had all their buttons but one disabled so only one channel could be selected. As we will see below, in the countryside there is only one official channel, so its button was the only one left functioning. If the TV had an old-style rotating channel switch, the switch was fixed on the officially approved channel of the Pyongyang Central TV which, as far as my defector friends remember, was channel 9. The switch was then plastered with paper and fixed with the seal of the local police office. TV sets and their seals were subjected to random checks to ensure that nobody would dare watch Chinese broadcasts. However, nowadays the authorities seem to be more relaxed in enforcing these regulations, and a large presence of smuggled Chinese TV sets makes this exercise meaningless anyway.

Currently the North boasts only three TV channels: Central Korean TV, Educational TV and Mansudae TV.

Central Korean TV is the oldest and largest of all the channels. It began broadcasting in March 1963 as Pyongyang TV and was renamed Central Korean TV in 1970. This is also the only channel which can be received across the country (reception is possible across some 75 percent of North Korea's territory).

Even in the better days of the energy-rich 1980s, the Central TV's daily programming was short: on weekdays Central TV broadcast only from 3 P.M. to 11:00 P.M., while on Sundays and holidays the broadcast began at 10 A.M. and continued until 11:30 P.M. During the famine and energy crisis of the late 1990s, the broadcast time was cut to a mere 2–3 hours a day.

The day's broadcast begins with the news, followed by the children's programs. Then there come hours of documentaries and features dealing with North Korea's fabulous successes in economy, education, science, agricultural production and the like. Of course, the deeds of the ruling dynasty are also extolled. Normally, there is also a movie or a TV drama. In recent years, the number of movies and TV dramas on the Central TV increased, and now these occupy some 30% of the broadcast time. However, the same programs are repeated very often: the repertoire of available movies, dramas and shows is too small even for short daily broadcast.

Another North Korean channel is the so-called Mansudae TV, which was officially inaugurated in 1983, after several years of experimentation. It broadcasts only on Saturdays, Sundays and public holidays and its programs can be received only in and around Pyongyang. Mansudae TV's programming is much less propagandistic (that is, less boring) than that of Central TV: it largely broadcasts shows and movies, including foreign content. Of course, only movies with sufficiently wholesome political messages are selected, with special preference given to old Soviet, Chinese and East European war movies.

According to rumors, Mansudae TV studio has another mission as well: it records foreign TV shows and movies for Kim Jong Il's edification.

From 1971, Kaesong, North Korea's second largest city, acquired its own TV station. Kaesong is located very close to the DMZ, and thus Kaesong TV had the dual task of conducting propaganda against the South while still catering to Kaesong's own needs. In 1997 Kaesong TV was split in two, one part becoming "Educational TV" while the other, specializing in psych-ops, came to be subsumed under Central TV.

Another way to reach a foreign audience is by satellite TV. While no dishes are allowed inside the country, from 1999 Central TV's programs have been broadcast by a satellite company in Thailand.

Perhaps TV is as high as it gets in the North as far as high-tech entertainment is concerned. There is no Internet there yet — and it is unlikely to spread under the current system. So, the North Koreans are fed a very meager information diet. But that will be our next story....

was explored

The Newscast

WHAT ARE NORTH KOREANS SUPPOSED to know about the world? Let us have a look at a typical news bulletin, the North Korea TV broadcast of April 25, 2005. I chose the day almost at random (almost, since there was a reason why I decided to watch the program on that particular day — but more of this later). The thirty-minute bulletin began with a long report about the world media's reaction to Kim Jong Il's visit to China. The announcer, a *hanbok*-clad auntie, spent a couple of minutes reading the long list of foreign newspapers that carried reports of the trip (including publications in Nepal and Cambodia, where news of Kim Jong Il is apparently hungrily devoured). Auntie's exalted tone would be an experience for most South Koreans — perhaps they have only witnessed such a spectacle when an especially frenzied pastor delivers a fire-and-brimstone sermon in church....

Without catching her breath, auntie moved to the second news item: the unveiling of a huge picture depicting Kim Jong Il and Kim Il Sung standing on Paektu Mountain. This event took place in the northeastern port city of Ch'ŏngjin and was attended by a large and remarkably well-organized crowd dressed in their Sunday best. After the speeches the masses were allowed to pay tribute to the sacral image.

The next item was a pretty female journalist interviewing some military officers. They were asked about how they felt on that special day. Indeed, in North Korea April 25 is Army Foundation Day. Each officer delivered a long speech extolling the wisdom and greatness of the "Three Great Generals from Paektu Mountains." Those great strategists are Kim Il Sung (a commander of a battalion-size guerrilla band), his son (not yet born during the campaign), and his wife (a cook and seamstress in the said band). Each soldier thanked the fate that had allowed him to serve the Great General and the Dear Leader, Kim Jong Il. The speeches each lasted several minutes, but not a single slip of the tongue occurred. One can imagine how much time it took to memorize and rehearse the texts.

The fourth item reported the great love that the military feels for the ruling dynasty. The military representatives attended the Kŭmsusan Palace where Kim Il Sung's body lies in state, and paid homage to the items once used by the late Great Leader: his personal railway carriage and his Mercedes. The news report also showed soldiers and dignitaries laying flowers at the feet of the 22-meter-high statue of the Great Leader and at other monuments in Pyongyang. Meanwhile, a new announcer (male) managed to spend nearly ten minutes on the greatness of the Kims and the selflessness of soldiers who are always ready to die for them.

Then the announcer informed the viewers that a concert had been held to commemorate Army Foundation Day. This was followed by footage of a public dance party held in a large open plaza in Pyongyang. While cameras were showing the uniform-clad lads and lasses, who were obviously having a good time dancing on an early spring evening, the announcer explained that they are very proud to be soldiers of the Dear Leader and ready to fight for the *Juche* revolution.

After two more news bulletins about the achievements of the workers and their love for the Dear Leader, a children's concert was reported. The announcer explained that this demonstrated the happiness of the Korean children who grow up under the wise guidance of the Dear Leader.

The next report also dealt with children. It showed students at a primary school making birds' nesting boxes. A laudable undertaking, indeed, but even this was spiced with proper ideological commentary: the kids were putting the nesting boxes near the old house of Kim Senior, in a forest where the dynasty's founder once loved to walk with his father.

The final story dealt with a begonia flower presented to Kim Jong Il by a Japanese admirer.

That was it. No news at all, only endless panegyrics of Kim Jong Il and Kim Il Sung. Nothing about the outside world and nothing about the events unfolding near the Chinese border.

Yes, all this was broadcast on April 25, when the world media were talking about a huge train explosion at Yongch'ŏn station and the remarkable efforts of Korean and foreign doctors, rescue workers, and engineers. Pyongyang admitted to the world that the disaster occurred, and this admission was widely hailed as a sign of change. But the news only consisted of the wind-up smiling mannequin-like dancers, and aging colonels delivering long eulogies to the superhuman wisdom of the Dear Leader.

People who are fed such news reports are remarkably ignorant about the outside world, and that is a travesty. However, people are not stupid, and information filters in somehow—more so in recent years with the development of technology and the disintegration of controls that brought about dramatic changes to North Korean society.

The Reel Thing

NORTH KOREA IS *THE* NATION OF MOVIE BUFFS—at least, that is what the available data seem to suggest. Indeed, in 1987 Pyongyang radio stated that the average North Korean visited the cinema 21 times a year. The South Korean sociologists who, in the mid–1990s, undertook a survey of defectors came out with a similar figure —15–18 times a year. Just for comparison, the average South Korean visits the theater merely 2.3 times a year.

What are the reasons behind this popularity? Of course, a major role is played by obligatory attendance. Indeed, everyone is required to view certain movies. Needless to say, these movies convey politically wholesome messages about the greatness of the Party and its Leaders.

However, in most cases people go to the movies of their own volition. This is by far the most easily available form of recreation. And it is cheap, too. Before the recent economic reforms and price hikes, a movie ticket would cost between 0.4 and 1.5 NK *won*, some 0.5–1% of the average monthly salary.

And, of course, the North Korea lifestyle does not provide much alternative to movie-going. Restaurants are rare, expensive, and beyond the reach of most people; computer game rooms are almost unheard of, and leisure travel is unusual and difficult to arrange.

The government is also supportive of the cinema. Long ago Lenin, the founding father of state socialism, remarked that from the propaganda point of view, the cinema is the most important of all arts. This maxim is still followed by the North Koreans. Indeed, Kim Jong Il himself has paid special attention to the film industry (perhaps partially because glamorous women play such a prominent role in it?).

As a matter of fact, the North Korean leader was a known cinema fan in his university years. In the early 1960s, Kim Jong Il used his position to arrange private screenings of foreign movies, which were imported in a very small number of copies. Eventually he initiated the so-called operations #100, which was aimed at acquiring copies of foreign movies and shipping them to the North, largely by the embassies. In the late 1960s, he took charge of the North Korean cinema. This provided him with opportunities to meet beautiful women (most of his known lovers were actresses), but he also used his political clout to improve the technical sophistication of the North Korean cinema, if not its aesthetic quality.

Revolutionary enthusiasm and the unremitting cruelty of the enemy — the U.S. imperialists and their South Korean puppets — have been the major topics of the North Korean cinema for many decades. However, the movie-goers are used to these ideological messages and somehow manage to filter them

A movie theater in downtown Pyongyang. Photograph by Andrei Lankov.

out, concentrating their attention on the depiction of "real life" with its problems of relationships and families.

Escapist movies are also popular. Of course, the baddies who have their asses kicked are all the usual suspects — U.S. imperialists, Japanese militarists, their collaborators or, for a change, the reactionary landlords of the more distant past. Nonetheless, North Korean movie-goers first and foremost enjoy a good action movie — even if the political message is swallowed as well (but the same is applicable to admirers of James Bond movies, isn't it?). The first such features appeared in the mid–1980s, and the North Koreans rushed to see action movies like *Hong Kil-dong* (a Korean analogue of the Robin Hood story, set in the 17th century) or *Order #027* (the North Korean commandos displaying their prowess during the Korean War).

Foreign movies were re-introduced to the North around the same time. In the 1950s, the Soviet, Chinese and other fraternal movies dominated the Korean screen. However, in the 1960s Pyongyang's relations with Moscow began to deteriorate and the increasingly liberal Soviet Union came to be perceived as a source of dangerous revisionism. Hence, for two decades the North

Koreans were seldom shown new Soviet movies, even if the ban was never complete and partially lifted in the early 1980s.

No North Korean statistics have been released, but it seems that one of the greatest box-office successes in North Korean history was *Pirates of the 20th century*, a 1979 Soviet action movie about Russian sailors who use their improbable martial arts skills to teach a lesson or two to the naughty pirates somewhere in the Southern Pacific. The story line is utterly implausible, the acting is primitive, but martial arts and special effects are abundant, and even semi-nudity is present (well, I am not sure if the latter scene survived the scissors of the North Korean censors).

On a more sophisticated note, the Pyongyang movie buffs enjoy romantic comedies by Russian director Riazanov, also a major hit among Russian middle-brow audiences (to which the present author proudly belongs!). Other hits are Soviet-era intellectual spy thrillers, based on numerous novels by the prolific author Yulian Semenov. They combine a correct ideological message (brave KGB agents thwart the intrigues of the U.S. imperialists) with a level of sophistication which would be impermissible in North Korean cinema (Semenov's cunning imperialists are by no means the one-dimensional wolf-like Yankees of North Korean films).

Indian movies are popular as well. While relatively unknown in the West, the studios of Bombay's "Bollywood" churn out an astonishing number of musicals and melodramas to be enjoyed across South Asia and some parts of the former Communist bloc. These movies are sugary, hyper-sentimental, with one-dimensional characters, predictable storylines, primitive dialogue and no acting worthy of the name. But they also have a lot of singing and dancing numbers as well as stunningly beautiful sets and scenery. It is escapism at its finest. Perhaps even the heavy dose of syrup in the storyline appeals to the North Korean public, who for decades have subsisted on a diet of ideologically wholesome movies where the major emotion is love for the Leader (and, perhaps, hatred for the enemies).

When talking to North Koreans inside the North it is impossible not to notice that one of the greatest praises for a movie is, "It is so interesting, it has no ideology." People are tired of ideological messages — at least, if those messages are put in a crude and one-dimensional way. It seems that not only movie producers, hardly happy about ideology themselves, but even their supervisors are beginning to realize this — at least, the most recent decade was *both* a time of economic disaster and political relaxation in North Korea.

Indeed, the major hits of North Korean cinema in the early 2000s were movies that paid only lip service to the obligatory political rhetoric. One of the recent sensations is the epic *Living Ghosts*, which deals with one of the worst disasters in Korean history — the tragedy of *Ukishima-maru*, the Japanese ship that sank in August 1945 while bringing Korean workers back home from Japan. Several thousand people died in the tragedy, whose scale probably surpassed that of the *Titanic*. The North Koreans since long ago have asserted that the ship sank because an explosive device had been planted by some Japanese extremists.

Indeed, *Living Ghosts* is obviously influenced by James Cameron's famous movie, which was not shown in North Korean theaters but was widely watched by VCR owners (that is, by the entire North Korean elite). *Living Ghosts* had the largest number of extras in the DPRK's movie history and made generous use of computer special effects, still a novelty in North Korean cinema. And, of course, it included a fictional love story heavily overladen with the obligatory set of propaganda statements.

The tragedy of *Ukishima-maru* is a part of rather distant history, and thus it now can be embellished and used as a background for a melodramatic story. However, there have been much more recent tragedies, and another movie triumph deals with the greatest of them. *The People of Chagangdo*, released in 2001, is probably the closest North Korean approximation to harsh realism to date. Chagangdo is the northernmost province of the country and it suffered greatly during the famine of 1996–1999. The movie was surprisingly frank when it depicted the local people eating a mixture of maize and charcoal. Of course, the harsh scenes are peppered with the expected rhetoric about the hard march of the faithful and their boundless loyalty to Kim Jong Il, but such a degree of openness was unthinkable until recently — and made the movie an instant success.

Will this period of frankness continue? And will the regime be able to survive more open forms of expression? The liberal era in the USSR lasted for three decades, while in China it is now some twenty-five years old (and counting). But rulers of those countries were lucky: they had no affluent capitalist half; there was no Southern China. This makes a difference, one might suspect.

The Workers' Paradise?
The Social Structure
of the DPRK

A Rank System

"I LOVED HIM, BUT MY PARENTS did not allow me to marry him: his *sŏngbun* was too bad." This is how a middle-aged North Korean refugee referred to her first romantic affair. It is an old story: parents will not allow young lovers to remain together because of some pragmatic reason. But what is *sŏngbun*, anyway?

Every North Korean knows only too well what *sŏngbun* means. Despite its professed allegiance to ideas of equality, the DPRK populace is divided into hereditary groups which are not much more flexible than, say, the "estates" of feudal Europe. These groups are largely hereditary and membership of a particular group (the above-mentioned *sŏngbun*) largely determines an individual's career path, school and marriage partner. Over the most recent decade, the *sŏngbun's* sway has slightly diminished — but it still remains a considerable force.

The development of the *sŏngbun* system began in the late 1950s, when Kim Il Sung eliminated his political rivals and established absolute control over the country. On 30 May 1957, the Standing Committee (Politburo) of the Korean Workers' Party adopted a resolution which bore the lengthy title: "On the Transformation of the Struggle with Counter-Revolutionary Elements into an All-People's All-Party Movement" (the "May 30th Resolution" for short). This document laid the foundations for one of the first large-scale purges in North Korea's history.

Although there had been purges before, the earlier campaigns had been different. They were either associated with clearly definable "enemies" (landlords, Christian missionaries, etc.) or targeted "erring" Party cadres who were real or potential adversaries of the regime as understood by Kim. This time it was decided to check the political credentials of virtually all North Korean adults. Every single citizen had to be investigated and allocated to a particular group.

This was a truly unique system. In other Communist countries, origin did play a role, and relatives of, say, a political criminal would have problems with getting some types of jobs. However, the system was never formalized to a comparable extent. In the Soviet Union of the 1920s and early 1930s, the system discriminated against the former gentry and other scions of the "hostile classes," but this approach lasted for less than two decades, and by the time the present author was born in the 1960s, many Russians openly flaunted their real or invented aristocratic origin. North Korea, however, was different.

At first, the campaign to "develop the struggle against counter-revolutionary elements into an all-people, all-party movement" was sluggish. It sparked up only in 1959 when a special organ was established within the KWP Central Committee to manage it. This coincided with a great upsurge of terror which resembled the Soviet "Great Purge" of 1937–38. This new investigation agency body was headed by Kim Yŏng-ju, the younger brother of Kim Il Sung. Similar bodies, employing almost 7000 people nation-wide, were created within the lower-level Party committees.

In the course of this campaign the entire population of North Korea was divided into three major groups: "hostile forces," "neutral forces," and "friendly forces"—a division which is largely retained to this day. A decisive role was played by one's family background.

Thus, North Korea began to develop a system of unequal hereditary groups. The system was influenced by Maoist China, where similar experiments took place in the late 1950s. However, in North Korea it was more elaborate and lasted much longer.

During the 1957–1960 campaign, many "unmasked counterrevolutionaries" were put on trial. About 2,500 people were executed, sometimes publicly, while about 100,000 received lighter punishments.

An important part of the campaign was Decree No. 149 of the North Korean Cabinet. According to this decree, people belonging to the "hostile forces" were prohibited from residing near the border or seacoast, closer than 50 km from Pyongyang and Kaesong, or closer than 20 km to any other large city. Given that North Korea is a fairly small country, this meant the forced transfer of "hostile elements" to inhospitable mountainous provinces in the north. About 70,000 people are believed to have been relocated to these regions.

Part 4: The Workers' Paradise? The Social Structure of the DPRK

68

By the beginning of 1961 the campaign of exposing and resettling "counterrevolutionaries" had been successfully completed. However, the increasing militaristic frenzy and further strengthening of Kim Il Sung's dictatorial rule required a new, more detailed check on loyalty. Thus, a new campaign was launched in 1964. Between 1964 and 1969, the campaign was conducted by "620 groups" which were specially created for this purpose. They redefined the system and created the division of the population into 51 groups which were broken into three main classes. This system still exists today, some 40 years later.

In order to give the reader a better feeling for the North Korean bureaucratic system I will name a few of the groups which are included in these strata.

Let us begin with the "goodies." The "primary" stratum includes 12 groups: (1) workers who originated from working families; (2) former farmhands; (3) former poor peasants; (4) the personnel of state organizations; (5) KWP (Party) members; (6) the family members of deceased revolutionaries; (7) the family members of national liberation fighters; (8) revolutionary intelligentsia (that is, those who received their education after Liberation); (9) the families of civilians who were killed during the Korean war; (10) the families of soldiers who were killed during the Korean war; (11) the families of servicemen; (12) heroes of the war.

The "uncertain" stratum includes 9 groups — whose descriptions I omit for the sake of brevity.

Then, as one might expect, it is the "enemies" who form the longest list. The "baddies" are: (1) workers of complicated origin, that is, people who though they had become workers after Liberation, had formerly been entrepreneurs and officials; (2) former rich peasants; (3) former small or medium merchants; (4) former landlords, that is, people who before the reform of 1946 had more than 5 ha of land; (5) people who participated in pro–Japanese or pro–American activities; (6) former officials in the Japanese colonial administration; (7) families of people of good social origin who fled to the South during the war; (8) families of people of bad origin who fled to the South during the war; (9) Chinese Koreans who returned from China in the 1950s; (10) Japanese Koreans who returned from Japan in the 1960s.

I will stop here since the complete list of "recommended suspects" is far too long. Among others, it also includes practicing Protestants, Catholics and Buddhists, descendants of shamans or courtesans, families of prisoners and the like.

There is considerable variation in rights and privileges not only between these strata, but also between different groups within each stratum. Of course, it is not as bad to be the grandson of a rich peasant than, say, the son of a political criminal. The position of the ethnic Koreans from Japan is even more controversial: the authorities keep these away from some sensitive jobs and closely watch them while courting them in order to extract money and expertise from the friends and relatives they have left behind in Japan.

A person's fate is determined by his or her group, by his *sŏngbun*. It influences his or her chances of getting a good job and a higher education, of being allowed to live in Pyongyang or another major city, and, hence, their standard of living, their punishment in the event of a criminal prosecution, and many other things. Thus, members of the "hostile stratum" normally have no chance of studying in prestigious Pyongyang colleges. *Sŏngbun* also determines one's marriage prospects: even if you were prepared to sacrifice yourself, your parents would not allow you to marry a person whose *sŏngbun* is too far below your own level.

It is sometimes possible to improve one's own station: for example, exemplary military service will vindicate a lad who was unlucky enough to be the grandson of a Protestant minister. Such "transformations" happen frequently enough, and it seems that there has been a kind of "upward shift," with a number of bad-*sŏngbuners* improving their standing over the years. However, it is also common for bad *sŏngbun* to last for generations, haunting the children and grandchildren of a supposed wrongdoer.

It is impossible to determine the number of people in each group, even approximately. The existing (and oft-cited) estimations are frequently patent nonsense. Perhaps we will not learn the truth until the collapse of the DPRK. Nonetheless, it is clear that the economic turbulence of the last decade has greatly damaged the system. The quasi-feudal system of *sŏngbun* is coming to an end, but within the few decades of its existence it has sealed many fates — and also rocketed a number of people to a life of prestige and privilege.

A Family Tradition

ONE OF THE MOST COMMON MISTAKES of the Korean Left is to see North Korea as the embodiment of social equality. Indeed, the dream of material equality was once the major driving force behind the Communist experiment — yet another noble experiment which went terribly wrong in the twentieth century. The Communists promised (and, in most cases, sincerely believed) that their victory would spell an end to material inequality, and make all citizens of their new societies equally prosperous. Unfortunately it did not work out that way. Most Communist societies retained a high degree of inequality even though it might be much less pronounced than in capitalist societies. And North Korea was no exception.

When the Communists took power, they often ushered in a period of hitherto unprecedented social mobility. The children of workers and farmers were recruited to positions of power while descendants of the former elite were discriminated against — even though they often still managed to come through eventually, thanks to their better education. The ambitious and the gifted from among the former underdogs used these opportunities to the full and naturally welcomed the new system.

But then there was a common problem: once the former underdogs took power, they did not necessarily act differently from their predecessors. In due time these "recruits of the revolution" grew old and became less enthusiastic about "affirmative action": like the old elite, they wanted their children to inherit their high status. This was, strictly speaking, against the official ideology which placed great emphasis on the egalitarian spirit and equal opportunity, but the ideology was able to be quietly discarded.

Thus everyone in the USSR by the 1970s knew the joke: "Can a general's son become a marshal? No way, the marshal has sons, too!" Indeed, by around 1970, social mobility in the USSR had noticeably decreased and the children of officials usually became officials — or dissenting intellectuals (a surprising number of the anti–Communist underground leaders were scions of prominent bureaucrats, KGB operatives and party functionaries). Meanwhile, workers' sons remained workers. There were exceptions to this rule, as the fate of the present author, the son of a single working-class mother, testifies. But these were increasingly rare exceptions.

In North Korea a similar process began very early — perhaps earlier than in any other Communist country. I have seen a 1950s document in which a Russian diplomat described his conversation with Yu Sŏng-hun, the then president of Kim Il Sung University. The man, a prominent intellectual and educator who soon afterwards ran afoul of Kim Il Sung, complained about the severe pressures on his university's admission policy. He said that there were "queues of cars" waiting near his office during the admission period — and cars were a sign of an extremely high position in the North Korea of 1956. The top officials lobbied for their offspring with such persistence that precious few places were left for gifted individuals who lacked powerful backing.

No comparative studies have been made, but it appears that North Korea remained more prone to such problems than any other Communist country. Perhaps the hereditary rule itself increased the opportunity for lesser officials to transfer their power to their children. If the Leader's superhuman wisdom and benevolence was transferred to his son, it is only reasonable to presume

that the "revolutionary enthusiasm" and "unbreakable loyalty" of his stead-
fast ministers and party secretaries was also inherited by their children. The
special role of one's social background, the notorious *sŏngbun* system, also
encouraged the process. Because of the *sŏngbun* system, North Korea was one
of the few Communist countries where hereditary privileges were officially
admitted.

The Kim family itself is well represented in the highest reaches of power,
with a dozen close relatives in the upper echelons.

Below Kim Il Sung's assorted relatives, there are two major groups at the
helm of the North Korean state. They are known as "people of the Paektu
Mountain" and "people of the Naktong River." The first group is considered
superior and includes the descendants of the guerrilla fighters who in the
1930s fought alongside Kim Il Sung. The second group consists of children
of prominent military leaders who led the North Korean armies during the
war. A large proportion of top officials either came from one of these two groups
or at least have close connections with it, usually through marriage.

The children of the elite spend their entire lives in a world which is very
different from that of the humble commoner. They attend privileged schools,
including Mangyongdae Revolutionary School, a boarding institution open
only to the elite and the occasional child of a national hero. They then go on
to prestigious schools, including Kim Il Sung University, from which they
proceed to high-level jobs. Of course, they are never required to subsist on
the mix of maize and low-quality rice which has been the staple food of the
masses since well before the Great Famine and has subsequently gone from
bad to worse.

North Korea has much in common with the aristocratic feudal state,
where the descendants of the ruling dynasty and those who once rode with
the founding warlord enjoy privileges as their birthright. This fact explains
a lot about the elite's indifference to the suffering of the populace: after all,
the inhabitants of medieval castles cared little for the destitution of their serfs.

Apart from the top officials, there is another group whose members enjoy
privileges in Kim Il Sung's North Korea, even if the authorities have sometimes felt uneasy about them. These are people with access to foreign currency.

In some cases, these privileges are approved by the authorities and are
granted as a reward for loyalty to the regime. For example, this group of affluent North Koreans has always included diplomats, crews of ships on overseas
routes, people employed in overseas projects (especially in the timber works
in Eastern Siberia) and the like. These individuals could use their dollars or
yen to purchase high quality goods in the currency shops that operated in
Pyongyang and some other major cities from the 1970s. Some of these goods

were then re-sold on the black market, reaping huge profits. In some cases people preferred to buy goods overseas and then bring them home. This was more profitable, since prices in the North Korean hard currency shops were well above international levels. During a three-year stint in the Siberian forests, a logger could easily earn one hundred times the annual salary of an average North Korean worker.

In some cases, the authorities' position was more ambivalent. Among the rich there were also ethnic Koreans from Japan who, in the 1960s, were lured by Pyongyang propaganda into moving to the North. Their relatives in Japan were ready to send money to them, and such transfers were encouraged by the state. These repatriates spent money in these same hard-currency shops. An especially generous donation could buy much more than a basketful of apples: in some cases, relatives purchased the right to live in Pyongyang and/or a flat in a good apartment complex, of the type normally reserved for cadres alone.

It is remarkable that the common North Koreans harbor few illusions about their own chances of social promotion. They despise this inequality, and they envy those who occupy top positions in the social hierarchy. But I am sadly cynical: even when (not if) the current system topples, commoners will not gain many more opportunities for social mobility. If the experience of other post–Communist countries is a guide, they will be probably ruled either by the same people (loudly professing a completely different set of beliefs), or by South Korean supervisors who are not likely to win much popularity. A sad prospect indeed....

A Woman's Place...

BACK IN THE EARLY 1900S FEW IF ANY major political movements could rival Marxism in its feminist zeal. In a world where women still had no voting rights and faced manifold legal restrictions, Marxism was unique in its commitment to gender equality in politics, society and the economy.

When in 1917 the Communists took power in Russia, they immediately introduced what was then the world's most pro-feminist legislation. All gender-specific legal restrictions on women's political and social activities were lifted, divorce rules were dramatically eased and abortion legalized. The Communist government for a while encouraged women to enter traditionally male occupations such as air force pilots, university professors or tractor drivers.

But this did not last. Communism in power proved to be covertly nationalistic and remarkably conservative with respect to social mores. By the late 1930s the mood in Moscow changed: traditional "family values" were loudly extolled once more, many family laws underwent conservative revisions, and Soviet women began to face a glass ceiling in their social advancement.

Thus, when the Stalinist system was brought to the North in 1945, it combined lip service to women's empowerment with much more reserved and ambiguous real politics. This approach was inherited by Pyongyang and has lasted until this day.

On paper, everything looked fine. In July 1946 the law of gender equality gave women electoral rights (admittedly meaningless in a Stalinist state), banned polygapolymous marriage and eased divorce. Soon afterwards, women were granted maternity leave. Currently, following several increases, this extends to 150 days: two months before and three months after childbirth. In the late 1940s, the government successfully wiped out prostitution, which did not make a comeback until recently.

North Korea's propaganda worked hard to uproot some centuries-old gender stereotypes. By the 1950s, primary schooling was obligatory for both boys and girls, and a number of girls proceeded to colleges and then to white-collar jobs. Some of the professions eventually came to be dominated by women — like, say, medical doctors or teachers, the social standing of both groups in the North being much inferior to that of their counterparts in the South.

However, throughout the first decade of its history, North Korea had no time for bold social experiments. Women's right to work remained largely theoretical: until the late 1950s, there were not enough jobs in the impoverished and ruined country to go around. Thus, whatever the official media said, most women remained housewives, like their mothers and grandmothers before them.

However, the postwar recovery resulted in dramatic shortages in the workforce. Thus women's participation ceased to be a question of principle and became a necessity. The major turning point was reached in 1958 when the North Korean Cabinet of ministers passed a resolution "On the increase of women's involvement in the various fields of economic activity." The decision meant that an ever-increasing number of women would be involved in the economy. In an ideal world, all women should work full-time.

Indeed, the number of working women increased in the 1960s and 1970s, peaking around 1980. Apart from propaganda and the need to earn money, there was another reason for women's participation in the workforce: the situation of the North Korean housewife had deteriorated dramatically. By the mid–1960s, the state reached every household through an elaborate system of neighborhood groups, known as *inminban*. Every woman who had no regular full-time job had to take part in *inminban* activities, and these activities were neither pleasant nor easy. The women had to clean public toilets, work as janitors, manufacture items in their homes and occasionally go to the countryside to take part in obligatory agricultural work.

In short, a housewife was nearly as busy as an employed woman, the only major difference being her infinitely lower income. In the North Korea of those days, income *per se* did not count for much, but rations did. And a housewife was eligible for a measly 300g of grain daily, while most women with proper jobs would receive 700g.

However, around 1980 the situation changed once again: the level of female employment began to slide. The reasons were clear: the North Korean economy entered an era of stagnation, and it did not need labor as it had before. Hence, the authorities eased their pressure and, in some cases, even discouraged women from holding down a full-time job after marriage.

However, even when the demand for workers reached its peak, the officially endorsed public opinion tacitly assumed that married women would take nearly total responsibility for all household chores. This made a career very difficult, especially in a society where household appliances were non-existent and no paid service could be hired due to both official emphasis on equality and social customs.

Very few women rose above the level of low-ranking managers or clerks, and even agencies which have a predominantly female workforce are usually run by male managers — in a typical secondary school, for example, most teachers are women but principals tend to be male. After an initial decade of bold social experiments, women's participation in politics also remains low: from the early 1960s virtually all women who were prominent in top-level politics came from the Kim Il Sung clan. But that is another story....

Women at the Top

WITHIN LIVING MEMORY, ELITE COMMUNIST politics has always had a distinctly male face. The top Communist bureaucrats are remembered as aging males, clad in badly tailored grey suits or Mao jackets, with virtually no women present in their secretive gatherings.

This was not always the case. In the early 1900s, in the initial stages of its turbulent history, the political world of early Communism was full of women, some of whom played important roles in defining the Communist doctrine. One could mention Rosa Luxemburg, a German-Polish Marxist thinker and politician, or Alexandra Kollontai, a radical feminist writer who eventually rose to become a prominent and successful Soviet diplomat, the first-ever female ambassador.

However, when Communism came to the North in 1945, it was already quite moderate with respect to women's rights. Still, formal legal equality had to be enforced, even though the right to vote was not terribly important in a Stalinist society where the approval rate of the officially endorsed candidates must be 100%.

The Supreme People's Assembly, the nation's rubber-stamping parliament, includes a number of women, who currently form 20.1% of the "legislature." However, their role is to obediently vote for the government's bills. These women are hand-picked by the authorities, largely from "exemplary workers," and cannot be seen as independent political actors in any true sense of the word.

If we look at the executive level, the situation is even starker. Out of some 260 North Korean ministers who have held portfolio between 1948 and 2000, a mere six were women.

Two female politicians were prominent in the North Korean scene of the 1940s and 1950s. One was Pak Chŏng-ae, a former Soviet intelligence agent who operated in Korea from the early 1930s and found herself in Pyongyang in the fateful year of 1945. Her fluency in Russian helped her to establish a good rapport with the Soviet military, and she obviously lacked neither ambition nor cunning. In subsequent years she became a Politburo member and from the late 1940s ranked within the top ten of North Korea's politicians. Pak Chŏng-ae soon became one of the most devout supporters of Kim Il Sung and proved instrumental in consolidating his power. This did not help, however: after all, she did not belong to Kim's "guerrilla faction" and was purged in the late 1960s. Fortunately her life was spared, and much later she made a moderate comeback.

Unlike Pak Chŏng-ae, Hŏ Chŏng-suk entered politics largely through her family connections: she was the daughter of Hŏ Hŏn, a prominent leftist intellectual. But she had developed her own track record as well: during the civil war in China, Hŏ Chŏng-suk fought as a political commissar in a Communist regiment. In the 1950s she occupied a number of important positions, including that of Minister for Justice. However, in the early 1960s she was purged. Like Pak Chŏng-ae, she made a comeback, but was never given any position of significance again, being relegated to largely ceremonial posts.

These two women were the closest approximations to Korea's Luxemburg or Kollontai. However, all women who featured prominently in the North Korean government circles after 1960 were somehow related to the ruling family.

In spite of her goddess-like posthumous standing, Kim Il Sung's first wife, Kim Jong Suk, was not prominent on the political stage during her lifetime. In contrast, the Great Leader's second wife, Kim Sŏng-ae, despite her low profile, held some official positions. She was the Chairperson of the Korean Women's Association, a powerful body responsible for "political work" among women.

Kim Il Sung's only surviving daughter (and Kim Jong Il's sister) Kim Kyŏng-hŭi was for a while probably the most powerful of all the "Kim women," but it remains to be seen what will happen to her after the downfall of her husband, Chang Sŏng-t'aek, who had even been considered an emergency replacement for Kim Jong Il in the event that the Dear Leader died before any of his sons were old enough to inherit power.

In recent years there have also been indications that another female Kim clan member, Ko Yŏng-hŭi, the long-time wife of Kim Jong Il, will assume some political standing.

But in general, North Korean politics is remarkable male-dominated — even by the standards of East Asia, which is not very well known for its political feminism.

PART 5

Pyongyang

The Mythic Capital

NORTH KOREAN OFFICIAL HISTORIANS have spent an impressive amount of
ink (they do not really use computers yet) to prove that Pyongyang has always
been the center of Korean polity. In East Asian cultures, capital cities were
very important, being an embodiment of the dynasty and its regime. The legitimacy is also associated with a long history, thus it is preferable to have a capital city which can boast a long pedigree.

However, even a cursory look at the city's long history confirms that this
is a gross exaggeration. From the first centuries of the Christian era, Pyongyang
was an important military stronghold, and in 427 AD it became the capital
of Koguryŏ, one of the three kingdoms that were fighting for supremacy over
the Korean Peninsula. After Koguryŏ collapsed in the late 7th century, Pyongyang remained an important local center. Nonetheless, the fate of the country was decided in the cities where the court and government were located — in
Kyŏngju, Kaesŏng, and, from 1394, Seoul.

In the colonial era Pyongyang was the largest city of what later became
North Korea. Nonetheless, even within the would-be North it could be rivaled
by two other cities: by Hamhŭng, with its huge steel mill and chemical plants,
then the largest in East Asia, and by Kaesŏng, the old capital of the Koryŏ
dynasty.

The fate of Pyongyang was sealed in late August 1945 — and, like many
other pivotal decisions of the period, this determination was made by the Soviets. On August 25, Marshal Meretskov had a talk with General Chistiakov,
the commander of the Soviet 25th Army, which had just finished wiping out
the last Japanese resistance in Korea. Among other things, Meretskov asked

The Pyongyang main street, until the 1970s known as Stalin Street. It is called Sŭngli (Victory) Street now, to commemorate the great victory over U.S. imperialism in 1953. Photograph by Andrew Salmon.

where Chistiakov would like to establish his headquarters: in Pyongyang or in Hamhŭng (Kaesŏng was a non-starter, since according to pre–1950 arrangements it was located to the south of the 38th parallel).

Chistiakov chose Pyongyang. Historical considerations hardly played any role: at the time Chistiakov did not have the slightest idea of Korean history. The central location of Pyongyang was a much greater factor in this decision.

The decision to locate the 25th Army headquarters in Pyongyang meant that the city became a magnet for the Korean leftists who were busy constructing the would-be Communist state in the North. Their efforts were encouraged, paid, sponsored, and protected by the Soviet Army. The somewhat misnamed Soviet Civil Administration (actually, a 100% military body) also ran the country from Pyongyang. When its duties were gradually transferred to the Korean agencies, the latter were naturally located in the same city.

The official declaration of the Democratic People's Republic of Korea took place in Pyongyang on September 9, 1948. The city has been the seat of the North Korean government ever since — with a short break during the Korean War. Nonetheless, the first North Korean Constitution of 1948 stated that the DPRK's true capital was ... Seoul. The DPRK (like its southern coun-

Pyongyang evening. Photograph by Christopher Morris.

terpart and arch-rival, ROK) claimed absolute legitimacy over the entire undivided Korean Peninsula.

From the official North Korean point of view, the South Korean government was an illegal puppet regime, to be exterminated as soon as the opportunity arose. After the victory, the capital of Korea was to be located in Seoul, not in Pyongyang. ROK officialdom had the same views — the only difference being that South Korean authorities had the opposite opinion as to which of the two rival governments had full and undivided sovereignty over Korea, and which one was an illegal puppet.

After the Korean War it became clear that the "liberation" of the South was not even on the horizon. Thus, the North Korean authorities began to promote the significance of their de facto capital. From the late 1950s the North Korean press began to refer to Pyongyang as "the capital of revolution"—not yet the nation's capital, but still something special. In order to prove it, it started to rewrite history in a way which would make Pyongyang appear far more important than it actually was.

The Koguryŏ cult was especially important in this regard. Koguryŏ was one of the three kingdoms that fought for supremacy on the Korean Peninsula between the first and seventh centuries AD. Since its territory roughly coincided with that of present-day North Korea, and since its capital was located in

Pyongyang crowd. Photograph by Anna Fifield.

Pyongyang, the North Korean authorities began to promote the Koguryŏ heritage as allegedly superior to that of other ancient Korean kingdoms. The Koguryŏ relics in the vicinity of Pyongyang were carefully (if not faithfully) "restored" to their alleged former glory.

In the early 1970s, Kim Jong Il reportedly criticized archaeologists for their inability to locate the tomb of King Tongmyŏng, one of Koguryŏ's most remarkable rulers. In 1974, archaeologists produced the required tomb — obviously a tomb which was an authentic burial of the Koguryŏ period was proclaimed without further evidence to be the final resting place of the great Tongmyŏng.

The message was clear: Koguryŏ was the first truly Korean state, and Pyongyang was its capital. In the East Asian cultural tradition, where the events of ancient history have always been used as tools of political propaganda, this was important.

In 1972, Seoul finally lost its position as the North Korean capital. The renewed constitution consecrated Pyongyang as the nation's capital city. The official propaganda began to compare the "impoverished and dirty" Seoul with "clean and affluent" Pyongyang, whose image was a living testimony to the wisdom of the Great Leader and his son, the Dear Leader.

The search for the "historical roots" of Pyongyang's supremacy continued. In the new climate, Koguryŏ, established merely two thousand years ago, was not seen as ancient enough. North Korean officialdom began to insist that Pyongyang was the capital of Old Chosŏn, the first proto–Korean state. This state actually existed in the first millennium BC, but nationalist "historians" both in the South and the North insist that its history began far earlier, in the 3rd millennium BC. Not much is known about Old Chosŏn, but most historians outside North Korea think that this state existed in what is now northeast China and the Liaodong Peninsula.

Around the same time, North Korean archaeologists claimed that they had discovered a new archaeological culture, named Taedonggang culture. According to them, this culture, associated with Old Chosŏn, was one of the most advanced in the entire world. According to the North Korean version of history, this remarkable culture, known only to North Korean "scholars," was equal or even superior to the cultures of Mesopotamia and Ancient Egypt and can be considered one of the few major sources of modern human civilization. Needless to say, this marvelous civilization flourished around the present-day Pyongyang.

The final coup came in 1993. Once again, the archaeologists were ordered to make a discovery by the Great Leader himself (this time, it was Kim Il Sung). Once again, the discovery was made immediately upon request — I just wonder how great life could have been had the North Korean scientists been able to produce, say, a high-temperature superconductor upon receiving the proper order from some Dear or Great Leader. The aging Kim Il Sung instructed them to find the tomb of legendary Tangun, the son of the she-bear and alleged founder of Ancient Chosŏn. The tomb was found — near Pyongyang, of course. This once again proved the city's credentials as the nation's capital for five thousand years!

But what if on that fateful day in August 1945, General Chistiakov had chosen Hamhŭng as his headquarters? Does it mean that in due time Tangun's tomb would have been discovered there? Does it mean that some "Hamhŭng culture" would have been proclaimed to be the predecessor of all important breakthroughs in the history of humankind? I suspect that the answer to this question is, "Yes, it would...."

Thanks for the Memorials

IN THE MID–1970S THE PYONGYANG leaders were confident as never before. The economic growth they presided over ensured the relative prosperity and

The Arch of Triumph, with the Kim Il Sung statue and Ch'onlima monument also visible. Photograph by Andrei Lankov.

stability of their country. Skillful political maneuvering by Kim Il Sung had allowed him to destroy all possible sources of challenge to his supremacy, and had laid the grounds for a transition of power within the family — something hitherto unknown in the Communist world.

This self-congratulatory mood probably played a major role in the decision to launch major construction projects that were to create "the eternal monuments to the era of the Korean Workers' Party." There are about a dozen of these ambitious monuments in Pyongyang and its vicinity, but two of them stand out because of their size and cost — the Arch of Triumph and *Juche* Tower.

The Arch of Triumph was unveiled in 1982 to commemorate Kim Il Sung's 70th birthday. It was constructed on the very site where, on October 14, 1945, Kim Il Sung was first introduced to the North Korean people by the Soviet military during a large public rally.

Official manipulation transformed this episode into a turning point of Korean history. Of course, no North Korean book mentions that the would-be Great Leader was just one of several speakers at this rally. Nor do they mention that the rally was called to "express gratitude to the liberating Red Army," not to Kim Il Sung.

The Arch of Triumph was modeled after the Arc de Triomphe in Paris, once constructed to commemorate Napoleon. However, the Korean copy exceeds the original in its size. French guides mislead credulous tourists when they habitually say that the Paris structure is "the world's largest Arch of Triumph." The Parisian Arch is merely 49.5 meters high, while its Pyongyang imitation is 60 meters high and 50 meters wide! It is decorated with sculptures and reliefs that depict the supposed "triumphal returning of the victorious Great Leader to the country." The 70 azalea reliefs remind the observer that the structure was built to commemorate the Great Leader's 70th birthday.

The two sides of the Arch bear the dates "1925" and "1945." In 1925 Kim Il Sung, then in his early teens, left his country for Manchuria, and in 1945 he came back.

However, the Arch pales in comparison with another structure, also unveiled in 1982. This is the *Juche* Tower, the major landmark of the North Korean capital for the past two decades.

Once again, its shape betrays foreign influences, even though these influences are never recognized in North Korean publications. The general shape of the *Juche* Tower duplicates that of the Washington monument in the U.S. capital, but exceeds it in size. The Tower is 150 meters high and is crowned with a huge gold torch that is illuminated at night. The torch adds 20 meters to the Tower's height, so the entire structure stands 170 meters high. It is equipped with a large observation platform, open for visitors.

The *Juche* Tower includes 25,550 granite blocks — one for each day Kim Il Sung had lived by the time the monument was unveiled.

On the foot of the Tower there is a sculpture that always makes the visitors from the former Soviet Union smile. Their smiles are understandable: while the guide is extolling the complete originality of the statue, they instantly recognize the source of the sculptors' inspiration. Indeed, this is an almost exact copy of Vera Mukhina's "Worker and Collective Farm Girl," one of the most famous visual icons of the Stalin era.

The only difference from the Soviet original is the addition of a third person, the Intellectual, who stands behind the Worker and the Peasant Girl, awkwardly raising an enormous writing brush. The brush is the same size as the hammer and sickle held by the Worker and the Peasant Girl. Like its Soviet prototype, the group is supposed to symbolize the unity of the entire population in support of the Party.

There are other sculptures as well. They symbolize the happiness of the North Koreans and their love for and loyalty to the Great Leader and his *Juche* Idea. Their titles are, perhaps, self-explanatory: *Juche* Industry, Bumper

Harvest, Land of Study, Land of Longevity, *Juche* Art, and Impregnable Fortress. The wall is also decorated with plaques donated by worldwide *Juche* study groups.

I often wonder what will happen to these monuments after the collapse of Kim's rule. Will they be destroyed as a heritage of the cruel past? I am afraid they will. Perhaps one of the most urgent tasks of the first post–Kim years will be saving the monuments of the era — or, at least, making exact descriptions of them. It is difficult to believe that the people of post–Kim Korea will be happy to live in the shadow of those structures. But they should be remembered nonetheless.

hey look cool

Go To, Let Us Build Us a City and a Tower, Whose Top May Reach Unto Heaven... (Genesis 11:4)

UNTIL THE LATE 1980S, MANY ASPECTS of life in North and South Korea were dictated by the relentless competition between the two Korean states. Now the competition is over: the South has won completely and undeniably. Nevertheless, the fierce competition had left behind traces in both Koreas, and some of these traces are here to stay as a reminder of passions long gone....

Arguably, the largest, or at least the most visible, monument to the North–South race for prestige and recognition is the mammoth structure which has dominated the Pyongyang cityscape for the past 15 years. Indeed, no visitor to the North can escape the sight of the unfinished Yugyŏng Hotel, a huge concrete pyramid which reaches the breathtaking height of 323 meters.

Its history began in the early 1980s when the gap between the two Korean states was much narrower than it is presently, and Pyongyang still felt itself capable of competing with the South. In South Korea, President Pak had a weak spot for high-rise buildings. A lot of skyscrapers were constructed under his auspices. The jewel in the crown of the South Korean projects was the Saengmyong building, better known as the "63-story building." It was completed in 1985, shortly before the Seoul Olympic Games of 1988.

Meanwhile, the leaders in Pyongyang were scarcely happy to learn about these successes. It seems that Kim Il Sung also saw high-rise towers as symbols of progress and economic might, and he wanted to have his own super-skyscraper. Thus the Yugyŏng project was born.

The building was meant to be used as a hotel. Economically this was

The unfinished pyramid of Yugyŏng Hotel has dominated downtown Pyongyang for nearly two decades. Photograph by Andrei Lankov.

quite a strange decision since the North Korean capital did not attract many visitors, and most hotels for foreign tourists had plenty of free rooms. However, the entire project was not about economy, it was about pride and prestige. The future hotel was given the name of Yugyŏng after an old name for Pyongyang itself (it means "willow capital" — and indeed willow trees are plentiful in the city).

After some delays, the construction work on the new hotel began in 1987. The delays made it impossible to open it by the time of the Youth Festival in 1989, but many still hoped that the Yugyŏng hotel would commence operations in 1992, when North Korea was expected to celebrate the 80th birthday of the country's founding father, the Great Leader Kim Il Sung.

The plans were grand indeed. The finished structure was to have 105 stories, 3700 guest rooms, and numerous large conference halls, restaurants, and other facilities. The total floor area of the hotel would be 430,000 square meters, and its highest point would reach a height of 323.3 meters — 40 meters higher than Seoul's "63-story building." The total volume of the building would be almost twice as large as its rival in Seoul. The hotel's shape was pyramidical, with the length of its base running to 160 meters. Technical assistance with the building would be provided by a French engineering company. In short, this was to equal the most sophisticated high-rise buildings in the world.

However, things soon turned bad. In 1989 a wave of anti–Communist revolution swept Eastern Europe. The Soviet Union, which had been a major sponsor of North Korea for many years, was going downhill. Although Pyongyang never admitted it, the country's economy was dependent on large-scale direct and indirect aid from other Communist countries. The loss of that aid and a lack of markets for North Korean goods led to a major economic crisis which soon became a real disaster.

The crumbling economy made the completion of the 105-story mammoth impossible. In 1989 work came to a halt. By that time, the outside structure was ready, but no internal equipment was yet installed. The French partners withdrew in 1990, after long quarrels over payments and other contract obligations (obviously, these people hoped to earn money by cooperating with the North Koreans — how naïve!). It is rumored that in the late 1990s the unfinished structure, exposed to the elements, began to disintegrate.

There have been several attempts to save the Yugyŏng. In 1998, the Hotel Kempinski chain, one of the major players in the international hotel market, was negotiating with the North Koreans, but the deal collapsed soon afterwards. In 1999, the North Koreans applied for technical assistance from Daewoo, and a few years later they approached LG with the same request. Finally, in 2005 there was talk of the city of Incheon being willing to take on the project, including bearing the enormous costs associated with re-starting it.

Perhaps the Yugyŏng, this largest of all North Korea's "prestigious" projects, is doomed. But it is still possible that one day it will be completed and remain a towering monument to its era — if someone is willing to outlay enough capital, of course....

Harmonica Houses

WHERE DO THE NORTH KOREANS LIVE? If the glossy North Korean official publications are to be believed, multi-story apartment houses are the favorite dwelling places of the urban population while farmers probably inhabit small but tidy one- or two-story buildings. The real picture is of course much different.

High-rise complexes do exist in the North, but these are heavily concentrated in Pyongyang. A handful of such structures exist in other large cities, while buildings in the smaller towns seldom have more than 3 or 4 floors. High-rise apartments are associated with progress and prosperity. Thus they are built in Pyongyang, where they showcase the alleged success of the North Korean social system.

In Wonsan, a major port on the eastern cost, there are also very few apartment complexes — and all are strategically placed along the coast in order to be visible from the sea (presumably by the crews of foreign ships). However, the city does not have an adequate water supply system, so these impressive showcase buildings have not been exactly popular with their inhabitants. Even in the relatively comfortable period of the 1980s, the water taps on the upper floors worked only fitfully, and the flush toilets did not always flush — because of a shortage of water. These days the problem is even more severe.

The earliest North Korean apartments were known as "harmonica houses," because their floor plan resembled the musical instrument. They had a long open gallery which ran along one side of the building. All flats were accessible from this gallery, so the entire floor plan was reminiscent of traditional Korean rural houses. This same floor plan can also be encountered in some South Korean apartment complexes.

Flats in the "harmonica houses" consist of one room and a small kitchen. These flats are very small, with the living area seldom exceeding 3 pyong (10 square meters). Nor are buildings of this type very tall — they hardly ever have more than four stories.

Another type are the so-called central corridor apartments. Their corridor is located inside the building, and runs through its entire length. All flats

An above-average North Korean apartment in Kaesong. Photograph by Byeon Young-wook.

on a particular level may be accessed from this corridor. In such apartments, flats tend to be larger, sometimes consisting of two rooms, but they are small by the standards of other countries — usually about 5–7 pyong (15–21 square meters). These are the most spacious apartments an average North Korean might hope to dwell in. More comfortable types of housing are reserved for the elite only.

The best apartments are the so-called section apartments. The floor plan of these apartments resembles the typical South Korean apartments of the 1990s. They have a staircase. On each floor there are 3–4 flats with separate entrances, thus affording the greatest degree of privacy to the apartment dwellers. There may be an elevator, although it would only operate a few hours every day even in the "good old days" of the 1980s. Such flats have up to 4 rooms with a total living area of 20–25 pyong (65–80 square meters). By North Korean standards this is a very spacious dwelling. However, such large flats are only allocated to the elite. This elite does not necessarily include only party bureaucrats or top military brass: prominent scientists, actors, or musicians have also been treated with great deference, although in recent years their standing in North Korean society has deteriorated.

In the new apartment complexes every flat has its own toilet and bath-

This is what one of the most privileged neighborhoods in Pyongyang looks like, in a picture taken from the Koryo Hotel and meant to be seen by foreigners. Photograph by Christopher Morris.

room, but in the older Pyongyang apartments, there are only public facilities. Typically, in the "harmonica houses" there was one toilet for every 10 flats. In smaller towns, multi-story buildings often do not have flush toilets at all, and their inhabitants must use outside conveniences. However, even in Pyongyang the water supply is unreliable, necessitating the installation of large water tanks to service the flush toilets.

Normally, apartments have only cold running water. The hot water supply is only switched on occasionally, and local residents are warned of this in advance, so they can take maximum advantage of this rare event. In many apartment complexes the cold water is also provided intermittently, according to a timetable, usually during morning or evening hours.

From the mid–1970s, the better apartment buildings have been equipped with locally produced elevators. All elevators come with a female operator whose duty it is to stay with her machine at all times. Most residents take great pains to be on good terms with this "elevator lady." The elevator lady knows a lot about their lives, and in a Stalinist society, such knowledge can be dangerous. However, over the last decade the significance of these women diminished: first, the authorities are somewhat more tolerant of minor deviations; and second, the elevators seldom work, since they are switched off to save the scarce electricity.

Well, what about property? Theoretically, all (well, nearly all) houses in the country belong to the state, and the state acts as a landlord. The only exceptions are individual houses which were built prior to the Korean War and have never been seriously remodeled: such houses still might be considered private property of their dwellers, but their number is very small.

However, the "tenants" have a right to swap their houses, if such an action is approved by a local government office. Such swapping has been common since long ago, but in recent years it is often used to cover actual trade in real estate. Owners of better houses, if they need money, move to smaller or less conveniently located dwellings, and draw money in compensation. This is unofficial, of course — like many other things going on in North Korea after Kim Il Sung's death in 1994....

Haute Cuisine, Kim Il Sung Style

KOREANS LOVE EATING OUT — as every long-time resident of Seoul knows from his or her own experience. Going to a restaurant is one of the most common leisure activities in the country. In this regard the North is not much different. Of course, decent restaurants are much more difficult to come by in the North: Communist economies have never been particularly successful in meeting consumers' demands in this area. Nonetheless, this does not mean that North Korean cities do not have good restaurants. Perhaps the very scarcity of such places, combined with the generally bad diet, makes eating out there an even more remarkable experience.

For the last 25 years two major restaurants have defined the culinary life of Pyongyang — Okryugwan and Ch'ŏngryugwan (the restaurants at the major international hotels also played an important role, one should admit).

Okryugwan, or the Jade Stream Pavilion, is located on the left bank of the Taedong River. It commenced operations in 1960, and since then has remained a major landmark of the North Korean capital. This large building, in mock traditional style, boasts a number of dining halls, including some special banquet rooms, and can seat up to 2,000 patrons. Obviously, a penchant for large-scale eateries is common to all Communist regimes (Soviet restaurants of the era, for example, tended to be of truly mammoth size).

Okryugwan has the officially recognized standing of the major guardian of traditional Korean cuisine, and functions as a type of living museum of

Ch'ŏngryugwan Restaurant, officially the best eatery in the North Korean capital. Photograph by Andrei Lankov.

culinary art. Recently it was reported that together with a local college, it sent special research teams to the countryside. The teams were to gather data on traditional Korean cuisine in order to introduce new dishes to the Okryugwan menu (I just wonder whether it was a good idea, or even particularly sensitive, to search for new recipes in a time of famine).

Ch'ŏngryugwan, or the Pure Stream Pavilion, is almost equally famous. It was opened much later, in 1980, in a new building shaped to resemble a ship. The Ch'ŏngryugwan sits on the banks of the Pot'onggang, a minor but capricious tributary of the Taedong River. It has two levels: the ground floor is occupied by a large dining hall, while the upper floor is used for small dining rooms and banquet halls.

Both restaurants specialize in traditional cuisine, with special attention given to cold noodles, a quintessentially North Korean dish. Generally, the cooking traditions in the North and South are slightly different, but South Korean visitors usually have a high opinion of the food cooked in both of these famous restaurants.

Both Okryugwan and Ch'ŏngryugwan are sometimes described in the

South as "mass restaurants," and this description is true. They are open to the average North Korean, they are not reserved for bigwigs or dollar-paying foreigners alone.

However, this does not mean that anyone can wander in off the street and enjoy a bowl of cold noodles at their whim. In order to get access, North Koreans initially had to get tickets, and these tickets were notoriously difficult to acquire. One had to have connections or endure hours in long queues — or, alternatively, tickets might be distributed through a work unit. The tickets are not free, but they give only entrance rights — the ordered food must be paid for separately. Only in recent years has the ongoing dollarization of the North Korean economy changed the situation: if one has money then tickets are available (that's a big "if," of course).

In the countryside there are local analogues to the two Pyongyang heavy-weights. Each major North Korean city has its own "special" restaurant. Their names usually include the characters "kak" or "gwan." Both words are of Chinese origin: they can be roughly translated as "pavilion" and "hall" and have been a part of the nomenclature of restaurants in East Asian countries for many centuries.

Apart from Okryugwan and its less successful rivals, North Korea has a number of smaller eateries. These are not as numerous as are eateries in the South, but in major cities they are not too difficult to find. In the past there was once a clear-cut difference between hard-currency restaurants, which were off limits to commoners, and establishments for the not-so-well-heeled. However, recent years have seen the gradual blurring of this once impenetrable border.

North Korean specialties are noodles and, of course, dog meat. Incidentally, the latter is not called "dog meat" (*kae kogi*) in North Korea. Kim Il Sung in his wisdom is said to have decided that this name was too unceremonious, and had it renamed sweet meat or *tan kogi*!

For somebody who — like the present author — lived in the Soviet Union, North Korea and South Korea, it is clear that North Korean restaurant food has been subjected to heavy influence of the Russian/Soviet gastronomic tradition. The menu often includes Russian-style salads — heavy and nutritious, generously mixed with mayo. The food which is served in the public eateries is remarkably different from what one would see in Seoul, and the restaurants' interiors vividly remind me of my youth in the Soviet Union of the 1970s (darkness and neon lights of bright, unnatural colors, white table cloths and somewhat mismatched furniture).

The restaurant industry was one of the first in which private enterprise was reintroduced. This occurred at a surprisingly early stage, in the late 1980s, when state control of the economy was still sound. In recent years, these private eateries have sprung up in very large numbers, reflecting the steady disintegration of the Stalinist economy.

Of course, there are other places where people with some money can eat very well. Hotels which are catering to the foreign tourists also serve the locals, and there are new restaurants popping up in the early 2000s. In 2005, a Western expat, permanently living in Pyongyang, even described the situation as a "restaurant boom."

According to a pro–Pyongyang newspaper in Japan, in 2005 there were 500 restaurants in the capital. Most of these charge prices well beyond the reach of the average North Korean, and cater to the tastes of the three major groups with money: foreign expats, black-market dealers, and officials. These groups are large enough to sustain a number of quite sophisticated eateries.

There is sashimi to be eaten in the Galaxy, barbecued ostrich at the Arirang, and a microbrewery where 5 patrons can feast on a locally produced dark ale and good noodles for a mere $15! A bargain, of course, at $3 per person — but not such a bargain when we remember that $3 is exactly how much the average North Korean worker is paid in one month....

On Ondols *and Moon Villages*

WHAT DOES PYONGYANG LOOK LIKE? North Korean publications depict it as a city of broad streets, high-rise buildings and great architectural monuments. This image of Pyongyang is projected by the glossy magazines which North Korean official agencies once disseminated worldwide free of charge (now they try to charge money for them — with little success, of course).

To some extent, this image is true. Pyongyang is a beautiful — even if somewhat artificial — city which has its fair share of high-rise buildings, parks and monuments. However, apart from this "official" city, there is the Pyongyang of small traditional huts, dirt alleys and communal wells.

Indeed, the large-scale construction programs undertaken by the North Korean government in the 1970s and 1980s have borne impressive results. Many districts are now host to an array of apartments which have become home to an estimated half a million Pyongyanites. But where do the other two million inhabitants live? The answer is simple: in single-story buildings, not unlike those which their parents once called home.

If the adventurous traveler ventures outside central Pyongyang, he or she will soon find an altogether different landscape. At first glance, the buildings in the more remote parts of the city are just a little less pretentious than those

A street crowd in Pyongyang. Photograph by Byeon Young-wook.

"downtown." Along the tree-lined streets one will see apartment blocks. Thus, if one is riding in a car or bus (the usual modes of transport for foreigners in Pyongyang), the illusion of a modern city may be sustained. However, this is only an illusion. Modern buildings are erected along the streets and shield from view the clusters of huts which are located inside these blocks. The small huts fill the entire space within blocks, safely guarded from the prying eyes of outsiders.

The further from the city center one roams, the less effort is taken to hide the huts. They are particularly numerous in the eastern part of Pyongyang, on the left bank of the Taedonggang River. Except for the new Munsu district where modern buildings form narrow strips along the left bank of the Taedonggang, as well as along Saesallim and Taedongwon Streets which lead towards the eastern edge of the city, the rest of eastern Pyongyang remains a sea of small brick-and-clay huts separated by dirt tracks.

The typical single-story Pyongyang house still appears very traditional. It is more or less the same as that which one can occasionally encounter in the poorest parts of Seoul — "moon villages" — although the Pyongyang variety appears much more destitute. These huts are low structures with tiled or slated roofs and plastered walls. Their windows and doors face a tiny courtyard with a back yard. Such houses would on average cover about 20 square meters, including the non-living space, while the back yard garden would scarcely be half that size.

Usually, such a dwelling consists of two adjoining rooms and a kitchen with *ondol* heating. The houses are so small that at night the whole floor must be used as a bed, while during the day they are deserted: the adults are at work, and the children are either at school or playing in the neighborhood.

Ondol hearths are fed with coal briquettes, made from coal dust by hand-operated presses. Until recently, these same coal briquettes could also be seen in Seoul, where they were known as yont'an. Perhaps the most striking features of North Korean houses are their chimneys. These are usually made of a piece of iron water pipe, often crooked and rusty, and emerge at odd angles from the wall, giving the quarters a quaint Dickensian appearance.

The housing density in the poorer districts is very high. Probably about 30–40% of all land is occupied by houses with space left only for small back yard and narrow dirt paths between the dwellings.

In such districts there is a very basic water supply but no sewage, so people are forced to use a common public toilet. Inside private houses there might be a water tap, but not always. Between the huts there can sometimes be seen elaborate pavilions. These are the well-houses, the center of the quarter's social life. Next to a well, there is often a small yard where children play while the women draw water, do their laundry or exchange gossip.

This side of Pyongyang is far more typical and genuine than the artificial and pretentious T'ongil or Kwangbok districts. Nevertheless, the new apartments for the privileged are interesting in their own right. But that is another story....

PART 6

Daily Lives

Bathed in Socialism

SOUTH KOREANS LOVE THEIR SAUNAS. It is therefore surprising to learn that public baths, now so ubiquitous in South Korea and attracting even foreign tourists, were first introduced only in the 1920s. What about the North? Does Northern poverty mean that North Koreans have never heard about saunas? Surprisingly, this is not the case. The North boasts a huge public bathing facility which probably exceeds anything one can find in the South in size and is not much inferior in service quality. This is Ch'anggwangwon, a mammoth bathing complex which opened for the public in March 1980. In early 2001 the North Korean media reported that over the first two decades of it existence Ch'anggwangwon had seen some 37 million visitors.

Ch'anggwangwon can be described as a "super-bathhouse." This granite and marble structure is complete with a swimming pool, an impressive array of spas and showers, saunas and the like. It has its own bars and tearooms. And it is open to the general public, not only to currency-paying foreigners or well-connected cadres and their offspring.

However, it does not mean that anybody can walk in: one has to have a ticket which allows a stay of a limited time only. Actually, the Ch'anggwangwon complex serves some 5,000 patrons a day, but it is not enough: many more people would like to get in. Thus people wait in the early morning from 4:00 A.M. in a long queue or, alternatively, get tickets via their work unit and/or neighborhood people's group. Foreigners are luckier: they have a special day (Saturdays) when the entire complex is reserved for their exclusive use — much to the dismay of the common people. However, foreigners pay hard currency for the privilege.

96

Palatial Ch'anggwangwon is unique — or almost unique. In the 1980s a handful of other top-class bathing houses were built in Pyongyang. These are modest compared to Ch'anggwangwon, but quite impressive by the standards of the "normal" North Korean public bathhouses. However, a visit to Ch'anggwangwon is a relatively rare event even for the inhabitants of privileged Pyongyang, while humble public bathhouses are for daily use.

In the countryside, a number of smaller bathing complexes were built throughout the 1980s, so every major city has its own scaled-down version of Ch'anggwangon — like, say, Ŭndŏkwon in the border city of Sinuiju.

And what about private bathing facilities? These are nearly absent. Almost all houses in the countryside have no bathing facilities whatsoever. This is often the case even with multi-story buildings, especially outside Pyongyang: a tap in the kitchen at best. Only a minority of North Koreans can wash themselves in their houses and then very seldom in a private bathroom. Some better apartment complexes have small bathhouses for the exclusive use of the residents, but only a handful of the best apartments in Pyongyang are equipped with their own bathrooms, and these luxurious dwellings are reserved for the elite alone.

Thus, the common North Koreans have a choice: either wash themselves at home, usually using a tank of hot water, or go to a public bathhouse or to a small bathing facility at the work unit. Most prefer the second option, since even a moderate public bathhouse provides more comfort than one's own kitchen. In cities, every ward (tong) is supposed to have its own bathhouse, and larger plants and factories also have their own bathing facilities attached to change rooms.

Once upon a time the North Korean authorities did their best to ensure that people would wash regularly. This was a part of a hygiene promotion campaign of the 1950s and 1960s. Those campaigns were successful but, by the standards of developed countries, North Koreans do not wash themselves too frequently: once every two weeks is seen as the norm. I would not criticize them for this neglect of personal cleanliness: it is easy to keep oneself clean when all it takes is the turn of a tap, and it is much more difficult when bathing requires a rather time-consuming visit to a bathing house.

A typical bathhouse is a large room with a small pool of heated water. People squat on the tiles or the cement floor around the pool and use small buckets to wash themselves with hot water. In better times, they were issued some better quality soap for personal use, with the products of the Pyongyang Cosmetics Factory being the best. In recent years, when the public distribution system ceased to function, people have to buy soap on the black market or use low quality soap, initially produced for washing clothes. There is another novelty: shampoo, once completely unknown. Nowadays, it is gain-ing popularity among the affluent families in Pyongyang, but the average North Korean still uses soap to wash his or her hair.

But one has to have hot water. Even in the more affluent times of the 1970s, the hot water supply was unreliable at best, and bathing facilities could use only cold water in summertime. In large North Korean cities they used the Soviet system of hot water supply: the water was not heated by small boilers attached to every house but by large thermal centers, each serving a large district and, ideally, combined with a thermal power plant. The heated water was pumped to the houses through a network of insulated pipes. This reliance on a centralized system made Korean urban dwellings particularly vulnerable in times of crisis.

The fuel crisis of the mid–1990s greatly aggravated the situation. Most public bathhouses are now open only a few days a month or before major holidays (like Kim Jong Il's birthday). In the late 1990s, when the crisis was at its height, the hot water was provided only for a few hours a day even in Pyongyang's best hotels, reserved exclusively for foreign visitors. Common people had to wash themselves in their homes, if they could afford to spend fuel on such niceties.

And, of course, there is the problem of washing clothes. Needless to say, a washing machine is a rare and exotic commodity — perhaps as rare as a private plane in an affluent Western country. Hence, most washing is done by hand with low quality soap instead of detergent, which is difficult to get even in the best of times. This means that North Koreans cannot afford to change their clothes too often: once a week seems to be the norm in the cities.

But then again, historians have long known that cleanliness does not come cheaply.

Crime and Other Misadventures

SOMETHING THAT IMPRESSES FOREIGNERS in Seoul is the physical security of this huge city. The crime level in Korea is indeed very low by the standards of most Western societies. This is especially true in regard to violent street crime. South Korea has its fair share of official corruption, fraud and embezzlement, but mugging or armed robbery remain rare occurrences in Seoul, and homicides are nearly non-existent. Vandalism, such a problem in Western cities, is also nearly absent from South Korea, and teenage gangs, while existent, are few in number.

However, the North is different. No criminal statistics have ever issued forth from the Kims' hermit kingdom, but anecdotal evidence leaves no doubt that violent street crime in the North is more common than in the South. Perhaps Pyongyang is a safe place by the standards of the urban West, but youth gangs are a part of life there.

Indeed, Northerners are different from the Southerners in their willingness to resort to force in confrontation. For a long time, I thought that it was my subjectivist and probably unreliable impression, but in recent years, as Southerners have been exposed to the defectors from the North on a much greater scale, a number of them have developed the same feeling.

Over the last few years North Korean defectors have been required to undergo a mandatory crash course in the Southern way of life. This course is run by a special training center known as Hanawon. This center acquired a notorious reputation due to violent fights between the students. In some cases staff members were attacked as well — something unthinkable in the South, with its ingrained reverence to teachers and social superiors! When I heard about it I was not surprised. Nowadays, defectors usually do not come from the elite as was the case until the mid–1990s. They represent a cross-section of the North Korean population, including commoners, and these people are ready to use their fists when they deem necessary.

The hoodlum subculture has been a part of the North Korean tradition from the 1970s, and a large number of young men from underprivileged households were members of such gangs before they went into the military (typically, at the age of 18).

The gangs are especially prominent in large provincial cities. Some of these cities are reportedly divided into zones, so nobody ventures into the turf of a rival gang. Such an incursion can lead to a violent fight with unpredictable results.

The gangs are engaged in criminal activities of various kinds. They pick pockets, steal food from food stalls, and take bicycles and household belongings left in yards. In recent years the hoodlums have been provided with new options and chances. There were some reports of muggings, although gang members are obviously afraid to attack foreigners. If they did they would attract the attention of the secret police, an organization that far exceeds the criminal police in resources, determination, and ferocity.

However, criminal activity is probably not the major part of a gang member's life. Group fights with "enemies" from other neighborhoods, daring escapes from the police patrols, and other risky undertakings provide the young Koreans with the thrill of adventure. In this regard, they are very different from their South Korean counterparts, who are too busy preparing for the college entrance exam to do silly things in their teenage years. Young North Koreans do not need to care that much about the future. With few exceptions, college admission and careers are determined by one's family origin, known as *sŏngbun*. This leaves a lot of free time, and less educated youth use this time in their own peculiar way....

The authorities generally turn a blind eye to the gangs, as long as their activities do not lead to social disruption. It is correctly assumed that most of their members will soon join the army and come back home as reliable members of North Korean society.

In the former Soviet Union and some other post–Communist countries these street gangs profited enormously from the social transformation, being involved in the protection racket and quasi-legal market activities. In the 1990s these hoodlums-turned-mobsters controlled many small and medium-size businesses in the post–Soviet states — at least, outside the capital cities. The North might follow the same scenario in the future, but so far it seems that the street toughs know their place, and that protection payments are more likely to be extorted by police, not by criminals.

However, the economic crisis resulted in a remarkable growth of crime, including robbery and theft. People are desperate, and they are ready to do what it takes in order to survive. What makes things worse is that the military is increasingly involved with violent crime — soldiers stealing food and fighting with civilians became quite commonplace in the recent decade.

Widespread participation in gang activity has begotten a school of violence and camaraderie which has few, if any, analogues in the South. I often wonder how the South Korean police, used to an obedient and soft type of criminal, would deal with the Northern toughs? But I am an optimist: sooner or later a piecemeal solution will be found. Koreans are good at solving seemingly impossible problems, and the fates of earlier generations of refugees from the North confirm this once again.

Strong Spirits

THE KOREANS CONSIDER THEMSELVES heavy drinkers. Is it really the case? Well, somebody with Russian (and Australian) experience might be of a different opinion, but it is impossible to deny that Koreans do drink alcohol and sometimes do so to excess. This is applicable both to South and North Korea, but the drinking traditions of the two parts of what was once the same country have become vastly different during the six decades of separation.

The most common types of alcoholic beverages in the North are soju and beer. The North also produces grape wine, but they are of inferior quality and do not enjoy much popularity. The traditional tastes are also conspiring against grape wine, which is either "too sweet" or "too sour" to the Korean palates. In South Korea, wine began to win some mass popularity only in 1990s, but even now South Koreans have not yet completely accustomed themselves to Western-style grape wine (and it does not help that most locally produced wine is, frankly, bad). In the North, Western-style grape wine remains a rare exotic, not much appreciated by many. Of course, there are great connoisseurs in the upper crust of the society, long used to foreign exotics, but those people form a tiny fraction of entire population.

On the other hand, North Korean beer is of relatively good or, at least, drinkable quality. Until the recent economic crisis, Pyongyang and some other major cities boasted beer halls which were run by the government — like all other retail and service outlets. Nowadays, one can easily order beer in numerous private eateries which have spread across the North over the last decade. But in general, beer is not well known in the North-traditional strong liquors are the drink of choice.

The best North Korean liquor is produced exclusively for export or for consumption by the country's tiny elite. It is somewhat of a paradox that many of these spirits are seen in the North as inaccessible symbols of luxury but, from the late 1990s, can be easily purchased in Seoul where they are neither particularly expensive nor particularly popular. Beverages of lesser quality are available for the North Korean secondary elite, while the worst ones are reserved for the general public.

Some of the North Korean spirits are very exotic indeed — for instance, "snake liquor" which is made with *real* snakes: the poor reptiles are placed in a bottle of strong spirit, the alcohol content of which is 60%. "Ant liquor" is produced in a similar way, with ants being the victims. In the North, "snake liquor" is seen as a symbol of utter luxury, and is available only for the cream of the elite (or for the hard currency earners). Needless to say, it is believed to be "good for men"—North Korean culture shares the unending quest for virility with cultures of the entire East Asia. But it is only a handful of the top cadres who can afford to enhance their libido by consuming such exotic beverages.

Ginseng liquor is slightly more affordable but is still clearly a luxury, beyond the normal reach of common people. Other expensive sorts of booze include Pyongyang and Taegŭkjang ("Great Theater," after a landmark building of early postwar Pyongyang) liquors.

The spirits for the masses were once produced from maize, but in 1984 the Beloved Leader Kim Jong Il decided that it would be an inappropriate waste of edible grain. Therefore, from that time on the mass-produced spirits were made from acorns. In some cases it is even allowed to barter acorns

Part 6: Daily Lives

for the spirits: a person who presents a certain amount of acorns to a local liquor factory could exchange this for a bottle of the local spirit!

Like everything else in the North, liquor is subjected to rationing. Every North Korean, depending on his or her position within the official hierarchy, is entitled to a certain amount of liquor of a certain quality. Only the lucky top bureaucrats are allowed to consume as much as they want. In order to enjoy this privilege, one has to belong to the "group of daily rationing distribution" or, in other words, be a Politburo member, Central Committee department chief (more or less equal to a Cabinet minister) or a general with the elite units. Lesser mortals — even the Cabinet deputy ministers — have to deal with some limitation.

Until the collapse of the state-run rationing system in the mid–1990s a common North Korean was entitled to have booze a few times a year, before the major official holidays (the most important ones, needless to say, are Kim Il Sung's and Kim Jong Il's birthdays). On the eve of an official holiday, commoners were issued rationing coupons which entitled them to buy one bottle of soju and three bottles of beer.

In case of some family event, like a wedding or a funeral, people had to go to a local office where they were issued some "special liquor." In order to prove their eligibility, they had to produce an official certificate which confirmed that their family was indeed having a wedding or a funeral. The norm was five bottles per family. In most cases this was not enough, and people had to resort to other means of acquiring alcohol. In recent years, when the public distribution system does not really function any more, spirits have to be acquired through alternative channels.

The easiest way to purchase booze is to go to a local market. For years, the North Korean authorities tried to stamp out the trade in home-brewed liquors, but eventually they had to give up this uphill struggle, and from the 1980s, the lively trade in homemade liquors became an essential part of North Korean markets' life. No statistics are known, but it seems that the privately produced liquors form an overwhelming part of all booze consumed in North Korea these days. They are made of all kinds of grain, including maize, acorns, potato and kaoliang, and are typically some 20% strong.

In recent years, when the nearly total control of the economy collapsed, small private drinking establishments appeared. Usually, these are simple and unpretentious places, somewhat reminiscent of South Korea's drinking tents. However, there are more expensive eateries which cater to the tastes of the expats or those Koreans who can pay in currency. Recently, there were reports about a microbrewery which probably operates with some involvement of the cadres and produces a quality dark beer for those who can pay a hefty price there.

Alcohol in North Korea serves as a social lubricant — pretty much as everywhere. A bottle of liquor might serve as a payment for some service, and it is advisable to keep a bottle while hitchhiking on the countryside roads. However — unlike South Koreans — people of the North have a strong resentment of female drinking. A glass or two might be OK for older women, but in most cases a decent woman should not drink at all.

Those lucky North Koreans who have access to foreign currency might prefer to go to a hard-currency shop. In the Rakwon ("Paradise") supermarket in Pyongyang or in its numerous local branches the lucky owner of hard currency can buy all the world-famous brands — but for a price which might be double the internationally accepted one.

Fortunately, booze and tobacco are the only addictive substances available for the North Koreans. Illegal drugs are not a major problem in the North. The DPRK is actively engaged in opium production, but this specific "product" targets overseas markets exclusively. It is not for the locals: this addictive substance is produced to poison outsiders only.

Communication Breakdown

FOR SOME REASON COMMUNIST GOVERNMENTS tended to neglect communication infrastructure. While the importance of steel mills, power plants, and even textile factories was well understood, most Communist governments perceived phone connections or efficient individual transportation as luxuries that could be safely ignored.

Alas, North Korea is typical in this regard. In the late 1940s it inherited the Japanese communications network, quite developed by the Asian standards of that era, and it relied on this for quite a long time. The growth in communications was very sluggish even in the best of the times when the country's heavy industry was developing with impressive speed and efficiency.

Indeed, the phone at home has always been and still remains a sign of unusual privilege. A recent estimate suggests that there are roughly 5.2 phone lines per every hundred North Koreans. However, this figure includes the office phones that form the overwhelming majority. Only 20% of all phones are installed in private houses.

The situation is exacerbated by the poor conditions of the existent network. Until the mid–1990s only Pyongyang had automatic phone exchanges. Over the last decade, the automatic exchanges were introduced to all major cities, but in smaller towns and in the countryside the connections are made

The public phone became common in Pyongyang around 2000. Photograph by Andrei Lankov.

manually, through a phone operator — a form of technology that disappeared from the developed world in the 1930s! The connections are unreliable, and calling outside the city is both expensive and time-consuming (it sometimes takes hours to get a connection).

Until recently a private phone was a sign of having a privileged position within the approved hierarchy: party cadres, police officers, and top management alone were eligible for this mark of distinction. However, in recent years the situation has changed. Now it is possible to purchase a phone line from the state-run phone company. One only has to pay an equivalent of some $200–$300. Such a sum is well beyond the reach of the average wage-earner, but for a successful black market operator it is quite affordable. The calls are charged per minute and are quite expensive — another reason why the phone is not for the average citizen.

There are some public phones as well, introduced only in the 1980s. They are located in but a few major cities, and their number is very small. Thus, if there is a need to make an urgent inter-city call, North Koreans normally go to a post office where the service is provided. In recent years of crisis and growing crime, one has to produce an ID and also pay a deposit in order to use the service. This is necessary since many people just disappear after they make the call.

International phone calls are expensive — $5 or more per minute. In other words, one minute of talk is enough to spend the entire monthly official salary of the average North Korean! In addition, not all countries can be called from within the DPRK. For example, most phones cannot be used to call the U.S., although major hotels provide such a service. South Korea is definitely off-limits. Incidentally, it is also impossible to call the North from the South directly (but one can use re-routing services through Hong Kong or other third parties).

Another peculiarity of the North Korean situation is the absence of phone books. Phone books are considered classified documents, not for use by common people. A limited number of such books have been smuggled from the North to be scrutinized by experts in the South and overseas: such books provide important data about the otherwise hidden structure of the North Korean bureaucracy.

Nonetheless, there are phone numbers known to everybody. One has to dial 110 to contact the police, 113 is for medical emergencies, and 119 connects to the fire brigade.

Many Pyongyang watchers believe that the present-day North Korean leaders understand the importance of modern communication much better than their predecessors, but the shortage of funds and the ongoing political crisis prevent them from implementing any substantive improvement.

Optimists hailed the growth of mobile communications as one of the signs of the North Korean changes. This service was introduced in the summer of 2002. Initially access was limited to top officials, and police and security personnel, but eventually commoners were also allowed to acquire mobile phones — as long as they were able and willing to pay $750 for the handset and initial connection fee, plus the high rates charged for every call. In summer 2002, there were an estimated 3,000 subscribers in Pyongyang.

However, this freedom did not last. In 2004 all mobile phones were confiscated by the authorities, and only a handful of the top officials probably use them under strict control. The reasons for such drastic measures are not clear, but there are persistent rumors that the crackdown on the phones was somehow related to the mysterious explosion on the Yongch'ŏn station in April 2004. A train loaded with explosive material was blown up, wiping out an entire neighborhood and killing hundreds of the local residents.

In a rare bout of openness, the North Korean authorities admitted that the explosion took place (normally, the North Korean press never mentions any disasters which happen in the country). The official reports insisted that the explosion was a result of some accident, but from the very beginning there were also persistent rumors that it actually was an assassination attempt: the heavily armored train of the Dear Leader had passed the Yongch'ŏn station a few hours before the incident. According to the rumors, the explosion, which was meant to crush the Dear Leader and his entourage, was triggered by a device which was activated using a mobile phone.

We are unlikely to learn the truth in the near future. But one thing is clear: in summer 2004 the North Koreans (a very small privileged fraction of them, actually) lost their right to use mobile phones. In late 2004, some foreign residents were allowed to re-connect, but as of July 2005 there were merely a hundred subscribers in all of North Korea.

The only exception is in the borderland areas where rich people widely use mobile phones which are connected to the Chinese networks. It became possible when the Chinese mobile companies built a number of new relay stations on the Chinese side of the border. This was ostensibly done to serve the local population, but the providers got some clients on the other side of the border as well.

Chinese mobile phones are smuggled from China where a friend, partner or relative makes all the necessary payments to the Chinese service provider. These phones are indispensable for the traders and smugglers who are so numerous in the area: they exchange information on prices, demand for goods, ways of smuggling and even movement of border guards.

These phones can be operated only near the border. The exact range depends on terrain and location of the nearest Chinese relay station, but as a rule such phones only work within a short distance of the border — maybe up to 10 or 15 km.

In some cases these smuggled phones are used to talk to relatives in China and even in South Korea. This worries authorities, who are used to controlling all exchanges over the phone, so there have been some reports about attempts to locate those using the Chinese phones. But obviously the efforts were not successful.

From the North Korean point of view, the development of a phone system presents a serious challenge. No modern economy is possible without a developed, accessible and reliable communications network, but the same network provides common people with ample opportunities to self-organize and exchange unauthorized information. The government correctly believes that such exchanges are dangerous for its political survival. Thus, they try hard to have the best of both worlds. To no avail, actually: apart from military technologies, Stalinism and high-tech do not really mix, and this is probably good.

The Northern Drawback

TOBACCO WAS INTRODUCED TO KOREA in the 1610s from Japan, and became an instant hit: in a matter of a few decades, all Koreans of both sexes smoked, and a long and thin smoking pipe became the powerful status symbol of the Korean gentry elite.

In the South, an anti-smoking campaign began to have an impact in the early 1990s, but South Korea still remains one of the world's most smoke-addicted cultures. In the North, the situation is even more dramatic: essentially, the North is every anti-tobacco campaigner's nightmare come true.

At least 90% of North Korean males smoke — and most of them are chain-smokers. It is not really that they are unaware of the associated dangers. North Korean schools teach their students that tobacco is dangerous and addictive, and this fact is occasionally mentioned in the press — but the message somehow does not get through. North Korean males take up smoking in their late teens, and do not quit until their death.

In contrast, smoking is an absolute taboo for young and middle-aged women. Women who smoke in the South are much disapproved of, but in the North the approach to the transgression is much tougher. As one defector put it: "A North Korean woman must be crazy to take up smoking." Only older women in their 50s and 60s are exempted, and many North Korean women who do smoke begin when they are in their late 40s.

The negative effects are aggravated by the North Koreans' fondness for truly strong tobacco. Filter cigarettes are almost unknown — they are reserved for the elite only.

The acute shortage of tobacco and the nearly universal demand for it has turned cigarettes into the product of choice for various gifts and bribes. Black market dealers know very well that a pack of cigarettes is the best way to persuade the soldiers at a checkpoint not to waste too much time on the papers of a traveling vendor and a couple of packs will usually make them look the other way when necessary.

North Korea produces some 30 types of cigarettes. Like all other consumer goods, they are subject to a strict and elaborate rationing regime. Every male is entitled to a certain amount of tobacco of a certain quality — depending on his position within the officially established hierarchical order. The tobacco used by Kim Jong Il and his immediate family is produced by a special laboratory in the Longevity Institute, a special research facility which is responsible for the Kims' precious health. Bureaucrats smoke "Ch'ilbosan" and "Rakwon"—filter cigarettes which are produced by the Taesŏng Tobacco Factory. This same factory produces tobacco for export — North Korean brands have recently also been available in Seoul, and for decades they were sold quite cheaply in the former Communist bloc countries.

It is not known which factories are involved in producing counterfeited branded cigarettes — another activity used by Pyongyang to earn an additional dollar. In 1995, the Taiwanese police discovered 20 containers loaded with counterfeit cigarette packaging material which were to be shipped to North Korea. One of the tobacco companies whose products were being counterfeited said the seized materials could have been used to make cigarettes with a retail value of U.S. $1 billion.

Foreign cigarettes are very popular in Korea. The top cadres, when they have a choice, prefer Camel and Rothmans to any local brand, even the most prestigious ones. Chinese and Russian tobacco is also quite popular.

Lower quality "tobacco for the masses" is produced by the Pyongyang Tobacco Factory. These cigarettes lack filters, but they are divided into two groups: the more expensive cigarettes are made with imported paper, while the cheaper brands are rolled using the local product.

Hard currency holders once again find themselves in a very privileged position: they can easily buy imported tobacco products in the hard currency shops. American filter cigarettes are currently the most popular choice, and smoking such cigarettes in public is the perfect way to show off one's wealth.

Since the officially allocated tobacco allowance is not enough for many smokers, the common people prefer to smoke leaf tobacco, which is easily and cheaply obtainable at the markets. Many farmers produce low-quality leaf tobacco in their plots while others sell the tobacco which they steal from the cooperatives' fields. Most popular are the tobacco leaves produced in the northern part of the country, in the mountainous areas adjacent to the Chinese border. This tobacco is especially strong, and thus it costs twice as much as the milder brands produced in the southern provinces. In the North, the approach is straightforward: the more nicotine, the better. The private vendors advertise their product accordingly: "strong tobacco," "very strong tobacco" and "so strong that you feel breathless!"

Apart from leaf tobacco, cigarettes can also be purchased in the markets. However, prices are exorbitant: a pack of locally produced filter cigarettes can easily cost half of the average monthly salary.

For the tobacco leaf users, the major problem is paper. The best quality paper is that of the *Nodong sinmun* daily newspaper, but it is difficult to obtain since this major North Korean daily may only be subscribed to by a secretary of a party cell. People who are not on friendly terms with the secretary have to use other newspapers — and they must also be careful not to tear up any pictures of the Great Leader! This would be seen as a serious transgression, perhaps even a political crime.

And another transgression is female smoking. Once upon a time, until around 1880, both women and men in Korea smoked, but towards the end of the colonial era, smoking came to be seen as an activity unbecoming for a decent woman — at least, a woman below a certain age. In the South it remains normal for the older aunties in their 50s and 60s to puff on a cigarette, but in the North, female smoking among women 50 or 45 or younger has been eradicated completely. There have been reports (somewhat doubtful I will admit) about women being arrested and sent to prison camp for smoking in the 1960s. Even if these stories are not true, all my informants agree that a female nicotine addict would find herself in deep trouble in North Korea. Fortunately, few if any women take the risk. But North Korea's chain smoking men certainly make up for them....

Keeping Up with the Kims

"THEIRS IS A DIRTY RICH HOUSE. They have all seven contraptions!" One can sometimes hear this statement in the North. It might appear enigmatic, but every North Korean knows what the "seven contraptions" or *ch'il gi* stands for. These seven gadgets are the major status symbols in the North. The list has changed, but now, in the early 2000s, it comprises the following: a TV set, a refrigerator, a washing machine, an electric fan, a sewing machine, a videotape recorder and a camera.

Only a tiny fraction of all North Korean households owns all of these "contraptions." In the mid–1990s, the average black market cost of the entire package was 30,000 *won* or, roughly, some 30 (!) times the annual salary of an average worker. Measured against South Korean criteria, this would be roughly equivalent to 600 million *won*! Nowadays, the figures have changed, but the ratio has remained essentially the same.

Of all these gadgets, TV sets are by far the most common. Nowadays, TV sets can be found in approximately 40% of North Korean households, even if they are spread across the country quite unevenly.

VCRs were at one time not included in the established list of the "seven contraptions," but it seems that the situation is changing. Until a few years ago, VCR ownership remained low, being merely a few percent. However, the situation recently underwent a dramatic change: the spread of DVD players in China led to a sharp drop in the price of used VCRs which are smuggled to North Korea. From around 2001-2002, VCRs became quite common with one house out of ten reputedly boasting one in Pyongyang. The machines are used largely for watching South Korean shows, illegally imported through China.

Cameras are owned by roughly 20 percent of all North Korean families. A vast majority of them are old Soviet-made manual cameras. While possessing fairly good optics, they are difficult for amateurs to operate. To take a good picture one has to possess the knowledge and skill which in advanced countries is to be found only among professional photographers. To obtain a picture of themselves for bureaucratic purposes, North Koreans usually go to special shops where pictures are taken and developed by professional photographers.

Electric fans are relatively common. Of course, air conditioning is unheard of, but even a simple fan helps to make the hot and humid Korean summer more bearable.

Meanwhile, washing machines and refrigerators remain luxuries. Washing machines have been locally produced since the 1970s, but even in Pyongyang few houses can boast such an appliance.

Sewing machines are important in the North since people still normally sew their clothes themselves. The situation there is akin to that of the West before the rise of the ready-to-wear industry in the early 1900s. When the rationing system still functioned properly, the North Koreans received their allotment in pieces of cloth which then had to be tailored. Thus, a sewing machine was very handy.

TV sets and some of the other "seven contraptions" were once distributed through government shops where prices were low, although one had to wait years for permission to buy a particular item, without which no shop would sell the item. However, neither washing machines nor fridges could be bought officially, even in the best of times. They had to be acquired via the black market. In recent years the distribution system has collapsed completely, and this market provides the only means of becoming an owner of the "seven contraptions"—if you can afford to spend some 30 average annual salaries, that is....

Uniform Trends

COMMUNIST GOVERNMENTS LOVE TO SEE their citizens in uniform, or so the common perception runs. No doubt, this perception is a stereotype—but most stereotypes do contain more than a grain of truth, and uniforms are not an exception. Indeed, the proportion of the population in uniform in most Communist countries is quite impressive.

Traffic lights were introduced in Pyongyang, but only briefly, and now the famous "traffic girls" have made a comeback. Photograph by Christopher Morris.

However, even amongst such august company, North Korea stands above all others. The number of uniformed people on the streets of North Korean cities is astonishing: sometimes up to a quarter of the people around you at any one time would be sporting some kind of military-style wear. I suspect that North Korea is currently the world's most uniformed country.

And who are these people in uniform? First of all, naturally, are the military personnel. North Korea maintains a very impressive army which numbers at least 1.2 million soldiers. No Communist government has ever been able to resist the temptation to use its army as an unpaid labor force, but North Korea went to extremes. The majority of the North Korean soldiers are perhaps more used to shovels than to rifles. Every spring, soldiers are sent to the countryside where they plant rice or maize seedlings, and these "operations" take at least two months. In autumn they participate in the harvest, and all year around they can be dispatched to construction sites across the nation.

The soldiers can be assigned a number of stunningly unmilitary tasks, like collecting medical herbs in the mountains or trucking civilian goods across the country. The armed forces are even expected to produce a large part of their own food. The KPA has its own large network of farms which is staffed by the conscripts.

Most projects where soldiers are involved are essentially of a civilian nature.

To name just a few, in the 1970s military units built the Pyongyang subway. In the 1980s, several infantry divisions were building the West Sea Barrage at Nampo. In the early 1990s, the soldiers laid the tracks of the Pyongyang trams. It is not an exaggeration to say that the KPA often plays the role of a large state-run building company.

It is estimated that the average North Korean soldier spends between one third and one half of armed service engaged in agricultural or construction activity. Only a few elite units, including those stationed near the DMZ, are excluded from this duty. KPA officers are soldiers, but they are farmers and builders too.

One can point at gross inefficiencies in the soldiers' work, but the same is true of most North Korean undertakings. In his Pyongyang memoirs, Andrew Holloway once cited his friend, a regular visitor to Pyongyang in the 1980s: "I have never known a people who work so hard or achieve so little. It doesn't matter whether it's handicrafts or bridges."

Pyongyang also has a number of soldiers on active duty. Many of them guard major government agencies or other places deemed important. For example, downtown Pyongyang boasts a large fenced-off area which is home to the members of the North Korean elite. The gates to this "small paradise" are zealously guarded by serious-looking stocky girls (for some reason, many of these guards are women) in military uniform, equipped with their Kalashnikovs. Many soldiers also staff the batteries of anti-aircraft guns which dot every hill in and around Pyongyang

Pyongyang also has its fair share of police men and women. Among other things, the policewomen direct traffic, an important duty in a city where there were no traffic lights until the early 2000s. Then traffic lights appeared on major crossroads, and the girls disappeared for a while. However, soon the traffic lights were switched off— obviously, the girls handled the traffic situation better, and their pay was too meager to worry about. A Pyongyang traffic controller, with her highly choreographed moves, has long been a source of inspiration for foreign photographers and North Korean official painters alike. Indeed, those girls are obviously selected for their looks and fitness!

At the same time, "normal" police who deal with criminals are not seen in Pyongyang too often. In Korea, both North and South, the level of violent street crime is quite low, and this makes the deterring presence of police on the streets largely unnecessary.

However, not all uniformed people are soldiers or policemen, since many other groups in the North are required to wear a uniform as well. First of all there are the members of the "shock detachments" or *tolkyŏktae*. These young men and women work mostly on construction sites and sometimes do unskilled work in factories.

In the subway. Photograph by Christopher Morris.

Young people are conscripted into these units after they graduate from high school. In fact, depending on one's academic success and family background, school graduates are assigned their careers: the best connected and/or most brilliant go on to colleges, the vast majority are shipped off to the army, and the less fortunate ones are allocated to the "shock detachments." There are several kinds of detachments, with the "high-speed battle youth shock detachments" or *soktojŏn ch'ŏngnyŏn tolkyŏktae* seen as more prestigious, more or less equal to respectable military units. Their personnel are involved in politically important construction projects, like, for example, erecting statues of the Great Leader or building monuments to his glory. But the majority of the conscripts are not so lucky and are consigned to far less prestigious *tolkyŏktae* units.

The "shock detachments" are organized in a military fashion, with a "brigade" considered the largest unit. Personnel of the "shock detachments" live in barracks, and receive some basic military training; in other words, their lives are very similar to those of the military draftees, but their supplies and social standing are generally much lower. The "shock detachments" personnel have military ranks and wear green uniforms with military-style insignia — but in the form of badges rather than epaulets.

Another uniformed group are the subway and railway workers. All subway staff are dressed in a dark-blue military-style uniform and wear signs signifying their ranks. Some subway staff members are enlisted into subway service as if into the army. Over their several years of service they too live in barracks and are subjected to military discipline. Most of them are women, young round-faced girls, obviously from the countryside. Although it includes a lot of hard manual labor, this is a quite prestigious occupation. But by any measure, any position whatsoever in Pyongyang is great by definition.

There are a number of other uniformed people as well. Miners, for example, wear uniforms (though they are rarely seen in Pyongyang). In the DPRK, miners are organized into "companies" and "battalions" and are subjected to military-style discipline.

Finally, of course, a uniform is required by all schools, including colleges and universities. In earlier times, students were expected to wear uniforms both in class and outside the school, but since around 1990 this requirement is not enforced with the same zeal, and nowadays uniforms are largely for school classes only. Students of the primary and middle schools are even required to go to school in formation, singing some marching song about the greatness of the Dear Leader!

All these uniforms create the impression of a highly regimented and controlled society. To some extent this is true, but only to some extent. The North Koreans are not robots, even if their government often tries hard to present them in a machine-like, individuality-free way.

PART 7

Recreation and Fashion

Fashion, After a Fashion

THE INGRAINED WESTERN IMAGE of a Communist city includes pictures of women clad in nondescript and ugly dress. To some extent, this imaginary depiction is correct, since light industry was never a success story under state socialism.

Some Communist countries — Mao's China being the most prominent example — deliberately wanted to clothe their womenfolk in the plainest dress possible. But this was rather an exception. Most Communist countries did not ignore fashion deliberately or out of some ideological considerations — they simply could not manage it well, even if they tried.

Surprisingly, North Korea was never a "hermit kingdom" at all as far as fashion was concerned. Worldwide fashion trends always found their way to Pyongyang — even if with some delay. In the 1950s, the more affluent Korean men and women largely imitated the dress style they saw in the Soviet and East European movies, and in those days the Soviets, in turn, were faithfully copying Western trends. Of course, these affluent and educated urban women were a tiny minority of all North Koreans: most women were too poor to afford anything but traditional dress.

If Korean fashion ever had a "bleak period," it was, in all probability, the 1960s. The nationalist purism, the deliberate attempts to do away with Soviet influences, and the impact of Mao's China conspired against imitation of the Soviet (read: Western) fashions. For a decade all women had to switch to the modified traditional dress: white blouse and dark skirt. The major change was that the "new" skirt was much shorter than the original one, only up to the knees.

However, in the 1970s, fashion made a comeback. In April 1970, Kim Il Sung produced an "instruction" which required the "production of more colorful clothes to satisfy the demands of the growing Pyongyang, and other cities." Of course, the persistent shortage of cloth remained a major obstacle for the North Korean fashion industry. Nonetheless, this was an official endorsement of the new approach to fashion, and during the 1970s an increasing number of women discarded their quasi-traditional dress in favor of the modern, Western-style one.

Around the same time, South Korean fashion began to influence the North. Of course, only a select few were allowed to see South Koreans, or read South Korean magazines, or watch movies from Seoul, but these selected members of the North Korean elite were quick to reproduce the latest Seoul fashions. Then the lesser beings emulated the privileged — and thus the "southern style" spread throughout the country. On account of this, North Korean urban women in the 1980s dressed in a manner eerily reminiscent of the South Korean fashions of the 1970s. This was yet another confirmation that South Korea was increasingly seen as a country to emulate — at least, in the field of consumer culture.

Of course, the government tried to control the process — as every Communist government should. In 1982 Kim Il Sung, while addressing the Supreme People's Assembly (the North Korean rubber-stamping parliament) stated his views on fashion: "It does not conform with the socialist lifestyle if women wear dresses without sleeves or a dress that shows their breasts!"

However, I would be wary of regarding this statement as an indication of the supposed "Stalinist stupidity" and holding it up to ridicule: at roughly the same time, the South Korean authorities were waging an uphill battle against mini-skirts, and even enacted laws which determined how short the skirts were supposed to be (not more than 17 cm above the knees). The North Koreans also tried to ensure that the skirts were of appropriate length to "conform to the socialist lifestyle." Even nowadays, in the time of relative openness, women's skirts should safely cover the knees of the wearers.

Another suspicious part of women's dress were trousers. For a long time women were not allowed to wear trousers in Pyongyang and other major cities. It was OK to work in trousers, but once the shift was over, decent North Korean women were supposed to dress in a "womanly manner"— that is, to wear skirts. Those who appeared on the street improperly dressed could be sent home by a patrol. Fortunately, in the mid–'90s trousers were partially pardoned, so now even in major cities women are free to wear them if they choose to do so (still, there are recommendations to avoid wearing trousers whenever possible).

Nonetheless, even under these purist restrictions, fashion survived in the

North. Another boost to the fashion industry came with the Pyongyang International Youth Festival of 1988. This large gathering of the world's leftist youth meant that an unprecedented number of foreigners came to Pyongyang and were seen by the locals, if not actually interacted with. The result was a resurging interest in modern fashions. In the early 1990s North Korea even introduced such a quintessentially bourgeois decadent cultural institution as a fashion show!

Of course, only a fraction of North Korean women are dressed as their South Korean sisters. Most of them are way too poor for that — but they often try as hard as they can.

In recent years, the gradual spread of South Korean videotapes smuggled through China has had an impact on the dress and hairstyles of Pyongyang's upper crust. The time lag between the North and South has never been so narrow, and now last year's Seoul fashion is a hit in Pyongyang.

In summer 2005 the traders interviewed in the Chinese city of Dandong, the main base of the legal, semi-legal and illegal trade with the North, said that peculiar shapes of tight trousers are a major hit among the North Korean women — "those who have a suitable figure," they explained. Most of the new clothes are sewn in China, but according to South Korean patterns.

This trend even became a matter of concern for the authorities. They believe that the youngsters' willingness to imitate the South Korean lifestyle indicates their growing fascination with the affluent and democratic South. The authorities are probably correct: I still remember the fashion for blue jeans and American music in the USSR of the 1970s. The Soviet government saw it as a political challenge — and this opinion, often ridiculed by the dissenting intellectuals in the 1970s, was eventually proven correct. It would be a gross overstatement to say that the USSR collapsed because it could not make good blue jeans, but the admiration for Western consumption goods was an important ingredient in the Soviet youngsters' disappointment with their system. Now it seems that the same story is being repeated in North Korea.

Time for a Holiday

PEOPLE LOVE HOLIDAYS. EVEN IF the rulers want to convey some lofty political or religious messages, the ruled have always seen holidays as a good occasion to have fun. This has been the case since time immemorial, and North Korea is no exception. Even though North Korean holidays are remarkably politicized even by the standards of the Communist countries, people love them nonetheless.

Generally, North Korean holidays are divided into three groups. The first one comprises the "political" holidays, for instance, the birthdays of Kim Il Sung or Kim Jong Il. Currently there are ten of them, but the list keeps changing all the time. The second group includes the traditional holidays which won recognition in North Korea in the late 1980s. For example, from 1988, Ch'usŏk or "Korean Thanksgiving" is a day off in the North. The third group includes "professional holidays," like Education Day (September 5) or Navy Day (August 28) and some others. These are not nationwide holidays, but people employed in the relevant areas have their day off.

The annual cycle of politically charged holidays starts on February 16 when Kim Jong Il's birthday is celebrated. The festivities last for two consecutive days, as is proper for such an important occurrence. The incumbent Great Leader was born in 1942 in the then USSR, but the official propaganda insists that this great historical event took place within Korea, on the slopes of the Paektu Mountain.

On March 8, the North celebrates Women's Day. In this it follows the long-established Communist tradition which is kept across the former Communist Camp. Once upon a time, this was a celebration of the revolutionary will of the "female masses," but when the Communist regimes gradually lost their initial pro-feminist zeal, the less political ideals of motherhood and wifehood came to be associated with this holiday.

In April the DPRK celebrates its major official holiday, the birthday of Kim Il Sung, the founder of the ruling dynasty. He was conveniently born in the village of Mangyŏngdae on the outskirts of today's Pyongyang, and this village, as well as countless statues of the Great Leader, Sun of the Nation, presents the North Koreans with places for the officially required pilgrimage. The heads of the "people's groups," small neighborhood units to which all Koreans belong, make sure that everybody goes to a designated statue and lays a bunch of flowers at its feet. Then the loyal subjects must make a deep respectful bow to the bronze likeness of the dynastic founder. The flowers, usually not to be found in North Korean cities, are specially distributed for this occasion.

Soon afterwards, on April 25, the North observes Army Day. This holiday became a nationwide day off only in 1996, obviously to stress the importance of Kim Jong Il's "army-first policy."

On May 1, North Korea celebrates May Day, the International Workers' Day, which used to be observed by the Communists and leftists worldwide as a symbol of workers' unity. Internationalist spirit was once typical for the Communist movement. Communism in power proved to be very nationalistic, and in few places more so than in North Korea. Nonetheless, some lip service to the internationalist tradition of past days is paid, even though this holiday is celebrated on a noticeably smaller scale than others.

On July 27, the North celebrates Victory Day. This is the day when in 1953 the Armistice was signed and the Korean War ended. Since the North has always insisted that the war was started by the South and the U.S., Pyongyang describes the outcome as a victory: the alleged invaders were repelled.

August 15, the day of Liberation, is the only non-traditional holiday which is celebrated in both parts of Korea. It marks the end of Japanese colonial rule in 1945. It is followed by DPRK Foundation Day, September 9. On that day in 1948 the Supreme People's Assembly in Pyongyang proclaimed the foundation of a Communist state in the northern part of the Korean Peninsula.

Then comes Party Foundation Day, October 10. Official history insists that on that day in 1945 the ruling Korean Workers Party was founded by Kim Il Sung (actually, this is one of many inventions of North Korean official historians).

The annual cycle of the official holidays ends on December 27, when the Day of the North Korean Constitution is celebrated.

Apart from ten political holidays, the North observes traditional holidays. Five are now officially recognized, but in the course of time this number has changed frequently.

Relations between the North Korean state and traditional culture have never been easy. A good example of the complexity of this relationships is the *Tale of Ch'un Hyang*—a classical love story of a courtesan's daughter and a young gentleman. The tale was first lauded as the embodiment of the Korean spirit, then vilified as a manifestation of feudal values and then lauded once again.

A similar degree of vacillation has been exhibited in the North Korean attitude towards folk customs. In the 1950s, most of the old rituals were rejected. The traditional rites were seen as essentially religious — and religion was an evil superstition to be uprooted at the earliest possible convenience. Therefore, the traditional holidays — like Ch'usok (Korean Thanksgiving) or Lunar New Year — did not enjoy official recognition.

The 1960s were a decade of radical attempts to eradicate this "reactionary heritage." The old holidays were abolished and those who observed the old traditions could be subjected to humiliating public criticism.

However, the traditions eventually made a comeback. The first concessions took place in 1972 when the authorities permitted observance of some of the traditional funeral rites. From that time onwards North Koreans could attend their ancestors' graves and put them in order, cutting the grass and making offerings to the ancestors' souls.

The next step was taken in 1989 when the "four traditional holidays" received official recognition and were made public holidays. However, they did not acquire an equal footing with the political holidays, such as Kim Il Sung's and Kim Jong Il's birthdays or Party Foundation Day. The eight political holidays (plus Western-style New Year) were unconditionally declared non-working days. The "four traditional holidays" were also declared public holidays, but the "working masses" were (and are) required to make up for the "lost time" on the forthcoming Sunday, which was considered a working day.

The traditions of merrymaking have been largely forgotten over the decades of bans, such that in recent years the North Korean media have tried to educate the people. Broadcasts and newspaper articles explain how to make ttŏk (rice cookies) or play yut, a traditional game, long associated with holidays. They also provide advice on how to dress and which holiday rituals may be conducted.

The first of the traditional holidays is the Lunar New Year, which is celebrated on the 1st day of the 1st lunar month (in late January or early February). It is marked by the same festivities as in the South although on a much smaller scale.

The second most important traditional holiday is Ch'usok. It is not incidental that Ch'usok acquired official recognition in 1988, one year before the same treatment was extended to the other three traditional holidays. Ch'usok is celebrated on the 15th day of the 8th Lunar month and is often described to foreigners as "Korean Thanksgiving." Like their South Korean brethren, on Ch'usok North Koreans try to attend their ancestors' graves, to put them in order and make traditional offerings. It is often much more difficult than in the South — the public transport system has a much lower carrying capacity — but people try hard to follow the custom.

Two other traditional holidays are not celebrated in the South or, more precisely, they do not enjoy the status of official holidays. These are Tano and Hansik. Like Ch'usok and Lunar New Year, these holidays have Chinese roots but became part of the Korean tradition long ago.

Hansik is celebrated on the 105th day after the winter solstice (in early April). Its name means "Day of Cold Food." It received this name because tradition prohibited the lighting of fires in hearths on this day. Tano is celebrated on the 5th day of the 5th lunar month. It commemorates the beginning of the summer and is dedicated to the spirits of ancestors.

Apart from these four traditional holidays, the North also has another holiday which is, strictly speaking, neither political nor traditional. This is the Western New Year, which is celebrated for two days — on the 1st and 2nd of January. The New Year events are not particularly lavish and the Pyongyang authorities have ensured that this seemingly innocent holiday also has political connotations. On the 1st of January the North Koreans are required to make a pilgrimage to the nearest statue of the Great Leader. They bow before Kim's likeness and pledge an oath of loyalty to him.

And are these oaths sincere? Once upon a time they most definitely were, but the situation has changed greatly over the last decade or two. However, the North Koreans still go — out of habit, out of fear, and out of residual devotion as well. Tradition, once established, can be remarkably resilient....

Having Fun

THESE DAYS, NORTH KOREANS DO NOT normally have time to enjoy themselves: they are too busy looking for food and income. However, this was not always the case: North Korea, which I saw for the first time in the mid–1980s, might have been a repressive dictatorship but this did not mean that people could not have some fun when they wanted.

How did North Koreans spend their leisure in the 1970s and 1980s when the economy was still functioning reasonably well, yet ideological pressures were so harsh? Some watched TV at home (if they had TV sets), some went to the movies (in North Korea, like elsewhere, this was a favorite place for dates). But most of this officially provided and approved entertainment was very boring. The TV told stories about the great love Kim Il Sung enjoyed among Central African farmers and South Korean clerks, while movies repeated the same sagas of assiduous workers, ever ready to follow a new order of their omniscient Leader.

However, one peculiar feature helped the North Koreans to have fun. This was their ability to organize a good time for themselves — and do it in public. This same tradition once existed in South Korea (and for that matter, across the world) but has been partially lost with the advent of TV sets and computer games — and with the general growth of prosperity and individualism.

One of the most popular pastimes was picnicking, still possible in the 1980s when at least simple food could be obtained without great difficulty. The Korean penchant for eating and drinking in the open air, preferably somewhere in the mountains, is shared by the inhabitants of both North and South. On their free days, large groups of people visited the parks of Pyongyang. Sometimes, a bus could be seen next to a large group of picnickers, meaning that a whole work unit was enjoying an outing with their families. There they

Playing Chinese chess is a favorite pastime of middle-aged men. Photograph by Byeon Young-wook.

would set up some makeshift tables or just place a cloth on the grass, eat, drink and have their fun. All participants would sing in turns, play games or engage in mock sporting competitions or, of course, dancing.

     Social dancing, once popular among the North Korean urban youth of the mid–1950s, was proclaimed a decadent pastime and banned in the late 1950s, not to be reborn until almost three decades later. In the 1960s and 1970s, only ideologically wholesome revolutionary dances were allowed — these dances were not for couples but for large groups. Some of them were based on ideologically sound topics — like, say, "My heavy machine-gun," often performed by primary school students. However, the public dances of picnicking groups were a much more refined activity — and around 1985 dancing in couples was once again permitted in public. Tape recorders were a definite luxury until the 1990s, thus clapping hands performed the role of music.

     Playing cards were also quite popular among merrymakers. Unlike South Koreans, who like to use the Japanese hwat'u (a variation on the sixteenth-century Portuguese cards), North Koreans largely use European-style playing cards, once imported from the Soviet Union. In the late 1970s, playing cards in public were forbidden (but were still played in the privacy of a friend's home). In the 1980s, this prohibition was lifted.

Fishing has been a favorite pastime of Korean males since long ago. Photograph by Christopher Morris.

Koreans are great singers, and this is true for the North as well. On weekend evenings, one would often see groups squatting around a guitar player. In general, the guitar appeared to be the most popular musical instrument.

On the streets, people often hummed melodies. Their repertoire was different from that which could be heard on the radio: they preferred lyrical songs, not militant marches. However, even these songs included the obligatory reference to the Great Leader Kim Il Sung or — from the early 1980s onwards — to the Dear Leader Kim Jong Il. There could not be such a thing as apolitical lyrics in North Korea! Only in the late 1990s, the South Korean tunes became popular and were finally approved by the government, becoming the first songs in decades free from political references.

During major festivities, in Kim Il Sung Square (near the Grand People's Study House) — the main square in the capital — public dances took place. Foreigners living in Pyongyang were invited to participate in this event. The dances started at 7 P.M. and lasted about an hour. Men would come dressed up in their best suits while women wore their most colorful traditional dresses.

The North Koreans are not brainwashed robots, whose idea of fun is to goose-step while singing songs about the greatness of the Dear Leader. They work, fall in love, earn their living, have sex, quarrel with bosses, enjoy good food (when they can afford it) or interesting conversation, get themselves drunk, bring up children, and do the thousands of other mundane things which normal human beings do.

PART 8

Family Matters

For Brokers or for Worse

WHO ARE THE MOST DESIRABLE HUSBANDS in the minds of the Pyongyang beauties — or their parents, for that matter? It is difficult to say since, being human, they are all different. Some of them dream about artists and pop singers (yes, North Korea does have its own pop idols); some of them do not care much about status or position and choose to marry the person they love; some others think that neither love nor social standing are as important as decency and humanity. People are different, but North Korea also has its "material girls" who marry for success, not to mention wealth and comfort.

The choices of these practically-minded girls have changed over the years — and these changes tell us a lot about North Korean social history. In the 1970s, the ideal husband was a Party cadre or military officer. These enjoyed great power and privilege. Their children had access to the best education available, and their generous rations ensured that their families were well-fed and well-clad while commoners were often undernourished (but not yet starving). The charisma of power was also a prime attraction for the North Korean gold diggers.

In the 1980s the situation began to change. Party officials were outclassed by diplomats, foreign trade specialists and ... sailors — in other words, by people who had regular access to foreign currency. Sailors were part of the list since they often visited foreign ports, and hence were eligible for small allowances paid in foreign currency (and they could make some additional money by buying things overseas and reselling them back home).

The life of the North Korean elite in the 1980s was increasingly defined by the currency shops, where the lucky owners of "imperialist" dollars or yen

Family on a walk. Photograph by Andrei Lankov.

could purchase goods and services beyond the reach — and even the dreams — of the average commoner. Those who by virtue of their jobs received their salaries in hard currency, attracted much attention, including the attention of prospective marriage partners and their parents.

In the last decade, the situation has changed again. The famine of the mid–1990s seriously damaged the social hierarchy that for many decades had been so carefully constructed by the North Korean authorities. One's position within the official hierarchy is increasingly meaningless, while money matters enormously. Nowadays, the rich black marketeers are seen as attractive by the material girls and their parents.

Many of these market dealers hail from families with "bad" *sŏngbun* (family background) — a stigma which people now tend to overlook. In the past, a bad *sŏngbun* could ruin one's life forever. For example, the second cousin of a defector to the South or a grandson of a pre–1945 landlord would normally be ineligible for any position of authority or even a white-collar job. Nowadays, such origins do not prevent them from making good money trading in a market or smuggling goods across the Chinese border — and money is what really matters today. For better or worse, money now really talks.

There have also been changes in the attitude towards another group — the families of some 120,000 ethnic Koreans who migrated to North Korea from Japan in the late 1950s and early 1960s. The position of this group has always been ambiguous: the authorities saw them as both politically unreliable and economically useful (for their expertise as well as their ability to attract money from Japan). They were shunned by the families with good *sŏngbun*, since the "Japanese" tended to get themselves into trouble with the authorities. The mothers-in-law of the Japanese families also had a notorious reputation of being tough on their daughters-in-law, and in a society like Korea, this was not a small problem. Nowadays, this fact is negated by their easy access to currency transfers from Japan, and the "repatriates" have become very desirable players in the marriage market.

Generally speaking, it is now quite common to see marriage alliances struck between individuals (or perhaps families), one of which has money but bad *sŏngbun,* while the other's political pedigree is untarnished but whose pockets are empty. In a sense, these marriages are reminiscent of the alliances between the rich industrialists and impoverished aristocrats which were so common in 19th century Europe. However, it is unlikely that the rich bad-*sŏngbun*ers will be able to gain much from the deal as a return to the old regime becomes more and more improbable.

People with particularly good *sŏngbun*, employed in the especially prestigious jobs (diplomats, sailors, pilots, etc.) should be very careful when choosing a marriage partner. Their wife's *sŏngbun* should be beyond reproach, since even a minor problem in a wife's family might ruin their careers.

Are we being too cynical? I hope not. But then again, thousands of North Korean youngsters do not care about these pragmatic considerations at all. Indeed, many North Korean men and an inordinate number of women have demonstrated a truly heroic spirit when their families were struck by disaster — and their stories are eminently worth telling as well....

Love and Propaganda

IN THE MID–1980S, THE EARLY DAYS of perestroika, there was a brief boom in direct TV conferences between the Soviet and American public. During one such conference, a Soviet girl famously reacted to a question about the sexual life of the Soviet citizens: "We do not have sex here, in the USSR!"

Early Communism was both pro-feminist and remarkably open about sexuality, but this freedom did not last. From the 1930s Soviet officialdom felt

Wedding visit to Kim Il Sung statue. The beginnings of a new family. Photograph by Andrei Lankov.

uneasy about the sexuality of its subjects, and tried to expunge it whenever possible. Thus in Stalin's Russia, the mores were defined by an extreme sexual Puritanism with more than a touch of patriarchal values. This mindset was essentially exported to North Korea in the late 1940s.

However, the labors of Stalin's bureaucrats were quite restrained when compared to the efforts of their North Korean colleagues. Sometimes it appears as if North Korea is indeed a place where they "do not have sex," but this is not the case....

Back in the 1980s, one of my Russian friends, who was then in her early 20s, worked as an interpreter at a joint venture between North Korea and the Soviet Union. She was by no means a prude herself (whatever the TV conferences claimed, the "sexual revolution" in the USSR had well and truly come before 1980), but she was somewhat shocked by the amount of sexual banter which her female North Korean colleagues engaged in. For the entire summer when the girls were on their own, they tried to learn as much as possible about the sexual habits of the then Soviet youngsters, and also graphically discussed related subjects among themselves. These sex-crazed North Korean girls made quite an impact on my acquaintance: it contradicted the more or less ingrained image of North Koreans as brainwashed, goose-stepping robots which was dominant in the USSR of the late Soviet era.

The official attitude to things sexual, however, is very different, of course. As every reader of North Korean novels can testify, sexual desire is invariably associated with "baddies." Sadistic U.S. soldiers, treacherous Japanese spies, cruel landlords, and scheming South Korean capitalists may be — indeed, must be — depicted as lustful. The "goodies," i.e., simple-minded, hard-working Koreans, are supposed to be completely free from such base urges. Their love is always "pure" and lacking any hint of carnal desire. North Korean society is depicted in its official artistic propaganda as completely sexless. Even suitably platonic love relationships have been seen as politically suspicious in certain periods of DPRK history (although in the last two decades the approach to "pure love" has softened considerably).

Is this asexual picture a true representation of North Korean mores? The answer is actually both yes and no. There is no doubt that the everyday life of North Koreans is governed by quite restrictive mores, though these mores are probably more Confucian than Communist in their origin.

This restrictive Confucian sexual morality was never obligatory for everybody, however: for centuries, these restrictions largely targeted women and the lesser orders. In old Korea, womanizing by the male elite was seen as a natural and even laudable pastime, and courtesans and concubines provided the powerful with necessary outlets through which to express this proclivity.

To some extent this is still true of North Korea. Stories about the sexual antics of Pyongyang's golden youth and the Dear Leader himself have been told and retold for decades. Of course, these tales can be discarded as propaganda disseminated by the South Korea rightists, as often really is the case. However, there are many independent reports which confirm that powerful North Koreans do not feel themselves bound by the officially proclaimed norms.

The recent research of a postgraduate student under my supervision has made me even more suspicious of the professed "sexual purity" of the North, at least where the elite is concerned. The investigation itself had little to do with sexuality; it focused on North Korean literature and writers of the 1950s. However, in the course of his research the student amassed a considerable amount of primary material including private letters, interviews, and unpublished personal papers. Among other things, these papers make it clear that the sexual promiscuity of bohemian Pyongyang in the 1950s was not very different from the Hollywood of the same era. In both cases lip service was paid to "lofty" standards, but this shrouded a substantially different reality. Some evidence leads me to suspect that this remained the case in later decades as well.

So much for the elite ... but the humble commoners' lives have been defined by a set of altogether different rules. Until the 1970s, an overwhelming majority of marriages were arranged, and women were expected to remain virginal until marriage. Peer pressure and persuasive political control helped a lot. It was a common practice in the 1960s and 1970s for apprehended lovers to be subjected to humiliating sessions of public criticism.

Even nowadays there are social groups where romance is not welcome. Public criticism sessions are held in camps if prisoners are discovered to be engaging in sexual liaison, and the authorities try to ensure that these sessions are as humiliating as possible, with the maximum amount of anatomical detail revealed by the lovers in public.

But in general there has been a considerable relaxation since the mid–1980s. The ideal North Korean romance is still supposed to remain platonic until formal marriage, but love *per se* is now seen as a completely natural thing. This reflects a change in marriage patterns: from around 1980 North Korea began to experience its own boom in "marriage for love," and nowadays most marriages among youngsters are these so-called love matches (coincidentally much like the South).

Nevertheless, public opinion is still very suspicious of women who openly consort with men — they are putting their reputations at serious risk. Of course, North Korea lacks what would be called a "dating infrastructure" — coffee shops or night clubs are almost unheard of. However, people find their way around this minor obstacle: the beautiful slopes of Morangbong Hill Park, or the poetic promenades beside the slow waters of the Pot'onggang River provide a suitable environment for the young (and occasionally not-so-young) lovers.

But if things get hotter, a solution is not easy to find: no hotels will accept an unmarried (or, for that matter, often a married) couple, and most North Korean hotels are essentially dorms with up to a dozen people crowded into a room. The only hope is to find a sympathetic friend who happens to be in possession of an empty room — or something even more adventurous. Nonetheless, premarital sex has become quite common among younger Koreans since the 1980s, and it seems that only a minority of males remain virgin until marriage which, incidentally, occurs very late, when they reach their late 20s. Women seem to be more bound by the traditional idea of "chastity," but even for them a premarital affair is less a taboo than it was for their mothers.

Nonetheless, the official ideology insists that the only proper type of sexual interaction is within marriage — and this union is often not concluded by the couple, even if they are not always unwilling participants. Which leads us to our next topic....

Marriage Lore

FOR DECADES NORTH KOREANS HAVE been forced to read tales which depict the miraculous wisdom and boundless kindness of the Great Leader or Dear Leader. In these hagiographies one can sometimes encounter the story of an orphan, a son or daughter of some failed hero of the guerrilla resistance or the Korean War. In such stories, Kim Il Sung or Kim Jong Il learns about the orphan and, upon finding that the orphan is not married, promptly arranges a marriage for the lucky person. Of course, the marriage partner is chosen from a family with unblemished revolutionary credentials, and the couple invariably live happily ever after, constantly praising the wisdom of the Great Leader.

When Westerners read such propaganda their reaction is quite predictable: they see these tales as yet another confirmation of the repressive nature of a North Korean regime which interferes with even the most private spheres of life. However, these stories do not target Westerners! They are written for Koreans — indeed for North Koreans of older generations — who know very well that finding a suitable marriage partner for his children is the most important obligation of a father. By providing a spouse for an orphan from a "good" revolutionary family, Kim Il Sung does what all good fathers are supposed to do.

Indeed, until the late 1970s, arranged marriages constituted the overwhelming majority of marriages in North Korea. In most cases the parents took responsibility for the choice of a suitable partner for their children — as it had long been the case in Korea. Quite often, a bride would be found by a boss or a party secretary (once again, for the old-school Koreans this act was associated with parental love, not with unwarranted involvement of the state in personal affairs!). Nowadays things are changing: the old-style arranged marriage or *chungmae* is being replaced by the love match or *yŏnae*, a marriage in which the would-be couple make the decision themselves.

In the North no sociological study is possible, but according to some estimates "love matches" form a clear majority of the marriages of the younger generation. Recent refugees believe that up to 70–80 percent of all marriages are initiated by the couples themselves, with formal approval being received from the parents. It appears that Northern twenty-somethings are, if anything, even more reluctant to enter arranged marriages than their South Korean peers.

However, among the elders the situation is different. In South Korea, the older people are, the higher the chance that they will opt for an arranged marriage. The same is true in the North.

Top: Next generation. They will probably sort out all this mess, somehow. Photograph by Bernd Seiler. *Bottom:* A family out on foot. Photograph by Andrei Lankov.

According to the North Korean Family Law, the marriageable age is eighteen years for men and seventeen for women. This was indeed the case until the 1960s, when the authorities introduced a new approach to marriage. As a North Korean newspaper explained: "The Motherland and nation hope and believe that the youngsters will uphold the beautiful tradition of marrying only after they have done enough for the country and people." In other words: when you are young, work hard, and do not let family worries distract you from glorious service to the Party, Motherland, and Leader! Indeed, such was the message of the North Korean propaganda from the late 1960s.

Kim Il Sung himself took care to provide special "instruction" on this topic. In 1971 he said: "It is good if women marry at 28, and men marry at 30." This indeed was the case for a brief while, but eventually the restrictions were relaxed, and nowadays North Koreans marry in their late 20s on average, later than their South Korean peers.

Some groups of North Koreans were subjected to even harsher regulations. For example, students are theoretically forbidden to marry, although this ban is sometimes ignored in these more liberal days. Army privates and many NCOs cannot marry, and I am aware of one case where a couple was dishonorably discharged from the army when they were discovered making love.

Perhaps the encouragement of late marriage was a part of the low-profile yet efficient family planning campaign that was waged in the North in the 1970s. A delay in marriage was an efficient way to cut down the number of births.

Around 1990, the old ban on early marriages was quietly lifted, but this did not mean that such marriages were endorsed: they were simply tolerated (as long as the couple reached the legal marriage age, of course). It seems that the North Korean public in general also does not think that early marriage is a good idea. But they now occur nonetheless.

And what about divorce? The divorce rate is growing in the North as well as it is in the South. As is usually the case with the North, all relevant statistics are secret, but judging from anecdotal evidence, divorce, which was almost unheard of until the 1970s, began to increase in the 1980s, and achieved record highs during the famine of the late 1990s.

This reflected the dramatic reversal in the family and gender roles which occurred in the North during the last decade. It was usually women, not men, who took responsibility for the survival of their families in the midst of the disaster. But that is another story....

The Main Event

ON SUNDAYS IN NORTH KOREAN CITIES, and in the more picturesque areas in particular, one can see newly married couples having their wedding photos taken. The choicest spots are usually occupied by statues of Kim Il Sung, which dominate cityscapes in most North Korean towns. The bride and groom are thus obliged to demonstrate their "fervent loyalty" to the dynasty. Perhaps, some of them are quite sincere in this demonstration, while others see it as a tradition to be followed without much deliberation. After all, this is their happy day, and the statues tend to be located in truly beautiful locations!

About a decade ago North Korea opened its first wedding hall in Pyongyang. Now it serves more than a thousand couples each year, and enjoys great popularity. There are some other halls in major cities, even if their numbers remain small. Incidentally, the established ritual starts from an appropriate reference to the Great Leader: "Under the auspices of Great Leader Comrade Kim Jong Il, Mr. Ch'oe and Ms. Park will be married today."

However, in most cases the wedding celebrations take place within the walls of the groom's or bride's home. This does not mean that the references to the greatness and wisdom of the Leaders and Party are absent from the home ritual; on the contrary, they are obligatory, even if not necessarily taken at face value by all participants. The wedding manager or *churye*— an important and honorary job in both the North and the South —*must* make reference to Kim Il Sung and Kim Jong Il while pronouncing the couple husband and wife. Often the ritual is accompanied by deep bows to the portraits of the Kims which are to be found in every North Korean house.

The *churye* himself is usually a local party cadre and/or industrial manager. He is often the director or general manager of the company where the groom or bride are employed (in the South the families also try to invite a respected person to be their *churye*).

The details of the wedding rituals differ slightly depending on the region. Generally, a wedding consists of two separate events: one party is held at the groom's house and another at the bride's. If the wedding takes place on a single day, the partying starts at the bride's home and after midday the participants travel to the house of the groom (assuming, of course, that both bride and groom live within a reasonable distance, which is normally the case in the North). If the wedding lasts for two consecutive days, the first is known as "women's day" and is marked by the celebrations in the bride's house, while the second day is spent at the groom's.

In most countries of East Asia weddings take place on days which are

Guests are arriving (for a wedding, perhaps). Photograph by Andrew Graham.

chosen by fortunetellers as "auspicious." It was also believed that the birth-dates of one's future spouse must be "compatible" when checked against special tables. Officially, North Koreans do not care about auspicious days, or about the compatibility of the bride or groom's birthdates. However, reports of defectors confirm that traditional superstition has undergone a dramatic recovery since the early 1990s and North Korean girls, unable to find a single professional fortuneteller in the country, must consult a "knowledgeable" auntie instead. Their families also show a keen interest in the opinions of fortune-tellers, and there have been cases where a bad prognosis resulted in the abandonment of the planned marriage.

Naturally the bride and groom dress up for the occasion. Brides put on the North Korean variety of Korean traditional costume (never called *hanbok* in the North), while grooms wear a Western-style suit. Both must sport the Kim Il Sung badges that all North Koreans are required to wear when they venture outside their homes.

The greatest style for a bride is to arrive at the in-laws' house in a *real* passenger car, which is a symbol of the utmost luxury for most families who do not belong to the ruling elite. Such a car can be provided by a sympathetic local bureaucrat, or a top manager of a factory where the bride or groom are employed. Needless to say, the car in question will scarcely be a limousine;

in most cases the couples must resign themselves to using a Kaengsaeng, a locally produced copy of a Soviet 4WD which, in turn, owes much to the Jeep of the 1940s.

However, in many cases even a hint at luxury is unattainable, and transport to the groom's house is provided by a truck. This is certainly the case for transporting guests. Although North Korean weddings are smaller affairs than their South Korean counterparts, some 30–50 guests seems to be the norm in the North.

It is remarkable that governments of both Koreas once waged very similar campaigns against lavish wedding ceremonies. From the 1960s, expensive wedding banquets were described by the South Korean authorities as a waste of money which would otherwise be saved and invested in industrial programs! The Seoul government introduced special laws which were to make weddings cheaper.

In the North lavish weddings, so usual in old Korea, also came under suspicion around the same time. Apart from their wastefulness, they were seen as politically subversive. In the 1960s, wedding banquets were described as breeding grounds for "factionalism" (read: forging informal connections between people) and, for some reason, "dogmatism" (this term normally hinted at the Soviet traditions, but in this particular case it obviously stood for anything bad). The situation changed only in the 1980s when the Pyongyang authorities decided to rely on the nationalist spirit even more heavily and began to promote so-called good traditional customs. Around the same time the South coincidentally began to soften its approach to "wasteful traditions."

However, weddings are indeed expensive. According to the old tradition, the groom's family had to take care of the newlyweds' accommodation while the bride's relatives provided the furniture. Nowadays most people live in houses which belong to the state and are rented for symbolic amounts of money (even after the recent reforms, the rent remains low by the standards of most other countries). Thus, the major burden falls on the bride's family, which begins to prepare for their daughter's wedding when the girl is still in her early teens.

More prosperous families provide furniture and other household items, including some or all of the "seven devices" — items, the possession of which are a sign of consummate prosperity in the North. The list includes a TV set, a fridge, a videotape recorder, a washing machine, a fan, a camera and a sewing machine. However, in most cases the bride's family has to limit itself to some kitchen utensils, blankets and a wooden blanket case.

In the modest interior of most North Korean houses, blankets are essential both for comfort and decoration. A popular joke says that guests attend weddings to look at the blankets rather than to look at the bride!

As a rule, the bride's family gives the groom his wedding suit while the groom's family, in turn, provides the dress for the bride — not a small expense in the North.

The attending guests are also expected to provide money gifts — pretty much like South Korea. However, the best friends sometimes present the bride and groom with some valuable items, instead of money. Until the outbreak of inflation in the mid–1990s, five to fifteen DPRK *won* (roughly 10–15% of the then average monthly salary) were seen as a sufficient contribution, even if close friends and relatives donated greater amounts. In South Korean terms, the equivalent sum would be 150–200 thousand *won*, much more than most Southern families donate when they attend weddings.

In the past a wedding was sufficient grounds to apply for additional rations — especially of liquor and rice. However, the recent crisis has changed the situation. In the 1990s, the authorities resumed the campaign for moderate weddings — and, among other things, prescribed that a wedding must not use more than 5 kg of rice. These limits place the hosts under considerable strain.

However, these days the North Korean state is increasingly powerless and unable to enforce regulations with its old efficiency. Thus, rich families flout these limitations. Meanwhile, the poor majority have to be economical anyway. But does it really matter? A wedding is a wedding when all is said and done, and the style of the occasion is but a small blip on the broad horizon of life, no matter whether it is lavish or modest....

Kisaeng *It All Good-Bye?*

MANY KOREANS BELIEVE THAT PROSTITUTION was completely alien to the Korean tradition until the early 1900s, when it was first introduced by those naughty Japanese. Unlike many other national myths, this one seems to be well-founded. Prostitution was known in old Korea, but largely in the elite form of *kisaeng* houses which were open only to the most affluent males. Cheap commercial sex for the lusting masses, while not completely unheard of, was not common. In this regard, Korea indeed was remarkably different from its Chinese and Japanese neighbors, and it appears that the idea of cheap mass prostitution was truly a Japanese "cultural import" of the early 1900s. But by the 1930s, it was fairly common nonetheless. The *kisaeng* also lost part of its earlier glamour and came to resemble professional sex workers.

Prior to the Korean War, the *kisaeng* houses — a cross between an elite club, a restaurant, and a brothel—flourished in North Korean cities, and in the years 1945–1950 even the leaders of the new Communist regime would occasionally choose a *kisaeng* house as a venue for a confidential meeting. Suffice it to say that the first encounter between Kim Il Sung and the leader of the North Korean Nationalist Right, Cho Man-sik, was arranged by the Soviet officers for Hwabang, the then famous *kisaeng* house. This meeting took place on 30 September, 1945, and its outcome to a large extent sealed the fate of North Korea. There are some pictures of the meeting: Kim Il Sung, Cho Man-sik and Soviet officers are seated in front of a table while the easy beauties can be seen in the background.

However, changes to the structure of North Korean society soon made *kisaeng* obsolete. In the late 1940s, the North Korean government embarked on an anti-prostitution campaign. The *kisaeng* houses were closed down by the beginning of the Korean War, and in the elaborate system of hereditary "class classification" of the late 1950s, their former employees were defined as members of the "hostile class." This meant that neither the ex-*kisaeng* nor their children had access to privileges—including, as a rule, a good college education and the right to reside in Pyongyang.

In the 1960s and 1970s, the North Korean authorities went to great lengths to promote the traditional mores of the Korean village community. Prostitution, promiscuity, extramarital or premarital sex would have no place within the utopia that they were constructing—and the government was usually strong enough to enforce its regulations. Nor was the task unnecessarily cumbersome, since these views were also shared by a majority of the population at the time. Obviously the spoiled brats, sons of the Pyongyang elite, could dally with pretty actresses and singers, but the exploits of young aristocrats can hardly be described as commercial prostitution.

It is not clear when and how prostitution made its comeback in the North. Perhaps the turning point was reached around 1980, when the authorities opened the so-called Ansan Club near the small but luxurious Pot'onggang Hotel. In this club the patrons (exclusively foreigners) were entertained by hostesses from southeast Asian countries. The authorities kept Korean women away from this dirty business and the club did not last very long.

Helen-Louise Hunter also mentioned that in the 1970s and 1980s there were known cases of liaisons between Western expats and their maids, but one can presume that the girls were not motivated by money alone: the thrill of adventure was perhaps equally important—and one cannot rule out that the North Korean secret services were behind at least some of these affairs. I also know of a Russian engineer who in the late 1980s boasted of having had paid sex with a pretty North Korean maid. But all these events remained isolated, even exceptional.

Things changed in the late 1980s when Pyongyang prepared to stage the 13th International Festival of Youth and Students. This gathering attracted several tens of thousands of foreigners, and some of these were interested in sex-for-sale. Rumors persisted that during the festival the North Korean police had instructions to turn a blind eye to sexual liaisons between local women and foreigners as long as these liaisons were conducted without attracting too much attention as casual affairs.

Around the same time, with the tacit approval of the police, professional prostitutes began to ply their trade in major international hotels. This is still the case. The girls' ranks are often swelled by hotel personnel — the allure of hard currency being too strong to resist....

And then the early 1990s changed everything. The dissolution of the Communist camp triggered a collapse in the North Korean economy. An estimated three quarters of the North's industrial plants ceased to operate by the mid–1990s. After the floods of 1995, the government was unable to issue rations, and most people in the countryside were left to their own devices.

Under the new circumstances the government was both unable and unwilling to enforce the regulations. Private commerce boomed, and millions of people began to make their living independently of the state. Crowds of small merchants hit the streets.

In this new environment, domestic prostitution was bound to appear and flourish. The merchants needed easy sex — and could buy it from the crowds of impoverished, displaced women. The hookers appeared in the markets, or near large shops and restaurants. Some private eateries began to provide "special services," sending girls to please their patrons after they finished their meals; the owners claimed a commission equal to 20% of the girl's fee. Prostitution became an important source of revenue for private inns — and such inns sprung up in great numbers in the last decade. In some cases, people make money by letting prostitutes use their houses.

The prostitutes are sometimes politely referred to as "flower-selling girls," but less decorous names are no doubt more common. In the mid–1990s their services would cost some 100–200 *won*. This amounted to about $2–5, depending on the time and place, but for the average Korean this was a good sum of money, so the temptation to enter this occupation was great. After the collapse of the North Korean currency and the explosive inflation of the early 2000s, the *won* prices increased exponentially, but their dollar equivalent has remained much the same.

By the late 1990s, hard-currency prostitution made a comeback as well. This was not the state run and supervised business of the Ansan Club era. This time, the hawkers troll for patrons near major international hotels and earn their $10 in the back seat of a car. The sum might appear pitiful, but it is still more than the average monthly salary in the city. The risks working girls are taking are also extraordinary. The Soviet experience leads us to suspect that many of them collaborate with police, either as informers or "bribe providers," but still, if caught, a girl is likely to be expelled from Pyongyang. And this is a heavy punishment indeed.

Thus even the world's purest Stalinist state has failed to eradicate commercial sex. Sin obviously pays.

PART 9

All Things Which Move

Letting the Bicycle Ride

EAST ASIA HAS A WELL-DESERVED reputation as the cyclists' paradise — indeed, in no other part of the world are bicycles so ubiquitous. Nonetheless, North Korea has been different. Until the early 1990s bicycles were outlawed in Pyongyang — and not much used in other North Korean cities. I do not know the reason behind this strange ban, which existed for decades. Perhaps, the North Korean "public relations" experts decided that bicycles were decisively low-tech — and thus inappropriate for the supposedly developed "capital of revolution"? Whatever the reason, for several decades the bicycle was not allowed on the streets of Pyongyang.

Nor were foreigners excepted from this ban. When in the mid–1970s a visiting Norwegian diplomat brought his bike to Pyongyang, he stirred up a minor diplomatic controversy. After painful negotiations he was granted permission to ride his bike ... on weekends only.

The situation changed in 1992, when the ban was suddenly lifted. Over the last decade, bikes have proliferated in Pyongyang. This policy change also affected the countryside, where the number of bikes visibly increased as well.

Nowadays, the city authorities not only allow bikes, but actively promote their use. In the late 1990s, the municipal authorities even began to construct special bicycle paths in Pyongyang.

However, not everybody is encouraged to ride a bike. In 1996, it was decided that the bicycle was not suitable for women. The North Korean press explained that "beautiful national customs" do not permit such debauchery, and women were banned from riding bikes. Allegedly, this judgment was the work of Kim Jong Il himself.

Cycling back home. Photograph by Byeon Young-wook.

Had it happened a decade earlier, such a ban would have been enforced at a day's notice and lasted forever, but nowadays things have changed. At first, police worked hard to enforce the ban, and some female riders had their bikes confiscated, but then things cooled down and some women began to defy the prohibition, but even now the sight of a cycling woman is somewhat unusual. The TV and print media occasionally ran quite disapproving stories and reports, and explain that such indecent and unladylike behavior is unbecoming of the female citizens of Pyongyang, the "capital of revolution." It seems that the ban was never really taken seriously in the countryside, where there are almost no alternatives to bikes.

North Korean bikes are required to display a registration plate, and their riders have to pass an examination with the local police in order to get a license. The number plates are small and round, with the name of the district which issued the registration, and a number printed in white against a red background. The registration plates are fixed over the front wheel of the bike.

The "riding license" system was first introduced in 1997 in Pyongyang, and from 1999 number plates and licenses became obligatory nationwide. But it seems that this requirement is sometimes ignored in the countryside. In order to obtain a license, North Koreans have to demonstrate their knowledge of traffic rules in a test. Once again, however, it seems that the number

Over the last decade, bikes — once prohibited — became ubiquitous in Pyong-yang. The small round plate on front is the registration. Photograph by Andrei Lankov.

of unlicensed riders is on the rise: in recent years, many bikes in the country-side do not have the required license plates.

For common North Koreans, a bike is probably the most expensive of all household items, and therefore a source of great pride — a bit like a car in a modern Western (or, for that matter, South Korean) family. It is not just a convenience, it is also a status symbol. Nor can every family afford one: according to current estimates, between one third and one half of all North Korean families have to do without a bicycle — not because they have no need for one, but because even the cheapest bike is beyond their reach. Thus, the current North Korean joke, "I can lend my wife, but cannot lend my bike," illustrates the general feeling well.

A real status symbol is a Japanese-made bike which costs several annual salaries of an average worker. This means that a specimen is affordable only to the privileged few and is the North Korean equivalent of a Jaguar or a Porsche. Most of these bikes come as second-hand imports from Japan, but they are still seen as vastly superior to the local product.

The most popular brand of locally produced bike is called the *Kalmaegi* or Seagull. These models are believed to be produced by the inmates of a large prison camp located near Ch'ongjin, in the northern part of the country. In the 1990s these bikes cost about ten thousand *won*— in other words, almost ten times the average annual salary. Nowadays, after the 2002 wage and price reforms, their price has skyrocketed, but the ratio to the average annual income remains largely the same (admittedly, these figures might be misleading since few people live on their official salaries these days).

There are cheaper local brands, like the *Chebi* or Swallow, which costs about 30–40% of the price of a real *Kalmaegi*, but is considered unreliable and clumsy. An even worse reputation is attached to the Chinese bikes which are also quite common in the North.

Bicycles are frequently stolen: the last decade has seen an upsurge in street crime, and bikes, being the most expensive individual item a North Korean possesses, naturally attracts the attention of criminals. I know of one case where a high-rise apartment dweller from Pyongyang sold his bike. Elevators never work these days, and it was difficult for him, a quite fit middle-aged man, to carry his bike to the 10th floor every day. It was also too risky to leave it locked on the ground floor so he had to sell it.

As a North Korean defector stated: "In North Korea you are upper middle class if you ride a used Japanese bicycle, wear a 'Kim Jong Il style jumper' and spend 5,000 *won* (US $3) every time you shop at the market."

In recent years, after 2000, the Chinese-style cargo tricycles also appeared on the streets of the North Korean cities. They are far less common than in China, but still used widely to move relatively heavy loads across the country. These are the North Korean quasi-vans, one might say.

And what about cars? To this day, private cars remain rare exceptions. The car is as affordable to the average North Korean as, say, a private jet would be to the average American. Nonetheless, the privileged few do own cars. And that is our next story....

A Fleeting Industry

ONE OF THE MOST RECURRENT FEATURES in the stories of foreign visitors to Pyongyang is the description of the North Korean capital as a "ghost city." The major reason is the near absence of the frenzy of car traffic which has become the trademark of large cities in modern "developed" nations, not least in Seoul. Taking into consideration South Korea's credentials as the world's fifth largest car-manufacturing country, this is perfectly understandable.

An old copy of a '50s Soviet truck is still a common mode of transportation. Photograph by Anna Fifield.

It is interesting that North Korean defectors also voice very similar impressions about the South: when I ask them what was the most striking experience in their first days in Seoul, the most common answer is the abundance of cars.

However, once upon a time the North Korean automotive industry was at least the equal of— if not superior to — that of South Korea.

The North Korean automotive industry was born in November 1958 when the Tŏkch'ŏn factory began to produce 2.5-ton trucks which were called Sŭngli-58, that is Victory-58. They were North Korean copies of the Soviet GAZ-51, then perhaps the most common truck in the USSR. Its primitive but robust design was quite suited to the postwar conditions in Korea. Generally, it was a major success, and in the 1970s the former Tŏkch'ŏn factory was renamed the Sŭngli factory. In later years, it also produced a 6-ton Sŭngli-1010 from 1960 and a 10-ton Chaju from 1964.

The North Korean media never mentioned that the design was a copy of the Soviet prototype, and that the more technologically difficult parts were imported from overseas. The Sŭngli-58 was extolled as the embodiment of the then new "self-reliance" policy. However, the mass production of cars was a major achievement indeed. In the South, the first attempts to start an automotive industry took place around the same time, but remained largely unsuccessful until the early 1970s.

Meanwhile, in the 1960s North Korea began to produce new types of cars, still largely based on the Soviet prototypes. Perhaps the single most important model was the Kaengsaeng or "Growing more." It was the North Korean copy of the GAZ-69, the hugely popular Soviet 4WD produced in Russia from 1953. Its sturdy design made this vehicle ideal for military use as well as operating in remote areas. Once again, it was an excellent choice, and Kaengsaengs are still widely used. For all practical purposes it remains the only passenger vehicle in North Korea which is locally produced in large quantities. It is widely used as a pickup, with a commercial load of some 500 kg.

In 1961 the Tŏkchŏn plant made an experimental passenger car, the Sŭngli-415. In the 1970s and 1980s there were further attempts to make passenger cars, and models such as the Paektusan and Pyongyang-410 rolled off the lines, but none were produced in large quantities. Both the Paektusan and Pyongyang-410 were greatly simplified copies of the Mercedes 190. However, the vast majority of passenger cars in North Korea are used as chauffeured vehicles for top officials and generals and these people were decidedly unenthusiastic about the local product. Pyongyang bigwigs prefer the foreign brands, and Mercedes, which is Kim Jong Il's favorite brand, is especially popular. It requires hard currency to buy these luxurious cars, of course, but this is hardly seen as a major obstacle by the top elite.

North Korea does produce its own trolley-buses, made at a plant in Pyongyang. This same plant also produces buses, partially assembled from Japanese parts. However, a large part of the bus fleet consists of imported vehicles, largely the Hungarian Ikarus and the Czech Skoda.

At present, there are four automotive plants in the DPRK. It is estimated that North Korean factories can manufacture 33,000 units a year. Roughly 20,000 units can be produced by the Tŏkch'ŏn factory alone. If compared to the South Korean production capacities, which are in excess of four million, this is a very small number — some 0.7%. The actual production is also much lower than the capacity: in 1999 the North Korean factories produced a mere 7,300 vehicles. Compared to the three million produced in the South in the same year, this amounts to a paltry 0.25%.

The entire North Korean fleet is estimated at some 270,000 vehicles, with passenger cars numbering merely 20–25,000 of this figure.

From the mid–1990s South Korean companies have been considering car production in North Korea. They are eager to tap the pool of cheap and pre-

Pyongyang streets do not have problems with traffic jams.... Yonggwang-ro Street in downtown Pyongyang. Photograph by Andrew Graham.

sumably obedient labor. Now it appears that at least one of these projects is slowly moving ahead — the first cars have already rolled from the factory amidst great publicity. Perhaps in a few years' time we will see a revival of the North Korean car industry — or at least that is what the enthusiasts for intra–Korean cooperation would have us believe. We will just have to wait and see: so far this "intra–Korean cooperation" has worked well only when the South Korean side has been willing to write off all losses and deliver all profits to their North Korean "partners."

Meanwhile, the streets and roads of North Korea remain largely empty, with the occasion gas-generator car passing by amidst clouds of thick smoke. But that is another story....

Hot Air Rises at a Snail's Pace

BELIEVE IT OR NOT, NORTH KOREA is probably the world's leader in the use of alternative automobile fuel. An estimated 70–80% of its cars run not on

Tractors often serve as buses in the countryside.

gasoline, but on an alternative fuel that is locally produced from sustainable resources. An environmentalist's dream come true? Not quite....

Every visitor to the North Korean countryside will have spotted a truck or bus equipped with a large drum-like device emitting thick clouds of dark smoke. This is a gas-generator vehicle. Less technically savvy journalists sometimes mistake it for a steam-driven vehicle, but actually it has nothing to do with steam. The vehicle does not consume gasoline, but uses charcoal or wood to produce a gas which is then filtered and fed into a slightly modified internal combustion engine. The large drums are the gas generators which produce the flammable gas, and the thick smoke is a byproduct of a chemical reaction when the gas is ignited.

The gas-generator car (or "charcoal car" as it is known in the North) is not a North Korean invention. In the 1940s, when the Second World War led to an acute fuel shortage in Europe, many European cars were refitted with gas generators to run on an ever-available supply of wood. Some countries (including Germany and Russia) even briefly mass-produced vehicles specially designed to run on this exotic fuel. The gas generator cars were also used in Japan and colonial Korea. However these cars went out of use as soon as the war was over and the normal oil supply resumed.

The oil problem has always been a painful issue for the North Korean economy. The country lacks oil deposits, and thus relies heavily on oil imports. Oil was originally sourced from the USSR and China. For strategic reasons, both countries charged Pyongyang so-called friendship prices which were well below the price on the international market. Nevertheless, the importation of oil remained a major financial burden even in the best of times.

Therefore, in 1978 it was decided to refit some Korean trucks with gas generators. The initial experiments were conducted with the Sŭngli-58 truck, which was the main workhorse of the country's cargo transport. The results proved successful, and in the mid–1980s a huge conversion program was launched. By the early 1990s, some 70–80% of the North Korean trucks and buses, including almost all vehicles in the countryside, ran on charcoal, wood, and even maize stems. Gas generators have been installed in many buses as well.

This was a fortuitous decision. In the early 1990s the "friendship prices" were suddenly abandoned, and former allies began to charge normal international prices. This shock was somewhat cushioned by the success of the conversion program.

However, if it was so simple to use sustainable fuel to run cars, why did all the world's automotive industry not rush to emulate the North Koreans? Alas, the gas generator will never become a viable alternative to the gasoline engine — as North Koreans can testify from their own experience.

First of all, the modified engine is remarkably inefficient. Normally, the Sŭngli-58 truck is designed to move a 2.5-ton load. However, with a gas generator it cannot carry more than 2 tons even under ideal conditions. The gas generator itself is heavy and unwieldy (a typical generator has a volume of 180 liters). In addition, drivers often have to carry some charcoal for the trip, and this bulky fuel further reduces the commercial load.

The generated gas is not as efficient as gasoline, thus the engine produces much less power. One of the results is a very low speed — 30 km/h at best. Quite often the vehicles really struggle when going uphill — a not inconsiderable problem in a country where 80% of the total area is covered by mountains.

Emissions from the gas-generator vehicles are quite serious, although this is probably not seen in North Korea as a major reason for concern. Despite occasional declarations to the contrary, environmental concerns are still quite alien to the North which, in this regard, is not very different from the majority of the world's poorer nations.

Another problem with the gas-generator car is that the equipment takes a long time to heat up. Even in warm weather it takes about half an hour to heat up the gas generator. Only when sufficiently heated up is it able to produce enough gas for the engine. North Korean gas-generator vehicles also require

A tractor serves as a bus, if the village somehow manages to get fuel. Photograph by Bernd Seiler.

an additional "crew member" — a technician who operates the gas generator when the car is in motion. It is looked on as a good job, but not as good a job as that of a real driver. Indeed, drivers are seen as privileged in North Korea, but that is another story....

To Be a Chauffeur

"BACK IN THE NORTH HE WAS rather privileged. He was a driver for the director of a research institute!" — I recently read this sentence in relation to a defector who failed to adjust himself to South Korean life. Alas, this is too typical a story for a defector. However, in this particular case one of the explanations was that the unlucky defector could not reconcile himself to the loss of his former semi-privileged position — that is, an automobile driver!

People who work with North Korean defectors to the South are also well aware that many of them do not think twice when they choose a profession

A chauffeured Mercedes is the vehicle of choice of North Korean elite. Sometimes these might be seen in numbers near major hotels (in this case, in front of Koryo Hotel, Pyongyang's largest). Photograph by Christopher Morris.

for vocational training. A disproportionately large number of the defectors want to become drivers — this is their profession of choice and is firmly associated with all kinds of privileges. This is not really the case in South Korea, of course, but it takes several years for this reality to sink in.

The idea of a driver as a member of the privileged or, at least, semi-privileged might be striking to Western readers. It is even striking to the present author, whose mother was a Soviet tram and bus driver. However, in the North there is good reason to count the drivers among the more affluent members of society.

Despite some recent changes (largely thanks to generous South Korean subsidies), in North Korea cars are few and far between. It is estimated that there are some 250,000 vehicles in North Korea — roughly one vehicle per 100 citizens, or some 25–30 times lower than the current South Korean level. It comes as no surprise that to South Korean or Western visitors the streets of Pyongyang appear ghostly and empty.

Almost all the North Korean fleet is state property. In the 1960s, some richer Koreans from Japan who visited the North took their cars with them, and were sometimes allowed to drive them during their stay. Eventually, most (or perhaps all) were pressed into surrendering their vehicles to the state. At any rate, keeping a private car on the road was a challenging job in a country which had virtually no infrastructure accessible to the individual motorist.

From the mid–1980s it became possible for private citizens to buy cars, but they had to pay hard currency, and normally at a much greater cost than a similar car on the international market. Car servicing and fuel also had to be paid for with the same "imperialist" currency. Recently there have been reports that the authorities began to allow private buses to operate, and that a small number of used buses have been imported from China to be run by North Korean entrepreneurs. If these reports are true (and this is a big "if"), this is a sign of serious change. But until recently, private cars have been a very rare sight indeed.

A majority of North Korean vehicles are trucks. Passenger cars are concentrated in Pyongyang and used by top officials only. Some of these cars are quite expensive: the penchant of the North Korean elite for the famous West European brands goes back to the 1970s. Volvo, Mercedes and BMW are their brands of choice. However, these vehicles are seldom seen outside Pyongyang, and for most North Koreans "passenger car" means a Kaengsaeng, a locally produced 4WD, or at best, a Volga, a 25-year-old Soviet-made contraption which was not synonymous with luxury even in its heyday.

Unlike most Western countries and, for that matter, South Korea, only a tiny minority of people in the North possess a driver's license. There are a few ways to gain a license. It appears that the most common method is to study at one of the special driving schools which are operated in every province and some major cities. In order to be admitted into such a school, candidates must produce recommendations from their superiors. It is also common for high school students to be sent there. This is a part of their military training: the army needs drivers, and the state ensures that some young men learn driving skills before they are drafted. At the end of the course the driving school students must pass an exam.

The school is an all-day institution. During the course, students must reside in the school's dormitory. They spend some six months studying traffic rules, learning practical driving skills, and training in vehicle maintenance. The North Korean driver is supposed to take care of his vehicle in all circumstances.

Another way to earn a license is through practical work. The low level of reliability of antiquated North Korean trucks means that they often carry onboard mechanics, also known as drivers' assistants. If someone works as such an assistant for two years, he (but never she) is eligible to apply to take a driving exam and, if successful, be granted a license.

There are four grades of driver's license in the North. In order to upgrade one's license, one has to work as a driver for a few years and then sit an exam.

The 4th level license qualifies its holder to drive trucks, the 3rd level permits the driving of buses and 4WDs and the 2nd level gives the holder the right to drive passenger cars as well. Indeed it is true: driving passenger cars is officially considered more difficult and demanding than driving trucks or 4WDs! But then again, passenger cars are used only by VIPs, and their precious lives can be entrusted to only the most experienced drivers.

Female drivers are almost unheard of. Back in the 1970s even foreign women, wives of diplomats and other expats, had serious difficulties in obtaining North Korean driver's licenses. Driving is meant to be an exclusively male prerogative!

So why then are drivers believed to be privileged? A driver can make a lot of money by allowing fee-paying passengers to board his vehicle. Over the last decade the booming black market has meant that most of these passengers are traders with merchandise and they are ready to pay handsomely. Another consideration is that passenger car drivers are close to the seat of power. They are essentially the butlers and valets of the Pyongyang aristocracy — and, like all servants, they are always able to glean a little something from their masters' tables.

Not So Airborne

IT IS A WELL-KNOWN FACT THAT South Korea is one of the world leaders in air travel. Despite its small size South Korea ranked sixth in the world for its volume of air transport in 1999. In North Korea it is a very different story, but this does not mean that this isolated state does not have a passenger air service.

The history of North Korean civil aviation began in December 1946 when North Korea and the USSR established a joint venture air company. The routes were served by Russian planes and flown by Russian crews. In the early 1950s these planes flew to the city of Chita in eastern Siberia via the Chinese city of Shenyang.

In 1954, the joint venture was replaced by a Korean national airline. The service acquired the name *Choson Air*— after the country's official name (North Korea officially calls itself *Chosŏn*, unlike its Southern counterpart which is *Hanguk*). This name was changed to *Air Koryo* in 1993, adopting the ancient name for the country. The new name was seen as politically more appropriate and had the added convenience of being easier for foreigners to remember: in most languages, Korea's name sounds more like *Koryo* than *Choson*.

A Soviet Tu-154 at the Pyongyang's Sunan airport. Photograph by Andrei Lankov.

Air Koryo has always been an agency of the Korean People's Army; it is subordinated to the Bureau of Civil Aviation, which in turn belongs to the KPA Air Force. Therefore all of the pilots are Air Force officers on active duty, and in case of war its small fleet can be switched to military use in an instant.

In 1958 the first air route connected Pyongyang with two major cities in the northern part of the country — Hamhŭng and Ch'ŏngjin. However, this first domestic service was far from an instant success. The restrictions on domestic travel combined with low incomes prevented North Koreans from becoming frequent users of domestic air flights, thus the service was cut back and eventually discontinued. The South Korean flag carrier, KNA, incidentally, experienced very similar problems in the late 1950s.

However, unlike the South, the North never managed to create a developed network of domestic air routes. In fact, the very existence of domestic air travel in the North is doubtful. Most international reference books insist that Air Koryo still maintains a domestic route between Pyongyang and Hamhŭng. However, I have never encountered a North Korean who has used this service, and most of the defectors confidently insist that North Korea does not have a domestic air service at all, nor has it ever had one within living memory. Thus, I would confidently surmise that the Hamhŭng route is not used regularly, except for the occasional charter flight for foreign delegations or local bigwigs. In the North there is only one dedicated civil airport — Sunan near Pyongyang. The infrequent flights to other cities all use military airfields.

From the late 1950s, North Korean planes began to fly international routes. The first international flight departed in February 1959. These services connected Pyongyang with the capitals of North Korea's two major allies and sponsors, the USSR and China.

Until the mid–1970s, Choson Air flew to these two countries alone. The isolated position of the DPRK within the world community meant that weekly services to Moscow and Beijing were more than sufficient. However, in 1974 a new route connected Pyongyang with Khabarovsk, a large Soviet city in southern Siberia. This new service was necessary because of the increasing number of North Korean loggers who were employed by the joint ventures in Siberia.

Around the same time, North Korea purchased their first jet planes — Soviet-made Tu-154s. This made possible the extension of the routes to Eastern Europe — to Sofia and Berlin. North Korean chartered planes also visited some other countries, normally as part of some diplomatic mission. However, until 1990 only five international routes (Moscow, Beijing, Berlin, Sofia, and Khabarovsk) were flown regularly, once or twice a week.

In the 1990s, North Korean planes also began to fly to cities in southeast Asia. New routes connected Pyongyang with Macao, Bangkok, and Hong Kong, but flights remained quite infrequent due to the low demand. So, at the time of writing, in late 2005, on a regular basis Pyongyang airport serves only five flights a week: two to Beijing, two to Shenyang and one to Vladivostok. Once upon a time, the air companies of the "fraternal countries" also used to fly to Pyongyang, but low demand, combined with increasing emphasis on economic efficiency, made them discontinue such services, so normally only North Korean planes use the airport. The five flights a week means that Pyongyang has by far the least busy capital airport in East Asia.

The Air Koryo fleet includes a number of old Soviet-made planes. One particular foreign tourist found this "charming," but he was an aviation history buff. Indeed, the entire fleet must be music to his ears: around 2000 the fleet included five old twin-turbo-prop AN-24s, two of which were delivered in 1966! It also boasted two Il-18s (an old Soviet turbo-prop airliner from the 1950s). Air Koryo also has a number of jet airliners: four or five larger Il-62s (one is exclusively reserved for use by the government), three Tu-134s and three Tu-154s.

For most North Koreans, air travel is a dream and a privilege. It is associated with the mysterious and beautiful "overseas world." The antiquated planes of Air Koryo are still seen as wonder machines, accessible only to the chosen few. For a vast majority of the population, trips to more distant places are associated with riding a train, which is another story....

The Beaten Track

MOST COMMUNIST COUNTRIES HAVE RELIED on railway networks as their major means of communication. The Communist takeovers occurred in the first half of the twentieth century, before the advent of the private car and its accompanying network of highways changed the lifestyle of the affluent West. However, the "car revolution" never really gained a foothold in the Communist-controlled parts of the world, a few countries in Eastern Europe notwithstanding. Perhaps cars were too individualistic for the Communist ideologues, or perhaps the general sluggishness of non-military technological development influenced the outcome.

Whatever the reason, North Korea retains an unusually heavy reliance on its railways. As of 2001, it possessed 5,224 km of track — roughly twice as much as the South. It is remarkable that unlike the South, where (with the important exception of the recent bullet train project) no major railway has been constructed in decades, the North has continued to build new lines. Therefore, the total length of railways grew steadily: from 4,043 km in 1970 to the present 5,224. The length of the South Korean track remained almost unchanged over this same period.

Approximately 4,500 km of the North Korean railways have the standard gauge of 1435 mm. Most of the remainder are narrow-gauge, although some 130 km was especially built to the standard Russian gauge. This track connects the Russian border station of Hasan with the Korean city of Ch'ŏngjin and is a reminder of the days when these countries were active trading partners.

The railroad accounts for an estimated 86% of cargo transport in the North. This is roughly the same level for the South back in the late 1950s. And indeed the picture of the North Korean railways is reminiscent of the South Korean network of the 1960s.

Most of the railways (98% of the total length) have only one track. The low level of signal equipment and technology (essentially unchanged from colonial times) further reduces the railways' carrying capacity. The average speed varies greatly, depending on the local conditions. On the best kept Pyongyang-Sinŭiju line it is about 60 kph, while on some secondary lines trains cannot move faster than 20 kph. A moderate 30–40 kph seems to be the national norm.

Steam engines are still common on the North Korean railways. Photograph by Bernd Seiler.

The North Koreans have been very persistent in their introduction of electricity. They obviously wanted to reduce their dependence on imported and expensive oil. To date some 80% of the railways are electrified against a mere 21% in the South. This makes possible the wide use of electric locomotives, but in some areas these still exist alongside ancient steam locomotives from the 1930s and 1940s. One can still spot a colonial-era Mika steam engine puffing along the tracks. It must be 70 years old!

While tracks and signal equipment constitute the greatest problem in any future reconstruction of the Korean railroads, the rolling stock also leaves much to be desired. First of all, it is old. Most of the locomotives and carriages were imported from the USSR decades ago or locally assembled following the Soviet blueprint. Second, it is severely under-serviced.

This situation has frequently led to disasters. The most notorious was the massive explosion in April 2004 which wiped out a large part of the city of Yongchŏn, near the Chinese border. According to the official report, the explosion was touched off by "electrical contact caused by the careless shunting of wagons loaded with ammonium nitrate fertilizer." Just nine hours earlier, the train carrying the Dear Leader Kim Jong Il had passed through this station, thus there was some speculation about an attempted assassination.

Technology of the 1930s still dominates in some parts of the North Korean economy. Photograph by Bernd Seiler.

While this may be true, I am inclined to believe the official North Korean pronouncement in this instance: it was much too late for an assassination attempt and, most likely, the explosion was a result of human error (though perhaps the havoc created by the transit of the Dear Leader's armored train did contribute to the accident).

It was not the first large-scale railway disaster in the North. Usually, such accidents remain unreported, since the North follows the established Communist tradition of hiding information about all industrial disasters. Nothing can possibly go wrong in a well-managed society! And if something does go wrong, "bad news should not be reported anyway since it might upset our people" (as a North Korean official recently explained to my Russian colleague).

Some 90% of passenger traffic in the DPRK is carried by the railways, and the great and powerful are no different from the meek and lowly. Both Kim Il Sung and Kim Jong Il were famed (and at times ridiculed) for their habit of traveling abroad by train rather than plane. Among state leaders, Kim Jong Il is probably unique in his aversion for planes — and he inherited this attitude from his father. Nobody knows for sure why he seldom flies, but the most likely explanation is a serious case of flight anxiety.

Common North Koreans travel by train for a different reason: they have no choice, since no other means of long-distance travel is available to them. Of course, in order to buy a ticket a North Korean must produce a travel permit, without which he is ineligible to venture outside his native county. Even in the best of times, these tickets are sold out, so the only way to get one is to approach the black market vendors, who first buy tickets from the official ticket office and then sell them at three times their face value or even higher. This business, which vividly reminds this author of the Soviet Union of his youth, began to grow in the late 1980s, following the general decline in public mores and the weakening of the government's control over the bureaucracy.

The tickets must be produced on entry to the platform, together with an ID and travel permit. Papers are checked by two people: a police officer (usually armed) and a railway clerk. Military personnel, who are quite common among the traveling public, use another entrance where the usual railway clerk is accompanied by an officer from the military police. In the old days of Kim Il Sung, control was very strict, but now the relaxation is obvious and sometimes a small bribe can buy entrance for a person without the proper travel permit, especially at smaller stations.

In the North there are three types of long-distance trains, depending on their speed and number of stops. The fastest trains are known as "special expresses" (t'ŭkküpch'a), the slower trains are "expresses" (sangküpch'a), and the slowest are known as "common trains" (ilbanch'a). Each train can consist of passenger carriages of three types. First-class sleeping cars are available only to foreigners and highly privileged passengers. These carriages generally imitate the Soviet sleeping cars with four berths in each compartment and toilets and wash rooms at each end of the corridor. Such carriages can be found only on certain express trains which connect major cities. The second-class carriages also provide sleeping berths, but without the comfort of a compartment. A vast majority of travelers, meanwhile, must use a third type of carriage: the regular carriage without sleeping berths at all.

The regular North Korean carriage is equipped with wooden benches for sitting. However, even in the best of times there are not enough seats and people have to sit on the floor. During the recent crisis, the situation has deteriorated and passengers have even been known to travel on carriage roofs. This makes for good photo opportunities for foreign journalists, but is hardly admired by the travelers themselves. The broken windows in most carriages also make a travel unpleasant — but passengers simply have no choice.

Traditionally, regular carriages had no seat numbers. As soon as boarding began, passengers rushed to the railway platform in an attempt to board the train ahead of their fellow travelers. I have witnessed these sprints, which produce quite a surreal impression: people of all ages, heavily laden with sacks and bags of all shapes and sizes, dashing to their trains. It was first come, first served!

In 2003 the government attempted to put things in order. A system of "seat numbers" was introduced. This reduced the carrying capacity of the railroads, but rendered the old dashes obsolete.

The North Korean railway system is not in an enviable state. Nonetheless, in recent years a large-scale reconstruction of the system has been widely discussed in the South. Its businesses now need North Korean railroads, but in order to restore them to working order they will have to invest a great amount of money. Restoration and reconstruction of the North's railroad system is bound to happen sooner or later, and it will not come cheaply....

The Marble Underground

STALINIST REGIMES HAVE ALWAYS BEEN notorious for their love of expensive and prestigious projects, and for decades the ornate yet strangely beautiful subterranean palaces of the Moscow subway served as the most common showcases of the supposed technological and artistic sophistication of the Soviet system. From Moscow, this special emphasis on subways was copied by other Communist regimes which saw it not simply as a convenient means of urban transport but also as a political statement in marble, concrete and granite. North Korea was no exception.

Since the early 1970s, the Pyongyang subway has been a vital link in the city's public transportation grid. However, it also serves two other less obvious purposes. First of all, the subway is a civil defense shelter of gargantuan proportions. And secondly, it is a showcase of North Korean architecture and design.

The military consideration was taken very seriously during the subway's construction. North Korea has spent the last few decades busily preparing itself for war — either defensive or aggressive — against the South and its U.S. ally. The construction of large-scale underground facilities was an integral part of these military preparations.

The Pyongyang subway is extremely deep — more than one hundred meters (reputedly, the world's deepest). All stations are equipped with hermetically sealing steel gates which can instantly quarantine the stations and tunnels. One of the subway stations — Kwangmyŏng — is never used. Trains invariably pass through this station without stopping. The station is located

In Pyongyang subway. Photograph by Christopher Morris.

beneath Kŭmsusan Palace, the former residence of Kim Il Sung, and was obviously meant to be used for the evacuation of the government in case of an emergency — perhaps to a bunker nearby.

Another military peculiarity is the presence of a long passage which connects the station itself to the underground exit from the escalators. Perhaps it is necessary for crowd control or to somehow otherwise improve the military value of the system.

Another part of the subway's mission is to showcase North Korea's "*Juche* socialism" in general and its architecture in particular. Like its Soviet prototype, the Pyongyang subway is lavishly decorated. The stations are adorned with polished marble, mosaics, stained-glass windows, frescoes, huge bronze chandeliers and other similar excesses.

Every station has its own particular theme. For example, Kaeson (Triumph) station is dedicated to the alleged "triumphal return" of Kim Il Sung to Pyongyang. It is located near the site where on October 14, 1945, the young Kim was first introduced to the citizens of Pyongyang. The station frescoes portray the great enthusiasm which, so the official propaganda insists, overtook the jubilant "masses" once they learned of Kim's return.

The very construction of the subway was also a political statement. The North Korean leaders went to great lengths to ensure that "their" subway would

An entrance of a subway station. Photograph by Byeon Young-wook.

commence operations before that of Seoul. They were successful: the first train departed in September 1973, and Pyongyang began using its subway almost exactly one year earlier than Seoul. However, ever since that time the subway has remained frozen in time: no new lines have been constructed over the intervening years, and the total length of the subway line is still only a modest 34 kilometers.

The subway is not only a fortification and a showcase, but also a means of transport. In this regard, however, its capacity is rather limited. The subway is quite small: it has only 17 stations and two lines which intersect at one point. Both lines traverse the western part of the city, and none of them crosses the Taedonggang River (there are probably unfounded rumors that an attempt at such a crossing resulted in a major disaster in the 1970s). This means that the eastern half of the city is cut off from the subway system completely.

The subway was constructed with Chinese technical assistance and its rolling stock was once imported from China, although the North Koreans have tried to downplay this fact. They even removed the plates which indicated the carriages' origin. North Korea was serious about projecting an image of a self-reliant country!

Opposite: An underground palace. Photograph by Andrew Salmon.

The trains are short and consist of only three carriages. They also run fairly infrequently, with 7–15 minute intervals between trains. The operating times of the subway change regularly. In 1999, the subway opened at 5:30 A.M. and closed at 11:30 P.M. while in the mid–1980s it ceased operation as early as 10:30 P.M. Nowadays, the closing time is 10:00 P.M.

Although normally not many people use the subway, during rush hours crowds can become dense and uncontrollable. The problem is that in the subway it is not customary to wait for disembarking passengers as is the case with boarding a bus. When a carriage stops, it is a free-for-all and as the outflowing current begins to ebb, the stragglers are often forced back inside by those rushing in. The battle is quite unceremonious, and greatly contrasts with the measured, pseudo-classical grandeur of the underground interior. But then again, Stalinism always did know how to make a good impression....

All Down the Line

IN THE WINTER OF 1990–1991, downtown Pyongyang was in the midst of a construction frenzy. Entire streets were taken over by soldiers who doubled as builders. Loudspeakers erupted with the usual mix of militant marches and regurgitated slogans. People had to work hard: the Great Leader had decided that Pyongyang needed a tram network, and the top officials ordered that the tram service commence by April 15, 1991, in time for Kim Il Sung's birthday.

For a brief moment it appeared that the builders would be unable to meet the deadline. Thus, in February the tempo of work was greatly increased. People worked around the clock, in all kinds of weather. Despite the bitter cold, many soldiers removed their padded jackets and worked in their undershirts alone. It was a much-trumpeted "high-speed battle" in its purest form.

As is the custom on North Korean construction sites, all work was done by hand. No earth-moving equipment could be seen. The soldiers used huge chisels to smash the asphalt and cement surface of the roads, then they moved the rails and laid them in order. The work was finished on time, and in April 1991 the Pyongyang tram was born or, rather, reborn.

Once upon a time, the would-be North Korean capital was one of three Korean cities to boast a tram service — the two others being Seoul and Pusan. The Pyongyang tram service was opened on May 20, 1923. However, the Korean War led to the destruction of the "first" Pyongyang tramway. In 1951–1953 the intense U.S. bombing virtually flattened Pyongyang, transforming the city into piles of smoking rubble. The tram service was discontinued

Early morning. The first tram. Photograph by Andrei Lankov.

and was not resumed after the war. In the mid–1950s, the tram was certainly out of fashion among city planners worldwide.

It is not clear why in the late 1980s it was decided to revive the half-forgotten tram. Of course the whim of Kim Il Sung, who either initiated or approved the project, played a major role. However, the decision probably made sense. Pyongyang was a large city, and its transport system needed improvement. The subway enlargement was difficult, especially when funds were running short, and the depth of the Pyongyang project made it doubly difficult and expensive. Meanwhile, buses were too dependent on imported fuel.

The first tramline opened in 1991 and was followed by a second line in 1992. The Pyongyang light rail system now boasts three lines with a total length of some 50 km. This is roughly equivalent to the length of the Seoul tram network in the early 1960s, shortly before the network was dismantled. The population of Pyongyang, incidentally, is also roughly similar to that of Seoul in 1955–1960.

Apart from two standard gauge lines, there is also the short Kŭmsusan line which connects Kŭmsusan Palace, where Kim Il Sung's embalmed body lies in state, with the nearest subway station. This is a narrow-gauge line which is not connected to the "normal" tramway network. It was built in 1995–1996 when the former presidential palace was reconstructed as Kim Il Sung's mausoleum.

The rolling stock for the lines was imported from overseas. The North Korean authorities did not advertise this fact, nor did they go to great lengths to hide it. This was a major departure from the practice in the 1970s, when Chinese-made subway carriages had all their plaques removed in order to obscure their foreign origin.

In 1990 the North Korean authorities bought 45 carriages from the CKD/Tatra works in the still Communist Czechoslovakia. CKD/Tatra was one of the largest and best manufacturers of trams in the world. Further shipments ensued, and altogether some 225 new Czech-produced carriages in three styles were shipped to Pyongyang.

However, the new carriages proved a costly purchase, and in the mid–1990s Pyongyang began to buy used carriages from Europe. The second line currently runs Czech trams which were bought from the former East Germany, trams which once plied the streets of Leipzig, Dresden and Magdeburg. Later these carriages underwent modification, an act which was predictably hailed by the North Korean media as "the production of a new type of tram for the capital of revolution."

The "special" Kŭmsusan line runs these imported used carriages as well. In this instance the stock came from Zürich in Switzerland. The narrow-gauge trams are half a century old (built in 1947–1954), but remain in good shape.

What will be the fate of the Pyongyang tram when the inevitable happens and crowds of cars flood the city's streets? I hope that it will survive, even if the recent Korean experience does not appear encouraging for the heritage conservation enthusiast: few countries discard the relics of their recent past as light-heartedly as South Korea. The tram may survive, but the chances of the trolley-bus, now the major means of public transport in Pyongyang, appears to be slim. Which brings us to our next topic....

Nostalgia for Trolley-Buses

PYONGYANG IS A RELATIVELY LARGE CITY, and this means that its inhabitants must commute to work. Of all the modes of transport available to them, the trolley-bus is by far the most common and reliable.

But what is a trolley-bus? Imagine a bus equipped with an electric engine.

A trolley-bus from early 1970s, still in operation. Photograph by Bernd Seiler.

The electricity is supplied through a pair of wires which are strung over the entire length of the route with the help of poles. In Pyongyang, the local trolley-bus system uses 600–650V electricity. On the roof of the bus there are two poles which touch the wires and provide the flow of electricity to the engine.

While this mode of transport might appear exotic to most readers of this book, it should be remembered that it was once common in cities of the developed West. In East Asia, Shanghai acquired such service first, in 1914, and still keeps its in operation.

In the USA and Western Europe, trolley-buses largely disappeared in the 1960s (in LA, for example, the trolley-bus service was discontinued in 1963), since they were seen as uneconomical and causing inconvenience to other traffic. Only in a few cities — Vancouver and Seattle, for example — do trolley-buses remain. They are also popular in South Africa, and there is a small trolley-bus service in Wellington, the capital of New Zealand. But the real trolley-bus heaven is the former Soviet Union and the ex–Communist states of Eastern Europe. As of 2000, some 190 ex–Soviet cities still had functioning trolley-bus networks. Perhaps the influence of the "fraternal countries" played a major role in Pyongyang's choice of trolley-buses as its principal mode of transport.

Waiting for a trolley-bus. Photograph by Andrei Lankov.

In the North Korean case, the choice was logical, since there are two major problems with trolley-buses which were not problems in a poor country with a Stalinist economy. Trolley-buses were uneconomical, but Stalinist economies are not famous for their regard for efficiency. They also created obstacles for other traffic, but then the North did not have much other traffic to worry about.

The first trolley-bus line in Pyongyang was opened in April 1962. It connected the Pyongyang railway station in the old eastern part of the city with the Industrial and Agricultural Exhibition which was once located on the western shores of the Taedongang (later this Exhibition was demolished to make way for the *Juche* tower). This initial line was followed by a dozen other lines until eventually all parts of the North Korean capital were connected by these strange electric buses. Apart from Pyongyang, trolley-bus services also operate in Hamhŭng, Kanggye, Ch'ongjin and P'yŏngsŏng.

The major advantage of the trolley-buses is their independence from imported fuel. Unlike diesel buses, they run on electricity, which once used to be quite plentiful in the North. Even in better times, well before the current economic crisis, the conventional diesel buses in Pyongyang operated only during rush hours. Outside rush hours these fuel-guzzlers were parked,

and all further transportation was the exclusive domain of electric vehicles —
trolley-buses, subway trains and, from 1990 onwards, trams.

Unlike the imported diesel buses, the trolley-buses are produced locally,
at the Pyongyang trolley-bus factory. The bodies of the trolley-buses are made
manually since, apparently, the factory does not have suitable hydraulic presses.
The sheet metal has to be hammered, and thus the surface of the Pyongyang
trolley-buses is invariably covered with dents. It should be said, however, that
this backward technology is partly compensated for by the diligent and consistent labor of the Korean drivers and repairmen who work devotedly to
ensure that their devices are reasonably roadworthy.

There are about a dozen trolley-bus routes in Pyongyang. These routes
are marked not by numbers but by the name of the last stop on the route.
Numbers are used as well, but they distinguish not the route but particular
stops along a given route. Thus, for example, there are three trolley-buses
which go from the First Department Store to the Sadon district. They travel
the same route but stop at different places and are marked by the numbers 1,
2, and 3. This system is not excessively inconvenient — and even if it were, it
would be difficult to change, since it was established on the personal instruction of none other than Kim Il Sung himself!

Trolley-bus tickets are sold in most shops. Until recently a ticket cost a
mere 10 chŏn (very roughly the equivalent of the South Korean 100 *won*), but
recently the prices have been increased to 1 *won*. If measured by the black market exchange rate, this is a negligible amount, well below $0.01.

Until the early 1990s, the trolley-buses carried conductors who checked
the tickets of boarding passengers. About a decade ago, these conductors disappeared, and passengers are now required to pay their fares up front. Unlike
the chaotic everyone-for-himself style of the subway, the trolley-bus stops
sport quite orderly queues, with rush hours often being an exception.

The conductors were once women, while the driver's job was almost
exclusively a male domain, but this is not the case any more: a majority of
Pyongyang trolley-bus drivers are now women as well.

Perhaps the trolley-bus system is doomed: the unwieldy vehicles do not
mix well with herds of cars which will sooner or later flood Pyongyang's
streets. But it will probably be remembered as a symbol of an era, of those
six or seven decades which the North Koreans spent under the rule of the
Kim dynasty. They will remember how they rode trolleys to the indoctrination meetings, military exercises, and public denunciations. But they also
used them to meet their loved ones, to go to a job which they liked and
enjoyed, or to explore new parts of their city. Even under the worst tyranny
most people manage to lead normal lives, and the trolley-bus may become a
symbol of this normality.

PART 10

Big Brother Is Watching

A Peep-Hole into North Korea

NO MAJOR STATE IS COMPLETE without a security agency, often derogatorily described as "political police" in less democratic countries or simply in countries we happen to dislike. And North Korea is of course no exception.

The core of the North Korean internal security system is the Ministry of the Protection of State Security (MPSS or *kukka anjŏn powibu* in Korean). Not much is known about this institution, not only because of its secretive nature, but also because of the peculiar position taken by the few people in the know.

In this respect, there is a remarkable difference between the "small" Cold War in Korea and the "large" Cold War which was once waged by the two superpowers. When the Cold War was at its height, American publishers churned out a tidal wave of publications about the KGB, and the Soviet official press produced an equally impressive amount of material about the CIA and FBI. These publications were heavily biased, but they still provided useful if distorted information. Nothing like this is happening with Korea. For some reason the South Korean authorities zealously guard all the information about the MPSS they undoubtedly hold.

Nonetheless, some things are known. The security police department operated within the Ministry of the Interior from the inception of the North Korean state. In February 1973, the political police functions were entrusted to the new Ministry of State Political Security. It was then headed by Kim Pyŏng-ha, a distant relative of Kim Il Sung who was seen as one of the most powerful dignitaries in the land.

However, connection with the Great Family does not necessarily help.

After all, under a dictatorship it is very dangerous to be a chief of political police, as the fates of Stalin's numerous henchmen testify. In 1982 Kim Pyŏng-ha was purged and disappeared. The MSPS was then subjected to a thorough purge, and thousands of officers who were deemed to be closely related to Kim Pyŏng-ha were sent to labor camps (together with their families — collective responsibility is a cornerstone of the North Korean system in a real sense). The guards recount how in the early 1980s new inmates arrived by the trainload. There they learned what had been the fate of the victims before them....

In 1993 the Ministry of State Political Security acquired its present name. The MPSS, together with the Ministry of Defense and the Ministry of Public Security, reports directly to the head of state and not to the Cabinet. It is not known exactly who is the current head of this powerful agency, but it is believed that these duties are assumed by Kim Jong Il himself. Perhaps this is really the case: the Great Leader is a known fan of spy adventures, with a penchant for all things clandestine.

Like the KGB, after which it was once loosely patterned, the MPSS deals with a number of tasks which in most other countries are entrusted to different agencies. It is responsible for overseas intelligence (together with the so-called Third Department and Room 35, of which more at another time), and it also deals with government communications and the protection of strategically important installations. However, its major task is to fight espionage and dissent within the country.

In tracking and uprooting "unreliable elements," the MPSS relies on an extensive network of informers. Special representatives of the MPSS are dispatched to all important factories and institutions to monitor the political reliability of the staff and also to run networks of police informers.

The North Koreans, like people under any dictatorship, have to mind their tongues. Even the most innocent remark can be easily represented as political subversion. For example, in the 1970s a vet was treating a pig when he uttered something like "in this world only pigs can live happily." This was interpreted as a counterrevolutionary statement; the culprit was arrested, tortured and shot, while his family was sent to a prison camp. We know this story from a camp guard who later managed to defect.

A network of prison camps for the real, potential, or imagined enemies of the regime is also managed by the MPSS.

I often wonder what will be the fate of the MPSS officers in the long run. I do not think they will ever be punished — save for a handful of the most notorious or unlucky ones. Too many people for far too long have participated in crimes in what is arguably the world's most repressive regime. Crimes on such a scale, committed over such a long period of time, are very unlikely ever to be investigated completely, and especially if these crimes were committed in some distant past.

Forget the Predators, Remember the Victims

KANG CH'ŎL-HWAN, ARGUABLY THE MOST prominent member of a small but growing community of former North Korean prison inmates who have managed to reach the South in recent years, recalled an episode he witnessed while incarcerated in "camp #15," North Korea's largest penal camp.

A woman wailed over the body of her son, who had died in detention. "Why did you die so quickly? Why did you depart this cursed world?" And then, without changing her tone even a little, she continued: "Why did you leave this world which has become so happy under the wise guidance of our Great Leader?" The reason for such a dramatic change in her worldview was simple: she had noticed that a known police informer was approaching her.

This is a good example of black humor, North Korean style. But it is also a reminder of the ubiquity of the police informers and their awesome power over human fates. Some 150–200,000 people are now incarcerated in North Korea's prisons, and many more have passed through the North Korean gulag.

The North Korean political police, the Ministry for Protection of State Security (MPSS), has an extensive network of informers. Officers of the MPSS who have defected claim that under normal circumstances there should be one informer for every fifty persons, while in more "politically difficult" environments the proportion is greater.

For example, Yi Su-ryŏn, daughter and wife of ethnic Korean repatriates from Japan, related a typical incident. During a drinking party, four out of the seven participants (including Yi's husband himself) admitted to being informers. They were all former repatriates from Japan, of course — a very dangerous group from Pyongyang's official point of view.

I often wonder what will happen to these half million spies in the future. It is often stated that Germany offers a good example of how the Communist past should be handled. Indeed, the files of the Stasi, the former East German security service, are now open to all concerned. A majority of the 2.4 million people who were tracked by the Stasi have checked their files. Why not do the same in a unified Korea as well?

Alas, I do not think that the German experience is relevant. The much-vilified Stasi appeared to be harsh only when compared to the standards of an affluent, stable, democratic Europe. What would happen to an individual in East Germany if a co-worker reported some words or actions deemed bad by the authorities? Such a person might lose the opportunity for promotion or the chance to travel overseas. However, in North Korea a similar report would often lead to the victim's execution, or a slow death in a prison camp. More often than not the victim's family would go to prison as well. There is a difference between a damaged career and the death of an entire family, isn't there?

Thus, all attempts to unearth the past are too likely to lead to an outbreak of hatred and revenge that will haunt the national psyche for decades to come. Is this a fair price to pay for the restoration of justice?

Furthermore, these secret informers do not necessarily initiate the persecution, even if that is what appears to be the case from the papers alone. Yi Su-ryŏn, whose husband was an MPSS informer himself, tells how he was once called on by his control officer to report a talk with a fellow repatriate. The talk was innocent enough, even though the person in question made some mildly critical comments. However, Yi's husband was ordered to rewrite his report so the remarks appeared much more subversive than they really were. He reluctantly did so, with the full understanding that a refusal would not help the targeted victim and would probably lead to his own arrest as well. Some weeks later the fellow was arrested and his family taken to the camps.

This particular story is real — Yi had no special incentive to disclose it, and probably did it to clear her conscience. Nonetheless, nearly all informers, if pressed, will insist that they were ordered to make false reports, and there will be no way of finding out the real situation.

Decades of North Korean rule have created a painful legacy that will not go away easily, even under the most benign of possible unification scenarios. Perhaps the best way to face the challenges of the future is to forget the predators but remember the victims. While this would appear to be a bad solution, I am afraid the alternatives may be infinitely worse.

Grannies in Charge

EVERY MORNING IN CITIES AND VILLAGES all over North Korea groups of women (sometimes together with a few men) emerge from their houses or apartments equipped with brooms and dustpans. They are not janitors. There

The morning cleaning, a daily routine arranged by a "people's group." Photograph by Andrei Lankov.

are no full-time paid janitors in the living quarters of North Korean cities. Indeed, the politically correct North Korean view is that "Janitors are incompatible with socialism!" — at least that is what one North Korean claimed to the present author a long time ago.

So who are these women? They are local inhabitants who are organized to perform daily cleaning services by their "people's group" (*inminban* in Korean). The activity of such groups looms very large in the daily lives of North Koreans.

A typical *inminban* consists of 30–50 families. In neighborhoods consisting of individual houses, an *inminban* usually includes all inhabitants of a specific quarter, while in apartment buildings such a group might include all families sharing a common staircase (or 2–3 adjacent staircases if the building is not large). No North Korean of any age or sex can exist outside the system of "people's groups." Everyone is a member of some *inminban* by definition.

Each *inminban* is headed by an official. Usually this is a middle-aged woman, known as the people's group head or *inminbanjang*. In Pyongyang and other major cities the heads receive a small stipend and large rations (in

North Korea, where until recently money was largely symbolic, the latter was far more important than the former). Typically, a non-working housewife was eligible for daily rations of 300g of grain, but if she was appointed the people's group head, her allowance would grow to 700g — a significant difference.

In the countryside, being an *inminbanjang* is an unpaid job. But even there the position is still made attractive by a number of small perks which these "heads" enjoy. For example, the *inminban* is the major unit for distribution of some consumer goods, like soap, and the head is always in a position to get more goods that she would normally receive, and often of better quality. This might be seen as a milder form of official corruption, but in recent years bribery has become quite common.

Still, not everyone wants to become an *inminbanjang*. The head's duties are numerous and occasionally onerous. First of all, she must keep an eye on citizens in her "territory" to ensure that nothing improper is taking place. It is her duty to keep track of all people who spend a night in "her" territory, check their papers and report their presence to the police. In apartment buildings she is responsible for the passage of all visitors: a specially appointed person, usually a lady in her 60s, must check the documents of all visitors and write their details down in a special book. It is the *inminbanjang*'s duty to make sure that records are compiled and kept properly.

In addition, she must conduct "ideological education" among those residents who do not have permanent employment — mainly retirees and housewives. These "aunties" are required to attend study sessions where they must discuss recent Party decisions on pig farming or the management of steel mills as well as patiently listen to long and boring lectures on a bewildering range of similarly intriguing topics. And, last but not least, the *inminban* and its head are responsible for maintaining the neighborhood.

Indeed, many activities which in most other countries are conducted by the municipal authorities, in North Korea are a part of the citizens' duties. Apart from the daily cleaning, the "people's group" is also responsible for garbage removal, upkeep of the water supply and sewage systems, and even repairs to public roads which run close to their neighborhoods. This is not always a rational delegation of responsibility, since the "aunties" who form the core of an *inminban*'s workforce are no substitute for professional technicians. Nevertheless, such an approach allows the government to save some money — or at the very least, the government believes that money is to be saved in such a way.

The removal of garbage is the *inminban*'s major task. North Korean cities lack garbage bins. Instead, in large cities there are special gate-like devices which are large enough to allow a truck to pass below them. The garbage is piled on the flat tops of such gates which are surrounded by a fence which prevents the garbage from being dispersed. On the appointed day, a truck arrives at the "gate." This is a normal truck, not especially modified for garbage removal. The truck is driven halfway through the gates, allowing the garbage on the top to be easily pushed into its tray. The whole procedure is, of course, executed by a group of local aunties, led by the *inminban* head. They all climb to the top of the garbage pile equipped with spades and shovels in military style. In the countryside the disposal of rubbish is less inventive, but the major workforce are these same aunties from the *inminban*.

Another unpleasant but unavoidable duty is that of "night soil" removal. Flush toilets exist only in large cities (a North Korean student in Eastern Europe once commented that he had never even seen a flush toilet before his arrival in Pyongyang). Even in the large cities there are large areas where the more traditional methods of human waste disposal are practiced.

In smaller towns and in the countryside the inhabitants use large public toilets and the manure has to be removed regularly. Trucks are provided by the local authorities, but the labor is supplied by the inhabitants themselves. Each *inminban* is attached to a particular village where it must collect its manure for subsequent use as fertilizer.

The daily routine is, of course, the "morning cleaning." Taking turns, local women tidy up their neighborhood every morning. As a rule, every house must send at least one person to take part in the cleaning.

From the 1970s, the *inminban* women were required to take part in all sorts of campaigns. They could be mobilized for few days of "patriotic labor" in the countryside or required to manufacture all manner of things in their homes. Normally only housewives are enlisted in these *inminban* activities — people with permanent jobs are given a reprieve.

The hyper-activity of the *inminban* is often cited by North Korean women as one of the reasons why in the 1970s or 1980s they did not see much sense in staying home. They say that the actual workload of the housewife who had to do her manifold *inminban* duties was not much different from the workload of a normally employed person, while her rice rations were dramatically smaller, some 300 g instead of the normal 700 g. Hence, staying at home simply did not make much economic sense — unless a particular lady was able and willing to become an *inminbanjang* herself, that is.

From the government's point of view, perhaps the most important part of the *inminbanjang*'s mission was to be enforcers and guardians of the surveillance regime, which had few if any parallels even in the Stalinist states. But this is our next story....

Guess Who's
Coming After Dinner...

THE SUDDEN RING OF THE DOORBELL, or a deafening knock at the door after midnight.... For a long time, such occurrences have been a symbol of the police state. Indeed, many a North Korean is awakened in the middle of the night by these sounds — and it is indeed the police. However, the chances are that these officers have *not* come to arrest the inhabitants and take them off to the gulag. Of course this might be the case, but it is much more likely that the police are doing their routine job — conducting a regular home check or *sukpak kŏmyŏl.*

Home checks are part of regular police work. Until recently, all North Korean households were subjected to home checks twice or three times a year. If for any reason it is necessary to heighten security, special additional checks are conducted as well. For example, if Kim Jong Il is going to visit a particular city, its inhabitants are subjected to a frenzy of midnight home checks. Quite often *sukpak kŏmyŏl* are conducted on the eve of official holidays — just to ensure that nothing improper happens during the holiday festivities.

The major aim of the home check is obvious: to find out if anyone is staying overnight at a particular address without proper permission. For many decades North Korea has maintained one of the world's most vigorous and efficient systems of surveillance, and control over population movement is an important part of this.

If a North Korean family has a visitor who intends to stay overnight, this must be reported to the head of the *inminban.* The *inminban* head must check the visitor's ID. If the person is permanently registered in another county, he or she must present a valid "travel permit" as well. Such permits are issued by the local police to every North Korean who travels outside the county of his or her residence — and of course, a mere desire to do so is not enough; one has to have compelling reasons to apply.

All overnight visitors are registered in a special book. Every evening the *inminban* head provides police with a written report which specifies the name, gender, place of registration, ID, travel permit number, as well as the length and purpose of the overnight visit.

To make sure that nobody breaks these regulations, the police conduct random "home checks." The typical search group includes a police officer and the head of the *inminban.* If in the neighborhood there are families of military officers, the groups are joined by military representatives as well, and in some cases a representative of the security police might also take part in the mission.

The best time for a *sukpak kŏmyŏl* is soon after midnight. A number of policemen take up positions near the door or on the streets, ensuring that no suspicious persons can escape, while the group begins its search. They knock on the doors and have a look around the flat or house. Nor do they limit themselves to a superficial examination, but search all places where a person might be hidden, including cupboards, chests, balconies, etc. Officially, they are looking for spies and criminals, but their usual quarry is different: relatives from the countryside, friends of the household owners, and, of course, a large number of unlucky lovers.

Being caught without a proper permit in somebody else's place is not a laughing matter in the North — it is a minor crime! Of course, every transgression must be reported to the work unit of both the visitor and the household owner. This means that they must deliver a full confession at the next public "self-criticism session" at their work unit or party cell. If there are aggravating circumstances, the visitor might be even be briefly sent for re-education through labor.

There are other things to be looked for as well — all kinds of prohibited items. The search group routinely checks to see if the radio is properly sealed and hence cannot be used for listening to foreign broadcasts, and they might also look for anything else suspicious. The presence of at least two officials from different agencies (a police officer and an *inminbanjang*) means that bribing one's way out of trouble could be risky or, at the very least, expensive.

In recent years the intensity of these "home checks" has reportedly diminished, even if they are by no means a thing of the past. However, a new danger has developed: the mobile police patrol group or *kyuch'aldae*. These groups were created to counter the growth of violent crime in recent years and they patrol the streets from midnight to early dawn. These groups also have the right to search houses if they believe that something improper is talking place inside — and often their search leads to problems. Thus, if one is listening to a foreign broadcast, then the volume must be turned down to an absolute minimum!

So does the North Korean constitution guarantee the privacy of the home, I hear you ask? Of course it does. However, the constitution is also very remote from the reality of life in this most secretive of nations.

Personal Identification:
It's on the Cards...

EVERY NORTH KOREAN MUST HAVE PROOF of his or her identity and produce it when required. I understand that this may give rise to a degree of sarcasm among the lucky inhabitants of democratic countries. But — wait a minute! Aren't Americans or West Europeans sometimes required to produce this very same proof? In our automotive age, the driver's license has become the most prevalent form of ID in most developed countries. Needless to say, this is not the case in the North.

The existence of an obligatory form of identification which must be carried on one's person does not necessarily transform a country into a police state. Nonetheless, dictatorships make good use of this device in their relentless quest for data about their subjects.

Like many other North Korean institutions, its ID system was initially designed to be a carbon copy of a Soviet prototype. The major ID is called the *kongminchŭng*, or "citizen's certificate," and until recently it looked pretty much like a passport: a small booklet with 12 pages, in a plastic cover, with the bearer's black-and-white picture on the first page. It was actually patterned after the Soviet ID of the 1940s. This is not surprising: the "citizen's certificates" were first introduced as early as September 1946, at a time when the Soviet military held almost complete control over North Korea.

From 1972 the "citizen's certificate" was issued when a North Korean reached 17 years of age, and it was renewed every ten years. This was the task of the Public Security Department, the North Korean police, the body which also handles any other changes to one's ID.

The small book contained a wealth of information about its bearer. Naturally it indicated birthplace, place of residence, and date of birth. But it also specified marital status. Upon marriage, a special stamp was placed in one's *kongminchŭng*, to record this important event. In the case of divorce, a further stamp announced the change in marital status.

In 1998 a new type of "citizen's certificate" was introduced. It contained basically the same information, but its appearance demonstrated a decisive break with the Soviet tradition. The present-day "citizen's certificate" is a small plastic card, reminiscent of its South Korean analogue. It is adorned with the picture of the Paektusan Mountain where Kim Jong Il was allegedly born (in fact he was born in the Soviet Union, where his father was in exile in the early 1940s, but that is another story).

An interesting peculiarity of the North Korean ID system is the clear distinction made between the "certificates" of Pyongyanites and the humble dwellers of other towns and villages. The right to live in Pyongyang has always been an important privilege because it offers access to a number of important perks, notably the much superior supply of foodstuffs and consumer goods. At the same time, the government has always limited migration to Pyongyang from the countryside. Therefore, all Pyongyang residents have a special type of "citizen's certificate" which indicates their right to reside in the capital. To facilitate police work, and to avoid mingling with lesser beings, these lucky few have "Pyongyang resident" written in their ID in large letters. Needless to say, a common country bumpkin has next to no chance of ever seeing the capital; one has to have special permission to enter Pyongyang, and such permission is notoriously difficult to obtain.

Yet a few other groups do not carry a regular "citizen's certificate." Following the old Soviet practice once again, North Korean authorities do not issue regular "citizen's certificates" to army personnel, nor to the members of the police and security services. They have their own IDs.

Another group whose members are deprived of their "citizen's certificate" are prisoners. If a North Korean is arrested, his "certificate" is confiscated by the police and is not returned until after release from prison or labor camp.

Children who have not attained the age of 17 years are issued birth certificates which must also be produced quite often. Among other things, these certificates are necessary when children are registered to receive rations from the public distribution system.

One's ID must be produced in any number of circumstances. One cannot, for example, buy a train ticket without producing the "citizen's certificate" along with a special "travel permit." In many regions, police conduct random ID checks. Thus, North Koreans rarely venture outside their houses without their "citizen's certificates."

The "citizen's certificate" might be the most important of all North Korean documents, but it is far from the only one. Indeed, every North Korean is expected to have a surprising number of certificates. But that is another story....

Gullible Travels

A NORTH KOREAN DEFECTOR RECENTLY remarked that he felt a sense of insecurity when he bought tickets at the Seoul station for the very first time. The reason was simple: he had no "travel permit." Buying a ticket without such a document went against all of his better instincts.

A square in front of the Pyongyang railway station. All these people must have their IDs and their travel permits ready. Photograph by Byeon Young-wook.

Indeed, no North Korean is allowed to leave his county of residence without such a document. The sole exception is for the trips to adjacent counties. Permits are obtained from the so-called second departments of local governments. These departments are staffed with police officers and are run jointly by police and the local administration.

The "travel permit," generally known as a *t'onghaengjŭng*, must be produced when train or inter-city bus tickets are purchased. The ticket sales clerk must carefully check the document as well as the prospective passenger's ID, and only after they are completely satisfied, issue a ticket. The "travel permit" is checked once again when the passenger is boarding his or her train or bus. It must also be produced during random checks, often conducted by the local police and especially in the vicinity of railway stations.

If one is found outside one's native county without such a permit the individual will be arrested and sent back to his native county after the appropriate punishment. An attempt to sneak oneself into Pyongyang is punished with two weeks of unpaid work at a special re-education camp for minor offenders. In other jurisdictions the punishment may be lighter.

The North Korean bureaucracy has developed an intricate hierarchy of travel permits (frankly, I think that a reconstruction of this system, which kept changing, will make a good PhD topic few decades down the track). The most prestigious are special passes that give unrestricted access to all areas of the country. They are held by the top cadres, police officials, and military officers. Such passes are very rare, since they must carry the imprimatur of none than Kim Jong Il or, before his ascent, Kim Il Sung. Any bearer of such a pass instantly commands respect and awe.

There are special passes issued to people who have to travel across the country because of their jobs. For example, there are special passes for the drivers which allow them travel in their vehicles, but do not give them right to use other modes of transportation.

The humble populace have their own permits too. For civilians there are separate passes for official or private trips. There is also a special type of "travel permit" which is issued for military personnel by the armed forces.

Travel permits for private trips are issued only if there is a valid personal reason — normally the funeral or wedding of some close relative. The fact of a recent death or impending marriage must be confirmed by the proper papers, and the entire process itself involves an impressive amount of paperwork. Travel permits of all types (apart from the special passes of the bigwigs) clearly indicate not only the name of the bearer, but also the trip's destination, and are valid for a limited period of time. It is fine to stay over briefly in some area en route to one's final destination, and many Koreans use this loophole to visit additional places.

However, visits are seldom motivated by curiosity. Domestic tourism is not completely alien to the North Koreans, but it remains a quite unusual pastime. Most tours are organized by various official bodies and their targets have more to do with ideological indoctrination than pleasure. For example, students often visit "revolutionary historic sites" where Kim Il Sung and Kim Jong Il allegedly conducted certain heroic exploits. Of course, the travel group has its own supervisor who holds the "group travel permit" with the group list attached.

A trip to Pyongyang is a rare privilege. In earlier, more orderly times, the local administration was allocated an annual quota of pilgrims who would be sent to Pyongyang on tour, sponsored by their party committees. The average North Korean from the countryside might have the chance to visit the "capital of revolution" once or twice in a lifetime.

In the 1990s, there were three types of travel permits, each valid for particular types of areas. Two of these are known as "confirmed number travel permits."

This seemingly strange name is explained by the fact that all these permits must be approved by the Ministry of the Interior's central headquarters in Pyongyang. Once the officials in Pyongyang make a check of the applicant's personal files, they issue a special "confirmation number" which is put on the travel permit form. Of course, this is done only if the reason for the trip is seen as serious enough by the Pyongyang bureaucrats.

So, which parts of North Korea are subject to this "confirmation numbers" regime? First, there are trips to Pyongyang and areas which house important military installations and other sensitive objects, like the nuclear research facilities or bases for the infiltration ships which deliver agents to South Korea. One can travel to these areas of high importance only if one is equipped with a "red strip travel permit." This is, of course, a type of "confirmed number permit" and is issued after the most rigorous checking. The name is derived from the fact that such travel permits have a reddish strip which crosses the paper diagonally — and, of course, a "confirmed number" on top.

The second confirmed number permit area is the borderland areas — those parts of the country which lie within a few dozen kilometers of the border with China and the DMZ. Access to these areas is only possible with a "blue strip" confirmed number permit, and readers will guess that the diagonal strip is blue in this case.

And finally, there are regular travel permits which do not have "confirmed numbers" and are issued by the local police at their own discretion. These are good only for travel in the countryside, far removed from any of the above sensitive or important areas.

The system of permits almost crumbled in the mid–1990s — the Great Famine rendered it unsustainable. Around 1996 the public distribution system collapsed, and millions of North Koreans began to move across the country looking for food. The government turned a blind eye to their activities. It is not clear to what extent the travel control system was officially relaxed, and to what extent the changes were a result of benign neglect or petty corruption. For all practical purposes, since around 1997 the North Koreans have enjoyed a de facto freedom to travel without permits, with Pyongyang and certain sensitive areas still being the exceptions.

After the Great Famine the system of travel permits was reintroduced, but its new version, in operation from around 2002, is less restrictive than the earlier regulations. Nowadays, the authorities issue travel permits within a week or two. Often they can be bribed to speed up the process, and in such cases the permit is produced almost immediately. The amount of the bribe varies, depending on the destination: from a mere $2–3 for a humble countryside destination up to $10 for one of the two types of "confirmed number permits."

However, something even more remarkable has begun to occur in recent years: the North Korean authorities have begun to issue certificates which allow their bearer to travel to China, crossing the border legally! The procedure to

Part 10: Big Brother Is Watching

obtain such a permit is time-consuming, taking about six months. As usual, it requires a special security check by the "competent authorities" (the same two departments of the MPSS). However, the outcome of such a procedure is not pre-ordained, so generous payments are helpful to steer officials in right direction. In this case, the bribes are much larger, up to $100 but usually about $50. For the average Korean this is a large amount of money, but a majority of the applicants are engaged in cross-border shuttle activities and for them $100 is not an exorbitant sum. They are quite happy to get hold of the permits and even if they pay bribes they still feel much more secure and law-abiding. Being Koreans, they obviously prefer the cloak of legitimacy, no matter how they may have come by their permit in the first place.

Go South, Young Man

ATTEMPTS TO STUDY REPRESSIVE SYSTEMS in non-democratic societies unavoidably run into a paradox: the more effective and tougher the control over the population, the less the outside world knows about the ongoing horrors within that county. When, in the late 1960s, the terror of Mao's regime reached its apex, information about the horrors which were being perpetrated by the regime was seldom reported by the Western press. When, under Mao's successors, the regime became much softer, the Western press began reporting the "abuse of human rights in China" in earnest. A few decades earlier, something similar had been happening in the USSR after Khruchshev's reforms.

In both cases, a major role was played by the then current ideological fashions among Western intellectuals: the self-appointed "progressive thinkers" of the 1960s loved Mao almost as much as their predecessors had loved Stalin in the 1930s. Many say now that it was Solzhenitsyn who "opened their eyes" in the early 1970s by his voluminous work on Stalin's death camps. This is not really the case: Solzhenitsyn was not the first to tell the world about Stalin's terrors — there had been earlier reports. However, leftist thinkers who reigned supreme in academic and intellectual circles ignored those unpleasant pieces of news and chose not to believe them. Solzhenitsyn's exposures in the 1960s and 1970s were taken seriously only because by his time the Soviet Union had gone out of fashion. In the meantime, former fans of Stalin switched their adoration to Mao....

At any rate, if a dictatorship is truly murderous and well-run, very little data will emerge from its prisons, torture chambers and execution sites. There are not many survivors who can tell the story, and even those lucky individuals have to keep a low profile. Everything is quiet, and some credulous outsiders might even talk about the regime's "remarkable achievements" while dismissing as "propaganda" the occasional reports about a few million farmers who have been starved to death or a wave of arrests in the cities. To make things even more complicated, the "remarkable achievements" might be quite real: cruelty towards one's own people is not necessarily incompatible with efficiency in some areas.

I know that my following remark might be seen as somewhat controversial, but it seems that the recent spread of information about the North Korean prison camps is also partially indicative of the regime's ongoing relaxation. At least, it is the collapse of border control in the northern part of the country which has made the escape of former inmates possible, and hence allowed them to reach South Korean and overseas audiences with their stories. It is also possible that the gradual and reluctant relaxation of the regime also increased the chances of former inmates to leave the camps alive, with the same increased likelihood of their escaping across the border.

Still, those stories do not necessarily meet much approval and interest in the South. In South Korea the Left is increasingly powerful in academia and the media, and the leftist intellectuals tend to dismiss reports of North Korean terror — much like the Stalin admirers and Mao-worshippers of European campuses once did in the 1930s and 1960s. However, in recent decades it has become quite difficult to ignore the growing number of testimonies coming from the North — including the evidence provided by the former inmates and prison guards. The recent books by Kang Ch'ŏl-hwan, the most prominent of all ex-inmates, attracted some attention outside South Korea, while inside the country these and other testimonies of the former prisoners are read almost exclusively by the people whose sympathies lie with the political Right.

All the new testimonies confirm what people in the know always suspected: in treating real or imagined political criminals, the North Korean government has out–Stalined even Stalin himself.

The North Korean camps can be divided into two groups: camps for political prisoners and camps for common criminals. The former are managed by the Ministry for the Protection of State Security (MPSS), the North Korean secret police, while the latter are run by the Ministry of Public Security — that is, the regular police force. Common criminals technically stand trial, while political criminals are send to the camps without such formalities.

Political prisoners might be told the length of their sentences, but some of them are kept in the dark even about this all-important information. This is a major departure from Stalin's dispensation of "justice": in the USSR, even at the worst of times, the authorities deemed a kangaroo court necessary and, of course, the prisoners were always told their sentences. The terms could be easily extended or cut short, depending on the political situation, but they nevertheless were spelled out.

Kim outdid Stalin in another regard: the incarceration of the whole immediate family of a purported criminal is obligatory as well. Stalin placed the wives and adult children of some of his enemies in the camps, but such measures were reserved for more prominent victims, not for everyone.

Initially, the camps were administered by the Ministry for the Interior, but from 1972, this responsibility was transferred to the security police. Currently the camps are managed by the Seventh Department of the Ministry for the Protection of State Security.

Until the late 1980s, there were about twelve political prison camps which carried the numbers #11 to #27. Nothing is known about camps #17 to #21, or #23 and #24, but this does not mean that such camps did not exist.

In the early 1990s, a large-scale reform of the prison system took place: many camps were closed and inmates were moved into just five major facilities. The two largest camps (#15 in Yodŏk and #22 in Hoeryŏng) have about 40–50,000 inmates each — an impressive figure even by Stalin's standards. Even taking into account the high mortality rate, it is reasonable to assume that some 3–5% of the entire North Korean population have experienced these camps. The camps are known by their numbers and are located in the northern part of the country, far away from the coast and at a reasonable distance from the borders with China and Russia. This is done to reduce the chances of an escapee crossing the border — even if in recent years some inmates have managed to do just that.

Of the known facilities, camp #15 in Yodŏk is probably the largest, with some 40–50,000 inmates. It occupies a mountain valley which has very steep sides, rendering escape almost impossible. The inmates are housed in villages, grouped according to their type of crime. Interaction with people from other villages is forbidden as well as any connection with the outside world. In North Korean prisons the possession of a local newspaper is a capital crime!

Camp #15 consists of two zones: the revolutionization zone and the absolute control zone. The former is populated by inmates who are seen as redeemable and have some chance of release, while the latter is a close analogue of the extermination camps of Nazi Germany. People are put into the absolute control zone for the rest of their lives. Most of the inmates in the revolutionization zone are the family members of some real or imagined political wrongdoer. They are allowed to live in a semblance of normality, if destitute and strictly controlled: families stay together, small gardens are allowed and there is even a local primary and middle school.

The inmates of camp #15 work in gold mines and a number of work-shops. The camp must also meet allocated quotas of foodstuff production which is shipped to other parts of the country. The inmates are given just 200–300 grams of corn per day, and augment their diet by hunting rats and gathering anything they can find which is edible.

Similar conditions exist in camp #22 in Hoeryŏng, which also largely houses the family members of victims of purges. This is the second largest camp in the country with only a marginally smaller number of inmates. Satellite photos of this camp were recently published by *Far Eastern Economic Review*. A correspondent, with the help of a former inmate, used old Soviet military maps to pinpoint the camp's precise location and then ordered the photographs from a commercial supplier. It is known that both South Korean and American intelligence have long held high resolution pictures of the camps, but these were never made public.

Despite the very high death rate, camps #15 and #22 are relatively liberal institutions. Other "political camps" are much worse. In camp #14, the worst of the known camps, the prisoners work in coal mines and live in barracks with no freedom to move even within the camp. There are no families there either, of course. The inmates also work at a glass factory and distillery. The death rate is very high because of malnutrition, constant beatings and frequent accidents in the mines.

What will happen to the North Korean camps in the future? Will they become museums, like the Nazi extermination camps? Or will the future Korean government make another choice: will they choose to forget this painful history for the sake of national unity and play down the significance and scale of the Kims' extermination system — not forever, perhaps, but for a few decades, until all torturers and victims are safely dead and the divisive issue is purely historical? Perhaps this second option sounds cynical, but could it be the best option? Only time will tell....

The Ideal World

THE HISTORY OF NORTH KOREA IS TRAGIC. Repression, famine, and large-scale terror have all been part of its history. But can the people who once created the North be described as monsters? Were they cold-blooded killers when they took power in the mid–1940s? I believe that both of these questions should be answered in the negative. Unfortunately, it was sincere idealists who founded this, one of the world's most murderous regimes. They yearned to create a better society — in fact a paradise on earth — and they believed that they knew how to do it. Nor did they tolerate any disagreement with their views: only an iron will and unbending belief would deliver the promised future. But the result was a disaster.

Who were the leaders of the North in the mid–1940s? In 1945, Kim Il Sung was a former guerrilla commander of some prominence. In the 1930s he had joined the resistance forces when he, a high school graduate, could have made a reasonably successful career in business. The same was true of Ch'oe Yong-gŏn, his trusted lieutenant. Kim Tu-bong (now forgotten, but then officially the head of the North Korean state and party) was one of the best Korean scholars, and also a long-time exile in the Communist-controlled part of China. Mu Chŏng was the highest-ranking ethnic Korean soldier in the Chinese Communist forces. Pak Hŏn-yŏng and other "Southerners," i.e. North Korean leaders with a South Korean background, were largely people who had been involved in the most radical and risky forms of anti-colonial resistance prior to 1945. In short, these people had demonstrated their willingness to sacrifice their own comfort and prosperity for what they saw as the happiness of their people.

It is not difficult to understand why the Korean intellectuals of the late 1940s were often ready to defect to the North. The Communist state broke so decisively with the colonial past, and was led by people with impeccable nationalist credentials. The leaders of the North came from the resistance forces or returned from long-time exile. This does not mean that ex-collaborators were not employed by Pyongyang. Contrary to the current myth, they were, but only occasionally and on a much reduced scale than was the case in post–1945 Seoul.

Thus, the people who took power in Pyongyang in 1945–1948 were largely idealists. But they were also zealots who believed that they knew the Only True Path. For the sake of the future happiness of their people, they were ready to do away with any who were seen as obstacles to this glorious path. No dissent would be tolerated. Indeed, in 1946 North Korean students learned painfully that open rallies against the policies of the new regime would be treated much harsher that they were in the 1920s or 1930s. The rally participants faced not only expulsion from school, but near certain arrest followed by a long involuntarily trip to Siberia (the North Korean state had no penitentiary system at that time, so it had to rely on the Soviets' fraternal help). All resistance was quashed with an iron fist. The Pyongyang dreamers had few misgivings about this action, at least as long as they did not witness the violence directly. After all, the victims were "class enemies" and "reactionary elements."

Then the logic of the system made it clear that a concentration of power was necessary. Personal ambition also ensured that a struggle for domination developed at the apex of the pyramid. This in fact would appear to be normal: the top levels of any human hierarchy tend to be the nasty seat of intense rivalry, hypocrisy, and intrigue. The difference was that in the Stalinist system the losing side was not simply deprived of power: it was physically annihilated. With rare exceptions, the system did not provide an opportunity for an individual to leave politics peacefully, even when that person wished to do so. This made the power struggle even more brutal, and soon the former idealists were at one another's throats.

Kim Il Sung eventually became a master of this cruel game, even if he initially was dragged into it somewhat reluctantly, and perhaps even against his own will (there are some reports that he was not very willing to act as the nation's leader in 1946). Initially, he made sure that all factions united against the most vulnerable Southern group, which was destroyed in 1953–1955. Its most prominent members were tortured into delivering absurd "confessions" at a public trial, while the less prominent simply disappeared without a trace. Then the same fate befell all the other groups that potentially could challenge Kim's supremacy — and finally, in the late 1960s, even a number of Kim's own ex-guerrillas were sent to the prison camps, probably to demonstrate that nobody was invulnerable.

Does this mean that Kim Il Sung was an especially nasty and skillful manipulator? Perhaps, but only to a certain degree. In other Stalinist countries different groups won the domestic clashes, but the results were invariably the same: an almighty leader could only be replaced via a palace coup, and the vilified losers were almost always presented as traitors and spies. Such was the logic of the system. And the most tragic irony of this story is that this system was created not by cynical manipulators, but by sincere idealists.

PART 11

How Does the System Work?

Treated Like Mushrooms

FOR DECADES, NORTH KOREANS HAVE BEEN told that their country is a beacon to a world whose inhabitants are envious of the North Koreans' prosperity and success. This was a bold statement for a country which even in the best of times was seen by its fellow Communist regimes as poor and underdeveloped. To be believed, this propaganda had to be free of any competition, and thus the North Korean authorities eliminated all sources of alternative information. Few if any Communist countries were as efficient as North Korea in cutting their population off from unwanted and unauthorized knowledge about the world beyond the nation's boundaries.

Few North Koreans were ever allowed to leave their country. The only non-privileged group of people with overseas experience were the Siberian loggers who were sent to the wilderness of southern Siberia from the late 1960s onwards. However, this part of the world is not famous for its highly dense population, so their contacts with the locals were kept at a bare minimum, and the North Korean authorities saw to this.

All other groups of North Koreans who were allowed to travel overseas formed the upper crust of society and by definition were carefully chosen for their supposed political reliability. These privileged few were diplomats, crews of North Korean ships and planes, as well as a handful of people who were allowed to participate in international exchanges, largely of an academic nature. These people had a lot to lose, and they also knew that their families would pay a high price for any wrongdoing on their part, thus they seldom caused trouble. These were also the least likely to relate much about life overseas to their fellow countrymen beyond their similarly privileged colleagues.

190

There were students too, of course. In the mid–1950s a number of Korean students studied overseas, largely in the USSR. These individuals were carefully selected either as academically successful youngsters or from the children of high officials. However, this did not render them immune to the seductions of the revisionist worldview. Some North Korean students defected when, in 1957-1958, Pyongyang refused to follow the Soviet policy of liberalization which was at the time imposed on all Communist countries. In 1959-1960 all students were recalled, and no North Korean was allowed to study overseas in the subsequent decade.

Pyongyang began to re-send students in the mid–'70s, but this time on a very small scale, with just a couple of hundreds of North Koreans studying overseas at any given moment. The students were also carefully selected and constantly supervised.

In the first 15 years of North Korean history, North Koreans could buy foreign books — but of course, only those published in fraternal Communist countries and largely from the USSR. However, from about 1960 the situation changed. The former "brothers in communism" came to be seen as another source of ideological contamination. Indeed, the USSR, and countries of Eastern Europe especially, were outrageously liberal by the then Pyongyang standards.

Needless to say, today no access to the Internet is allowed. Perhaps North Korea remains unique in being the world's only country which has almost no Net users. Kim Jong Il himself is said to be an enthusiastic surfer, but outside the elite's top crust (perhaps a few dozen families), access to the Net is unheard of. The scholarly institutions have their own digital network which operates within the North but it has only limited connections to the Web. Moreover, this network can be accessed only from one's workplace. Only in late 2004 did some Western companies and missions in the North acquire access to the Internet — at a high price, of course, and the access was strictly limited to foreigners.

From around 1960, all foreign news publication, including that of the supposedly friendly countries, ceased to be sold freely. Major libraries subscribed to foreign newspapers, but they kept them in special departments. In these departments the subversive materials could be accessed only by trustworthy people who had obtained special permission from the secret police. All printed material from overseas was treated in this way. This system was actually patterned after the Soviets, but in the Soviet Union the approach was never so strict.

Of course, radio was a major headache for the North Korean leaders. They discovered an ingenious and probably unique way to keep radio politically safe: in the North, they sell radios without tuning. The radios are fixed on the frequency of the official Pyongyang broadcasting stations.

But citizens must be cut off from the past as well, for their own protection. George Orwell cannily realized that a truly thorough Stalinist dictatorship should control the past — or rather public perception and memory of the past. Hence all publications more than 5 or 10 years old are to be confined to the same special departments which are used for the subversive foreign material.

Even speeches of the Great Leader are no exception. They are rewritten from time to time to meet the demands of an ever-changing political situation. If the great man mentioned someone who subsequently became a victim of a purge, one can be sure that such references would be edited from later editions. But common folks are not supposed to know this: after all, the Leader and Party cannot change their opinions since they are always unfailingly correct in everything they say and do.

Foreign tourists who arrive in Pyongyang are isolated from the locals and kept under constant supervision. To play it safe, a tourist group or even an individual tourist is accompanied by two tour guides. The guides are tasked with controlling not only the tourists, but one another as well. Such tight supervision must be paid for by the tourists themselves, thus the North Korean operators charge exorbitant fees to their foreign partners. Few people agree to pay $1,300 for a week in Pyongyang, of course. However, a shortage of tourists does not seem to worry Pyongyang greatly. Despite all the talk about the development of international tourism, North Korean leaders obviously believe that the hard currency brought in by the tourists will not compensate for the political risks incurred in letting these dangerous individuals in!

Most of these policies were common in other Communist countries, but few if any of them went to such extremes.

The events of the recent decade, however, provide us with a good lesson. Repression and control cost money, and can be supported only by a robust economy. The hordes of supervisors and policemen devour resources, but do not produce anything (apart from political stability, of course) in return. Since the early 1990s, when the North Korean economy nose-dived, the above-mentioned measures have been somewhat relaxed. It seems that this relaxation is not a result of some policy, but simply a reflection of the government's inability to find the money to pay for these programs. Of course, this means that unwanted information is flowing in, and the common people are beginning to doubt that they live in a workers' paradise, as well as many other "facts" which their government continues to feed them....

Boot Camp, Forever!

WHEN I VISITED PYONGYANG IN THE 1980S, one of the most striking peculiarities of the city was the omnipresence of the military. People in uniform could be seen everywhere: marching across the street, working on construction sites, guarding anti-aircraft batteries and doing many other things, not necessarily associated with their military duties.

There were good reasons why the army was so visible. Despite its relatively small population, North Korea supports the world's fourth largest military. The Korean People's Army or KPA is estimated to be 1.2 million strong. Few if any other countries have ever reached such a level of mobilization in peacetime: suffice it to say that, in terms of numbers, North Korea's armed forces roughly equals that of India, the world's second most populous nation.

In order to maintain such a huge standing army, North Korea drafts its citizens into the military for an unusually long time: since the mid–'90s male soldiers have been required to serve until they are 30, with servicewomen remaining in uniform until they are 26. This means that the average North Korean male spends over a decade in uniform — for a male, 13 years as a draftee seems to be the norm.

The children of the North Korean elite have long been willing and able to dodge the draft. A major escape route is provided by North Korean laws which exempt college and university students from the draft, a practice which was incidentally copied from similar Soviet laws, also widely used by the Soviet elite. Students are supposed to attend obligatory reserve officer training courses which can be arduous, but they pale into insignificance when compared to the hardships of real armed service.

Nonetheless, people from less-privileged backgrounds are surprisingly eager to serve in the army — at least, such was the case until the mid–1990s. A large factor in this attraction was the intense propaganda which promotes the heroic image of the KPA. However, there are less idealistic motivations as well.

First of all, those who serve in the military are well-provisioned. Before the disastrous 1990s, the boys and girls in uniform were well-fed and had good warm clothes in winter. Those who remained on farms fared much worse. Military discipline was harsh, but North Koreans spent their entire life under harsh discipline anyway, so military discipline was neither new nor special for them, and was seen as a small price to pay for good rations and the chance of social advancement.

The soldiers' families back home enjoy preferential treatment from the local authorities as well. The military also provides forms of training which

Young soldiers in Pyongyang. Photograph by Christopher Morris.

would otherwise be beyond the reach of many. People leave the service with skills as drivers, radio operators and the like, and this liberates them from the dreaded routine of the hard life of a farmer or miner.

And last but not least, the KPA is a good place from which to enter the ruling Korean Workers' Party. Party membership renders a discharged soldier eligible for some low-level managerial work back home. In general, even people with relatively bad *sŏngbun* (the hereditary background which determines one's perceived political reliance and career) have some chance to improve their social standing through military service.

Thus, it comes as no surprise to find that people whose *sŏngbun* is exceptionally bad (descendants and close relatives of political prisoners, defectors to the South and the like) are not drafted at all. The same is true of the families of repatriates from Japan who returned to Korea in the 1960s. With few exceptions, they are seen as politically too unreliable to be trusted with weapons.

When teenagers are still attending high school, they are registered with the local Mobilization Depot, which is managed by the DPRK Ministry of Defense. They undergo some medical checks, and the security police check their family relations to ensure that no one with a suspicious relative is assigned to an elite unit. The grandson of a landlord's nephew will not be trusted to

The old military uniform is worn by many North Korean males. Photograph by Byeon Young-wook.

guard Pyongyang or patrol the DMZ while he and his peers can be used as a substitute for earth-moving equipment at some local construction site.

The KPA has an unusually high proportion of women, who form about 10% of all military personnel. Women are not normally drafted, but they are encouraged — and often positively pressed — to volunteer. In some cases they can be drafted as well, but this does not happen very often.

The girls are attracted by the same opportunities of education, promotion, party membership and, of course, by the ideological and material incentives as well. They are usually employed as radio operators, clerks, or medical personnel, but many of them staff the anti-aircraft batteries, or serve with the coastal defense units. Some anti-aircraft and anti-ship batteries have exclusively female crews.

Nowadays, however, it appears that military service is losing its once formidable lure. The new "army-first" policy may enrich some senior officers and boast the political standing of the top brass, but for the rank and file the recent economic disaster has brought serious deprivation. While the elite units are still well fed (after all, one of their tasks is to put down any food riot or army mutiny), common soldiers are often severely undernourished. And in the new, increasingly market-driven society the old *sŏngbun* system counts for much less.

The Health of Totalitarianism

GENERALLY SPEAKING, COMMUNISM WAS a costly and bloody failure. However, this does not mean that all Communist regimes failed in every area of state management. The world is too complicated to be reduced to a simplistic black-and-white analysis. Even the worst social systems have some features any normal person would appreciate, and even the best social system has its ugly side. Stalinism was no exception, including its North Korean Kim Il Sung incarnation.

One such field is health care, or at least basic health care. Communist propaganda sometimes exaggerated the successes in this area, but they were real nevertheless. Life expectancy in Communist countries was generally higher than it was in comparable capitalist societies. The same is true in regard to infant mortality, and many other key indicators of public health.

North Korea was no exception. Before the famine of the 1990s destroyed the country's infrastructure, life expectancy in the North was quite high. In the early 1990s it peaked at 70, which was not too different from life expectancy in the much more prosperous South. Now the World Health Organization estimates the figure to be 66 years, but this relatively low level results from the recent crisis which wreaked havoc on the health system.

Child mortality is now estimated at 45 per 1000 live births. This is slightly higher than China, but much lower than most developing countries. And, once again, this level has been measured after a profound social shock. In the early 1990s the infant mortality in the North was only marginally higher than in the South (21 vs. 25 per 1000 live births).

These achievements appear to be even more of a paradox if we take into account the serious underfunding of North Korean clinics, even in the best of times. Most of the hospitals occupy derelict buildings with small crowded rooms (a dozen inpatients in one room is the norm), and their equipment is roughly the same as Western doctors enjoyed in the 1950s, if not the 1930s.

The doctors certainly do not constitute a privileged or well-paid group in North Korean society. Unlike their pampered Western counterparts, medical professionals in the North are no different from average white-collar clerical staff in their social standing and remuneration. In the still-patriarchal North Korean society this leads to a drain of males away from the profession, and doctors are overwhelmingly female.

Access to drugs is also limited. Since modern drugs are seldom available in hospitals, antibiotics are one of the major items traded on the black market. Only a handful of special clinics for top government officials can afford to administer antibiotics on a regular basis.

Since this is the case, how can the North Koreans maintain such impressive standards of public health? The basic answer is, surprisingly, the ability of the government to control everyone with little concern for privacy. This is an essential feature of a police state, but it can also be very conducive to maintaining public health.

The entire population is subjected to regular health checks. The checks are simple — like, say, chest X-rays at most, but they help to locate health problems at an early stage. The checks are obligatory, and no North Korean can avoid an inspection, since the entire state machine sees to it (at least until the social disruption of the late 1990s). The same was the case with immunization. Sanitation and the water supply are also monitored carefully.

Even the low salaries of the doctors is not necessarily a bad thing. This allowed this rather poor state to support a large number of doctors — one doctor per 370 persons, roughly the same as in the U.S.! Medical services were free for decades, even if in recent years corruption has taken its toll such that now, in order to get treatment, one usually has to pay a doctor privately, and drugs are not free any longer.

The management of the health system follows the Soviet model, which was able to deliver good results despite persistent underfunding (at least by Western standards). Each small area, usually consisting of 100–200 households, has its own doctor who has treated the locals over many years. There is no freedom to choose your doctor: if you have a problem, you have to attend the person who is allocated to your area. With the ratio of patients to doctors so high, a medical professional is always nearby.

If things turn really nasty, the doctor will refer a patient to a local hospital, whence he can be referred to a better clinic if it is deemed necessary. The patient might even be sent to Pyongyang, to some specialized clinic dealing with a specific type of disease.

In the established Communist fashion, the top officials enjoy their own hospitals which are beyond the reach of lesser folk. The members of the Kim clan attend a clinic at the Longevity Institute (Mansumugang yonguso) while top cadres are treated in the luxurious and well-staffed Ponghwa and Namsan clinics.

Of course, there are serious problems with high-end medicine. Sophisticated surgery is available only in the exclusive hospitals for top bureaucrats, like the Ponghwa clinic in Pyongyang. The absence of ambulance services is another problem. Over the recent decade or so, drugs, which were never abundant, have become very scarce, and whatever the official instructions say, patients have to buy the necessary drugs themselves.

However, the majority of threats to life come not from complicated diseases but from seemingly minor ailments which can be easily treated if recognized early enough, and if there is a doctor nearby. And the North Korean health care system is proficient at doing just that.

The Party Game

LIKE ALL OTHER LENINIST STATES, the North Korean state machine is built around its ruling Leninist party. In North Korea this party is known as the Korean Workers' Party (KWP), but its structure and function are carbon copies of the Communist parties that once existed throughout the entire Soviet bloc.

The KWP is large, although no outsider knows exactly how large it is. The latest available figures are not recent: they date from 1980. In that year it was officially announced that the KWP had "some three million members." Since then, the number of KWP members has increased to approximately four million, but the exact figure is still one of the numerous carefully guarded North Korean state secrets.

Thus, in 1980, one out of six North Koreans (or one out of four adults) was a Party member. This 16% was among the highest proportions in the Communist bloc, where Party members usually comprised less than 7 to 8% of the entire population. To a large extent, this reflects a North Korean tradition: from the late 1940s Kim Il Sung wanted his party to be large!

Why do people become KWP members? Official ideology is quick to explain that they are driven by their burning desire to work and fight for the country and its Great Leader. Indeed, that is precisely what they are supposed to say in public. Perhaps some people are indeed motivated by sincere loyalty to the country and join the KWP. Once upon a time, in the 1940s and 1950s, such motivation was commonplace.

Nowadays, in most cases the actual reasons are different and the motivation is a little less lofty. A KWP membership card is necessary for career promotion: KWP membership is the necessary prerequisite for acquiring any managerial job in the DPRK. Even some of the more prestigious blue-collar jobs cannot normally be occupied by a person not in possession of the much-coveted membership card. I have also heard statements to the effect that one has to be a Party member to become a professional driver.

However, the common Western perception that all Party members are privileged is wrong. Becoming a Party member makes one *eligible* for but not inexorably *entitled* to privileges. But then again, non-members are ineligible for any of these privileges!

In theory, every North Korean citizen is allowed to join the KWP. He or she needs to produce letters of recommendation from two KWP members who will be then held responsible for his or her behavior (at least to some extent). The aspiring member's candidacy is then discussed by the would-be fellow members of the KWP cell to which the application is relevant. After formal approval the new member is placed on probation for a period, and then he or she subsequently receives a membership card, a card that must be guarded with the utmost care.

In practice, a major role is played by the admission quotas, which are distributed from above. The Party secretary and his local cronies select the candidates to fill the quota and few refuse to join if approached. A person's origin and family connections, the notorious North Korean *sŏngbun*, are also taken into account.

The admission quotas are quite generous in the armed forces, so a number of North Koreans try to use their service period in order to enter the KWP and then return to civilian life with a better chance of success. In factories, and especially government agencies, the quotas are much more restrictive, and there are reports of people bribing officials to be allowed to join the KWP.

The authorities expect that KWP members will be tractable and reliable. Indeed, they must endure even more meetings and indoctrination sessions than the average person. They can also be criticized for transgressions which are regarded as trivial by the normal North Korean standards.

And Party members are subject to their own system of punishment. A "warning" or "severe warning" stamp in their membership files adversely influences their career in perpetuity — unless these marks are overridden (an act which also occurs quite often, thankfully).

The worst punishment is expulsion from the KWP. This is a rare event, and normally it comes as, so to speak, "part of the package" following one's arrest and sentencing. Criminal conviction for political or common offenses always means expulsion from the Party: no convicted criminal is allowed to remain a KWP member. After release from jail, one is also not normally welcomed back into the Party.

Can these four million people be counted as devoted supporters of the regime like both Pyongyang's friends and foes often assert? I am not so sure. Some of them are truly loyal to Kim Jong Il out of conviction. However, for the vast majority, membership is a simple opportunistic gesture and it hardly bears much relevance to their actual world view.

Belt-Tightening

ONCE UPON A TIME, STALIN COLORFULLY described the role of trade unions, student bodies, and other associations which would be called NGOs (non-government organizations) in the modern West. He said that they would serve as the "transmission belts" of a Communist society. The Communist Party was its main and, indeed, sole engine, while all the NGOs had to transmit the party energy to the populace (later, Chairman Mao would describe the populace as "cogs in a wheel").

Such an approach was typical of all Communist societies, but in different places and different times it was pursued with varying intensity. As usual, North Korea went to extremes in following the teachings of Comrade Stalin and Chairman Mao. Every adult North Korean must belong to some organization and take part in its activity. This is a major difference from other Communist countries, where the major burden of meetings, indoctrination sessions, and unpaid "voluntary" work fell on the shoulders of the Party members and, to a lesser extent, the members of the Party's youth organization. In Korea, the system of obligatory (and very time-consuming) meetings, campaigns, and similar activities reach everybody. In the North Korean parlance, this is known as "organizational life" or *chojik saenghwal*.

The members of the Korean Workers' Party form a sort of potential elite, even if the ordinary Party members (that is, at least 90% of the total) hardly enjoy much privilege at all. The party members have to attend their own special indoctrination and study sessions, and they also take part in many activities organized by their work unit.

All young people aged between 14 and 30 are members of the KWP's youth organization, known as the Kim Il Sung Socialist Youth Union (Party Youth). Some of them join the "adult" Party before they turn 30, and thus relinquish their Youth Union membership. For people older than 30, "organizational life" is managed by the Federation of Trade Unions if they work in industry, or by the Federation of Farmers if they work in agriculture.

Even housewives, quite numerous in the North, are not left without proper ideological guidance. They are, by definition, members of the Women's Union, and have to attend meetings arranged by the Union's neighborhood committees.

These five bodies — the Korean Workers' Party, Party Youth, the Federation of Trade Unions, the Federation of Farmers, and the Women's Union — form the five major "transmission belts" which ensure that the entire population moves in accordance with the leaders' will.

The major content of the "organizational life" is endless meetings. In the

1970s, during the worst (or best?) period of relative economic stability and tight political control, such meetings could occupy several hours every day. At the meetings the participants would listen to long lectures on the Kims' *Juche* theory, and sometimes take part in "discussions" where one has to reproduce memorized slogans and quotations from the Leaders. Meetings of mutual criticism were held regularly and in them the members of the same work unit had to denounce their co-workers' wrongdoings and deliver public repentances for their own.

The "organizations" are also responsible for supplying people for mobilization campaigns, for planting and harvesting rice, or for doing unpaid work on construction sites.

The "transmission belts" ensure that a large part of the individual's spare time is spent with members of his or her work unit. Some of these activities are quite innocent, like group excursions to the mountains, or *t'aegwondo* lessons. Others are less attractive, like obligatory participation in government-sponsored rallies. The government promotes such activities for the sake of better social cohesion, but also because individualism is seen as dangerous and an essentially wicked phenomenon which should be discouraged.

Admittedly, the level of pressure varies greatly between different organizations. The toughest job is to be a party member. Even today this can mean countless hours spent in all kinds of meetings and mobilizations. The Party Youth have it somewhat easier, while the trade unions and farmers' unions are relatively relaxed bodies. The women's union is the least stringent of all: housewives and old retired ladies are thankfully spared some of the pressures which other people have come to consider unavoidable.

However, one must not believe that all North Koreans are great admirers of this "organizational life." While it may appear that the Northerners are indeed less individualistic than their South Korean brethren, a defector nonetheless recently remarked: "All the best times in my life were when I was able to escape the 'organizational life,' and spend some time with my friends or family."

Belonging

THE OFFICIAL NORTH KOREAN IDEOLOGY of *Juche* insists that every human being has two identities — one biological and the other political. The biological identity is determined by one's parents while the far more important political identity is provided by the Party and the Great or Dear Leader who, in their infinite wisdom, assign every "good" member of society a political task.

More organization This means that virtually all North Koreans are required to be members of some political organization. For those who are still too young, ideological leadership is provided by two closely connected bodies — the Children's Union and the Youth Union (Party Youth).

The Youth Union was founded in January 1946, a carbon copy of its Soviet counterpart, the Komsomol or Party Youth. Originally known as the "Democratic Youth Union," the body was renamed the Socialist Workers' Youth Union in 1964. Later, in 1996, it acquired its present name — the Kim Il Sung Socialist Youth Union.

Once upon a time, in the late 1940s, membership of the Youth Union was both a privilege and a duty. Nowadays it is to all intents and purposes compulsory, and embraces all young North Koreans: in the mid–1990s, the Youth Union had approximately five million members.

North Koreans are allowed to join the Youth Union in middle school when they reach 14, but such early membership is open only to a handful of the best students whose admission is approved by the school administration. Later, when the students are 15 years of age, more are allowed to join. For even older students membership is obligatory. Thus by graduation, practically all students are members. The North Korean bureaucracy acts on the assumption that every Korean between 16 and 30 is a Union member, thus nobody is allowed to dodge membership.

North Koreans remain Youth Union members until they reach thirty. *Not very young* However, there is no age limit for the Union's bureaucrats, most of whom are far from youthful! Its current First Secretary, Kim Kyŏng-ho, was born in 1943 — not exactly a young man and, perhaps, the world's oldest chairperson of a youth organization.

Structurally, the Youth Union generally follows the KWP. It is governed by its own Central Committee and boasts a full-blown hierarchy of regional committees, down to the school, factory or battalion level. All students in the same class, soldiers of the same company or young workers in the same department belong to a particular Union cell.

The Youth Union committees are technically elected, but there is only one pre-selected candidate for each position, so for all practical purposes the committees and their heads are appointed. One of the Union's major tasks is to act as a training ground for aspiring officials. A majority of younger North Korean administrators began their careers in the Youth Union.

For the rank and file, obligatory membership in the Youth Union means additional — and often quite onerous — duties. Members are required to attend regular meetings which might be held several times a week. In the not-so-distant past, these meetings were held almost daily. Among other things, the Youth Union cells are also charged with conducting the infamous "mutual criticism meetings." All members of a cell must be present and they spend hours confessing their own transgressions — and reporting on the transgressions of their fellow members.

There are less grim aspects to the Union's activities as well. The Youth Union committee is responsible for overseeing the members' leisure time, so they organize outings and trips, taking their members to concerts and many other kinds of youthful activities. And what about younger North Koreans? These are not left without proper spiritual guidance either. All North Korean children are members of some political organization which is tasked with infusing them with a "revolutionary spirit" and, of course, a "love of the Great Leader." This body is the so-called *Sonyŏndan* or Children's Union. It was founded in June 1946 and from the mid–1950s onwards, membership has been virtually obligatory for students between the ages of nine and thirteen. However, to be one of the first *Sonyŏndan* members in one's class is a great honor, and children vie to be among the chosen few.

Sonyŏndan was closely modeled on its Soviet counterpart, once known as the Young Pioneers. The main *Sonyŏndan* rituals also closely follow the Soviet pattern, although the North Koreans will not admit to this, since any foreign influence is anathema to this staunchly nationalist regime. But neither were the Soviets themselves original: back in the 1920s the founders of the Soviet Young Pioneers borrowed heavily from the Boy Scouts — and they too were most reluctant to admit it!

The highest *Sonyŏndan* unit is at the school level. *Sonyŏndan* extensively employs military terms: the school organization comprises "detachments" which, in turn, consist of "groups." Normally, each class forms a "detachment," while a "group" consists of some five to ten members. Members of the *Sonyŏndan* wear special uniforms and their main symbol is a triangular red necktie. Traditionally, this necktie is considered to be the symbol of the eternal unity between the Korean Workers' Party, the *Saroch'ŏng* or Party Youth and the *Sonyŏndan*, while in reality, it is an article also borrowed from the Soviet Young Pioneers. Nor were the Young Pioneers the inventors of the necktie — back in the 1920s, once again, they simply made good use of the Boy Scouts' necktie!

Sonyŏndan is a deliberately ritualistic organization which skillfully exploits children's love of ritual, oaths, and parades. The *Sonyŏndan* induction ceremony is an especially important event in North Korean school life. This solemn ritual is awaited with great excitement and anticipation. The ceremony is normally held in some public place, with the participation of teachers, parents and local officials. A party functionary reads the Solemn Oath, which is repeated by the children, then parents and teachers approach the children and present them with red neckties.

Needless to say, the Solemn Oath includes pledges of loyalty to the country, the Party and, naturally, to Kim Il Sung. More recently, Kim Jong Il has been added to this hallowed list as well. The *Sonyŏndan* motto is "Be prepared!" and its members exchange a special greeting which vaguely resembles a military salute (sound familiar to any former Boy Scouts out there?).

And what about the everyday activities of the *Sonyŏndan*? *Sonyŏndan* members perform many public services such as collecting old iron and paper for recycling (not out of environmental concerns, a concept which is generally alien to North Korea, but in order to provide industry with more raw materials), cleaning streets and yards annexed to their schools, raising rabbits for meat and fur and involving their members in military training of all kinds.

Nor does *Sonyŏndan* activity cease during vacations. Vacation trips are not affordable to North Korean families, thus children have to spend their summer in the vicinity of their schools. *Sonyŏndan* also runs its own summer camps where children spend some time, typically a week. The camps are run by the local educational institutions with a special emphasis on *Sonyŏndan* activities.

Of course, *Sonyŏndan* is heavily militarized, so military exercises and games constitute a large part of its members' activity. Apart from shooting, grenade throwing and trench-digging, the children are taught how to act in an emergency, how to find and cook food in a forest, how to treat wounds and provide urgent medical assistance. And, of course, they are fed with heavy doses of stories about young heroes who died fighting the treacherous Japs, wolf-young Yankees and other eternal enemies of the Korean nation.

So does this mean that North Koreans are brainwashed from childhood? Yes and no. The *Sonyŏndan*, like other similar bodies, goes to great lengths to ensure that the next generation of North Koreans will consist of "steel soldiers" ever loyal to the "Great Leader." However, no amount of indoctrination can make a human being oblivious to the realities of life. Therefore, it is very likely that in a few decades, the former *Sonyŏndan* members will remember not the political content of their upbringing, but those wonderful evenings they once spent together in the summer camps....

North Korea's Missionary Position

NORTH KOREAN DEFECTORS TO SOUTH KOREA were recently asked about the fate of those escapees who were apprehended in China and sent back for interrogation to North Korea. Their treatment is harsh but they are not necessarily doomed. If an arrested escapee does not make any dangerous confessions while being subjected to relatively mild beatings, he or she is likely to be set free very quickly. While not very nice, this is still a vast improvement over the situation that existed a few decades ago. This author asked, "What do interrogators see as dangerous activities?" and the answers were virtually identical across the board: "Contacting missionaries and bringing religious literature into North Korea."

For three decades North Korea and Albania were unique in being countries without any organized religious worship and without a single temple or church of any religion. But this is changing fast — and the Pyongyang authorities obviously worry that they do not have complete control over the fast-developing new religious environment. The central authorities are losing control as cracks appear in the country's "Stalinist" ideology.

Once upon a time, Christianity played an important role in North Korea's politics. Indeed, few people are now aware that in the colonial era, between 1910 and 1945, the present North Korea was a stronghold of Korean Protestantism. Protestant missionaries came to Korea in the 1880s and achieved remarkable success in conversions. By the early 20th century, Koreans had come to associate Protestantism with modernity and progress, and many early Korean modernizers came from Protestant families. Although Christians composed just 1–2% of the population, they were overrepresented among the intellectuals and professionals. It helped that Korea was colonized by a non–Christian nation, Japan, so that in Korea the teachings of Jesus avoided those associations with colonialism which proved to be so damaging in many other parts of Asia.

There was a time when relations between early Korean Communism and Christianity were much closer than either side is willing to admit nowadays. Kim Il Sung himself was born into a family of prominent Protestant activists. His father graduated from a Protestant school and was an active supporter of the local missions, and his mother was the daughter of a prominent Protestant activist. This was fairly typical: it seems that a majority of early Korean Communists had Christian family backgrounds, even though Christians were few and far between in the general populace.

By the early 1940s Pyongyang was by far the most Protestant of all major cities in Korea, with some 25–30% of its adult population being churchgoing Christians. In missionary circles this earned the city the nickname "The Jerusalem of the East."

Thus, throughout the first years of North Korean history, the nascent Communist government had to reckon with the power of the Christian community. Even Kim Il Sung's own family connections with the Protestants was able to be put to a good use. A major role in the North Korean politics of the 1940s and 1950s was played by Kang Ryang-uk, a Protestant minister who also happened to be a relative of Kim's mother. He even became the target of an assassination attempt by rightist agents, specially dispatched from the South.

Nonetheless, left-wing Christianity was not a success in North Korea. Most Protestant preachers and activists were enemies of the new regime. There were a number of reasons for this. Most pastors came from affluent families and were not happy about the redistribution of wealth during the land reforms of 1946 and the subsequent nationalization of industry. In addition, many Christians had personal connections with the West and admired the United States as a beacon of democracy, and thus were alienated by the regime's intense anti–American propaganda. The increasingly harsh and repressive policies of the new government did not help either.

Thus in 1946–50, Protestants formed one of the major groups of refugees who moved to the South. When the Korean War began, the remaining Protestants often helped the advancing American and South Korean troops. Such incidents once again demonstrated to the Pyongyang leaders what they believed anyway: that Christians were politically unreliable.

In the 1950s anti–Protestant propaganda reached fever pitch. All kinds of religious worship were banned, but Protestantism was particularly singled out as a "wicked teaching of the US imperialists." All churches were closed by the mid–1950s, and those Protestant leaders who were unlucky, naive or foolish enough to stay in the North after the Korean War, were purged in the late 1950s as "American spies." Even those who renounced their faith, while doing so usually saved their lives, were not completely off the hook: under North Korea's elaborate system of hereditary groups, such people became members of "hostile group No. 37" and remained branded until the end of their days.

Meanwhile, the official media bombarded North Koreans with ranting anti–Protestant propaganda. The educational efforts of the early missionaries were explained as part of their scheme to pave the road for the long-planned U.S. invasion. Pastors and activists were portrayed as spies and saboteurs on the payroll of the U.S. Central Intelligence Agency, or as sadists who killed innocent and naive Koreans with their own hands.

Works of fiction depicted missionaries killing innocent Korean children in their "clinics" in order to sell their blood, eyes or body parts, which was most improbable in the era before body-parts transplantation, but made good propaganda anyway. The "regeneration" of the Korean Christian was another favorite topic of North Korean fiction of the late 1950s. The protagonist of such stories would be initially misled by scheming missionaries and their willful collaborators and foolishly become a Christian, but then some incident or bitter personal experience would help him or her discover the depraved nature of Christian teaching. Of course, he or she would then reject this "imperialist ideological poison" and lead others to eventual enlightenment.

Even nowadays, in Sinch'on Museum, a propaganda center dealing with largely invented U.S. atrocities, one can see a collage of photos of all the prominent American missionaries active in Korea around 1900, accompanied by the caption: "The American missionaries who crawled into Korea, hiding their daggers in their clothing."

By the mid-1950s, not a single church was left functioning. As usual, the Korean Stalinists outdid Stalin himself: even in the worst days of Josef Stalin's rule, a handful of churches remained open in Soviet cities, and some priests avoided the gulag, more often than not through cooperation with Stalin's secret police.

Some North Korean believers continued to worship in secret. The precise scale of the North Korean "catacomb church" is likely to remain unknown forever. Serious research is made impossible by the secrecy of the church, and in the post-unification future, the picture is likely to be distorted by the exaggerations and myth-making to which religious organizations are often so prone. A lot of stories of martyrdom are certain to emerge in the post-unification Korea, and some of them are certain to be true, but none of these stories should be taken at face value without careful checking. Nonetheless, the existence of the Protestant underground is beyond doubt.

In the early 1970s the North Korean approach to religion was softened, but this liberalization was initially designed for export only. By the 1970s, Pyongyang had given up its earlier hopes of a Communist revolution in the South. Long and persistent efforts would be needed to bring the "Seoul puppets" down, and cooperation with "progressive religious forces" in the South would be useful.

Thus some Christian associations had to be created under the auspices of the North Korean government, to be put to good use as propaganda organizations. In 1974, the Korean Christian Association reappeared on the political scene. This association was established in 1946 to steer religious activity in the right direction, but in 1960 it was disbanded. Of course, the restoration of the KCA did not mean much for the few surviving underground Christians. Its sole task was to influence South Korean religious circles and provide a convenient outlet for dealing with them. Indeed, the KCA conducted a number of remarkably successful propaganda exercises which targeted credulous Southern lefties.

The real turning point came in 1988 when the first North Korean church was opened in Pyongyang. This was accomplished under pressure from overseas religious circles, but was significant nonetheless. For the first time in 30 years the North Korean authorities admitted that there was some religious activity in the land of *Juche*. However, many inhabitants of Pyongyang were somewhat surprised to see how a building with Christian crosses, long seen as symbols of dark imperialist designs, was constructed in the middle of the North Korean capital.

Nowadays, North Korea has two Protestant churches with 150 alleged believers. This figure is suspect, however; one should not be surprised to learn eventually that these people were appointed to be "believers" after careful selection by the party and screening by secret police. After all, their major role is to be props during the frequent visits by foreign delegations. However, some people who visited the church expressed the opinion that it is rather genuine if strictly controlled. Well, we are unlikely to know for sure until after collapse of the North Korean system.

The existence of two churches is hardly a sign of revival in a country that once boasted 3,000 churches and some 250,000 believers. Nonetheless, it could be a sign of liberalization. North Korea has also opened a Catholic church, also located in Pyongyang.

Recently, Pyongyang suggested opening an Orthodox church as well. The hitherto unknown "Orthodox Committee of the DPRK" contacted Russian church leaders — and no one was surprised at the fact that nothing had been heard of North Korean Orthodox believers for six decades. Even in 1945 they scarcely numbered more than a few hundred. The Dear Leader, Kim Jong Il, assured a Russian official who expressed some doubts in this regard: "Do not worry, we'll find believers!" No doubt they will — the North Korean "competent agencies" know just how this can be done.

However, there are signs of a genuine Christian revival in North Korea. From the mid–1990s an increasing number of South Korean missionaries have been traveling to northeastern China, adjacent to the almost uncontrolled border with the DPRK. These missionaries are overwhelmingly Protestant, of various denominations. They preach among the refugees, and their mission is remarkably successful. This is understandable: Christian organizations are among the few organizations that take note of the refugees and work hard to help them — much to the annoyance of the North Korean authorities. Newly converted North Koreans often go back to their country, taking Bibles and religious literature with them. The North Korean authorities take the problem very seriously. As mentioned above, defectors extradited from China and then interrogated by North Korean political police are always asked whether they have been in contact with Christian missionaries.

There are reports of the growing Christian underground. Alas, these reports cannot be verified. Still, it seems that some sort of catacomb church is fast developing in North Korea — a development that has nothing to do with the elaborate performances staged by the authorities in the officially approved churches.

It is remarkable how successful Protestantism is among Northern defectors who are currently living in South Korea. Many of them converted in the first months of their sojourn. Once again, this can be partially explained by the active involvement of right-wing Christians with the refugee community while the secular Left and South Korean society in general are quite indifferent if not hostile to these people. Still, it is also clear that North Koreans are willing to embrace religion with exceptional zeal.

Perhaps this is a sign of things to come, and Pyongyang is on the verge of regaining its old title of "The Jerusalem of the East." The collapse of Kim Jong Il's rule someday is likely to leave a serious ideological and spiritual vacuum, which can be easily filled by Christianity. Nor do the associations between Christianity and South Korean prosperity go unnoticed — along with the right-wing sympathies of mainstream Korean Christians. The Left is unlikely to be popular in a post–Kim North Korea for at least a generation. And it seems likely that in many cases the newly emerging North Korean Protestantism will take some rather extreme forms.

Honoring the Order of Medals

ALL STATES DECORATE THEIR CITIZENS for certain exceptional acts of bravery and courage — and North Korea is no exception. If anything, its system of orders is especially elaborate when compared to that of most other countries.

For the author, a former Soviet citizen, the North Korean system of decorations appears quite familiar. Indeed, it has much in common with the Soviet system. Such was the situation in most other Communist countries as well. However, the North Koreans never admit this fact: all kinds of foreign influences are taboo for a regime which tries to present itself as the embodiment of the "true" national spirit.

Like the former Soviet Union, North Korea has a three-tier system of decoration. On the top are two special honorary titles while the second level includes several "Orders" and lastly, there is a multitude of various "medals" for the least distinguished.

The highest of all decorations is the honorary title of "Hero of the DPRK." This honor was first introduced in 1950 and once again was a copy of the Soviet title which had been introduced in 1934. Every recipient of this title is also automatically decorated with the Order of the State Banner. The bearers of the title are also issued with a special "Gold Star" medal.

The other top honorary title is that of "Labor Hero of the DPRK." This title, awarded for exploits in labor, rather than the military, is less prestigious than the "Hero of the DPRK" but still well above all other regular decorations. Its recipients are also issued with a special medal.

Most of the "Heroes" received their titles during the Korean War. In later decades the title was awarded for acts of especial bravery — quite often, posthumously. For example, in the 1970s the title was posthumously awarded to a secret police officer. And what was his heroic act, I hear you ask? He was supervising some underground construction work when things went terribly wrong — the workers realized that an explosive device would detonate prematurely. However, the brave officer did not run away: he used his own body to cover the sacral letters of Kim Il Sung's name which had just been affixed to the wall. He was killed in the ensuing explosion.

In the USSR the "Gold Star" of a "Hero," while formally considered a mere "medal," was above all "orders," and being awarded a "Hero" also meant automatic decoration with the Order of Lenin, the highest in the USSR. In North Korea the situation is different, and the Kim Il Sung Order, which is used only in exceptional circumstances, is considered superior to the title of "Hero."

The next level of state decorations consists of the "orders" or *hunjang*. For a long time the Order of the State Banner was the highest decoration in the land. First introduced in October 1948, the order has three degrees. In March 1972 the newly introduced Order of Kim Il Sung became the top decoration in the North. In addition to this, North Korea also has two other government decorations — the Order of Labor Achievements, and the Order of the Banner of the Three Revolutions. These are usually awarded to people who have distinguished themselves in "revolution and construction" — that is, in peacetime labor.

Below the regular orders there are many "medals." Some of these are issued to commemorate particular events — like, say, a major military campaign — and are awarded to people who distinguish themselves on such occasions. Others are simply "minor orders," less prestigious than the above-mentioned categories.

The North Korean state has been quite generous with decorations. Over the last half century, it has given away some six million orders — excluding medals. Therefore, a high-level bureaucrat or the army's top brass can easily sport a dozen different orders. This makes for a rather peculiar picture, since North Korean orders tend to be quite large in size. The suit of such an official is somewhat akin to medieval armor, ablaze with stars both large and small. Most North Korean orders take the shape of a star.

The North Korean system of state decorations has another peculiarity which was also derived from the USSR. Schools, factories and military units, even cities, can also be decorated with an order. For example, in March 1998, the editorial board of the *Korean Annual* was decorated with the Order of the State Banner, First Degree!

The orders entitle their bearers to a number of privileges. A person who has been decorated with the Order of the State Banner, First Degree, for example, is entitled to free public transport. He or she is also given a monthly subsidy. Nowadays, in the era of runaway inflation, this does not mean much, but until the early 1990s such subsidies were significant, amounting to some 15% of the average salary. And, last but not least, such a person is eligible for an early retirement: men can retire at 55, and women at 50.

Absurd system of elevation& ennobling.

PART 12

Schools

Schools Both Great and Small

FROM ITS INCEPTION, THE NORTH KOREAN state has been very serious about education. Indeed, education is one of the few fields where Pyongyang's achievements have been genuinely impressive. Despite the sorry state of the country's economy, North Korea has provided basic education to all its citizens, and its universities — while seriously lagging behind the world standard — are nonetheless doing extraordinarily well for a country with a per capita GNP similar to that of Mozambique.

The reason is simple: since the late 1940s, the North Korean state has invested heavily in education. This was influenced by at least three different sets of factors. First, an unusual reverence for education has been a part of Korean culture for a long time. Second, Communism inherited from the European Enlightenment the strong belief in the redeeming power of education. As a rule, all Communist countries have boasted much better-educated populations than non–Communist nations of roughly similar economic strengths. Third, Communist countries were quick to recognize that an educated population was a necessary precondition for military advancement.

Nowadays, there are some 300 colleges and universities in North Korea. The DPRK inherited from the old Soviet Union a clear distinction between universities (*chonghap taehak* in Korean) and colleges (*taehak*). The universities train scientists and scholars, experts in basic knowledge, while colleges were supposed to educate more practice-oriented specialists — engineers, interpreters, agronomists, schoolteachers and so on. The number of colleges far outstrips that of universities — and are, normally, much less prestigious.

For decades, North Korea had only one university, the Kim Il Sung Uni-

212

In a few years they will join the Children's Union. Photograph by Byeon Young-wook.

versity in Pyongyang. This university is even depicted on the 5-*won* bank note, a bank note which is entirely dedicated to the theme of education. The university was founded in 1946 and still remains the most prestigious school in the DPRK. In the late 1980s, the number of Universities increased to three. Kim Ch'aek Technological College in Pyongyang became the Kim Ch'aek Technological University and Kaesŏng Technological College was upgraded to Sŏnggyungwan University.

Colleges are far more numerous. Some of them rival and even surpass the universities in popularity. For example, the Foreign Languages College and the College of International Relations are equal in prestige to the most popular departments of the Kim Il Sung University. Their reputation is driven by pragmatic considerations: their graduates become diplomats or interpreters, who are stationed overseas or deal with foreigners inside Korea. Such people are likely to have access to foreign currency and consumption goods which are symbols of luxury and worldly success in the present-day DPRK.

However, a majority of the colleges are situated far lower on the prestige ladder. As a rule, every provincial capital has a Pedagogical College which trains teachers for middle and high schools, as well as a medical college for would-be doctors.

Another peculiarity is a number of "factory colleges" which are maintained

Public performances, often attended by the "foreign guests," require months of hard training. Photograph by Byeon Young-wook.

So is that a good thing?

by large industrial enterprises to train their engineers and skilled technicians. The studies in such schools are closely connected with on-the-job training, and students spend a large part of their time on the factory floor as workers. In most economies these graduates would be described as technicians rather than engineers, but this is not the case in North Korea.

Indeed, the heavy emphasis on technological training which has always been a mark of the Communist education system, has been taken to extremes in the DPRK. This has been done deliberately and Kim Il Sung himself has made several remarks to this effect. More than 90% of all students are trained in science and technology while the humanities are implicitly seen as almost useless niceties.

The period of study in the North Korean schools varies from four to six years. In most colleges students study four years, while in the universities it varies from four and a half to six or even seven years. Recently the study period was shortened, but it still represents a substantial commitment by any student planning to enter the hallowed halls of Northern learning.

The Studied Life

KOREANS ARE SERIOUS ABOUT COLLEGE-LEVEL education. In the South, graduation from a top-level university means that one's future career is more or
less guaranteed. In the North, graduation is somewhat less important — but
important nonetheless.

After graduation from secondary school, a young North Korean may either
seek employment or continue education at a college or university. However,
it is not a matter of making a simple choice. First of all, North Koreans are not
allowed to leave their counties of residence without a permit issued by local
police. And, unlike the South, only a minority of high school graduates are
allowed to compete for places at the nation's best universities.

In the North, the processing of prospective university students consists
of two separate stages. A high school graduate must first receive the approval
of his or her local Board of Education. This Board recommends only a small
proportion of applicants (about 20%) to continue on to further college studies. Others usually take up manual work or, if they are males, go into the armed
forces, but they have the right to reapply for recommendation later.

From 1980 onwards, permission to sit college entrance exams was granted
according to the results of a special test, administered annually in secondary
schools — much like it is done in the South or, for that matter, in China. The
subjects examined are mathematics, physics, chemistry, foreign languages and,
of course, the "revolutionary history of the Great Leader."

So, the lucky 20% or so go to don the students' uniform — in the North,
students are required to wear uniform when attending classes (and many wear
it outside the school as well).

College and university students are also required to stay in their dormitories unless they reside in the city which hosts their institution. Indeed, in
the past the college administration often encouraged students to live in the
dormitories even when their parents' house was very close by, but this is not
the case any more. Students seldom rent rooms in private houses: until recently
this was impossible, and still remains quite unusual. The Northern communal
lifestyle is encouraged as a part of the "nurturing of the collective spirit" and,
indeed, it helps to foster strong and lasting bonds between the students.

Their accommodation is hardly luxurious — but still not bad by North
Korean standards. Usually four to eight students share a room in a good school
while in less well-provided colleges, dorms with 15–20 students in one room
are not unusual.

The students eat in the dormitory canteen. Even in better times, before
the crisis of the 1990s, the food was moderate — essentially, rice or corn gruel

and *kimch'i*, with meat or even fish almost unheard of. The dormitory accommodation is free, and the government also provides college students with a free uniform and textbooks, as well as with a small stipend.

Until the early 1990s this assistance was sufficient to support a simple life. However, the recent crisis has wiped a great deal of value from the North Korean currency, and many students have begun to look for supplementary income. However, the North Korean economy does not provide many venues for readily available, appropriate, and reasonably paid part-time work. Thus one cannot really apply to the North Korean students the South Korean saying which states a student's life should consist of "three things —*arbeit* (a part-time job), romance and study."

The romance part is a little complicated. In the 1960s and 1970s, the North Korean authorities preached a very restrictive approach to relations between the sexes. Not only was sex outside marriage outlawed, but even platonic relations between male and female students were condemned as distractions from the glorious task of socialist construction. If couples were caught together — even engaged in innocent talk — they risked the humiliation of a "public criticism session" or even expulsion from their college.

This is still the case, but the ideological controllers seem to be willing to turn a blind eye to whatever happens between couples in private — as long as appearances are kept up.

These rules appear to be even more demanding if one takes into account that North Korean college students are no teenagers. Most male students come to schools after their military service, which takes over 10 years, and they are in their late 20s or early 30s.

However, in the mid–1980s the situation began to change. The government ideologists suddenly discovered that love was not necessarily incompatible with "revolution and construction." Love was once more mentioned in North Korean movies and fiction. However, there was one important caveat: love is supposed to remain platonic until formal marriage takes place — much in accordance with the Confucian tradition. But is this really the case? Not always....

There are other restrictions. Pyongyang does not have many places suitable for dating, and public opinion is still opposed to such a decadent habit. Thus students have to be careful, and — as is the case in patriarchal societies — women face a much greater risk even if the relationship is completely platonic. Students were once completely forbidden to marry. However, as early as the 1980s this ban was quietly disregarded by older male students who entered college after their military service and hence were in their late 20s. The marriage of such a student is seen as a transgression, but it does not result in his automatic expulsion from school.

Apart from the near-ban on sex and marriage, there are other bans North Korean students must take into account. Drinking within colleges is forbidden, completely and unconditionally. If a student is seen drunk in public, he or she is almost certain to be expelled from school, and will have little chance of landing a decent job. In theory, students are not supposed to drink alcohol at all. In practice, they do so in the security of their own — or their friends' — private houses. Smoking is a serious transgression as well.

And what about the studies, the third component of the ideal student life? Generally speaking the North Korean college students work harder than their South Korean counterparts. To a large extent this is determined by differences in culture: in the South, entering a university requires tremendous effort, but the years of college life are usually seen as a time of well-deserved relaxation. By the standards of most Western countries, South Korean professors are singularly undemanding, and students do not spend much time hunched over textbooks. But in the North the assumptions are different.

Vacations are short: North Korean students study for 35 weeks per year. On average they take 30–35 hours of classes a week — once again, more than their South Korean counterparts. Finally, the period of study in North Korean colleges is often longer — up to six years in some cases.

However, there are two major obstacles the North Korean students have to overcome on their path to wisdom. First, a large part of the classes (some 25% of all teaching time) is spent — or should we say wasted? — on political indoctrination. Furthermore, additional periods in spring and autumn are spent on obligatory "labor mobilizations," when students are dispatched to work in the countryside. The first such mobilization starts in early May and lasts until late June: students are required to plant rice or maize seedlings. The second mobilization is shorter: throughout September students participate in the harvest together with the farmers.

The second problem is the shortage of equipment, materials, and books, which also impairs teaching efficiency. Nonetheless, one has to admit that the overall standards of North Korean education are quite good for a country with an economy in such a sorry state.

The students sit exams at the end of each semester. The marking system follows the Soviet prototype and is based on only four marks: "5" (very good), "4" (good), "3" (pass) and "2" (fail). The unsuccessful students have one semester to re-sit the failed examination — and, if they are lucky, get a better mark.

College life is managed by the local committee of the Kimilsungist Communist Youth Union. This committee can be seen as a rough equivalent of the Students' Committee which is so influential in the South Korean universities — but with two important differences. First, the "election" of the

Committee members and its chairman are a pure formality. There is always only one candidate per seat, and this candidate is always elected regardless of any other considerations. These persons are pre-selected by the college administration and Party. Second, the Committee is not engaged in any independent activity, but remains a proverbial "driving belt" that provides the regime with an additional channel of influence over the student "masses."

This does not mean that North Korean students are wholehearted supporters of the regime, even if they avoid discussion of political subjects as too dangerous. This indeed used to be the case a long time ago, until perhaps the 1970s, but in recent decades enthusiasm has waned and has been replaced by disillusionment, cynicism, even secret dissent. Some fifteen years ago I was told about leaflets allegedly distributed in Pyongyang colleges by an underground student group — and recently these stories have been confirmed by defectors. Of course, the apprehended dissenters received harsh treatment and, once arrested, are very unlikely to ever see freedom again. But resistance does exist.

However, young North Koreans largely perceive politics as an exercise in outright demagogy to which they have to pay lip service for the sake of their future careers. University culture in recent years has been liberalized, and students spend less time on indoctrination — and more on partying.

Both exam marks and involvement with the Communist Youth are important in determining a student's future after graduation. At the end of their study period, students sit what are known as "state examinations" in their subjects, and also submit a major research paper which is a rough equivalent of a BA thesis in Western schools.

When the thesis is submitted and state exam passed, the 4 or 5 years of a student's life are over. The graduates cannot choose their own jobs. They are dispatched to work units by a special committee which takes into account their academic achievements, their political credentials and, unofficially, their connections.

But, of course, despite all the restrictions, students remain young, ambitious and hopeful — like students anywhere. The recent decade has seen many hardships come their way, but also a major liberalization in the mores and lifestyles of the younger North Koreans, and the universities have served as major engines of this liberalization.

Liberalization for the future?

PART 13

It's Economics...

A Tenderly Legal Currency

NORTH KOREA IS OFTEN DESCRIBED as the most repressive of all Communist regimes. Generally, this unflattering description is correct: in some respects the Pyongyang leaders out–Stalined even Stalin himself. Nonetheless, in certain other areas the North Korean state has demonstrated a surprising degree of leniency.

Hard-currency transactions are one of these areas. Indeed, in most Communist countries the use of foreign currency by the local citizens was outlawed. In the USSR, private trade in foreign currencies was a crime which carried the maximum punishment of death even in the 1970s, during the more liberal era of Soviet history. In most Communist countries citizens returning from overseas were required to exchange their currency immediately upon crossing the border. Needless to say, the exchange rates were determined by the government, and were heavily distorted in its favor.

Of course, Communist countries also boasted government-run currency shops which sold goods otherwise unavailable to the populace, often even to privileged groups. The shops were provided exclusively for foreigners. In some cases, locals who had been overseas were allowed to shop in special shops where they could use special certificates issued in lieu of their surrendered currency. Such shops carried far better goods than normal and the illegal exchange of certificates was strictly forbidden.

North Korea is an obvious exception to this trend. The North Korean authorities did not mind if their citizens used hard currency in the specially designated shops. Foreign publications often state that this policy was first introduced in 1984, but that is not really the case. Judging by the recollections

of many a veteran expat, the hard currency shops had been a common feature of North Korean life since the mid–1970s — probably from around 1975.

Nonetheless, early 1985 was an important turning point: at that time the Pyongyang hard-currency shop entered a joint venture with a Japanese company which was run by ethnic Koreans. It was reborn as the Rakwon Department Store. Rakwon means "paradise," and the shop indeed appeared to be a consumer's paradise when compared to the average North Korean store. It is located in downtown Pyongyang, and reminds one of a small Japanese department store, albeit with markedly higher prices.

By North Korean standards, this lady is quite well dressed, and she might even have access to hard-currency shops. Photograph by Byeon Young-wook.

There have been some reports in foreign media that in 1986 the authorities finally allowed everybody with hard currency to shop there. Well, maybe — but as early as 1984, foreign observers in Pyongyang had no doubt that the shops were already open to anybody who was in possession of dollars or yen, with no questions asked. To the foreign observers, the practice appeared outrageously liberal.

The Rakwon Department Store is the most prominent of all North Korean currency shops, but it is by no means the only one. The number of currency shops increased dramatically in the late 1980s, on the eve of the "World Festival of Youth and Students" in 1989. At that time it was decided that every city, province and even county was entitled to a currency shop. Sometimes several smaller or poorer counties shared a common hard-currency

opening up?. Only one great store

An office building, North Korean style. Photograph by Byeon Young-wook.

outlet. Then the government tried to cut the numbers down, closing many shops in 1992. However, they soon made a comeback.

Dozens of lesser hard-currency shops operate throughout the country today. Pyongyang alone has an estimated 20–30 hard-currency outlets. In recent years, the old Rakwon chain has been supplemented by newer ventures, catering to the tastes of the small but growing community of Western expats.

And what are the reasons for such a liberal approach to the currency regulations, you might ask? Initially, this network of hard-currency shops was created in order to tap the financial resources of the ethnic Koreans from Japan who were persuaded to move to North Korea in the 1960s. This was a large community, and even today it numbers some 150–250,000 people, including children, grandchildren and spouses. Many of them stay in touch with their relatives in Japan and regularly receive money from them.

After some consideration and experimentation, the North Korean authorities concluded that it would be unproductive to force these people into changing their yen into North Korean won at grossly distorted rates. They decided that government-run currency shops with overpriced but otherwise unavailable merchandise would be a smarter solution. Indeed, the prices in the North

Repression because of convenience

Korean hard-currency shops are roughly 20–50% higher than the prices of identical merchandise in Japan.

Thus, the former Japanese-Koreans are encouraged to shop in the Rakwon and its analogues. Almost all goods come from Japan and other developed Western countries, and the general layout of the shops shows the strong influence of Japanese managerial traditions. The profits are divided between the Korean-Japanese owners and the state. Actually, the Rakwon is believed to be one of the very few economically viable joint ventures in the DPRK.

Of course, not all shoppers come from these Korean-Japanese families. The North Korean state has never been very harsh on private money exchangers, even in the heyday of Kim Il Sung's rule. Thus, anyone with enough money can buy hard currency—at the black market rates. These rates, incidentally, were many times higher than the officially recognized ones, and even the 2002 reforms changed the situation only for a brief while. With hard currency, the individual could then go to the hard-currency shops and buy whatever he or she wished. Nowadays, when currency exchange is legal, it is even easier. While this sounds too good to be true, it should be remembered that only a fraction of the population can avail themselves of this service. After all, the average North Korean monthly salary is just a few U.S. dollars.

In order to facilitate hard-currency commerce, the North Korean government even issued a special type (actually, two types) of bank notes, which are the local equivalent of the hard currency. But that is our next story….

So basically the economy sucks! doesn't exist

Show Me the Color of (North Korea's) Money

APRIL 1979 SAW THE INTRODUCTION of a new, multi-tiered system of currency in Korea. It was not truly unique: the DPRK followed the example of China which, in turn, emulated some earlier experiments of the Soviets. Nonetheless, in the North the new system acquired a special sophistication.

In fact from 1979 onwards, the DPRK had three types of money. They all bore the same names and, initially, a very similar design, but had vastly different forms of purchasing power.

The lowest type was often known as "Korean money"—the equivalent of the Chinese *renminbi* (literally "people's currency" in Chinese). This money formed a sizeable majority of all bank notes and was used in all daily transactions by commoners whose salaries were paid in these bank notes as well.

Not even a western tiered currency system.

However, these bank notes could not be legally exchanged for foreign currency, even if the black market dealers were increasingly ready to break this ban.

The two other types of bank notes were issued in exchange for foreign currency, and could be freely changed back to yen, dollars, and francs. They came to be known as "pakkunton" (literally, "changed money") and were used in specially designated shops where no ration coupons were required, and where polite sales clerks waited near shiny rows of foreign-made consumer goods. As a rule, pakkunton was foreigners' money, the Korean analogue of the Chinese FECs or Foreign Exchange Certificates, still well remembered by those who traveled in China in the 1980s and early 1990s.

But why did the North Koreans issue two types of FECs/pakkuntons while China managed with just one? This reflected North Korean specifics. A large number of the foreigners in North Korea in the 1980s came from countries with "soft" currencies, i.e. currencies which could not be freely exchanged. Such closed monetary systems existed in all Communist countries, as well as in a number of Third World states. Therefore, people who could not bring "authentic" hard currency to the DPRK, had to content themselves with a lower-valued pakkunton, while the lucky holders of imperialist greenbacks and militarist yen were rewarded with a higher type of pakkunton.

Initially, the "soft currency" pakkunton were known as "blue *won*," while the higher level were called "red *won*." I actually suspect that the now commonly accepted "blue" is a mistranslation. The Korean "p'urŭn" means both "blue" and "green," and the imprints of the so-called "blue" *won* were salad-green in color.

Then in 1988, the names of the two currencies were swapped. Perhaps the revolutionary red color was deemed more suitable for the less fortunate foreigners from the Communist and "progressive" countries with inconvertible currencies, while the equivalent to the capitalist currency would be more properly named "green" (mistranslated "blue") after the evergreen U.S. dollar! Never though Of the DRK as so artstic

So what was the difference between the two types? Once again ... buying power. The lower-level pakkunton (let us call them "red," following the post–1988 convention) could only be used in special shops where the merchandise was light years ahead of the usual North Korean standard of goods, but still much inferior in quality to items sold in the real hard-currency shops where the "blue" *won* were accepted in lieu of dollars, yen, and francs.

Until 1988 the pakkunton looked similar to "normal" money. The only difference was a large rectangular imprint, a sort of stamp in green or red, which indicated that the banknote was a pakkunton. Until 1985 the pakkunton were issued only as paper currency, but in January 1985 pakkunton coins for denominations less than one *won* were introduced. The coins did not distinguish between the two "blue" and "red" *won*, and had small stars which differentiated them from the usual North Korean coins.

During the 1988 reform, the DPRK Central Bank introduced new types of pakkunton which were much more different from their common-currency analogues. However, subsequent events changed everything. The collapse of the Communist bloc made the "red" *won* largely unnecessary, while the demise of state control over commerce meant that the real dollars, yen, and euros began to take over their North Korean analogues. So the pakkunton bills are now just an interesting quarry for collectors, I suspect.

The North Korean "Salaryman"

"HOW MUCH DO THEY EARN THERE, in the North?" "What are North Korean salaries now?" These questions come naturally, even if people are aware that in a socialist economy the formal size of one's salary is a much less significant indicator than it is under capitalism.

Under socialism access to goods is at least as important as the amount of money in someone's possession. Since retail prices in the socialist economies tend to be fixed and subsidized, this means that many goods are not readily available in shops, but are instead distributed by the state bureaucracy. Thus, people who are deemed more deserving have access to goods that are not available to the "less valuable."

A party bureaucrat and a skilled worker often might earn roughly similar salaries in a state socialist economy, but their actual consumption levels are vastly different, since the bureaucrats go to shops and distribution centers which are off limits to mere mortals. Apart from bureaucrats, another group of people who have privileged access to commodities are people employed in the retail system. These individuals can always divert some goods from the public distribution system and use them either for their own consumption or for barter with those who control other valuable commodities. Thus, a sales clerk is seen as a very prestigious occupation in the North.

For several decades between 1970 and 2000 the average salary of the North Koreans remained fairly stable, steadily increasing from about 60–70 *won* to roughly 100 *won* per month. Comparisons with Western currency values are actually meaningless, since the price structure in the North is very different, but we can roughly say that this equaled about $10. This may not be as bad as it appears since in those days one cent would buy a bus ticket, and rice, the major source of carbohydrate, was essentially distributed free of charge as long as one had ration coupons.

In the late 1980s, just before the collapse of the old certainties, an unskilled worker was paid 60–70 *won*, a skilled worker or technician brought home about 80–120 *won*, about 150 *won* was the usual monthly income of an engineer, and high-level bureaucrats and other very privileged groups could be paid up to 250 or even 300 *won* per month. But then things changed: rampant inflation, the collapse of the public distribution system and famine paralyzed the old system, and only a few years ago the government "adjusted" salaries to the new reality.

The 2002 reforms (which were never called "reforms" in the North Korean press) dramatically changed the structure of wages and prices in the country. For a while it was not clear what the current price and wage levels were, but recent research by the World Food Program seems to answer a few questions. We now know what was regarded as "normal" wages in 2004 when the unofficial exchange rate approximated 1800 *won* per U.S. dollar.

According to the survey, most types of low-paid workers earn between 1,700 and 2,500 *won* per month, with an average estimated at 2,100. Low-level professional jobs such as clerks and teachers at nursery and primary school earn between 1,400 and 2,000 *won* per month. The old age pension for the average person does not exceed 900 *won*; women, in particular housewives, sometimes get pensions as low as 300–400 *won*. The talks to the defectors I myself had seemingly confirm those figures.

It is also remarkable that after the 2002 increase, the elite salaries have remained relatively low, seemingly never exceeding the level of 10,000 *won* per month. A senior officer in the army or a factory general manager is likely to receive some 5–8,000. For all practical purposes, this is a subsistence income and the salaries of lesser folks are even below the subsistence level.

Throughout 2004, the exchange rate fluctuated between 1,600 and 2,200 *won* to the Euro, and in 2005 and began to grow with awesome speed. To play down the significance of the "imperialist dollar," exchange rates are usually quoted in euros. The official rate was fixed at 154 *won*, but this was essentially meaningless. This means that in 2004 the average old age pension was something like 50 cents a month, with a nursery teacher earning as little as one dollar a month. This is not as bad as it sounds, since prices are also cheap — one can buy one kilo of apples for 5 cents. But it is still bad.

According to the FAO report, "the income of cooperative farmers from the annual obligatory crop sales to the Government varies greatly from one farm to another, resulting in monthly incomes per person ranging from 500 *won* to 4000 *won*." But farmers can also substantially increase their income by selling the produce from their gardens, and by hillside farming which is done on the steep slopes of mountains. The latter activity has become common in the North over the past decade. It is formally forbidden but practiced nonetheless, and it seems that a large part of the hillside produce is exchanged outside the public distribution system.

Unemployment is quite high, but it is hidden. Formally, everybody has a job, but a persistent shortage of raw materials, spare parts, machinery, and power supplies means that few factories actually operate at full capacity. In many cases people go to their factories and offices and sit there idly, spending just a couple of hours a day doing some meaningful work. They still have to attend, since otherwise they could lose access to food rations, and this would make their situation impossible, probably even threatening their physical survival.

According to interviews with officials and other information garnered, the WFP estimated that some 30 percent of North Korea's workers are either permanently or temporarily under- or unemployed.

As usual, women are more likely to be unemployed. But perhaps they do not mind. Why? Well, is it possible for a family to survive, even on two salaries, if one's official income can only buy eight kilos of rice to augment one's distributed 200 grams? Of course the answer is "no." The official salaries are meaningless and are scarcely more than token payments these days. If people survive, it is not because of their official salaries....

On Cheeses and Other Matters

FROM THE EARLY 1970S OUR FAMILY lived on the outskirts of Leningrad, the second largest Soviet city, near a large new supermarket. We went there to shop, and I still remember how its shelves changed year after year. There were ups and downs, but the general trend was clear: every new year, the choice of goods available to consumers was getting smaller and smaller. Supermarket fridges, which around 1970 offered four or five kinds of cheese, by 1975 had only one or two, and by 1980 they were empty. The Soviet economy was crumbling under the weight of the arms race and its own inefficiency, and one type of consumer good after another disappeared from the shelves.

I could not help but return to those memories of my childhood when I was reading about the results of a research project undertaken by Ch'oe Pongdae and Ku Kap-u, two South Korean scholars who painstakingly checked which goods were available to North Korean customers in three towns located in the northernmost part of the country, near the Chinese border. The choice of those cities is explained by the fact that most defectors in the last decade have arrived from that area, and this provides researchers with a large amount of data which can be cross-checked. The picture is of the gradual but unstoppable disintegration of the government-owned retail trade, and it is very similar to what I experienced in the USSR some 25 years ago. Of course, in North Korea this long slide downhill began from a much lower point: compared to the North, the former Soviet Union was always a very prosperous country indeed.

The rationing of cereals was first introduced in North Korea in March 1946, although initially only the state employees were issued with ration coupons. As a result of the "socialist transformation" of 1946–1957, by the late

Commerce and services, socialist style: an empty state-run tailor's shop and a stall where they sell bad ice cream.... Photograph by Byeon Young-wook.

1950s virtually all North Koreans came to belong to this category: industry was nationalized and private shops were closed down. Thus, in 1957-58 rationing was remodeled to encompass all North Koreans, although in the countryside the system worked somewhat differently. This has been the case until the recent reforms of 2002 — and their impact remains to be seen.

Private trade in grain was prohibited in 1958 and was not either formally lifted or quietly disregarded until around 1993. All grain had to be collected by the state from the farming cooperatives and then redistributed through the public distribution system. City dwellers were issued rationing coupons which were to be exchanged for grain. Money was to be paid as well, but the price of grain remained fixed and essentially symbolic.

The prices of cereals and other daily necessities were kept at a very low level. For decades, the price of rice was fixed at 0.08 *won* (over this time the average monthly salary grew from some 50 to about 100 *won*). But the prices did not matter a great deal: even if a person had money, he or she could not buy more than was permitted by the state.

Every North Korean was (and still formally is) entitled to a certain amount of cereal. The largest amount — 800g daily — was reserved for workers engaged in hard manual labor: steelworkers, miners or loggers. The majority of the population was entitled to a daily ration of 700g. College and high school students were given 600g, and younger students received 300–400g, depending on their age. Retirees and housewives were also entitled to 300g of cereals. And North Koreans were given some other foodstuffs including cabbage, soy sauce, etc., but in terms of nutrition, almost all calories in their diet came from rice and other cereals. *Not nutritional*

The rationing coupons were issued by employers — or more precisely, by the payroll office of the state company which employed the particular person. Normally, his or her dependants also receive coupons there. The retirees received their coupons — small rectangular pieces of low-quality colored paper — in their *inminban* or "people's group," while students were given coupons at school. To deter fraud, the color of the coupons was frequently changed. Actual sales of rationed goods took place in a special distribution store and there was one such store for every 1000–1200 families.

Normally, every ward or *tong* had one distribution center which served all companies operating in the area. Twice a month each company provided the distribution center with data about their current number of employees and their dependants. The data about dependants was required since as a rule, the entire family received their rations in a center to which the "work unit" of the family head was associated.

The rice rations were delivered every 15 days. On the appointed day, a family representative, usually a housewife, since it was a daytime, went to the distribution center with her ID and the ration coupons of the entire family. She produced the coupons, paid the price and then took home her family's rice for the next 14 days.

If a North Korean ate away from home (say at his company's cafeteria or on a business trip), he or she should produce the rationing coupon for the eatery. The same was true even for patients in hospitals.

Let us imagine a middle-aged housewife who enters a distribution center in, say, 1971. She produces three sets of ration coupons. Her husband, a clerical worker, is eligible for 700g of grain a day, her son in Year 6 of primary school can receive 400g and she, being a humble housewife, receives the lowest adult ration of 300g. This lady would be issued with (15 × 0.7)

10.5 kg of grain for her husband, (15 × 0.4) 6 kg for her son and (15 × 0.3) 4.5 kg for herself, a total of 21 kg. If it were Pyongyang in 1971, some 70% of this amount would consist of rice.

The 700g might appear a generous amount — at least as far as calories are concerned — however, even in the late 1970s, undernourishment was an *Aha!*, acute problem in North Korea. The reason is that the 700g was an increasingly theoretical norm, more and more remote from the harsh realities of the country.

In the 1960s, the economic situation was relatively sound. However, the economy began to slide downhill in the mid–'70s, and this was soon felt by everybody.

The first downsizing of the rice rations took place in 1973 when the country's economic growth began to decelerate. In September 1973 it was announced that, "due to the dangerous international situation," the rations would be reduced: every month two daily rations would be sacrificed for the strategic reserves. In 1989 the rations were cut a further 10%: this was necessary, the authorities explained, to prepare the country for the forthcoming International Youth Festival. In 1992 a new 10% cut arrived, and around 1994-95, grain ceased to be provided to the population of more remote areas. These cuts meant that on the eve of North Korea's Great Famine of 1995–1999, the average worker received less than 500g of cereal and a retiree was forced to subsist on 220g, which was not exactly a generous amount.

During the Great Famine, the PDS almost ceased to function for a few years, but in recent years it has obviously made a moderate comeback. Since all data in the secretive North is classified, nothing is known for sure, but it seems that in early 2005, the Public Distribution System was "the main source of cereals for the 70 per cent of the population living in urban areas" — according to an estimate by the FAO, a UN food agency.

Still, the official rations are hardly generous. According to the WFP, in early 2005 rations were cut to 250 grams per person per day or 40 per cent of the internationally recommended minimum. And people must purchase their food on the markets, and this food is expensive, with rice costing some 500 *won* a kilo.

It is not incidental that we keep talking about cereals instead of rice. Actually, the rations consisted of a mix of different grains. In the 1970s, rice constituted up to 70–80% of the allowance in Pyongyang, but in more remote areas the rations consisted entirely of corn and barley — even in those relatively prosperous times. These cereals are popular with some dieticians for the exact same reason that they are unpopular with the North Koreans: they are less rich in calories; obesity has never been a problem in North Korea.

Foreign missions always kept a close eye on the proportion of rice to other cereals in the rations within the public distribution system. It was seen as a major indicator of the country's real economic health.

In most cases, maize grains were boiled and eaten, but they were occasionally made into flour and used for more complicated dishes. Maize noodles, born out of necessity and a shortage of rice and buckwheat flour, became a common item in the North Korean diet — and in recent years an entrepreneurial North Korean defector named Pak Ch'ŏl-song even tries to market this product in South Korea as a "health food."

A reliance on maize has led to some consequences for the health of the less fortunate North Koreans. They suffer from pellagra, a disease common to consumers of maize and once common among some native American tribes. This condition is characterized by skin sores, diarrhea and mental confusion. Pellagra has been a very common problem in North Korean prison camps, where inmates subsisted on maize alone even in the relatively prosperous 1970s.

Initially it was only grain which was distributed by the state, but by the late 1960s the increasing food shortages led to an increase in government control. In the borderland cities, almost all foodstuffs came to be rationed from around 1967. From that time onwards, soy paste, salt and sugar could be bought only upon presentation of a coupon, and sugar soon disappeared completely. Pyongyang and the more privileged large cities switched to this system in the 1970s. Thus until around 1980 it was still possible for people from the countryside to mount shopping expeditions to Pyongyang and other major centers. The same phenomenon was common in late Soviet Russia with its "sausage trains" running from Moscow to the countryside. However, in North Korea the travel permit system made such trips accessible only to the privileged few: while a Russian of the Soviet era could go to Moscow when he or she wished, for a North Korean, a trip to Pyongyang is a rare privilege.

This situation did not last long, however: the scope of the distribution system kept growing such that by 1980 virtually nothing could be sold or bought freely in Pyongyang and, needless to say, across the entire country. The state shops were not really retail outlets but rather distribution centers, places where ration coupons of all kinds could be exchanged for food. This tendency to replace trade with rationing could be seen in almost all state socialist countries, but in North Korea it reached its theoretical limit.

More prestigious items were also subjected to rationing, but of a special kind: the rationing of luxuries masqueraded as "gifts from the Great Leader." Quality cloth for clothes, good leather footwear, not to mention wristwatches or TV sets, which were very expensive items in those days, were distributed or, better still, "awarded" to North Koreans as "gifts" from Kim Il Sung.

Of course there were goods in the shop windows, but as an older North

Korean defector recalled: "In the 1960s, the goods displayed in the shop windows were of a better quality but still basically the same as what could be bought inside. But from 1974 it became impossible to buy goods like those displayed in the shop windows."

At that time there was no starvation in the country, even if very few people ate their fill. However, by the early 1990s the slow slide downhill accelerated and soon a famine, the worst in Korea's entire history, struck North Korea with great ferocity.

And how about that large supermarket near my old house in Leningrad? I visited recently and was amazed to find one hundred or so kinds of cheeses where even in the best of times there used to be three or four....

Russia vs. DPRR
Communy (again)

Rason Sez: A Good Bet

ONE OF THE THINGS TO WHICH ALL long-time Pyongyang watchers have grown accustomed is the announcement of "historic breakthroughs." Indeed, every two or three years the international media erupt with reports about a new "dramatic change" which has supposedly just occurred in North Korea. To date none of the predictions have withstood subsequent analysis....

I still remember how in the mid–1980s Western journalists loved to speculate that North Korea was on the eve of dramatic changes. The reason for this hope was a Joint Venture Law passed by the North Korean parliament in September 1984. The Law was adopted at the same time as the new Chinese investment-oriented policy began to bear fruit, and it was only logical for North Korea to follow the example of its long-time ally and sponsor.

However it soon became clear that no serious investor was showing an interest in North Korea. Almost all the joint ventures were opened by ethnic Koreans from Japan, active supporters of *Ch'ongryŏn*, a powerful front organization of the North Korean government in Japan. And even these people whose pro–Pyongyang sympathies could be taken for granted did not rush to the North with really serious money, limiting themselves to small-scale investments. They were prepared to pay for their patriotism, but not too much.

Between 1986 and 1992 a mere 140 joint ventures were agreed upon — and only about 65 actually became operational. More than 90% of these ventures were controlled by the *Ch'ongryŏn* — and nobody else showed any interest in investing in the North. All ventures were also very small — like a coffee shop in downtown Pyongyang. Frankly, it was a fiasco.

The industrial landscapes of North Korea often remind one of Victorian-era technology. Photograph by Bernd Seiler.

Nevertheless, in 1991 North Korea undertook its first attempts to establish a special economic zone, or SEZ in the economists' parlance. The idea was modeled on the Chinese SEZ, a huge success story of the 1980s, even though North Koreans, true to their tradition, vehemently denied that the inspired decisions of the Great Leader could possibly have something to do with the schemes of foreigners. The SEZ was to be developed in the Rajin-Songbong area, in a remote northeastern part of the country where the borders of Korea, China, and Russia meet.

Once again, there was much hype about the pending breakthrough. Even South Koreans, the traditional opponents of Pyongyang, joined the chorus: by the mid–1990s, an increasing number of South Koreans wanted the North to survive and prosper, and they wanted to persuade themselves that the Rajin-Songbong SEZ would soon become a first step towards prosperity.

The choice of this area for a SEZ was understandable. It was believed that the area would attract substantial investment from the booming China as well as from a Russia which was then in much better shape than in later years. Pyongyang proclaimed that in due time the Rajin-Songbong area would become a "transport and manufacturing hub of North-East Asia." On paper, the investors were indeed welcome. Suffice it to say that the tax rates and other regulations were even more favorable than similar regulations in China.

From the North Korean point of view, the Rajin-Songbong area (renamed Rason after the merger of the two cities in August 2000) had the added convenience of being remote from major population centers. This meant that the sprouts of capitalism could be more easily controlled and isolated from the "masses," whose spirits the new developments would undoubtedly spoil. There were even rumors that all politically suspicious inhabitants of the area would be shipped elsewhere, to be replaced by trustworthy model workers. Perhaps it was indeed thus planned, since a similar policy was officially adopted several years later when the Sinuiju Project came to be discussed.

In the early 1990s the Rajin-Songbong area was frequented by foreign businessmen. However, the visitors usually limited themselves to ritual speeches or, perhaps, signing a non-binding letter of intent. As of 2000, the total volume of actual investment was a mere 35 million dollars even though the letters of intent initially promised an investment of more than 2 billion!

So what went wrong? Many things. First of all, the North Korean authorities greatly overestimated the attractiveness of their country to foreign investors. Foreign businesses flocked to the Chinese SEZs in the early 1980s largely because these areas were seen as stepping stones to a market of some 1.2 billion consumers. The 24 million North Koreans comprised a much smaller, and hence much less attractive, market.

There were also serious problems with the infrastructure. The only paved road in the area connects Rajin and Songbong, and even this is only a single lane. It takes some 30–40 minutes to travel 17 km along the area's finest road. The bridge which connects the area with China has remained unchanged since colonial days. Obviously, Pyongyang expected that the rich foreigners would pay for the upgrading of the infrastructure. They did, but only on a very limited scale.

Of course the bad credit rating of the DPRK, the only Communist country to have ever defaulted on its loans, did not help either. The few foreigners who were brave enough to invest in the North were further discouraged by uncooperative bureaucrats, as well as by the unrelenting attempts of the locals to squeeze a few additional dollars out of them. And, last but not least, the recurring nuclear crisis also drove investors away.

Thus, by 2000 most foreign observers concluded that the entire Rajin-Songbong project was a failure. However, in recent years there has been some cause for hope. Perhaps the Rason area has finally found its market niche. It began to attract growing numbers of Chinese tourists from the booming cities of the Chinese northeast. Most of them were lured there by the opportunities for gambling, something which was strictly controlled back home. A large new casino and luxurious hotel were built by the Emperor Group from Hong Kong to cater to the tastes and demands of these visitors.

The visitors enjoy more innocent pleasures as well. Northeast China is landlocked, and many Chinese come to the area because they want to spend a day or two by seaside. And to be sure, they also enjoy the thrill of being "overseas," a new feeling for most Chinese.

Of course, the casino and seaside resort enclave was a far cry from the once promised "hub of North-East Asia," but it was better than nothing. Alas, it did not last for long: in early 2005, after a scandal which involved some Chinese bureaucrat who had gambled away large quantities of embezzled money, Beijing took a new tough stance against gambling tours to North Korea. The business collapsed immediately, the casino equipment was shipped back to Hong Kong and the SEZ remained what it had always been: a poor enclave in the middle of a destitute country, away from all major communication networks.

But the optimists continue to profess their belief in the brilliant future which awaits the North Korean economy. This time, the next historical breakthrough is supposed to occur in the Kaesong area, where the South Koreans are busily constructing an industrial park. Maybe this time it will indeed be different. Perhaps — so long as the South Koreans are ready to bear all major expenses, I suspect....

An Accidental Sez

IN SEPTEMBER 2002 THE WORLD learned that North Korea had finally embraced capitalism and reform — or so the foreign media informed their readers and viewers. The Sinuiju Project, an ambitious plan to develop a special economic zone on the Chinese border, was seen as a sign of great change.

People who were enthusiastic about this idea chose to forget the deplorable history North Korea had had with foreign investment. "This time it will be different!" they chimed (and do we not hear it now too when they discuss the Kaesong Project?). This one was sorry indeed. The first attempts to lure direct foreign investment took place in 1984 when the North Korean parliament rubber-stamped the Joint Ventures Law. The foreign media immediately proclaimed this "a historic breakthrough." But, like many other alleged "breakthroughs" in North Korean history, this one ended in nothing.

In the early 1990s the North Korean authorities developed another project. This time they decided to establish a special economic zone (SEZ) in the Rajin-Songbong area, in the remote northwestern corner of the country. Once again, the offer had no takers.

Taking all these lessons into account, Pyongyang decided in 2002 to be as bold and radical as it could. They decided to establish a new SEZ in the city of Sinuiju. The city is conveniently located on the railway lines and roads which connect North Korea and China, and has an infrastructure which by North Korean standards can be described as good.

From the very beginning the plan had some twists which made it appear, well, North Korean. It was stated that the entire population of Sinuiju, estimated at 400–500,000 people, would be relocated to other areas. These people were not good enough to enjoy the fruits of capitalism. They were to be replaced by 200,000 model workers, hand-picked by the authorities for their skill and political reliability.

The most unusual act in this drama was the decision to appoint a foreigner as the SEZ governor. The North Koreans' choice was Yang Bin, a Chinese entrepreneur with Dutch citizenship and reputedly the second richest man in China. He was 39 years old at the time.

On September 12, 2002, the Supreme People's Assembly, the North Korean pseudo-parliament, adopted the Basic Law of the Sinuiju Special Administrative Region, as the SEZ was officially known. The Law consisted of six chapters (government, economy, culture, fundamental rights and duties of residents, structure, and the emblem and flag of the region), and an impressive total of 101 articles. The plans even envisioned that the SEZ would have its own emblem and flag!

The basic law proclaimed that the legal system would remain unchanged for fifty years, and that foreigners would enjoy the same rights as North Koreans in the area. Foreign judges were to be invited to solve disputes and oversee the enforcement of the laws.

For a while the usual hype about a "breakthrough" was all the rage. The North Korean vice-minister for foreign trade called the SEZ "a new historic miracle." The South Korean authorities, already in the middle of a "sunshine policy" frenzy, also assured the world that "Prospects are Bright for Foreign Investment in the Sinuiju Special Region" (such was the title of the Yonhap press agency's report wired on September 24, 2002).

However, the entire Sinuiju affair hardly lasted fifty weeks, let alone the promised fifty years, and its flag is nowhere to be seen.

It was probably the Chinese who sank the project. Beijing was not amused by the turn of events. There are at least two known reasons for their unease. First, Yang Bin wanted to transform the city into a gambling center, a Macao of the North. This was not welcome. It is also likely that China did not want competition between Sinuiju and its northeastern cities. It did not help that the North Koreans, following their *modus operandi*, did not bother to liaise with the Chinese beforehand.

Disagreement between chinese guy and DPRK, so no liberalization after all

Yang Bin was already under investigation — perhaps not so much on account of any wrongdoings but owing to some intrigues in Beijing. It is not clear whether Yang Bin wanted to use the grand dreams of Kim Jong Il to slip out of a legal tangle, or whether his willingness to participate in the scheme was his crossing of the Rubicon, but he was arrested for fraud and eventually sentenced to 18 years in prison.

For a time the plan was in limbo. Then in September 2004 there was talk that Julie Sa (Sha Rixiang) had been approached to become the new chief of the SEZ. Indeed, the Chinese-American businesswoman appeared to be a good choice due to her unusual background: an ethnic Chinese born in South Korea, she had been mayor of Fullerton, California. However, Julie Sa scotched the rumors. She admitted that she had been approached by Pyongyang, but by the summer of 2004 she had not heard about the proposal for long enough to assume that the idea was no longer on the table.

Obviously, by early 2004 the Sinuiju plan had been shelved for good. This was finally confirmed in late 2004 when, in their usual circumlocutory way, the North Korean authorities quietly notified the interested parties that there would be no SEZ in Sinuiju.

At least inhabitants of the city avoided a forced relocation — an unpleasant procedure under any circumstances, and positively dangerous in the North Korea of the early 2000s. Nowadays, Sinuiju plays a major role in the international exchanges of North Korea, but these exchanges have nothing to do with the ambitious and bizarre plans of Pyongyang officialdom. Sinuiju has become a stronghold of North Korea's "capitalism from below," the major base of an intense private trade with China. But this trade has nothing to do with the grand schemes of a declining Stalinist socialism.

The Currency of Currency

COMMUNISTS HAVE ALWAYS PROFESSED their intention to abolish money — and for a while they took this promise seriously. The first years of Communist rule in Russia were marked by bold experiments aimed at the abolition of cash, which was to be replaced by "direct labor exchanges." However, the ensuing bitter experience was a harsh lesson and so in later eras, Communist regimes only paid lip service to the anti-monetary rhetoric. They did not reject their earlier promises to do away with money altogether, but this was to be done at some unspecified point in a very distant future.

North Korea became Communist at the time when the earlier dreams were long forgotten, so the new regime began to pay great attention to its financial system.

For the first few years after Liberation, the North Koreans continued to use Japanese bank notes and coins. However, in December 1947, the nascent Communist authorities launched a currency reform. Needless to say, this was done with full Soviet endorsement, and the practical management of the reform was entrusted to a Soviet-Korean financial expert, Kim Ch'an.

Within the week of 6 to 12 December, 1947, all the old bank notes were to be exchanged for new ones. According to contemporary Soviet reports, trade on the Korean markets came briefly to a complete halt as shopkeepers panicked. Only in January, with the issue of the new bank notes, did shops resume normal trade.

The 1947 bank notes were printed in the USSR. There were four denominations: 1, 5, 10 and 100 *won*. These early bank notes were peculiar in many regards. First of all, they were issued before the official proclamation of the DPRK—and thus did not bear the name of the state which issued them. They only carried the inscriptions "Democratic Korea" and the name of the issuing institution—the Central Bank of North Korea. Another peculiarity was the use of Chinese characters, soon to be banished from North Korean life.

In 1949, the bank notes were augmented with currency for small transactions. This "small change" was issued not as coins, but as paper money—with values of 15, 20, and 50 *chŏn* (a *chŏn* is 1/100 of the North Korean *won*). However, rampant inflation soon made these small bank notes unusable.

The Korean War created complete havoc with the currency systems of both Koreas and in February 1959 Pyongyang launched a new currency reform. This time, the "old" *won* were exchanged for "new" at a rate of 100:1 (what used to be a hundred *won*, became one *won*). This was necessary to encourage stability and make the Korean currency more manageable. Indeed, until the dramatic changes which followed the Great Famine of 1996–1999, it had been easier to handle the North Korean currency than its South Korean counterpart: in the North nobody was forced to operate with five- or six-digit numbers for every small transaction!

The 1959 bank notes depicted industrial and agricultural landscapes. As a rule the front of each bank note displayed something industrial, while the reverse sported largely agricultural topics. There were six types of bank notes, valued at 50 *chŏn* (0.5 *won*), as well as 1, 5, 10, 50, and 100 *won*. In addition, the first North Korean metal coins were minted as well—with denominations of 1, 5, and 10 *chŏn* (later to be followed by 50 *chŏn* denominations). The coins were made of a light aluminum-based alloy, and all had a similar design: the DPRK coat of arms on the reverse and the denomination on the front.

In this respect the coins largely followed the patterns of the coinage in other Communist countries.

The next reforms took place in 1979. While the old coins remained in circulation, bank notes were replaced. The new bank notes (once again, with the values of 1, 5, 10, 50, and 100 *won*) had a dramatic and highly politicized design. The 100-*won* bank note was decorated with a portrait of Kim Il Sung, who thus became the second Korean leader to be depicted on a Korean bank note in his lifetime. The dubious honor of being the first goes to the South Korean President Syngman Rhee, who put his face on South Korea's bank notes as early as 1950. The reverse of the 1979 100-*won* bank note depicted Kim Il Sung's childhood home in Mangyŏngdae.

The 50-*won* bank note had representations of a worker, a farmer (the only female in the picture), a soldier, and an intellectual (the latter lurking in the background), all of whom were holding high the symbolic torch of Kim Il Sung's *Juche* ideas.

However, by the late 1980s the old currency was losing its value fast. This necessitated a new currency reform. But this will be our next topic….

Currency Reforms

ON THE MORNING OF 15 JULY, 1992, the entire North Korean population was thrown into a state of frantic activity. Radio and TV broadcast an official communiqué which confirmed some long-circulating rumors. The government had unleashed a new currency reform — and many people ran to save what was left of their money.

In the centrally planned economies, inflation took a peculiar shape: since prices for goods and services were set by the government agencies, they could not increase automatically with the amount of currency in circulation. There was "classical" inflation as well, to be sure, but prices could rise only on the black market, beyond government control. In the official government-run economy, inflation led to shortages of everything, since people rushed to purchase every possible commodity, stripping the shops virtually bare.

Two solutions were advanced to rectify the problem. First came rationing — and few countries could rival North Korea in its enthusiasm for rationing. Rationing — combined with very low, almost token, prices — made money essentially unnecessary. For decades the North Korean government decided how many calories would be allocated to members of a particular social group.

The same was true of consumer goods which were distributed by officials on the basis of a citizen's perceived "worthiness."

However, the amount of currency in circulation continued to grow—and this was felt keenly in the black market, which became especially prominent in the late 1980s. It also became next to impossible to buy those few goods which were not rationed: such goods were seen as a kind of investment and hoarded in huge quantities. Therefore, the second proposed solution was ... currency reform. *Good way for govt to control economy*

In all Communist countries currency reform more or less followed the same pattern. One day—all of a sudden—the government informed its citizens that their old currency would become worthless paper the next day. Only a certain amount of the old money could be exchanged for the new, and this could be done only within a very limited period of time (usually a few days). This meant that any surplus currency was neutralized in one fell swoop—and a semblance of financial stability restored. This also meant that most people instantly lost at least part of their savings. And the black marketeers suffered a devastating blow—but this was precisely the reformers' goal. The financial system was rebooted, so to speak, and things started anew.

The 1992 reform was a very typical set of measures which had been followed a number of times by many other Communist (and, as a matter of fact, not only Communist) governments.

The North Korean authorities announced that the new bills would be issued while the old coins remained in circulation. The old bills could be exchanged for new ones—but only in the following five days. And of course, there was a ceiling—not more than 400 *won* per person could be exchanged (roughly, four average monthly salaries). This limit led to some grumbling, but there was little people could do about it. After all, they had been through this process before and expected something like it to happen again.

Thus, the current North Korean currency was introduced. The design of the bank notes did not change greatly when compared to the earlier bank notes of 1979. The 100-*won* bill is still adorned with the face of Kim Il Sung and depicts his childhood home. The 50-*won* bank note has the same 1979 trio of a worker, an intellectual and a farming woman (for some reason farmers are frequently represented by women in Communist propaganda). Fortunately, this time they were not visibly struggling to hold high the torch of *Juche*, but one has to be well versed in Communist symbolism to guess that one of the two men in nearly identical dress represents the workers while the other is supposed to be an intellectual.

The 10-*won* bill presents a worker operating some kind of heavy machinery with a number of smoking chimneys in the background. The 5-*won* bill features a student, and a 1-*won* bill, the smallest paper denomination, presents a scene from *Flower Girl*, a lavish political musical.

The 1992 reform effectively wiped out most of the cash in circulation. However, contrary to the hopes of the North Korean economic managers, the reform did not usher in financial stability. The economy continued to deteriorate after the loss of aid from the USSR and China, and within a year or two the problem of excess currency in circulation was as acute as ever. This time, however, no reform was attempted: since the economy began its free-fall, ordinary measures would not work.

Trying to counter inflation, the Central Bank of Korea began to issue bank notes in greater denominations. In 1998 a 500-*won* bill was introduced, and after 2002 it was joined by banknotes valued at 1000 *won* and 5000 *won*. These bills are meant for larger transactions, but nowadays most North Koreans prefer to pay in dollars. The imperialist currency has won the day, even in Kim's *Juche* socialist paradise.

So economic reforms screw with citizens just so the gov't has a firm grip on the ppl.

PART 14

*SoVS vs DPRK again, very diff
this time*

Foreign Affairs

Keeping an Eye on the Foreigners

IN 1985 I RETURNED TO THE Soviet Union from North Korea, where I had spent a year as an exchange student at the Kim Il Sung University, and was met by a barrage of questions about my experiences from friends and colleagues. Even in those days, and even in the former Soviet Union, which was hardly a paragon of political freedoms, North Korea was seen as an exotic and somewhat bizarre place.

It became clear that my fellow Soviet citizens did not understand the basic rules of North Korean life. Even those elders who still remembered life under Stalin could not comprehend just how isolated foreigners were in Pyongyang and to what extent their every move was controlled by the authorities.

Admittedly, the 1990s saw some relaxation in this social ostracism. But for a few decades, from the early 1960s to the early 1990s, foreign residents of Pyongyang had next to no interaction with the "locals." No exceptions were made for citizens of the supposedly "friendly" nations like the Soviet Union or China either, and in fact, with very rare exceptions, the citizens of the "unfriendly" nations were seldom seen or heard of in Pyongyang.

When we lived in the North in the 1980s, we needed a Korean "supervisor" and special permission to visit most public places. For some reason, even movie theaters and many (but not all) city museums were off-limits to foreigners. When a fellow student and I decided to visit the Pyongyang Revolutionary History Museum, we had to apply for permission and then wait two weeks until proper arrangements had been made. We were then assigned a supervisor and a car, and driven to the museum where we were accompanied by both our supervisor and a guide.

lots of supervising

The border guards which are often seen by foreigners and South Koreans are an elite force. They are well-fed and well-dressed but should remain vigilant. Photograph by Byeon Young-wook.

It was not possible to talk to North Koreans unless they belonged to the lucky few who were specially selected to work with foreigners. In the 1970s North Koreans would not answer even the most harmless questions and would invariably dart away if approached by a foreigner. *(brainwash?)*

In the 1980s the situation improved, so it was possible to strike up a short conversation on the street or on a trolley-bus, but these interactions never led to any lasting contact and were usually very short and superficial. At best, we could spend a few minutes talking about the weather or some equally innocuous subject. It was out of the question to visit North Koreans in their houses.

Even when we took a ride on the subway, an empty space a couple of meters wide magically formed around any larger group of foreigners, but one or two foreigners could move about reasonably freely.

All trips outside the city limits were forbidden, and we could only go on organized tours, constantly supervised by the North Korean staff. Foreigners who had cars needed to ask special permission for any trip outside the city, and the greater part of North Korea was unquestionably off-limits for foreigners. Once again, nationality did not matter much; citizens of both "friendly" and "hostile" countries alike were restricted in their movements.

We had to be careful when taking pictures as well. In the 1970s foreigners who tried to take "improper" pictures were frequently attacked by "unknown persons," and had their cameras smashed or disabled. These incidents were recurrent enough to warrant an official statement by some East European embassies who requested that these attacks be stopped. The statement helped, but there were a number of occasions where North Korean officials still prevented us from taking "incorrect pictures." Once when an East German student took a picture of a woman with a child on her back, the official insisted on having the film exposed immediately. North Korean women were not supposed to carry their children around in such an archaic manner!

Foreign students at the Kim Il Sung University lived in special dormitories and attended separate classes, organized strictly according to their nationality. Students from the same country were allocated to the same group, even if they came from different schools and had different levels of language proficiency. Only in exceptional cases were foreigners allowed to attend classes together with North Korean students. Even in such cases, North Koreans did not talk to foreigners. We did not blame them: the 1980s were a relaxed time in the USSR, but we knew from our parents how it used to be under Stalin, and understood that our Korean peers were concerned about their futures.

The most surprising thing was that we were not even allowed to use a university library. Being foreigners, we were not allowed to enter the room where the library catalogue was located. The student guards prohibited us from approaching such sensitive information and would not let us in. Books on topics of interest to us were selected for us by the officials who decided what could and could not be seen by foreign eyes. SO, MUCH, CONTROL,

In the dormitories, a foreigner usually shared a room with a specially selected Korean student. For language practice, this was very useful, although in fact the authorities had a different aim in mind. In theory, our roommates had two major tasks: to propagate *Juche* ideas among us (nobody showed much enthusiasm for this lofty mission), and to report on us. Eventually our roommates ceased making a secret of this obvious fact. Every evening at 6:30, a police security officer, responsible for foreign students, summoned our roommates for their daily report. However, though our roommates were supposed to spy on us, many of them turned out to be clever and interesting people, and I still remember them with great respect.

Things have changed a lot since then. The short-time visitors to the North are still much restricted in their actions, but the famine of the late 1990s meant the arrival of a large international crowd, officials from assorted NGOs and agencies. Reluctantly, the authorities gave them some freedoms they had denied foreigners for decades, including the right to visit some parts of the country (always escorted by minders, of course).

However, for three decades North Korea was, indeed, a hermit kingdom, possibly the most isolated society on the planet. The legacy of this period may outlive the now crumbling regime for many decades — and will create a number of problems for the future rulers of the North, whoever they will be....

Your Mission, Should You Choose to Accept It...

OF ALL THE DIPLOMATIC POSTINGS in the world, Pyongyang has always been among the most difficult and challenging. The veterans recount horror — yet absolutely real — stories about electric lamp globes mysteriously failing every few days, strange crackling sounds coming from the skirts of maids (the unreliable old eavesdropping devices malfunctioned regularly), a *very* irregular supply of hot water, and North Korean opposite numbers who, on being asked a question, took a clipping from *Nodong sinmun* and read it aloud for 20 minutes, oblivious to any remarks or gestures of their guests.

Nonetheless, there *are* foreign missions in Pyongyang — well, at least there are a few of them. The total number of embassies in Pyongyang has been remarkably stable for decades, even if, in accordance with the changes in politics of different countries, the list keeps changing. From the early 1970s onwards Pyongyang has hosted between 20 and 25 embassies. In 2001, for example, they numbered 23. Pyongyang has diplomatic relations with some 135 nations, but most countries are satisfied to have their ambassador to China act as ambassador to North Korea as well. In recent years, it has been possible for smaller countries to appoint their ambassadors to South Korea to act as their representatives in the North as well. These diplomats are based in Seoul, of course.

This small representation is understandable: the economy of the North is roughly the same size as that of Mozambique, and prior to the outbreak of the nuclear crisis the list of countries that had a serious stake in the Korean situation was very short indeed. Over the last few decades it has included the USA, the USSR/Russia, China and Japan (and, of course, South Korea — but the South is not technically considered to be a "foreign country"). Of these four, neither the U.S. nor Japan have diplomatic relations with the North.

Thus, the Soviet (from 1992, Russian) and Chinese embassies are by far the largest diplomatic missions in the North. They have a couple of dozen diplomats each, as well as an even larger number of technicians, secretaries, guards, and doctors. They are also very much self-contained and self-sufficient. These two "great embassies" are located in downtown Pyongyang, just a few minutes' walk from the major government agencies. Once upon a time, in the 1950s, when Kim Il Sung considered it convenient to be informal and friendly, he would sometimes even drop in on one of the embassies, without much prior warning, to have lunch with an ambassador or just play billiards. Those days are long gone now, of course....

Almost all the other embassies are clustered in a special quarter in the Munsu district, some seven kilometers from the downtown area. The embassy quarter is not fenced off, but it is remarkably empty: North Korean commoners know only too well that this is not a place to wander without a thoroughly valid reason.

With the notable exceptions of the Russians and Chinese, the embassies are small, with usually between two and four staff in each one. What exactly are these people doing in Pyongyang, you ask? I suspect that in some embassies the staff would be more than a little embarrassed if they were asked this blatantly undiplomatic question. Nonetheless, there is usually some rationale behind a particular country's decision to dispatch an ambassador to North Korea.

First of all, one should mention the countries that have significant commercial relations with Pyongyang. More often than not what the North engages in is not conventional trade. From the late 1970s North Korea has been making money by sending weapons and military technology to countries that could not buy them elsewhere. This lively if clandestine trade in rifles, tanks, missiles and, occasionally, nuclear technology, has brought ambassadors to Pyongyang from such countries as Iran, Egypt, Libya, and Pakistan.

Then there is a handful of Western embassies. Their number increased recently, but from the mid–1970s or for two decades, the developed West was represented only by a small Swedish mission. The Swedes were there partially because they naively hoped to recover the money North Korea owed them from the 1970s, but their involvement with the armistice regime also played a major role. Until the dramatic changes in the armistice regime in the 1990s, Sweden was one of the four neutral observer nations whose representatives controlled the DMZ. The Swedes also acted on behalf of the USA whenever necessary.

Another group includes the "friendship embassies" which are there just to show their governments' solidarity with Pyongyang. Thus, until the collapse of the Communist bloc in 1989-1990, virtually all Communist regimes of Eastern Europe maintained permanent missions in Pyongyang. Their real interests were minimal, but the embassies were there to show their symbolic support for the DPRK. Some radical Third World governments also dispatched missions to Pyongyang.

I still vividly remember a Maltese ambassador who in the mid–1980s spent his days in the hard-currency (read "foreigners only") bars and tea shops of Pyongyang. At the time Malta was ruled by a radical left-wing government, and they had decided to send a mission to Pyongyang. The mission comprised the ambassador only, and the gentleman apparently felt very isolated in the bizarre world of "diplomatic Pyongyang." He found some solace in flirting with women — expat ladies, of course, since North Korean girls inhabited a different universe, completely off limits to any foreigner.

Culture is just so DIFFERENT

Family Allowance

IN THE 1960S AND 1970S WHEN THE Cold War was at its height, the South Korean (and, to some extent, American) press often described the North as a "Soviet puppet," which was hardly the case. In fact, out of some 15 or 20 Communist states which then existed, only two or three were less dependent on Moscow than North Korea.

The frictions between Moscow and Pyongyang were seldom made public, of course. Officially, the "Soviet-[North] Korean friendship" was described as "unbreakable" and "eternal," and diplomats smiled while shaking hands before camera crews. In reality, the relations between the two countries turned sour in the late 1950s and never completely recovered. Moscow was annoyed by Kim Il Sung's policies, and especially by Kim's personality cult which was seen as an embarrassment to the Communist cause.

There was a great deal of personal friction between Brezhnev and Kim Il Sung, and even the more conservative Soviet officials viewed North Korea's ultra–Stalinism with great disdain. According to a recently declassified East German paper, Oleg Rakhmanin, the Deputy Head of the Soviet party's Central International Division (and by no account a liberal or reformer), commented on the North Koreans to an East German diplomat in the early 1970s in the following terms: "In the interests of our common tasks, we should sometimes overlook their stupidities. None of us agree with the idolatry of Kim Il Sung."

The North was remarkably unpopular with the general Soviet public as well. The Soviet intellectuals of the 1960s and later decades looked at North Korea with great unease. For them, Pyongyang embodied everything that was wrong about the Communist system. In short, it appeared to them as a caricature of the then USSR. Unlike the West, where many intellectuals toyed with Maoism and similar versions of the extreme Left, virtually no one in the Soviet intellectual circles of the 1960s or 1970s felt positively towards either

Mao or Kim. The memories of Stalin's terror and its horrors were still too fresh to render the East Asian Stalinists attractive.

It might come as a surprise, but the lavishly illustrated but badly translated *Korea* magazine was subscribed to by many Soviet people since it was subsidized by the DPRK government and was thus very cheap. The Pyongyang propagandists would be shocked to learn that their publication was normally used as inspiration for countless jokes about *Juche*-style socialism and Kim himself! Their magazine was seen as an unintended crude caricature of the Communist method and official mindset, and as such was widely admired by dissenting intellectuals — as a sort of example in reverse. As a prominent right-wing politician and former underground activist recently remarked: "*Korea* magazine was the only anti–Communist publication on sale in the Soviet news stands."

The great popularity of this magazine is confirmed by the fact that now, in 2005, there are two major Web sites in Russia consisting exclusively of articles taken from the old North Korean propaganda periodicals. Needless to say, they present only those parts which look particularly bizarre and amusing to the post–Soviet Russian reader.

Of course, the Soviet intellectual world of the 1960s and 1970s did not consist of liberal-minded intellectuals alone. There were also hard-liners and nationalists, hawkish admirers of the strong state. In this group, however, North Korea also enjoyed little popularity. The hard-liners were probably quite happy about Kim's Stalinist policies, but they did not like his intense nationalism or his anti–Russian tendencies. For these "neo-imperialists," Kim Il Sung was, first and foremost, an unreliable ally.

Soviet officials, including a majority of diplomats and Leonid Brezhnev himself, were not fond of Pyongyang either: they disapproved of its brutal and inefficient Stalinism and saw it as an unreliable, costly and scheming ally.

Nonetheless, despite the friction between the states, the flow of Soviet aid never ceased. It is difficult or even impossible to calculate the scale of this Soviet aid; the rough estimate is some 2.2 billion dollars over the 1948–1984 period.

One of the factors which makes a correct estimate impossible was the indirect nature of the aid. The Soviets (and, for that matter, the Chinese) shipped to the North industrial equipment and weapons as well as oil and gas, and in most cases this was not officially seen as "aid," since the North supposedly paid for these shipments. However, North Korea paid not in hard currency, but in kind. The USSR and China shipped to the North oil and other items which could be sold on the international market. In exchange, they often received low-quality consumer goods which were virtually unsaleable on any normal market. In other words, a large part of the trade between

North Korea and its fellow Communist countries may be described as barter-ing avionics and oil for bad tobacco, pickled cucumbers and padded cotton blankets. When North Korea saw a chance to sell something for hard cur-rency, these items were never shipped to its Communist brother states — even if this meant an obvious breach of its existing agreements.

The importance of this aid was vividly demonstrated in the 1990s when the changed political environment caused erstwhile allies to lose interest in subsidizing exchanges with the DPRK. The sudden withdrawal of the aid triggered a complete collapse of the North Korean economy. For almost a decade, the North Korean GNP shrank. The process was reversed only in the late 1990s when Pyongyang found a new politically motivated donor — and this time, it was the South.

However, the scale and significance of the foreign aid which the North received was never recognized by the official propaganda. Quite often the North Korean media told blatant lies: when they reported the successful com-pletion of a new industrial project, they never mentioned any foreign partic-ipation, even if it was large and, in some cases, decisive. Nor did the Korean press ever mention that locally produced cars were copies of Soviet proto-types. In some cases the North Koreans went even further and simply removed any labels which could show that a particular item had been imported from overseas!

Why then did the Soviets provide for a regime which they did not really like, and did not perceive to be a reliable ally? Altruism has no place in the world of international diplomacy, and no nation is ready to sacrifice a con-siderable slice of its wealth for nothing — and of course, the Soviet Union of the 1960s and 1970s was no exception. Its policy towards North Korea from the early 1960s to the early 1990s was driven by three major considerations, two of which were totally pragmatic and had nothing to do with ideology.

First of all, North Korea was seen as a bulwark against the U.S. military and political presence in East Asia. The North Korean armed forces formed a protective shield between the U.S.F.K (U.S. Forces in Korea, some 60,000 strong in the 1960s) and the vital industrial areas of the Soviet Far East. In the event of World War III or another major confrontation with the U.S., the North Korean army would distract a number of U.S. troops, and thus the Soviet strategists wanted to keep it in good fighting order. The North Korean economy was also to be supported — otherwise, the country would be unable to maintain an efficient army.

However, this policy was not free of risks. The Soviet diplomats were always afraid that some reckless actions by the North Koreans might spark an unnecessary confrontation with the U.S. A couple of times in the late 1960s and mid–1970s this almost happened — the capture of the USS *Pueblo* in 1968 being the most notorious example. At the time, Washington believed that the Soviets had instigated the attack, while the opposite was in fact true: Moscow employed all means at its disposal to push Pyongyang to the negotiation table.

The second imperative related to the ongoing Sino-Soviet feud. Moscow provided Pyongyang with aid since the DPRK made it clear that without such aid it would probably join the Chinese side. From the North Korean point of view, the rift between the USSR and China was a godsend. It gave North Korea enormous leverage over both Communist giants. And Pyongyang diplomats used this leverage with admirable skill, extracting additional aid from both Moscow and Beijing without actually joining either side.

Thirdly, despite its ideological differences, North Korea was seen as a socialist nation, eligible for at least a minimum of support because of its professed allegiance to the Communist doctrine. The stability and relative prosperity of such a country would be useful for the eventual worldwide victory of Communism. Even though in the 1960s, not to mention the 1980s, very few people in the Kremlin were seriously interested in the future of the World Revolution, the propaganda value of this fiction still influenced Soviet policy towards the DPRK to some extent.

Money Grows on Trees

WHEN IN MARCH 1967, THE USSR and North Korea signed an agreement about cooperation in logging, few expected that this would become by far the longest and most successful joint business project ever undertaken by the two countries. Most of the other joint industrial undertakings ended in failure: from the very beginning these projects were driven exclusively by political expediency and were seen by Moscow as yet another way to keep the struggling North Korean economy afloat. Pyongyang was happy to squeeze more money from its major donor, but economically the cooperation proved disappointing.

The timber project was unique in being based on a genuinely complementary arrangement between the two countries' economies. When the gulags were emptied after Stalin's death, few people were willing to go to fell trees in remote corners of Siberia of their own volition. The North Koreans possessed an abundance of cheap labor but almost no good timber. Thus, the idea of cooperation came naturally. In March 1967, when the relations between the two countries began to recover after a serious chill, the logging agreement was signed.

According to the agreement, the North Korean loggers were allowed to work in designated areas of the Russian Far East. They were housed in special labor camps, run by the North Korean administration. The timber produced was divided between the two sides: the Russians got 60% and the Koreans 40% of the harvest.

Initially, North Koreans were not eager to go to Siberia. Thus, only people with a "bad class background" were dispatched to work in the timber camps in the 1970s. Many of them were minor criminals who were sent to Siberia with the promise of full exoneration upon their return.

However, by the mid–1970s it became clear that these people did not make good workers. The North Korean authorities decided to change their approach and emphasize carrots rather than sticks. The strategy worked. Around 1980 they began to pay wages in rubles, not in the almost meaningless North Korean *won*. To an outsider, a Soviet ruble in the early 1980s did not look like a mighty currency, but it was this switch which finally transformed the logging into a highly prestigious occupation. The Soviet internal market was well-stocked when compared to North Korea's, and rubles could buy things beyond the wildest dreams of the average Northerner.

In those days, when no private businesses were tolerated, it was perhaps the only way for the average North Korean to earn really serious money. North Koreans began to compete for the opportunity to go, often bribing responsible officials. By the early 1980s even college graduates lobbied hard to be selected for a work trip to Siberia.

In the 1980s a logger would receive the rough equivalent of some $30–40 a month, of which about a third would be deducted as various payments (including a "voluntary" contribution to the Great Leader). However, for a North Korean this still represented a fortune. Within a year such a worker could save enough money to buy a color TV and a fridge — items that were beyond the wildest dreams of most North Koreans at the time. Around 1985, the black market price of a Soviet-made fridge was about 15,000 NK *won*— some 15 times the *annual* salary of an average worker. One of these items would probably go to the official who arranged the employment selection, but as the normal length of a trip was three years, the loggers made enough money for themselves as well.

At their peak in the late 1980s, the Far East joint logging projects employed over 20,000 North Korean workers. Since the workers were rotated every three years, it is likely that up to a quarter of a million North Koreans have taken part in this project over the decades.

The Soviet Union had far higher standards of living and was a much more liberal and permissive society than the North. This meant that the North Korean leaders always saw it as a potential source of troublesome information.

However, the timber project was not as dangerous as it might seem: the North Korean workers were placed in the middle of nowhere, and kept under the watchful eyes of their supervisors in isolated camps. People who broke the rules were arrested and sent back to the North. If this was deemed too difficult or impractical, they could be killed on the spot — the Siberian forests provided enough spaces for secret burials and the Soviet authorities usually turned a blind eye to anything the North Korean administrators thought it "necessary" to do.

In the heyday of the operations, there were 17 logging camps, divided into two zones with head offices in Chegdomyn and Tinta. The system still exists today, in the 2000s, even if the scale of operation and number of camps is smaller. Each camp consists of a number of "companies" — North Korea is known for its penchant for the militaristic terminology; even miners form "battalions," "companies" and "platoons." There are "communication companies," "transportation companies," "road maintenance companies" and the like, but the major unit is the "field company" or *sanji chungdae* which consists of workers who do the main job — the logging itself.

The loggers are divided into groups, each consisting of 5–6 men. They live in small trailers which provide just enough heated living space for 6 berths and are 2 meters wide and 4 meters long. There are portraits of Kim Il Sung and Kim Jong Il, of course, strategically hung in the dormitory. The trailers are located near the logging area and even many miles away from the dubious comfort of the main camps. A lot like the girls in foctories

Logging has to be done in winter, between November and April, when temperatures in this area drop to -40° C (and below). The conditions are harsh, and loggers cannot wash themselves for several months in a row. They cook their own food, using rice rations which are quite generous by the North Korean standards: 800 grams of rice per day. They augment their rations by hunting, but their habit of hunting pet dogs for food has always been one of the major causes of clashes with the local villagers.

Around 1990, in the heyday of perestroika, investigative Russian journalists began to report on the conditions of the North Korean workers. The exposure of a secret prison maintained by the North Korean security police in one of the logging camps led to a particular public outcry in Russia. In those times the Russians felt almost universal enthusiasm for democracy and believed that Kim Il Sung's regime would collapse soon.

There were also publications about secret opium plantations and the illegal harvesting of protected species of plants and animals — both frankly long-established parts of North Korea's currency-earning programs. On top of that, some loggers used the change in the international situation to defect to the South. In those days, defectors were still rare and thus welcomed in Seoul.

Needless to say, this political danger led Pyongyang to wonder if sending workers to the Siberian wilderness was not the same as shipping them direct to Seoul.

In 1993-1994 it appeared that the entire timber project would be discontinued because of these manifold political pressures. However, the situation changed quickly. The events of 1992–2005 made Russians quite skeptical about democracy and suspicious of idealistic crusades of any kind. Thus, the North Korean camps were left alone — to the great relief of the local Russian administrators and businessmen who make good money out of the projects. For them, the North Koreans are just a cheap labor force, and they do not care how these "Orientals" are treated by their supervisors. When the initial Russian enthusiasm for a free press died out, the local politicians also learned how to keep journalists away. *we see they before?*

By the late 1990s, it also became clear that South Korea was not going to encourage the defection of the loggers. On the contrary, anecdotal evidence indicates that those loggers who managed to escape, find some shelter (usually with help of sympathetic Russians) and then approach the local South Korean consulate, were turned away in the most unceremonious manner. Seoul does not need these impoverished and potentially troublesome brethren in these days of the "Sunshine policy" of engagement and unilateral concessions to the North! Of course, some loggers still manage to run away, but largely in order to find better job opportunities in Russia's black economy. There are about a thousand such runaways hiding in Russia now, but the authorities tend to ignore their presence.

Then in the 1990s the joint projects diversified. There are some 11–12,000 North Korean workers in the Russian Far East today — and about a thousand North Koreans are in hiding, mostly runaways from the camps. The number of loggers in the area shrank to 8,000, even though logging still remains the most significant industry in which North Koreans are employed.

Businessmen in the newborn capitalist Russia are eager to get their hands on cheap laborers who can be easily disciplined. Thus, the North Koreans are employed on vegetable plantations and, especially, on construction sites. Small groups of North Korean workers are even allowed to seek their own employment. They must pay the North Korean state a fixed amount of cash (reportedly, about $10 per head per day), and then use the rest as they wish. After paying this tax and buying food for himself, the average worker can easily save $100–150 a month — a very large amount of money by North Korean standards.

This means that the North Korean workers now enjoy much more freedom of movement than in the heyday of the logging operations of the 1980s. This has not led to political problems either, since their plight does not evoke much sympathy in Russia, and since the South Korean consulates and other official representative make it clear that common defectors should not count on their help.

If the North Korean laborers are mentioned at all by the Russian press, they are portrayed as either troublesome illegal immigrants or as predators who prey on the vulnerable resources of the Far East. While not necessarily wrong, this reflects a remarkable change in the attitude to North Korea which has occurred in Russia over the last decade. It also reflects the remarkable cynicism which reigns supreme as long as human rights issues are concerned in contemporary Russia, like it or not.

Russian attitute towards DPRK

A School of Thought

PORTRAITS OF KIM IL SUNG AND Kim Jong Il adorn a small school square. Crowds of school children in Young Pioneer uniforms are about to begin their parade, with the obligatory goose-stepping and flag-waving. The loudspeakers erupt with the usual mix of marching tunes, militant slogans, and eulogies to the Great Leaders. Is this a typical festival at a North Korean school somewhere in Pyongyang or Kaesong? Yes and no. The school is North Korean all right, but it is located in Japan and is attended by the children of the so-called Chongryon Koreans, supporters of the pro–Pyongyang General Association of Korean Residents in Japan, better known as Chongryon or Soren.

Education has been important to Chongryon since its foundation in 1955. In those days two thirds of the 650,000-strong ethnic Korean community opted to staunchly support the pro–Pyongyang Chongryon rather than its pro–Seoul competitor. One of the reasons driving this was the persistent educational efforts of Korean leftists in post-war Japan.

Nowadays, Chongryon operates some 140 Korean schools across Japan. At least in the major cities it is possible to provide Korean-language education at all levels, from kindergarten to high school. Their educational system is crowned by the Korean University in Tokyo, established in 1956. Most Japanese companies and agencies do not recognize certificates from this university, and thus the university largely trains people who will work within the Chongryon-sponsored network of businesses, credit unions, youth and sports unions, etc.

The graduates of high and middle schools also face serious problems if they want to continue their education in Japanese universities. Only recently were they allowed to sit the exam for entrance to the national universities. In

Korean & Japanese cultures clashing

the past the more ambitious students had to transfer to Japanese schools to prepare them for college entrance. However, for decades this did not matter much: Koreans were strongly discriminated against, and only a small number of them continued their education at the university level.

The curriculum and textbooks for the Chongryon schools are compiled by Chongryon's Education Department. For at least four decades this department emulated the North Korean textbooks and were overloaded with the peculiar North Korean vocabulary. Sonya Ryang, the leading authority on the ethnic Korean community in Japan, once remarked that in the past, students of a Chongryon school knew how to address an agricultural cooperative manager in North Korea, but were unaware of the names for the many Japanese institutions they dealt with on an almost daily basis.

The deification of the Kim dynasty also found its way into these ethnic Korean schools. It was especially prominent in the two decades between 1973 and 1993, the changes coinciding with the revision of the curriculum, which is revised once a decade. Until last year the portraits of Kim Il Sung and Kim Jong Il had graced every classroom, and students spent several hours every week studying the "revolutionary history" of the Kims.

This was part of a general effort to imbue students with a mix of *Juche*-style leftism and Korean nationalism. Needless to say, North Korea was portrayed as a stronghold of the "true Korean spirit," while South Korea was a land of hunger, poverty, and repression. When, in the early 1990s, the utter implausibility of such propaganda became too obvious, the South Korean topics were simply dropped from the textbooks and students' contacts with things South Korean were discouraged.

The regular dispatch of "education money" from North Korea is an important part of the propaganda campaigns. Children, and for that matter, most Chongryon supporters are led to believe that these funds are crucial in running the schools. This is of course not the case: although the Chongryon budget is a closely guarded secret, there is little doubt that remittances from Chongryon to North Korea far exceed any contributions made by the North Korean government towards the schooling of Korean children in Japan.

Despite their shortcomings these national schools have been popular for decades. The selfless work of the teachers and administrators has provided ethnic Koreans with an education in their native tongue, and helped to keep the language alive for two or three generations. Even pro–Seoul families send their children to these institutions. South AND North

However, the number of schools is dwindling, and in 2000 they only had half as many students as they had in 1967. The almost unbreakable "glass wall" of discrimination which once surrounded the ethnic Koreans in Japan is beginning to crumble as well, and this, combined with the influence of South

Korea's success and news about North Korea's misery, continues to undermine Chongryon. Nevertheless, the fact remains that for many decades, Koreans in democratic and affluent Japan chose to associate with one of the world's most brutal governments, and did so completely of their own volition. This is one of the paradoxes of North Korea.

Woah.
weird choice (considering)
they have the option not to

PART 15

On Spying, Smuggling and Kidnapping

Cigarettes, and Whiskey, and Wild, Wild ... Diplomats

EARLY IN 1976, DANISH POLICE BEGAN to monitor a jewelry shop in Copenhagen. Its owner, they suspected, was involved in some illegal dealings. They soon noticed that a black Mercedes with diplomatic license tags often appeared near the shop, and that the car's passengers handed bags to the shop owner. The Mercedes was identified as belonging to the North Korean Embassy.

The suspicious meetings focused police attention on the diplomats' activity, and on October 13, 1976, the North Korean diplomats were caught handing 147 kg of hashish to local drug dealers. The entire Embassy staff of four diplomats was promptly expelled. This was the beginning of the "Scandinavian smuggling crisis" which is still well remembered by many — not least due to its bizarre nature.

This was not the first time North Korean diplomats had been caught moving illegal drugs. In May 1976, a group of North Korean diplomats, once again smuggling hashish, were intercepted by Egyptian customs. The loyal soldiers of the Great Leader even drew knives, but they were overwhelmed and of course, their diplomatic passports saved them from prosecution.

But it was in Scandinavia in the mid–1970s that the North Korean embassies became involved in illegal activities on a massive scale. And this was not just good old espionage, long tacitly recognized as an integral component of the diplomatic trade. No, the North Koreans were engaged in something far more intriguing: the large-scale vending of smuggled merchandise!

256

Soon after the Copenhagen debacle, in late October 1976, the Norwegian police caught North Korean diplomats selling 4,000 bottles of smuggled liquor and a large quantity of smuggled cigarettes. *Where for,*

Liquor was to feature prominently in the Nordic crisis. In order to control the drinking habits of the population, and also to increase tax revenues, the northern governments imposed exorbitant taxes on alcohol. I still remem-*got it* ber one by-product of this policy — the wild Finnish drinking parties of the 1980s which were often held in my native St. Petersburg, where they could enjoy the cheap booze. This system made the importation of tax-free liquor an extremely profitable business. Pyongyang officials soon discovered that this was a way to make easy money, and began to transport tax-free liquor and cigarettes in their diplomatic luggage.

In Norway, for example, it was estimated that the DPRK Embassy sold liquor and cigarettes with a black market value of some one million dollars (at present day prices, this would be at least three times this amount).

After Norway and Denmark, a similar network was discovered in two other Nordic countries — Finland and Sweden. The scale of operations in Sweden was probably the largest, and the affair was widely discussed in the local press. One night, some mischievous Swedish students put a sign reading "Wine and Spirits Co-op" on the entrance to the DPRK Embassy — to the great annoyance of its inhabitants.

However, Sweden did not follow Denmark and Norway's lead and break diplomatic relations with the North. As a Swedish official explained at the time, "There were other considerations involved." His nebulous remark was easy to interpret: of the Scandinavian countries, Sweden was the only one that had real interests in North Korea. In the early 1970s, when Pyongyang widely borrowed on the international market, Swedish businessmen shipped a large amount of equipment to Pyongyang.

Obviously they acted on the then-common assumption that Communist countries made good borrowers. It was only when, around 1980, North Korea became the first Communist country to default on its loans, that the Swedes belatedly learned to their chagrin that the pickings were not as good as they had assumed. However, the vain hope of recovering some money prevented Stockholm from officially breaking off relations. The fact that Sweden also had a representative in the Armistice commission might also have had some bearing on the decision.

Thus, the rather inept attempt to use diplomatic privilege for smuggling backfired. This does not mean that these activities ceased. From the mid-1970s, the North Korean missions overseas were under permanent pressure to earn money to pay for their expenses and, ideally, send some currency back to the home coffers. All legal and illegal methods were permitted: after all, foreigners were outsiders and hence fair game for *Juche* warriors. Nor were Pyongyang's allies and sponsors exempted — all were fair game.

All these activities probably created far more problems than the amount of money earned warranted. In essence, it was a mistake. But the occasional erratic behavior or miscalculation by North Korean diplomats should not lead us to underestimate their skills. They might be inept tacticians, but they are good strategists who have managed to outsmart many a powerful adversary.

The Secrets of Room 39

EARLY IN 1996 A RICH JAPANESE VISITOR attracted the attention of the Thai police. The attention was probably unwanted but certainly well-deserved: during his visits to Thailand, this man paid for his expenses with counterfeit U.S. $100 bills. The suspect was intercepted when he was trying to cross from Cambodia to Vietnam in a North Korean Embassy car. Inside the car police found a bag of counterfeit U.S. $100 bills. The man's identity was discovered as well: the rich Japanese was none other than Yoshimi Tanaka, one of the Japanese extremists who in 1970 had hijacked a Japanese plane and forced it to land in North Korea. He had resided in the North ever since.

A long trial ensued. Tanaka denied that he had anything to do with the 1,238 counterfeit bills found in the car. Since it was impossible to prove otherwise or, for that matter, arrest the North Korean diplomats who accompanied Tanaka, Tanaka was acquitted of the counterfeit charge in 1999 on the grounds of insufficient evidence. He was extradited to Japan to stand trial for hijacking, however....

The Tanaka affair was just another reminder of the scale of the "unconventional economy" practiced by the North. Indeed, North Korea has acquired a notoriety as a country which uses quite unusual methods to fill the coffers of its treasury. The first incidents of this kind took place in Scandinavia in the mid–1970s and have been described above. But smuggling liquor and cigarettes in the diplomatic luggage was only the beginning of an enduring and well-established enterprise supervised by a special agency in the North Korean bureaucracy.

It was recently reported that over the years 1976–2003 there have been 50 documented cases of North Korean diplomats involved in drug trafficking. The actual figure is much higher, since the North Koreans targeted not only the "hostile" West, but the "friendly" Communist bloc as well. The North Korean embassy in Moscow was engaged in smuggling from the early 1980s, with North Korean students in the then USSR used as sales agents. Due to "national interest considerations," these incidents were never reported by the Soviet and later Russian presses, but they were always a thorn in the relations between Moscow and Pyongyang.

Over the recent decade this activity has increased. In a number of countries North Korean officials have been caught trying to sell counterfeit U.S. dollars, illegal drugs (largely methamphetamines), or ivory. Of course, similar things have happened with officials from a number of other states, but in these cases it is normally the result of the penetration of the state bureaucracy by some criminal rings. In North Korea, the opposite is the case: it is the state itself that has decided to use criminal methods to increase its revenues.

And why do they need to do this? Because North Korea badly needs money and cannot get enough revenue through the normal channels. They have no currency to pay for imports, and their industry is largely unable to manufacture products that are marketable overseas.

Most of the illicit trade is coordinated by an agency called Room 39, a special department in the KWP Central Committee bureaucracy (in English it is usually rendered as "Division 39," but I choose to stick to the more literal translation). Room 39's main goal is to acquire hard currency through any legal or illegal means.

Room 39 is especially active in Macau, the former Portuguese colony which has become a major base for North Korean illicit operations. In 1994 the Macau authorities arrested the head of a North Korean trade company and four other North Koreans for making a deposit of a large amount of counterfeit $100 bills. Of course, they were loyal to the Great Leader (or rather to their own families who were hostages back home), and did not say anything. The investigation came to a standstill, but similar activities certainly did not. In 1998 a North Korean official was caught while trying to pass U.S. $30,000 in counterfeit bills in Moscow. In 1999 another incident took place in Macau. A number of similar incidents have taken place in Thailand over the past decade as well.

Coincidentally, U.S. experts believe that the Pyongyang-produced U.S. dollars are of exceptional quality, which is assuring — at least we know that some North Korean products are of international standard....

Another Room 39 favorite is ivory. Diplomatic immunity provides Room 39 with wonderful opportunities to move ivory around the globe, from the African poachers to the rich consumers in South Asia. A North Korean diplomat was once intercepted in Moscow smuggling 600 kg of ivory! And they do not care how many elephants die in the process. Endangered species? Bah, humbug!

North Korea also appears to be a major producer and exporter of drugs, with Japan being its major target. Pyongyang's logic is simple: international politics is a struggle for survival, and no holds are barred!

Intelligence Quotient in North Korea? High!

NEAR THE KIM IL SUNG UNIVERSITY, in the Moranbong district of Pyongyang, stands an intriguing group of official buildings. They do not bear any signs, but there is nothing special about that: even the most innocuous North Korean agencies do not advertise their whereabouts. However, in this particular case there are good reasons to be discreet. The Moranbong complex houses a powerful part of the North Korean intelligence community.

Communist countries typically followed the Soviet example of having two distinct, and sometimes competing, intelligence services. One was responsible for political intelligence and for industrial espionage in non-military areas (in the USSR it was the foreign branch of the KGB; in later decades of Soviet history it was known as the First Directorate), while another was gathering military intelligence (in the USSR this was the Armed forces' Main Intelligence Administration, better known as GRU).

The North Koreans augmented this duo with another service which can be described as the party's own intelligence. Nothing like it existed in most other Communist countries.

This peculiarity is a result of North Korea's history. The ruling Korean Workers' Party or KWP is not, technically, a *North* Korean party. It was created in 1949 when the North Korean Workers' Party merged with the (then illegal) South Korean Workers' Party. The united party was supposed to operate across the entire Peninsula.

The 1949 merger meant than the KWP inherited a large underground network in South Korea. It included numerous party cells, groups of agents, guerrilla detachments, and clandestine presses. In those days, the Communist underground still hoped to overthrow the South Korean government by means of domestic rebellion, and was engaged in large-scale guerrilla warfare in the South (as newly discovered Soviet documents testify, this was done with the full support and encouragement of Moscow).

Running this secret network required a special agency which would be responsible for subversive activity in the South. Such a department had to be created within the Korean Workers' Party structure, since the clandestine operations in the South were run by the KWP.

Thus, the KWP Central Committee acquired what was known as a "Liaison Department." This Department was principally set up to liaise with the South Korean underground, and keep it provided with weapons, instructors, radio stations, and what not.

By the mid–1950s, after the end of the Korean War, the South Korean Communist underground ceased to exist. Most of its activists had been killed or imprisoned, while others had moved to the North where, more often than not, they eventually felt victim to Kim Il Sung's purges. *[handwritten: chonic]*

However, the Liaison Department outlived the structures which it was initially supposed to run. For a while, it was deemed necessary to preserve it since the North Korean leaders hoped to restore the Communist underground in the South. Even when this dream died sometime in the 1970s, the Department survived. Now the Department coordinates operations aimed at undermining the Seoul government and bringing a *Juche*-style revolution to the South. It is also responsible for "revolutionizing" the overseas Koreans, and using them as a channel of influence in the South. For example, the powerful pro–Pyongyang "Association of Korean Residents in Japan" (better known under its Korean name of Ch'ongryŏn) is controlled by the Central Committee's United Front Department, a part of the "Third Building" bureaucracy.

Of course, not much is known about this structure, not least because the South Korean intelligence services, which presumably have a wealth of data, are not eager to leak it to the press.

The "Third Building" bureaucracy is presided over by a KWP secretary who is responsible for dealing with the South. The "Third Building" also houses three or four interconnected, specialized departments of the Central Committee.

The former Liaison Department is still the center of bureaucracy. It is now known as the "Department of Society and Culture" (a nice name for a spy agency, is it not?). It trains the people who are to be dispatched to the South, and runs a network of underground agents there. Its efforts are augmented by the "United Front Department" which manipulates a number of seemingly innocuous front organizations, operating both in North Korea and among ethnic Koreans overseas. The Operational Department deals with technical questions relating to the dispatch of agents.

The Foreign Intelligence Analysis Department, often known as "Room 35" (or "Bureau 35") used to be a part of the "Third Building," but according to some reports it has become independent from the "Third Building" even though it remains a part of the KWP Central Committee bureaucracy. This department is responsible for acquiring and processing foreign intelligence not necessarily related to South Korea.

In addition to the "Third Building," North Korea has two other intelligence services: the Military Intelligence and the Ministry for the Protection of State Security.

Of Disappearing Maidens and Fisherfolk

NORTH KOREAN SPY AGENCIES LOVE KIDNAPPINGS. Of course, many of their colleagues worldwide would also love to abduct a person or two, but in most cases there are perceived urgent reasons for such dramatic actions: the victims are prominent opposition leaders, or wanted criminals who cannot be extradited through normal channels, or people who are unlucky enough to know something far too important to be allowed freedom of movement or speech.

However, some of the North Korean abductions are different: they are often surprisingly random and target people of no apparent significance. The very randomness of most abductions was once cited by skeptics who used to rebut these accusations as "Seoul-inspired falsities." Indeed, why should the secret services of a Stalinist state spend time and money to kidnap a Japanese noodle chef or a tennis-loving teenager? Nonetheless, in 2002 none other than Kim Jong-il himself, the Dear Leader and son of the founder, confirmed that these seemingly meaningless abductions of average Japanese men and women did take place. This led to a major scandal which put additional strain on the already tense relations between North Korea and Japan.

Of course, North Korean spies did not limit themselves to the Japanese. The North Koreans began to snatch their own dissenters, abducting them from the Soviet Union and other communist countries in the 1950s and 1960s. Then they applied their new experience and skills to a wider choice of targets, including, of course, South Koreans.

It is known that since the end of the Korean War in 1953, at least 486 South Koreans have been forcibly taken to the North and never returned. These statistics do not include a large number of North Korean refugees who were abducted from China over the past decade. Nor does it include a far larger number of South Koreans who were taken to the North during the Korean War, either as prisoners or draftees for the North Korean armed forces.

There are four major groups of South Korean abductees: fishermen, navy personnel, and the passengers and crews of hijacked planes. The abductees also include a number of known victims of covert operations. Currently the latter are said to number seventeen, but there is little doubt that the actual number is much higher. If the abduction is planned and conducted well, the victim simply disappears and is sooner or later presumed dead.

A good example is the case of five South Korean high-school students who disappeared from island beaches in 1977-78. They were all believed dead (presumably drowned) for two decades, but in the late 1990s it was discovered that the youngsters were working in North Korea as instructors, introducing would-be undercover North Korean operatives to the basics of South Korean culture and lifestyle.

It is remarkable that the kidnappings of these South Korean students roughly coincided with similar abductions in Japan. In both cases the abductors obviously targeted randomly selected teenagers who were unlucky enough to be on a lonely beach at the wrong time, and in both cases abductees were later used to train espionage agents. Perhaps teenagers were seen as ideal would-be instructors for the spies: still susceptible to indoctrination but with enough knowledge of local realities to be useful. But one cannot help but wonder how many teenagers who are still presumed to be drowned or lost in the Korean Peninsula's mountains were actually taken to North Korea. And how many of them have survived to this day? Just a training act, v/+?

Quite a few of the kidnappings took place overseas. In April 1979, a young South Korean walked into the North Korean Embassy in Oslo. His name was Ko Sang-mun and he was a schoolteacher back home. Why and how he did this is not clear. As was usually the case, the North Korean side insisted that Ko had defected, while the South Koreans alleged that the young teacher was the victim of a taxi driver's mistake: he took a taxi to the "Korean embassy" and the driver delivered him to the embassy of the *wrong Korea*.

At that stage, it is impossible to say whether this highly publicized case was abduction, a defection or something in between. However, in 1994 it was revealed that Ko was in a labor camp. A small propaganda war ensued. Ko was made to appear in North Korean broadcasts assuring everybody that he was free, happily married and full of righteous hatred for the U.S. imperialists and their Seoul puppets (most of his broadcast speech consisted of standard anti–American and anti–South rhetoric). We do not know where he disappeared to after delivering this speech — to an apartment in Pyongyang or to a dugout in a prison camp, but the latter option appears more likely. Meanwhile, Ko's widow in the South committed suicide, unable to cope with the stress of the situation.

There were also more convenient cases of abduction: the North Koreans kidnapped people who possessed important intelligence. In 1971 Yu Song-gun, a South Korean diplomat stationed in West Germany, was kidnapped in West Berlin together with his wife and their two children. Perhaps a few other

South Korean officials who went missing in Europe in the 1970s were also abducted by North Korean agents, but at this stage only Yu's case is certain.

In the 1990s most abductions of this sort took place in China, and the victims were political activists, missionaries and real or suspected South Korean spies. All these abductions occurred in China's northeast, near the North Korean border. In early 2005, the South Korean government finally admitted that pastor Kim Tong-sik, involved in aiding North Korean refugees in China, was kidnapped by North Korean agents in January 2000. He was transported to North Korea, where the intelligence officers tried to extract information from him — presumably by applying good old Stalinist interrogation techniques on him. The pastor died.

A vast majority — 90% of the confirmed cases or 435 out of 486 abductees — are fishermen who were taken to the North with their vessels after they were intercepted at sea by the North Korean navy. After such incidents, the North Koreans usually insisted that the vessel had deliberately crossed the demarcation line between the two Koreas, while the South Korean side either denied this or asserted that the trespassing had been an innocent navigational mistake. It is not possible to say who was responsible for a particular skirmish, especially since the navigational techniques available to Korean fishermen back in the 1960s and 1970s left much to be desired.

In some cases the captured crews were eventually repatriated, but often Pyongyang alleged that at least a few crew members had "chosen to stay in the socialist paradise and not to return to the living hell of the capitalist South." In some cases this may have been true, while in many others it was a blatant lie. This is a common problem with abductions or defections. When an incident happens, South Korean authorities and the family members of an abductee have an incentive to present the incident as a kidnapping while the North Korean side insists that the person in question has defected voluntarily. One suspects that even in the future it will be impossible to discover the truth with absolute certainty: human motivations can be mixed. There will be new pressures as well: in post–Kim Jong Il Korea, few people will be ready to admit that they or their close friends once voluntarily defected to the Stalinist regime.

The first known interception of a fishing boat took place in May 1955 and the most recent incident occurred in 1987, when 12 South Koreans became the prisoners of the North. During subsequent interceptions the crews were always repatriated.

Some people were kidnapped in the air, not at sea. The first such incident took place in 1958 when a group of hijackers flew a South Korean plane to the North. Most of the passengers and crew were returned, but Pyongyang in its usual manner stated that two passengers (and six hijackers, of course) chose to stay in the socialist paradise. In 1969 another plane was hijacked. Most of the South Koreans were repatriated, but twelve crew members and passengers were held in the North. Eventually, two stewardesses became announcers in the North Korean propaganda broadcasts which target South Korean audiences.

Generally North Korean authorities wanted to utilize the knowledge and skills of their abductees. Of course, the fishermen hardly had access to valuable intelligence, but they could still be trained as spies and sent back to the South. They were also used for schooling would-be North Korean intelligence operatives. The better-educated abductees could be employed by institutions responsible for waging propaganda campaigns against the South in, say, their broadcast facilities.

Most of the abductees were dispatched to work somewhere in the countryside. Some led lives which could be described as normal or even successful, at least by North Korean standards. For example, Kim Pyŏng-do, whose boat was intercepted in November 1974, was forced to stay in the North, where he became a factory worker. Eventually he became a foreman, was decorated for exceptional work, and otherwise enjoyed a life not so very different from that of the average North Korean worker. In 2003 he crossed the border into China and returned home. Others were much less lucky. There have been reports about abductees being sent to prison camps as "unmasked spies" or "reactionaries" (the above-mentioned story of Ko Sang-mu being one of many examples).

But one cannot help but wonder why there is not much said about the abduction issue in Seoul. After all, there have been fewer than 60 Japanese abductees — even if one were to believe the highest available estimate. Nonetheless, the issue is central to Japanese politics and stirs high emotions in Tokyo. Meanwhile, only family members and some right-wing groups seem to care about South Koreans who have vanished in the direction of Pyongyang. So what is the matter?

This reflects the general approach to the North in present-day South Korea. The abduction issue used to be much cited by the official propaganda of the military regimes of the 1960s and 1970s, but middle-aged Koreans are seriously (and, one suspects, incurably) allergic to anything that reminds them of this propaganda. The political Left, which increasingly dominates South Korean internal discourse, is remarkably positive towards the North. The logic is simple: if one raises uncomfortable issues with the North, it is unlikely to help, and will doubtless make things more complicated instead.

The left-wing journalists love to say, "Development needs come first, and human rights second." This might well be true, but these same ideologues are incensed when a similar logic is applied to the authoritarian regimes of

South Korea's own past, even if South Korean strongmen, unlike the North Korean dynastic rulers, delivered truly exceptional economic growth, and even if the human-rights violations in the military-ruled South were on an infinitely smaller scale. This can probably be described as a betrayal of political freedom committed by the South Korean Left — but admittedly, throughout the world's history, freedom has been sacrificed to political expediency both by the Left and the Right a countless number of times.

It is important to note, however, that isolated attempts to raise the issue are largely ignored by the general South Korean public, or at least by the majority. They long to nurture their newly acquired illusions about the North. According to the currently prevailing mood, North Korea should be seen as a tragically misunderstood brother in need of help, not as a cruel kidnapper of teenagers or torturer of priests on humanitarian missions.

Sometimes, the present-day South Korean public opinion (or rather the now dominant sections of it) conveniently forgets the most outrageous examples of North Korean action. Few people remember, for example, the attempted abduction of two South Korean artists which took place in Zagreb — even if the documents recently found in the archives of the former Yugoslavia shed new light on this story. Which brings us to our next topic....

Perhaps too blind to know better

Piano, Piano

IN EARLY JULY 1977, PAEK KǑN-U, a young but famous Korean pianist residing in Paris, received a rather unusual proposal. He was told that a Swiss multi-millionaire would like a private concert to be given in his home, and Paek Kǒn-u had been selected as the artist to play this concert. He was invited to go to Switzerland together with his wife, the famous beauty Yun Chǒng-hŭi, who was one of the leading stars of the South Korean movie industry of the 1970s.

The proposal arrived via Mrs. Pak In-gyǒng, the wife of a prominent Korean painter who also lived in Paris. Mrs. Pak did not make a great secret of her leftist views, and her husband was soon to become one of the very few overseas Korean painters who was permitted to hold an exhibition in Pyongyang. However, in this case Pak In-gyǒng said that she was driven by a purely material interest: the mysterious millionaire was allegedly a buyer of her husband's paintings. Initially Paek was not enthusiastic about the idea, but besieged by Pak In-gyǒng's unrelenting persuasion, he finally gave his agreement.

On July 29, 1977, the couple, accompanied by Pak In-gyǒng, arrived in Zurich where the concerts were to take place. Then things began to take a strange turn. At the airport, the group was greeted by a woman who introduced herself as the millionaire's secretary. She explained that the venue had been changed, and that the private concert would take place in Zagreb, in *Croatia* Yugoslavia. While technically a Communist country, Yugoslavia always was a dissenting member of the Communist bloc and was on relatively good terms with its capitalist neighbors. Nonetheless, it had strict visa regulations. The "secretary" assured them, however, that everything would be taken care of.

When the trio arrived in Zagreb, Paek Kǒn-u and his wife noticed an unusual sight: a North Korean passenger plane standing on the tarmac. Zagreb had a small airport, and had no regular service to Pyongyang (no East European country had such a service in 1977). At the airport Paek and Yun also noticed an Asian woman who appeared to be a North Korean. As promised there were no visa problems: the group was met by a Yugoslav official who let them skip the usual immigration procedures. However, no one greeted them at the airport. Following the instructions they had received in Zurich, they took a taxi and went to a villa located on the city's outskirts. *Bad idea*

By this time Paek Kǒn-u was quite suspicious, and he asked the taxi driver to wait for a moment. He also had his wife remain in the taxi. The villa was empty and did not appear to be the house of a leisurely businessman. However, after a few minutes Paek encountered a man. Judging by his dress and manners, the man was North Korean, so Paek took flight, hotly pursued by the stranger.

Near the gates, the pianist jumped into the car and locked the door before the North Korean could grab the handle. The taxi then drove off. Being the holder of U.S. permanent residency rights, Paek Kǒn-u went straight to the U.S. consulate. The American consular official put them up in a local hotel, next to his own room, and arranged air tickets for the first available flight to Zurich. At dawn, a group of Asian people tried to break into their room, but Paek and Yun did not open the door, and the following morning they flew out. The North Korean plane still stood on the tarmac.

Obviously, Paek's vigilance, courage and good luck (as well as the decisive actions of the American consular official) prevented Yun Chǒng-hǔi and Paek Kǒn-u from becoming the first prominent South Korean artists to be kidnapped by the North Korean secret service.

The late 1970s were the heyday for North Korean kidnappings, and strangely enough, South Korean movie stars appeared to be one of their favored targets. Perhaps this was the personal imprint of a well-known North Korean movie buff who was supervising the secret operations while being groomed to become the new Dear Leader. In 1978, Ch'oe Ǔn-hǔi, one of Seoul's major movie stars, was abducted in Hong Kong, soon to be followed by her husband, a movie producer. It appears that the same fate was to befall Yun Chŏng-hŭi and Paek Kŏn-u.

In the 1990s more details emerged. It is known that some Yugoslav officials were bribed by the North Korean operatives to facilitate the abduction. But a lot of things remain unclear — like, say, the role of Pak In-gyŏng. Seoul conservatives accuse her of being a Pyongyang agent who tried to lure her "friends" into captivity and perhaps death, while the Left lauds her "progressive pro-democratic activities." We are unlikely to learn the truth anytime soon. But in South Korea, being a "progressive" and even a "human rights activist" does not necessarily preclude an enthusiasm for one of the world's most repressive and murderous regimes. Such are the vagaries of Korean history.

Kidnapping 101

ONE NOVEMBER DAY IN 1957, those who happened to be in the courtyard of the old North Korean embassy in Moscow, witnessed a remarkable episode. All of a sudden, a window on the second story was broken from the inside, and a man in his late 20s jumped from the window onto the roof that covered the entrance to the basement of the building. The next jump put him on the ground, and then the man rushed to the embassy entrance. "Stop him!" "Close the gates!" "The bastard is getting away!" "Start the car!" But it took several minutes to start the embassy cars, and by the time they began the pursuit it was clearly too late: the runaway had disappeared into the Moscow streets. One of the first abductions undertaken by the North Korean secret services had gone awry.

The "Japanese abductee" issue recently once again attracted attention to a bizarre feature of the North Korean spy agencies: their penchant for kidnapping. Among their victims number Japanese and South Korean citizens, but the least known part of the North Korean operations is the kidnapping of North Korean citizens who begin to show traces of dissent while overseas. To avoid the political problems caused by an open defection, these persons are either lured back, abducted, or killed.

Most of these operations took place in the Soviet Union. The Communist superpower had always had a number of North Korean sojourners — students, officials, technical experts, and loggers. The experiences of these people in the USSR often made them skeptical about the omniscience of the Great Leader, or the wisdom of his policies. Such unbelievers had to be dealt with.

We are unlikely to ever learn the precise details of all these operations.

The relevant documents are now buried in the Pyongyang archives, and I am not sure whether these papers will survive the turbulent future events of Korean history. After all, paper is highly inflammable, as every keeper of secrets knows only too well. At any rate, in the early 1990s, several hundred Koreans (largely loggers from timber camps in Siberia) were officially considered "missing" in the USSR. Some of them were indeed victims of crime or miscellaneous incidents, but the Soviet security services believed that many had been kidnapped or assassinated by Pyongyang agents.

The first incident of this kind occurred in 1957, soon after a major scandal rocked relations between Moscow and Pyongyang. Influenced by the Soviet ideas of non–Stalinist socialism, a dozen North Korean students from the prestigious State Institute of Cinematography (VGIK) in Moscow refused to go back to Korea and asked for Soviet asylum. The asylum was granted. This decision of the Soviet authorities was both a humanitarian step, and a clear warning sign to Pyongyang indicating Soviet disapproval of Kim Il Sung's policies.

The VGIK students were led by Hŏ Chin (Hô Un-bae). In spite of his young age (he was 30 years old in 1958), Hŏ Chin was a Korean War hero and also a grandson of Hŏ Wi, a famous Confucian scholar and independence fighter. In Moscow Hŏ Chin became a vocal critic of Kim Il Sung's dictatorship, and the decision was made to kidnap him. The North Korean agents managed to get him into the embassy, but there Hŏ Chin, a man of great fitness and courage, jumped out of the toilet window and disappeared into the city.

Another incident took place in the autumn of 1959, and once again it was the abduction of a dissenting artist. Yi Sang-gu, a North Korean postgraduate student at the Moscow School of Music, applied for Soviet asylum and even sent a letter critical of Kim's regime to Korea's rubber-stamping parliament. Retribution was swift. On 24 November, Yi Sang-gu was abducted by North Korean agents. This incident happened in the center of Moscow in broad daylight, virtually at the feet of the Tchaikovsky monument (a suitable place to kidnap a promising musician). Yi was forced into a car and flown to Pyongyang the next day, visibly drugged and unconscious.

This incident triggered the personal intervention of Nikita Khrushchev, the then Soviet leader. The North Korean ambassador was recalled to Pyongyang and the DPRK government was required to make a formal explanation. As one might guess, the entire affair was blamed on over-zealous officials, but this did not help Yi Sang-gu: the hapless musician disappeared into the Pyongyang prisons forever.

And what happened to Hŏ Chin? He stayed in the USSR where he became a journalist and writer. In the 1970s he undertook a daring project: braving the threats of the North Korean spying agencies, he conducted interviews with numerous North Korean exiles in Russia. These interviews were used in a book which he published in 1982 in Japan — one of the first serious studies of North Korean history.

Almost Brought the House Down

ON JANUARY 16, 1968, A BUS LEFT a top-secret North Korean military base in Hwanghae Province. The passengers were officers of the elite "unit 124," young and fit soldiers in their mid-20s. That evening they departed for a special mission in Seoul.

Their morale was high: the soldiers believed that their operation would hasten the collapse of the "puppet regime" in the South. They were given the password for passing through the DMZ on their way back, but they understood that the chance of their ever using the password was close to zero. Theirs was a mission of no return. The 31 North Korean commandos were tasked with attacking the Blue House, the official residence of the South Korean president.

At some point in 1966 the North Korean leaders (in all probability, Kim Il Sung himself) decided that the South was ripe for a Vietnamese-style revolution. This was a gross misjudgment, but for a few years Pyongyang acted in accordance with this assumption. Hundreds, if not thousands, of Koreans on both sides of the DMZ paid with their lives for this miscalculation.

"Unit 124" was trained for guerrilla and terrorist activities in the South. The unit included a number of Southerners who had moved to the North with their parents prior to or during the Korean War. This is yet another reminder that the entire Korean conflict was essentially a civil war where Koreans fought Koreans.

It took almost two years to train the would-be assassins. In early January, the participants in the raid were trained in a specially constructed model of the Blue House. Everything was well rehearsed.

Initially the operation went smoothly. The commandos crossed the DMZ unnoticed, changed into South Korean army uniforms and began their advance on Seoul. They slept during the day and moved at night. And then the unexpected happened. On January 19 they came across a group of woodcutters. The logic of this operation required any unlucky civilians whom they met to be killed on the spot. But "unit 124" were an idealistic bunch. They fought to liberate the South, not to kill innocent people! Thus, the woodcutters were set free after a crash course in Communist ideology. Once released, they rushed to the police. The lesson was learned, and in later decades North Korean commandos treated unwanted witnesses in a more conventional manner....

However, even though they had been tipped off by the woodcutters, the South Korean police did not manage to intercept the group. Of course, the scale of the problem was underestimated also. In the years 1966–1968, North Korean raids were a common part of border life; security was, however, tightened up.

By early Sunday morning, January 21, the group approached its destination. Everything now was going to plan. After a daytime break, they marched toward the Blue House.

At 10:10 P.M. the North Koreans were a mere three hundred meters from the Blue House gates. Suddenly they were stopped by a police patrol and asked for identification. They insisted that they were soldiers of a special counter-intelligence unit returning to their barracks. However, Ch'oe Kyu-sik, the commander of the Chongno police station, found the group suspicious. In the midst of the argument, one of the North Koreans lost his nerve and opened fire; a gunfight ensued.

Ch'oe Kyu-sik was killed on the spot but he had raised the alarm, so the Southerners were not caught unprepared. The Northerners began to withdraw under heavy fire. About a dozen commandos were killed on the spot. During the fighting, a North Korean soldier threw a hand grenade into a city bus, killing and wounding its passengers.

Eventually, 27 of the 31 North Koreans were either killed or committed suicide to avoid capture. Some 40 South Koreans died in the fighting as well. The fate of the remaining three commandos remained unknown. Much later it was learned that at least one of them managed to return safely to the North, where he later became an army general. There was only one prisoner — Kim Sin-jo, the son of South Korean migrants. He was the commander of a squad responsible for killing everybody of the ground floor of the Blue House. Nowadays, he is a popular Christian minister in Seoul.

The Blue House raid was one of the most bizarre incidents in the history of the two Korean states, but more attempts to assassinate the South Korean top executive followed. The most prominent of them took place in Rangoon in 1983, 15 years after the Blue House raid. But that is our next story....

Okay, Maybe more like enemies... or 'least govt-wise [handwritten note]

Red Faces in Rangoon

ONCE UPON A TIME, THE NORTH KOREAN spy agencies loved to hunt South Korean presidents. Indeed, over the 15-year period between 1968 and 1983, there were at least three assassination attempts against South Korean leaders

by the North Korean secret service. All three attempts were a close shave —
and we can surmise that there have been a number of plans which remained
unknown because they were canceled or went completely wrong.

The last known attempt to kill the chief executive took place in late
1983, in Burma. In the early 1980s South Korea was in turmoil. After the
death of President Pak, power was grabbed by another military strongman,
Chun Doo-hwan.

In early October 1983 a large South Korean delegation was scheduled to
visit Burma, one of the few countries which at that time had diplomatic relations with both Koreas. This opportunity for the North was not to be missed;
the North Korean embassy would be an ideal base for an operation.

On September 22, 1983, a North Korean cargo ship docked in Rangoon
harbor. Apart from the crew members, it had three very special passengers:
Major Chin Mo and Captains Kang Min-ch'ŏl and Sin Ki-ch'ŏl were officers
of the North Korean elite special operations squad. They left the ship unnoticed and were met by a guide, a North Korean woman who worked for the
embassy. The woman escorted the trio to their safe house, the apartment of
a North Korean diplomat.

In the six-story apartment block the officers spent the next few days
waiting for an explosive device to be delivered to them. On October 5 they
left the relative security of the safe house and moved to the scene of the
intended assassination.

Standard Burmese protocol required visiting foreign dignitaries to pay
their respects at the mausoleum of Aung San, the founder of the modern
Burmese state. Despite an ongoing civil war, in 1983 Rangoon itself was a relatively safe place. Thus, the mausoleum was poorly guarded, and at dawn on
October 7 the North Korean agents easily installed the bomb under the roof.
They then prepared an observation post a few hundred meters away. From their
hideout they could activate the device at the right moment. They then spent
the night in a park, and took up their positions at dawn on October 9.

Around ten in the morning, the South Korean dignitaries began to gather
near the mausoleum. They were waiting for the president, who was on his
way. And then the unexpected happened. A Mercedes 280 belonging to the
South Korean ambassador stopped near the mausoleum. It was the last opportunity to rehearse the ceremony, and the Burmese officials decided to make
sure that everything would go according to established protocol. A bugler blew
his trumpet....

When the agents saw these movements, heard the trumpets and saw a
large car carrying the South Korean flag, they assumed that the president had
arrived. Chin Mo, who was the head of the assassination squad, pressed the
button. It was 10:28 A.M. on October 9, 1983.

The huge explosion instantly killed 20 people — 3 Burmese and 17 Koreans. The list of victims included a number of Cabinet ministers. The Vice-Premier, the Minister of Foreign Affairs, and the Minister of Trade and Commerce, as well as a number of other officials were killed in the blast. But, contrary to Kim Il Sung and Kim Jong Il's expectations, Chun Doo-hwan survived — actually, he was well away from the spot when Chin Mo detonated the charge. *[handwritten: Could that start a war?]*

The assassins tried to run away. However, they were soon hunted down by the Burmese police and taken following a fight. Sin Ki-ch'ŏl was killed in the shootout while Chin Mo suffered serious injuries.

Pyongyang denied any involvement, but after the capture of the team, it all became glaringly obvious. Burma broke diplomatic relations with the DPRK, and even official newspapers in China, North Korea's major ally, published the official Burmese reports without any comments, indicating that in Chinese eyes the North Koreans had gone beyond what was acceptable.

Chin Mo, who refused to cooperate with the investigation, was sentenced to death and eventually executed. Kang Min-ch'ŏl had his sentence commuted to life imprisonment. He is still an inmate at Insein Prison. Kang became a devout Buddhist, mastered Burmese, and is studying English.

The Rangoon incident was the last known North Korean attempt to assassinate a South Korean leader. Soon the changes in the political situation made such attempts both impossible and meaningless. After all, over the last decade the survival of the Kim regime was made possible largely by the generous amount of aid provided by South Korea, a country which is technically still at war with the North.

Still Waters Run Deep

FOR THE 50-ODD YEARS THAT FOLLOWED the armistice of 1953, both Korean states have been locked in an intense rivalry. It was a local cold war, a minor version of the global Cold War, but much more emotional, since it was a war between one people. On some occasions this cold war became very hot. Indeed, those decades were an era of daring raids, complicated intrigue, botched and successful assassinations and, of course, of covert naval warfare.

The major role in this quiet warfare was played by North Korean infiltration craft, used to land agents on the South Korean coast. There are three major types of vessels used by the North Korean navy for this purpose. Throughout the history of the quiet naval warfare, two ships of each type were lost due to enemy action.

The most unusual and imaginative contraptions are the semi-submersible boats. These can be described as a poor navy's submarines. They are small boats, with a displacement of some 5–10 tons and a top surface speed of 40–50 knots. They have ballast tanks, and when these tanks are filled with water the craft submerges almost completely, with only the small conning tower visible above the water. In this semi-submerged state the craft is much slower, but it is also almost invisible both to human eyes and to radar. Perhaps they are not as good as a real midget submarine, but they are much cheaper and easier to maintain, and can carry up to six people.

The first battle with such a craft took place in December 1983 when one was discovered not far away from Pusan, and after a chase was sunk by the South Korean navy. Later it was recovered and now can be seen on display in a military museum in Seoul.

Another semi-submersible was lost in action, in 1998. The South Korean signal intelligence discovered the semi-submersible near Yŏsu in the early hours of the morning of December 18. The South Korean navy mobilized a number of planes and ships, which approached the boat, demanding the crew surrender. But North Korean special forces are famous for their unwillingness to give themselves up alive, so they opened fire using small arms. There was no possible doubt about the outcome: the boat was hit by artillery shells and sank, only to be salvaged the following year.

A semi-submersible infiltration boat cannot operate at a great distance from its base, and in most cases it is carried close to the target destination aboard a specially designed mother ship. Such ships are disguised as fishing boats, but they have powerful engines and a built-in dock for a semi-submersible or a more conventional speedboat. The dock is equipped with outward-opening double doors on the stern, allowing the boat to be safely hidden inside the hull.

There have been two cases in which such a ship has been discovered and sunk by hostile forces. The first incident of this kind happened in August 1983 when a South Korean patrol boat discovered just such a ship operating near Ullung-do Island. The ship was sunk after a short shoot-out.

Another incident took place in December 2001, and this time the ship was discovered by the Japanese navy near the Japanese coast. This was not the first discovery of its kind, but on previous occasions the North Koreans ships always managed to flee, taking advantage of their superior speed. This time, however, the ship could not move fast enough — perhaps the disintegration of the economy has influenced the navy as well. As could be expected, the ship's crew refused to surrender and opened fire, injuring two Japanese sailors. The Japanese returned fire and in less than four minutes the ship sank, along with its entire crew.

The North Korean navy also possesses a number of submarines, including the Yugo class vessels. These are specially designed midget submarines whose major task is infiltration. The Yugo boats are small, with a displacement of just 70 tons when submerged.

One such submarine was caught in a fishing net near Sokcho on the east coast on 24 June, 1998. Its propeller and periscope had been fouled. The vessel was captured by the South Korean navy but sank while being towed. The submarine was soon salvaged but all crew and commandos (nine of them — more than usual for a submarine of this type) were found dead. They had committed group suicide.

Larger Sango class submarines are also sometimes used for infiltration. It was just such a submarine that was involved in the most high-profile case of military confrontation between the two Koreas in the 1990s. In mid–September 1996, a North Korean Sango submarine was on a routine infiltration mission: a group of commandos from the so-called Reconnaissance Bureau, the major military intelligence agency, were to conduct a surveillance of the military installations on the east coast. However, in the early hours of 18 September, the submarine ran ashore and was discovered by a taxi driver. The crew and commandos attempted to break through to the DMZ. A long spy hunt ensued, with heavy losses of life on both sides (among the victims there were local farmers whom the commandos killed as dangerous witnesses) as well as with the usual group suicide of the North Korean soldiers.

Indeed, one of the most remarkable features of this quiet war is the unwillingness of the North Korean soldiers to surrender. Few sailors and commandos have ever been taken alive. Does this reflect the exceptional valor of the North Korean warriors? To some extent it may, but there are also other reasons behind such behavior. But that is our next story....

Of Midgets and Fish-Nets

ON THE 22ND OF DECEMBER, 2001, a North Korean spy ship was being chased by Japanese patrol boats. The North Korean crew knew that they were in serious trouble: the engines did not work well, and soon it became clear that they would not be able to escape to the security of their own waters.

When the Japanese boats approached, the North Koreans opened fire with automatic rifles and grenade launchers. Two Japanese sailors were wounded, but the return fire sank the ship in a matter of minutes. Some survivors managed to stay afloat for a while. But they refused any help and even reportedly tried to shoot at their would-be rescuers. They did not last long: in December the seawater is a swift executioner.

In June 1998, the South Korean navy captured a North Korean midget submarine which had been caught in fishing nets. They towed it to a navy base and broke into the hull. They found nine dead bodies: the North Korean crew and commandos destroyed all classified material and committed group suicide. This is all pretty recent

In September 1996, a North Korean submarine ran ashore near Kang-nung on the eastern coast while trying to recover a reconnaissance team which had completed its covert mission. It was less than a hundred kilometers from the DMZ, so the crew attempted a breakthrough. However, their chances were slim. Thus, the commanders ordered the suicide of those who were not fit enough. On September 18, 11 bodies of North Korean sailors and marines were discovered in a forest.

In November 1987, two North Korean agents were apprehended after they had bombed a South Korean passenger jet, killing all 115 people aboard. Both agents took poison: the younger one was saved while her older partner died on spot.

The list of such incidents goes on and on. The North Korean commandos and espionage agents are seldom captured alive — in most cases they die fighting or commit suicide when capture appears imminent. Even during large-scale operations very few prisoners have been taken. Of the 31 commandos who raided the Blue House in 1968, for example, only one was captured. Of the 26 sailors and commandos aboard a submarine which ran ashore in 1996, only one was captured alive.

What are the reasons for such behavior? Of course, one should realize that North Korean warriors are often ready to die for their country — like the warriors of any country should. It does not matter that their country is a repressive and impoverished dictatorship. After all, throughout history, millions of people have voluntarily sacrificed their lives for far more dubious causes. But apart from patriotism, a sense of duty and honor, there are material factors which make the North Korean soldiers remarkably unwilling to surrender — and these factors are probably more important.

How can a dead man be pressured by "material factors," I hear you ask? Very simple: dead people have families — and their responsibility to their loved ones is often far stronger than their responsibility to the imagined community of a nation.

There was a wonderful Soviet joke of the 1970s which nicely captures the essence of the problem:

U.S. President Carter and Soviet General Secretary Brezhnev, while visiting Niagara Falls, started to argue about whose bodyguards were better.

Brezhnev said: "Let's have a check. Let's order them to jump over the Niagara!" They gave the order. The American Secret Service guy said: "No way! I have a wife and kids!" The Soviet bodyguard rushed to jump but was stopped at the last moment. An American colleague asked: "Why didn't you refuse to jump?" He replied: "No way! I have a wife and kids!"

This story captures the spirit of the system very wryly yet succinctly, even if in the USSR after Stalin's death it softened up considerably.

Indeed, if a North Korean commando or spy surrenders, it means that he or she will be branded a traitor, and thus places his or her family back home in serious trouble. Most of these people are recruited from mildly privileged families. The real upper crust do not want their children to risk their lives in the tiny compartments of midget submarines or under the hail of South Korean bullets. On the other hand, the common people are not trusted enough, so the operatives are overwhelmingly the children of the mid-level elite: army colonels, mid-ranking party officials or university professors. In other words, their families have something to lose. A "betrayal" by a captured spy or commando would probably lead to the loss of all privilege and to exile, perhaps even to imprisonment of his or her immediate family: parents, spouse, children, and maybe siblings as well.

In contrast, a heroic death means that the family back in the North will improve its status. Children of a "dead patriot" are admitted to the best schools, perhaps even to Kim Il Sung University, his wife receives generous rations for the rest of her life, and his parents will also be seen as members of a "heroic family" with all the requisite perks.

The North even has a special bureaucracy which is charged with taking care of people whose providers died for the Dear Leader — the so-called 11th department. The heroic dead also have their own hierarchy, so a commando who committed suicide to avoid capture is well above, say, a soldier who was killed in a traffic incident while on military duty. Their families are treated according to this difference in status.

The family responsibility system works wonders, keeping people in line. The collective responsibility system might be seen as immoral, but it certainly gets results.

PART 16

North Koreans Overseas, Foreigners in North Korea

International Relations

ON DECEMBER 13, 2002, A LARGE HALL in the Vietnamese capital of Hanoi hosted a lavish wedding banquet, attended by almost one thousand guests. The bride and groom were not local movie stars or children of some dignitary. And they were not young: both were in their 50s. However, the event was indeed unusual, since the bride came from North Korea. This was perhaps the first officially endorsed marriage between a North Korean citizen and a foreigner in many decades.

Yi Yŏng-hŭl met her future Vietnamese husband, Pham Ngoc Cane, in 1971 when he studied in North Korea. When returning home, he promised to marry her. But soon they learned that this was next to impossible. Indeed, few if any countries were ever as hostile towards mixed marriages as the North Korea of the 1960s, 1970s and 1980s. During these decades, citizens were bombarded with racist propaganda which extolled the alleged racial purity of Koreans.

To some extent, this propaganda continues to these days. As recently as 2005, North Korean official radio explained that miscegenation is one of the most abominable acts committed by the "U.S. imperialists" in South Korea. The Pyongyang broadcast said: "U.S. soldiers indulge in bestial sexual assaults against South Korean women, and have polluted the bloodlines of our race, which remained unbroken for 5,000 years, and sullied the purity of the race." Indeed, from the 1960s Pyongyang insisted that Koreans were united by their blood. In 1998 Kim Jong Il said: "The Korean nation is a homogeneous

278

nation that has inherited the same blood and lived in same territory speaking the same language for thousands of years." Historians would laugh at such a statement, which is patently wrong on all accounts, but it is the official North Korean line, and it is not very conducive to mixed unions.

Such an approach was not always the case. In the 1940s and 1950s a large number of Korean students went to study overseas (the USSR alone accepted some 1,800). These people spoke foreign languages, and were free to interact with the locals. Romances were certain to occur, and a number of young Koreans came back with foreign wives. I say "wives" since very few, if any, Korean female students married foreigners (there were not many females among the students, anyway). No statistics on such marriages between Korean men and foreign women is available, but they undoubtedly numbered in the dozens if not hundreds.

I have personally met some of these foreign women. For them their move to North Korea was often a huge shock. Cultural differences, a difficult language, and problems of daily hygiene made their lives difficult enough. Many had troubles with their in-laws: North Korea in the 1950s was still a patriarchal society where daughters-in-law must know their proper place and behave themselves. And, of course, the living standards were very low, even if compared with the then Soviet Union which itself was not exactly an affluent country. However, as long as their husbands remained supportive, many women fared quite well.

The situation deteriorated in the early 1960s when Kim Il Sung began to distance himself from the USSR and other East European countries. Foreign wives were dangerous since all overseas connections were deemed subversive. The increasingly nationalist, even racist, public mood also meant that men who "polluted the blood of the nation" were looked upon with disdain.

Thus, the authorities placed mixed couples under pressure. The husbands were denied promotions, and were told that only divorce would save them from worse trouble. If they then did not fall into line, the husbands were sent to the countryside, without being permitted to take their families with them. One after another, foreign wives moved overseas with their children. In some cases the foreign wives were even forcefully deported back to their native countries. By the late 1960s, nearly all of them had left.

From the 1960s, international marriages became a virtual impossibility. If a North Korean national overseas was suspected of having an affair with a foreign woman he would be immediately recalled and never allowed to go overseas again. More likely than not, his career would be ruined forever. Perhaps a more serious punishment would follow as well: after all, his lechery placed the Korean racial purity in danger!

There were rumors about a North Korean who was allowed to marry a woman from the former Yugoslavia in the early 1980s, but in this case permission was allegedly issued by Kim Jong Il himself. At this stage, these rumors cannot be confirmed but they do sound plausible: the Dear Leader has his romantic side. The above-mentioned couple of Yi Yŏng-hŭi and Pham Ngoc Cane were also able to marry only after intervention at the highest level.

But to return to their remarkable story.... When Pham Ngoc Cane returned to Vietnam in the early 1970s, he soon ceased to receive letters from Yi Yŏng-hŭi. This was not surprising: North Koreans were not normally allowed to send letters overseas, even to supposedly friendly countries. The authorities thought that their "love would cool down." In this particular case, however, they were wrong. Pham Ngoc Cane continued to visit the North Korean Embassy in Hanoi, pressing for permission.

Finally, the North Korean diplomats told him that Yi Yŏng-hŭi had married. Then they began to insist that she was dead. However, in the mid–1970s Pham Ngoc Cane went on a business trip to the North, and discovered that Yi was alive and single. He once again promised her that sooner or later they would marry. They did — but only after lobbying at the highest level. Their fate was discussed during a summit between their nations' respective leaders in May 2002, and permission was finally granted. The couple had had to wait 30 years.

And they were lucky: in 2004 the relations between Vietnam and North Korea entered a new crisis stage, since Vietnam allowed a large group of North Korean defectors to be flown to Seoul from its territory. North Korea was outraged. Had not Pham Ngoc Cane used the short window of opportunity in the late 1990s, his marriage would have been impossible.

Nonetheless, there is another relatively large group of foreign women who are married to North Korean men — the Japanese wives who came to the North during the large-scale "repatriation" of ethnic Koreans in the 1960s. An estimated 1,830 Japanese women came to North Korea during that migration. But that is our next story....

To Take a Wife ...
(And Not Return Her)

In November 1997, the major Japanese newspapers ran photos of old women embracing their relatives, walking the streets of their native towns, and bowing to the ancestors' tombs. There is nothing particularly strange or unusual about an old woman going to her native village to meet relatives. However, these ladies had been deprived of such options for decades, and they were unlikely to see heir native places ever again. These women were the "Japanese wives" whose fate was (and to an extent still is) one of the many stumbling blocks in relations between North Korea and Japan.

The problem of the Japanese wives has its roots in the late 1950s, when a large number of ethnic Koreans in Japan chose to be "repatriated" to North Korea. Strictly speaking, this hardly can be described as "repatriation" since the overwhelming majority of these migrants had never been to North Korea before. They or their parents once came from the southern part of the Korean Peninsula. In the 1930s and 1940s they moved to Japan — often against their will, being forcefully drafted as laborers by the colonial authorities.

Once in Japan, they found themselves subject to discrimination. This made them quite sympathetic to North Korean propaganda, and in the late 1950s and 1960s approximately 93,000 of them decided to move from the "capitalist hell" of Japan to the "socialist paradise" of North Korea.

In the 1950s, the Koreans in Japan largely lived an isolated ghetto life-style, but some of them married Japanese women. One has to admire these women, since in most cases by marrying a Korean they challenged the powerful chauvinistic assumption of Japanese superiority. And some of them were brave or reckless enough to follow their husbands to the "socialist paradise." According to Japanese migration statistics, some 1,830 Japanese women followed their husbands to the North.

While very few of them understood it, by boarding a ferryboat to North Korea they had crossed the Rubicon. Once a repatriate was in the embrace of the Great Leader Kim Il Sung, he or she was not supposed to go overseas again for any reason, for any length of time. People were stuck there for the rest of their lives, and even retaining Japanese citizenship made no difference.

Of course, relatives back in Japan felt as if these people, both Koreans and their Japanese spouses, had been kidnapped (and with a slight stretch of the definition one can actually describe this as a kidnapping in disguise). However, the ethnic Koreans usually remained silent — partially out of national solidarity, and partially because they had little leverage in local politics. It was the relatives of the "Japanese wives" who were positively outraged. They insisted that the Japanese government request Pyongyang allow these women to come home, at least for a short visit.

In the 1990s, the "Japanese wives" began to loom large in the Pyongyang-Tokyo negotiations. Pyongyang demanded aid, but Japan cited a number of problems, including visits by the "Japanese wives."

It was too politically risky to give in, but money was badly needed, so the North Korean leaders agreed to a compromise. The first such visit was arranged in November 1997. Fifteen "Japanese wives" were handpicked by the authorities according to political criteria. They had to be reliable, and had to say only what Pyongyang wanted them to say. The visit lasted for less than a week. The old ladies, aged between 55 and 84, visited their relatives, prayed at the ancestors' tombs, and then returned. In exchange, North Korea received a $27 million aid package — quite a bargain for a week-long tour by 15 aged ladies. In January 1998, another group of 12 "Japanese wives" visited their native country. WHY!?

It was promised that such visits would continue, but it soon returned to business as usual. Obviously, the supply of politically reliable "Japanese wives" was short, and Pyongyang could not afford to risk a scandal which could happen had one of the visitors refused to go back or made a critical statement. Thus, the visits were rare and the number of participating women remained small. In June 1998 the North Korean media stated that "Japanese women in North Korea retracted their applications to visit Japan on their own initiative." The reasons cited were "obstacles" allegedly created by the Japanese authorities and the "unsympathetic" coverage of the visit by the Japanese press. No visits took place for the next few years, until 2002 when another group was allowed to make a visit — obviously, a sign of North Korea's intention to re-establish ties with Japan.

However, in 2002 a miscalculation by North Korean diplomats led to the "abduction scandal," which led to a new interruption of these exchanges. Perhaps exchanges will resume, but it is unlikely that many Japanese wives will ever be able to see their native country again. Like billions of other women in human history, they are paying a hard price for the ambitions, emotions, idealism and, frankly, sheer stupidity of their men....

A Sea Change

On December 14, 1959, two North Korean ships departed from the Japanese port of Niigata, carrying 975 ethnic Koreans from Japan. They had chosen to move to North Korea for good. This trip heralded the beginning of a large-scale migration of ethnic Koreans from Japan to the DPRK.

In 1959 the Japanese and North Korean Red Cross signed, in Calcutta, an agreement that made it possible for ethnic Koreans in Japan to move to North Korea if they wished to do so. At that time most of the 650,000 Koreans residing in Japan were affiliated with the staunchly pro–North General Association of Korean Residents of Japan (better known as Chongryon or Soren), and many of them were technically North Korean citizens, even though a majority of them came to Japan in the '30s and early '40s from what later became South Korea.

Over the next two decades some 93,000 ethnic Koreans used the opportunity to move to the "socialist paradise." This constituted almost 15% of the then entire Korean community!

Nowadays, this appears strange, almost unbelievable. Indeed, almost 100,000 people voluntarily moved from a country which was well on its way to becoming the world's second largest economy to a country which was poor then and eventually became a locus for humanitarian disasters. Politically, this was a move from a nascent, if imperfect, democracy to a Stalinist dictatorship.

Authorities in Seoul have long asserted that skillful Pyongyang propaganda was the major culprit for this move. There is a great deal of truth in this assertion. Indeed, in the late 1950s the ethnic Koreans in Japan were bombarded with grossly exaggerated sugary stories of the DPRK's alleged success and prosperity. The Chongryon newspapers depicted the North as a "socialist paradise." Of course, this resonated well with the Chongryon followers, who believed their leaders and rejected all critical remarks about the North as "fabrications of the reactionary propaganda of the U.S. imperialists, Japanese militarists, and their Seoul puppets."

However, one should not judge the late 1950s equipped, as we are, with hindsight. Around 1960 the choice of North over South was understandable. To a large extent it reflected the indifference of the Seoul governments to the fate of ethnic Koreans in Japan. Pyongyang spent a lot of time and effort in helping the ethnic Koreans and won their support, while Seoul largely ignored them. Nor was the economy of the South very impressive either. It was also important that the Koreans, an underprivileged and discriminated-against group, had long nurtured a serious sympathy for the Japanese Left and were traditionally overrepresented among the Japanese Communist Party.

Chongryon was founded on the 25th of May, 1955, at a meeting of Korean activists in Tokyo. A huge portrait of Kim Il Sung in his marshal's uniform beamed down on the inaugural meeting's participants, and two large North Korean flags clearly indicated the meeting's leanings to everyone. Chongryon Koreans were, first and foremost, "proud overseas nationals of the DPRK." Indeed, all Chongryon Koreans were technically citizens of North Korea, even if only a tiny fraction of them originated from that part of the peninsula. In fact, more than 95% of all ethnic Koreans in Japan originated in the South!

From its inception, Chongryon began a large-scale campaign advocating a mass "return to the homeland." However, even without intense propaganda, the "Northern choice" of many Japanese Koreans was reasonable on purely rational grounds. In the late 1950s the South was lagging behind the North in terms of per capita GNP. This did not necessarily translate into higher standards of living, since vast amounts of American aid boosted consumption in the South. Nonetheless, the North demonstrated greater economic dynamism.

The North Korean propaganda insisted that in the "glorious socialist motherland" the children of migrants would be able to become university professors, musicians, or medical doctors. There was considerable truth in these statements: many of the migrants' children eventually achieved career success.

However, whatever truth there was in some statements was only one side of the picture. Once in the North the migrants soon made two unpleasant discoveries: first, life in the Stalinist country was not as carefree as they had been led to believe; second, they had passed the point of no return. The trap was closed, and under no circumstances would the migrants be allowed to return to Japan, even for short visits.

As newly found evidence testifies, the Japanese authorities were not very unhappy about such a turn of events: they too wanted to get rid of the Koreans. Traditional Japanese nationalism treated Koreans with contempt, and the Tokyo establishment perceived the ethnic Korean community (not without reason) to be a hotbed of left-wing anti–Japanese nationalism. Hence the Tokyo leaders were very happy to ship the potential troublemakers to where they so yearned to belong — even if Pyongyang and the local Left loudly accused them of sabotaging the return of these "Korean patriots."

For the North Korean leaders, the arrival of the ethnic Koreans was a problem, but also a heaven-sent gift. The repatriates were prone to trouble since they had lived in a far more prosperous and liberal society, and knew only too well that a large part of the official propaganda consisted of patent lies. They could not discard their "decadent bourgeois habits," including their penchant for smart dress or Japanese pop music. And, of course, it took some time (and more than a few arrests) to teach them to mind their tongues.

For all these reasons, the repatriates were placed quite low on the *sŏngbun* grade, the elaborate feudal-like system of hereditary groups which determined one's career and lifestyle in Kim Il Sung's North Korea. To borrow the Northern expression, "their *sŏngbun* was bad." The repatriates and their children were banned from politically sensitive jobs, and they even had some restrictions on college admission or might not even be allowed to serve in the army.

However, the real situation of the repatriates was much better than that of their fellow "bad-*sŏngbuners*." The "repatriates" had access to hard currency and this mattered enormously, even when the North Korean anti-market drive reached unprecedented heights.

This made the repatriates a very special group, both despised and privileged. Their houses boasted color TV sets and tape recorders back in the 1970s when even top cadres did not have such items. They could eat fresh fruit, sweets and even meat almost daily. In the 1980s they became the only group of North Koreans who could own private cars!

In special cases, the "repatriates" could purchase something even more attractive than Japanese canned tuna, American cigarettes or even a Romanian-made Dacia subcompact. A sufficiently generous donation by a relative from Japan could buy pretty much anything: the right to permanently reside in Pyongyang, a good flat, a place in a prestigious college or even an enviable official position. For example, a repatriate in Wonsan became the head of a large transportation company after his relatives donated to the North Korean state 50 trucks. Another became a journalist when his relatives presented the authorities with a factory.

Even the North Korean political police had to restrain themselves when dealing with the repatriates. While being carefully monitored and overrepresented among the prison population because of their propensity for incautious statements, they could still get away with minor transgressions, and there have been rumored cases of repatriates who were released from the prison camps because their relatives quietly pressed Pyongyang or bought their freedom with donations. For better or worse, money has always talked, even in the worst times of Stalinist repression. The only difference is that now it talks even louder.

In recent years, the power and influence of the repatriates has increased greatly. Their easy access to money, often combined with a residual experience of the capitalist enterprise, has helped them tremendously now that the old system is crumbling under pressure. Perhaps some of them are now future *chaebol* owners in the making. These people or their parents, who once moved to the North to build socialism, appear to be ending up busily building capitalism. But then again, history is full of paradoxes.

PART 17

Defectors

Trade Across the Water

WHEN THE FUTURE HISTORIANS ANALYZE the history of North Korea in the 1990s and early 2000s, what will they see as the most important events of the era? Is it likely to be remembered as the "demise of Kim Il Sung's *Juche* social-ism"? I do not think that serious historians will spend too many pages (or rather megabytes, since traditional paper books are unlikely to last for centuries) describing the never-ending soap opera of the "nuclear crisis." Perhaps some still unknown clashes within the North Korean palaces will grab their attention. And of course, the melodrama of Kim Jong Il's convoluted personal life will remain popular among the less-than-highbrow readership.

However, it is very likely that most historians will concentrate on the social changes in North Korea, and, among other things, the near collapse of the border control on the northern frontiers of the country. This collapse laid Korea open to foreign influences and international exchanges of all kinds, to a degree which was unthinkable for many decades.

It is a bit of an overstatement to say that the North Korean border with China is now "open." It is not "open" in the same sense as, say, the border between Canada and the U.S., let alone borders between West European states. But it is porous to the extreme, and this situation is quite new.

Most Communist countries heavily guarded their borders against both intruders who tried to get in and defectors who wanted to run away from the not-so-perfect Communist paradises. From this point of view, the North Korean border with China constitutes a serious challenge. It follows two rivers — the Amnok (the Chinese read these same characters as Yalu) and the Tuman. Both are shallow in their upper reaches, and completely freeze every winter. Thus the determined defector or smuggler can always find his or her way across the border.

The ethnic composition of the region is favorable to anyone who wishes to cross the border clandestinely for whatever reason. There are two million ethnic Koreans in China, and most of these live across the Chinese side of the border. Many ethnic Koreans of the People's Republic have relatives in North Korea, and a small part of them are even technically DPRK citizens — the so-called *chogyo*.

However, for decades the cooperation between the DPRK and Chinese police authorities ensured that defectors stood little chance of finding asylum across the border. Sooner or later a Korean defector would be arrested by the Chinese police and extradited back to the North, where he or she would be prominently sent to a prison camp. Everyone, including aspiring defectors, were aware of this.

But this system collapsed in the 1990s, following changes both in China and North Korea. The disastrous famine of 1996–1999 made countless North Koreans leave their native places and go to look for food elsewhere. Meanwhile, the booming Chinese economy, capitalist in everything but name, created many opportunities for those immigrants who were ready to work hard for meager pay. Chinese police also could not exercise the same level of control as was common in the bad old days of Chairman Mao.

At the same time, North Korean authorities have been unable to dramatically improve border control even if they have made some attempts to do so. Sealing the borders is expensive, and North Korea has a serious shortage of money and resources. Underpaid and even undernourished border guards are also quite willing to look away if they are paid to do so.

Hence, in the late 1990s the adjacent areas of China were quickly flooded with North Korean refugees. Their number in 1998-1999 reached some 200,000, though their numbers are much lower now at approximately 50,000.

In the early 2000s, the number of people who crossed the border every day (or rather night) could be counted in their hundreds. Most of them were refugees who fled the destitution and hunger of their Korean villages. Others were smugglers, engaged in the somewhat risky but profitable business of moving valuable merchandise across the border. And some others are engaged in more unusual types of activities.

There are professional matchmakers, for example. While ethnic Korean girls from the Chinese northeast try and sometimes succeed in marrying South Koreans, the girls of the North normally do not mind a Chinese husband either — but often of Korean origin. China with its abundant food supply appears to be a dream land for them.

Such marriages are quite common: according to one study, in 1998 some

52% of all North Korean refugees (overwhelmingly women) were living with local spouses. In most cases such marriages are arranged via Chinese (Han or ethnic Korean) brokers, and sometimes these brokers contact girls and their families while they are still in North Korea. If a girl is interested in the idea, a matchmaker or his/her agent crosses the border and then escorts the would-be bride to her new place of residence.

In such cases the girls' decision to marry into China is sort of voluntary, even though the disastrous economic situation in the North does play a major role in such a decision (but, after all, is not the same applicable to most mail-order brides in the affluent West?). However, in many cases the women move to China to find food and jobs — and then are kidnapped by mobsters who sell them to the highest bidder.

Whether the woman volunteers for marriage or is kidnapped, the brokers still receive their commission. The fees range widely: depending on the girl's looks, age and education, a woman might fetch anything between one and ten thousand yuan (roughly, between $120 and $1,200). A typical "purchase price" for a woman in her late 20s is said to be some 3–5,000 yuan (400–600 dollars). The sum is paid "upon delivery" by the husband. The entire amount goes to the intermediaries: neither the woman nor her family gets anything even if the marriage was initiated by them. The family's reward is that a daughter is saved from starvation and there is one less mouth to feed back home.

There are reports about North Korean women sold to Chinese brothels, but such cases, fortunately, remain a rarity — not least because the sex industry is less developed in the Chinese northeast than, say, in the coastal areas.

Most of the "husbands" are people who, for a variety of reasons, have had difficultly in finding a wife by more orthodox methods: widowers with children, habitual drunkards or the disabled. In many northeastern villages the mass migration of young women to the booming cities has resulted in a "bridal shortage," such that North Korean wives are in high demand — especially among the less fortunate sections of the male population.

Of course, being illegal aliens, the North Korean wives face the risk of deportation, and there are problems with children born of such unions. Their children, as a rule, cannot be formally registered — with all the consequences flowing from this predicament. The authorities do to some extent, however, take into account the real situation: if a refugee is facing deportation she is often permitted to choose whether to take her children with her, or leave them in China, and most women prefer to leave children with the fathers. Nonetheless, usually a bit of caution and a hefty bribe can often solve some of the problems, winning a much-coveted local registration for a baby and buying the local constable's willingness to look the other way.

Frankly, this picture is depressing, but some of these marriages are obviously happy. The press has reported some cases in which women, once apprehended by police and deported to the DPRK, have eventually found their way across the border and returned to their husbands despite all of the dangers involved. However, such happy unions are not very common. Many more women have found themselves at the mercy of drinkers or gamblers, often twice their age.

Another business is getting people from the North to China and, ultimately, to South Korea. Nowadays, there is a large and growing community of the North Korean refugees in Seoul. Many of these people save their every cent in order to bring their families from North Korea — to the great dismay of the Seoul authorities, who tacitly discourage defections while still providing those North Koreans who manage to reach Seoul with some assistance and the full rights of a South Korean citizen.

Since South Korean missions do not even want to talk to the aspiring defectors these days, some go-betweens are necessary to arrange a trip to the South. It is much easier to do so if some relatives have already defected. When those relatives have enough money, they pay brokers who arrange the escape of the rest of their family. A few thousand dollars will be enough to ensure that a professional agent will cross into North Korea, locate the person and escort him/her across the border. A $10,000 payment is the price for retrieving a resident of Pyongyang, but for the less remote areas, the fees are smaller. Then an additional payment will be necessary to get the person to Seoul (this costs between $2,000 and $10,000 extra, depending on a number of factors). However, in most cases it does not cost that much, since the family members of defectors are usually already in China, waiting for the money to arrive.

And there are money transfers aplenty, both from the North Korean refugees doing well in China, and from South Korea. Money has to be sent in cash, through reliable couriers, and there are many ways to confirm that the transfer has been delivered safely.

Take, for example, the case of Ms. Yim, a 31-year-old refugee, happily married to a Chinese man and engaged in a small business. Twice a year Ms. Lim sends about $400 to her parents in the North. Being a retired officer of an elite unit and a devoted supporter of the regime, her father initially refused to accept the money from this "daughter who had betrayed the country," but then he changed his mind. Nowadays, these transfers keep the family alive and even prosperous by North Korean standards.

From around 2003-2004 it has been common for North Korean defectors in the South to not simply remain in touch with their families, but send them money, widely using this same "Chinese connection." Nowadays, people in borderland areas of North Korea are beginning to realize that a family's affluence is secure if it has a close relative who is doing some casual unskilled work in China. And it seems that soon they will learn that having a relative in South Korea, this hell-hole of imperialist exploitation and land of destitution, is even better! It is easy to guess what impact this discovery will have on their worldview.

A large proportion of the refugees is sooner or later discovered by the Chinese police and deported back to the North. Until the mid–1990s, such a deportation would lead to a long prison term perhaps, accompanied by the arrest of the entire family.

However, nowadays the situation has changed — to some extent, at least. When faced with an exodus on such a scale, the authorities chose to treat illegal border crossings as a relatively minor offense. Although occasional reports of the execution of apprehended defectors do surface, these appear to be the exception, and often involve those who, with or without reason, are accused of subversive activities. The majority of the defectors who are extradited from China are first sent back to their native counties where they are investigated by the Minister for Protection of State Security, the North Korean security police. This investigation is not meant to be a pleasant procedure. The interview sessions are routinely accompanied by severe beatings, sleep deprivation and similar confession-extracting techniques — after all, torture is a commonplace in political investigations in the DPRK.

However, the investigation does not last for long: typically, the unlucky defectors spend only a couple of weeks in custody. Most of them are not accused of any serious political offense (like, say, contacting South Korean officials while in China) and thus are sent for three of four months of "re-education through labor" — a standard euphemism for a stint of forced labor in an improvised prison camp. Some people, and especially those with bad health, die in custody, but the majority survive. Of course, their CVs, their reputations, are damaged forever, and they will have no chance of getting a white-collar job. But these days most of the defectors are poor farmers and workers who would not dream of such a promotion anyway. Many people cross the border a second time. According to a recent study, an astonishing 40% of them return to China after their release from detention.

A minority of refugees who are found to have had some interaction with foreigners — especially with South Koreans — are sent for further investigation. The investigators try to make them confess to spying for the South. If a person breaks under torture and makes such a confession, he or she is likely to face the firing squad. If the defector's real or imagined crimes are deemed less grave but still politically significant (like, say, attending prayer meetings arranged by Christian missionaries or talking to South Koreans), he or she is

[handwritten margin note: Really? I thought it was the other way]

sent to prison camp for years. Nevertheless, such unlucky individuals comprise only a minority of all apprehended refugees.

Perhaps this does not sound like a very liberal approach, but by the North Korean legal standards, the refugees are nowadays treated with remarkable leniency. And why? Probably, the South Korean unwillingness to accept refugees persuaded Pyongyang that the political risks involved are relatively low. The exodus of the more restive part of its population might save the bankrupt state from the troublesome necessity of caring for people whom it is unable to feed anyway.

The returning refugees have now become the first statistically significant group of North Koreans to have had first-hand overseas experience. They have seen the results (both good and bad) of the market reforms in China and they are aware of North Korea's backwardness and poverty. They might even have some inkling of South Korea's prosperity. All these will undoubtedly have a serious impact on North Korea's future.

A New Life: Fully Furnished

NOWADAYS, THE SOUTH KOREAN PRESS often writes about the social problems associated with the relatively small but fast-growing community of North Korean defectors. The stories and interviews that are reported do not sound encouraging. The defectors feel lonely and guilty, they are relegated to badly paid and unskilled jobs and are often misunderstood by their countrymen.

Most of these problems would be completely alien to their predecessors, the defectors of the 1970s and 1980s. It was nice to be a North Korean defector in the South 20 or 30 years ago — as long as you could forget about your immediate family, who were likely to be shot or sent to certain death in a prison camp. But at least you could not complain about a lack of attention or generosity from your hosts. In those times, defectors were lionized by the press and the establishment, paid generous lifetime allowances, and provided with lucrative book contracts and lecture tours. Those who brought with them particularly valuable intelligence were paid special bonuses — often of truly obscene proportions.

Then what has changed? In a word, much. First of all, the numbers of defectors were much smaller back in the 1980s, averaging a mere 5 to 7 defections a year! Until the mid–1990s, only members of privileged groups had any chance of leaving the DPRK. Among the early defectors were pilots who flew their fighter jets to the South, diplomats who defected while stationed overseas, and soldiers of elite units who knew how the DMZ was controlled and could thus outsmart the guards. Secondly, these rare defectors were of great propaganda value. North Korean socialism was still seen as a viable alternative to South Korean capitalism, and the authorities tried to utilize defectors to prove Seoul's social and political superiority. Thirdly, the North remained a serious military threat, and encouraging defections has been a good tactic in dealing with the enemy from time immemorial.

Under such circumstances the defectors were treated with remarkable generosity. In 1962 South Korea introduced a law which regulated the treatment of defectors. This was the "Special law on the protection of defectors from the North." In late 1978 the South Korean parliament passed a slightly revised version which, with some modification, remained effective until 1993. Needless to say, all defectors were immediately given the full rights of a South Korean citizen. Since the ROK government maintained (and still maintains) that it has legal standing as the only legitimate authority for all Korea, all North Koreans are, by definition, potential South Korean citizens.

Every defector was also eligible for a generous aid package. After their arrival in the South, defectors would receive an allowance. The size of this allowance depended on which of the three categories the particular defector was assigned. A person's category was determined by his or her political and propaganda value, as well as the quality of the intelligence which he (or, very occasionally, she) provided to the authorities.

Apart from this allowance, defectors who delivered especially valuable intelligence or equipment were given additional rewards. These rewards could be very large. For example Yi Ung-p'yŏng, a fighter pilot who defected with his MiG-19 fighter jet in 1983, received a reward of 1.2 billion *won*. This was an astronomical sum, about 480 times (!) the annual salary of the average South Korean — in today's terms it would be some 8–9 million U.S. dollars. Interestingly, prior to 1997 the payments had been fixed in gold, not in Korean *won* — probably to reassure defectors who might have had doubts about the stability of paper currency. Perhaps it was also influenced by Taiwan, which once paid defectors from mainland China in gold as well.

However, even without generous special awards, the payments received by the ordinary defector were more than sufficient for a comfortable life. Then there were other perks as well. The state provided defectors with good apartments which became their personal property at no charge. Anyone who wished to study was granted the right to enter a university of his or her choice, which was not a small privilege in South Korea. Military officers were allowed to continue their service in the South Korean military, where they were given the same rank as the one they had held in the North Korean KPA. For a period of time after their arrival the defectors were also provided with personal bodyguards.

This situation changed in the early 1990s, soon after the collapse of the Communist bloc. Communist ideology ceased to be a serious danger to Seoul, and the ailing North was less and less perceived as a direct threat. On the other hand, the stream of defectors began to grow just as the political need for them began to diminish. In the new circumstances, the Seoul authorities began to have second thoughts, and around 1995 tacitly ceased to encourage defections. From that time on, only well-connected defectors, with access to valuable intelligence, could count on some South Korean assistance — and even in these instances, Seoul was becoming increasingly choosy.

In 1993 the laws dealing with the treatment of defectors were revised dramatically with further revisions to follow in 1997, and yet more in 2005. The new law stipulated a radical reduction in the aid packages and other benefits available to defectors, and in every new version the payments were reduced further.

Gone are the times when an ordinary defector could comfortably live off his or her benefits. Nowadays on their arrival in the South defectors are eligible for three kinds of payments. First, the authorities pay a rental bond for a small apartment. Second, a defector receives a lump sum payment. From January 2005, this sum was fixed at 10 million *won* or U.S. $10,000 for a single defector. Families are paid more, depending on the number of family members. A lump sum of 3 million *won* is first paid upon arrival while the remaining amount is paid in quarterly installments over the first two years of the defector's new life in the South.

Especially valuable defectors are eligible for a third kind of payment — a "special prize" which can be quite significant. For example, Yi Ch'ŏl-su, a North Korea Air Force captain who in 1996 flew his antiquated MiG-19 to Seoul, received an award of 478 million *won*, which at that time was equivalent to U.S. $600,000. Out of this total, 442 million was his "special prize." This is a very good sum, but still well below that once paid to Yi Ung-p'yŏng, another North Korean pilot who flew a similar jet to the South in 1983. After all, 442 million *won* equaled only 24 average annual salaries in South Korea in 1996, while in 1983 Yi Ung-p'yŏng was given the equivalent of 480 average salaries! This signified not only the diminishing military value of MiG-19s, but also the diminishing political value of defectors.

Former KWP Secretary Hwang Chang-yŏp, after his famous escape from the North, was paid the smaller but still significant sum of 250 million *won*, which was the maximum sum payable as a "special prize" under the 1997 law. However, these figures are far from typical: in recent years, 95% of the defectors were deemed ineligible for any "special prize."

From 1998 onwards, the number of defectors doubled each year, but after 2002 the figure stabilized at some 1,000–1,500 defections a year. By summer 2005, the total number of North Koreans living in the South reached some 6,700. The South Korean press describes this influx as an "exodus," but actually it is a very small number: after all, in 1961–1989, in the Berlin Wall era, West Germany accepted 21,000 East German defectors in the average *year*!

Defections are not newsworthy any more either. Korean newspapers have long ceased to report ordinary defections. The media still pays some attention to group defections, or to defections of prominent individuals, but even these hardly make headlines.

Meanwhile, defection remains a very dangerous business. Few people arrive by sea or across the heavily protected DMZ. The vast majority of defectors these days travel to the South via China. The South Korean diplomatic missions overseas are remarkably reluctant to assist these would-be defectors, thus the defectors are forced to rely on their own skills, or the financial assistance of their relatives in the South or in the U.S.

And what happens to those North Koreans who fight or buy their way to the Republic of Korea and are not captured or killed in the process? Immediately after their arrival in the South, defectors are debriefed by South Korean agencies, normally by the National Intelligence Service (the former South Korean CIA) and the Ministry of Unification. The debriefing takes weeks or even months. It is done in what is known as the Taesŏng building, which is specially dedicated to this purpose. During this period fugitives are isolated from the outside world — in fact they are placed in custody, although quite a comfortable one.

After the debriefing process is over, most defectors attend special classes which prepare them for their future life in a capitalist society. Since August 1999, such classes have been operated by a special educational center, located in Ansŏng, a county town some 70 km from Seoul. The center's official name is the "Center for Supporting the Adaptation of North Korean Defectors," but it is commonly known as *Hanawon*.

By late 2001 some 600 defectors had graduated from *Hanawon*. The study period in *Hanawon* lasts two months. Initially it was meant to last longer, but in late 2001 it was cut back since the center could not handle the larger than expected number of students. Approximately half of the teaching hours are allocated to the study of South Korean culture. The rest are occupied by more practical training: the basics of computer literacy, driving skills for men — even cooking for women, since many of the foodstuffs found in Seoul shops are unknown to the North Koreans. The defectors are also taught some basics of everyday life — how to ride the subway, use a mobile phone, and buy goods in supermarkets. Lectures in the center are given by both its regular staff and professors from some Seoul universities.

Obviously, there are serious problems with *Hanawon*. Within the allocated time it is impossible to equip the defectors with any vocational skills which could be expected to facilitate their employment — even for low-level jobs. The South Korean press and government agencies are critical of the institution, but we must not be too harsh on it: it is definitely understaffed and under-funded.

After graduation from *Hanawon*, defectors are given the lump sum payment of their "settlement money" and allocated a place of residence. Their first place of residence is determined by the authorities, who now try to settle the defectors away from Seoul — much to their displeasure. From this point on, the defector is almost completely left to his or her own devices. And thus the most difficult part begins — but more of these problems in our next story....

The Fate of Defectors

IN SEPTEMBER 1994, A YOUNG North Korean named Kim Hyŏng-dok arrived in Seoul. It was the end of a long trip: he had spent two years trying to secure a passage to the South. He succeeded against all odds and came to Seoul full of expectation.

Two years later Kim Hyŏng-dok made another escape attempt — this time he tried to flee back to the North. He was apprehended and jailed, since any attempt to travel to North Korea without proper permission is still a crime under South Korean law. In 2001 Kim Hyŏng-dok, who was by that time a university graduate and clerical worker in parliament, remarked: "I shall not escape any more. Utopia does not exist anywhere." Alas, the realization of this fact strikes most North Korean defectors with great pain.

We must admit it: North Korean defectors do not fare well in the South. Their crime rate (per 1,000, of course) is 1.7 higher than the national average. Their income is about half that earned by the average South Korean. They complain about discrimination and an inability to find and keep a decent job and difficult relations with the locals.

Naturally, the press sometimes reports remarkably successful adaptations as well. Yi Chong-guk has established his own restaurant chain in the South. Sin Yŏng-hui became a moderately successful actress. Her husband Ch'oe Se-ung founded a highly successful company which deals in currency exchange. Yo Man-ch'ŏl opened a small restaurant in Seoul. The restaurant industry for some reason is especially popular among defectors.

However, a closer look at these stories reveals an unpleasant discovery.

Who are these lucky people? They are a far cry from the former loggers, peasants or fishermen who form the majority of the defectors of the last decade.

Restaurateur Yi Chong-guk used to be a cook at Ch'ŏngryugwan, the most famous of all Pyongyang restaurants. His colleague, Yo Man-ch'ŏl, is a former captain in the Ministry of Public Safety, the North Korean police — not a bigwig, but unequivocally a member of the elite. Sin Yŏng-hui was a dancer in the Mansudae troupe, the North Korean equivalent of the Bolshoi. Her husband Ch'oe Se-ung — perhaps the most financially successful of all defectors — worked for many years in the overseas offices of a number of North Korean trade companies. In North Korea this is a telltale mark of a very high social position. Indeed, his father was the head of the finance department in the Party's Central Committee, and this safely puts his family in the top 0.01 percent in that country.

Defectors who have found employment in research centers and universities also commonly come from the DPRK ruling elite. Chang Hae-song, a former North Korean playwright and journalist, nowadays works in the Institute of Unification Policy and writes about North Korea. His daughter also attracted some attention when she posted an exceptional score in the South Korean version of the Scholastic Aptitude Test. Many ex-officers continue to serve in the South Korean armed forces, mainly in the intelligence agencies or psychological warfare units. For example, Yi Ung-pyŏng, who in 1983 fled in his MiG-19 fighter jet to Seoul, taught at the Air Force academy until his death in 2002.

Indeed, almost all of the "success stories" of North Korean defectors come from the elite. There is nothing surprising in this. Members of the North Korean upper crust have a good education and possess leadership skills, they know how to learn, and last but not least, they have social ambition.

However, this does not bode well for the future political transition of North Korea. It appears that the only leadership material available in the North will be found within the existing elite. Local Party secretaries will become democratically elected mayors and will avow their loyalty to democracy with the same persuasive zeal that they once expressed in their professions of loyalty to the Great Leader. The secret police operatives will become successful entrepreneurs, and the children of people who sent hundreds of North Koreans to prisons will graduate from the best universities to lead the sons and daughters of their parents' victims. We have seen this reality play out far too many times in other ex–Communist countries, including my native Russia.

But is this to be condemned? Perhaps. But what is the alternative? Will it be possible to prosecute all those who played a part in the crimes of the regime? It is unlikely. There are far too many of them. And who will become the administrators, teachers, policemen, and engineers in the post–Kim North

Korea, whenever it arises? And should unification occur, would not the whole-
sale replacement of the elite by Southern carpetbaggers be an even greater evil?
The only thing we can say for certain is that the next few decades of Korean
history are unlikely to be tranquil....

The Plane Truth

IF YOU ARE A NORTH KOREAN WHO, for some reason, decides to defect, how
would you extricate yourself from the loving bosom of the Dear Leader? These
days, defection is no longer so difficult. The border with China is all but
open, and every North Korean can virtually walk through — only to discover
that nowadays getting into the South is much more difficult than getting out
of the North.

But back in the 1970s or 1980s the situation was different. China had
no relations with the South, and its police still worked with great efficiency.
Thus, a fugitive would soon be apprehended and immediately sent back to
certain death. In those days the North Korean authorities treated an attempted
escape as a capital crime. The landmine-infested and heavily guarded DMZ
was an insurmountable obstacle as well, and only a handful of soldiers from
the elite units could attempt to cross the DMZ by land.

Thus, until the early 1990s, defectors predominantly came from those
few small groups of North Koreans who had the wherewithal to do so. One
of these groups were air force pilots. There have been six such escapes so far,
involving seven North Korean military pilots.

The first such air escape took place very soon after the Armistice. On
September 21, 1953, Lt. No Kŭm-sŏk of the North Korean air force flew his
MiG-15 to the South. For the Americans, this was an intelligence bonanza,
since this fighter plane was then the best the Communist bloc had — and
arguably the best plane in the world. No Kŭm-sŏk was awarded the then
exorbitant sum of U.S. $100,000 and the right to reside in the United States.
He still lives there, a retired professor, who wrote a book about his experience.*

The next air escape took place quite soon afterwards. On June 21, 1955,
the then major Korean airport on Yoido witnessed an unusual arrival. A North

---

*The book is No Kŭm-Sŏk with J. Roger Osterholm, A MiG-15 to Freedom: Memoir of the War-
time North Korean Defector Who First Delivered the Secret Fighter Jet to the Americans in
1953 (Jefferson, NC: McFarland, 1996).

Korea trainer Yak-18 approached the airstrip. Aboard the plane were two friends, North Korean officers who had decided to defect to the South. This is the single instance when a defecting pilot did not arrive aboard a fighter jet.

North Korean pilots later continued on occasion to turn south. In 1960, Lt. Chŏng Nak-hyŏk flew his MiG-15 to the South. In 1970, Major Pak Sun-kuk was ordered to return a recently repaired MiG-15 from a repair workshop to a North Korean air base near Wonsan. He used this opportunity to fly it to the South, crash-landing in Kangwon Province.

The event of 1983 is probably still vividly remembered by many. Captain Yi Ung-pyŏng of the North Korea Air Force used a training exercise to defect and landed at a South Korean airfield. According to the then common practice, he received a commission in the South Korean Army, eventually becoming a colonel.

And finally, in 1996, another MiG-based escape took place: on May 23, Captain Yi Ch'ŏl-su flew his MiG-19 fighter jet across the DMZ and arrived in Seoul. Incidentally, the Seoul air-raid alert center failed to react to the aircraft's approach, and some of its staff were later charged with negligence.

But it has not been all one-way traffic. Some dissatisfied South Koreans have used this same exit option as well. On Feb. 17, 1955, ROK Air Force Captain Ok Hum took his trainer L-19 to the North. The resourceful Ok also managed to take his wife along with him as well.

Two other incidents involved the hijacking of civilian planes — something quite impossible in the North. On Feb. 16, 1958, a DC-3 of the KNA, the then Korean national air company, was hijacked in flight by a group of North Korean sympathizers and diverted to Pyongyang. The government insisted that they were Pyongyang spies, but this is rather doubtful. There were also foreigners among the 28 passengers and four crew: an American pilot and 3 foreign (two German and one American) passengers. After negotiations, the foreigners and most South Koreans were returned home, but eight passengers, including the six hijackers, remained in the North. This incident dealt a heavy blow to the already struggling KNA and contributed to the bankruptcy of the nation's first air carrier.

The next plane hijacking took place a decade later, in 1969, when North Korean agents (and this time it seems that they were genuine agents rather than sympathizers) took over a KAL plane and diverted it to Wonsan. The plane had 51 people on board. Once again, not everyone came back: the North claimed that 12 of the 51 chose to stay in the "warm embrace of the socialist motherland."

In 1970, the North offered a "warm embrace" to a group of international hijackers as well. But that is our next story....

Still Waiting for
the Japanese Communist Revolution

On March 31, 1970, Japan, which is normally a remarkably violence-free country, was shocked to learn about the hijacking of an airliner, the first ever such event in the nation's history. A group of nine young people used antique samurai swords and a bomb threat to take over a JAL Boeing 727 on a domestic flight between Tokyo and Fukuoka. Since the plane had a name of its own, Yodo, the hijackers came to be known as the "Yodo Group." They ordered the pilots to fly to Seoul, where they released most of the hostages, and then proceeded to Pyongyang, where they asked for asylum.

The Yodo hijackers were members of a small Japanese radical Left group known as the Red Army Faction. They advocated guerrilla warfare in Japan as a means of bringing about the triumph of the Japanese Communist revolution. They achieved a level of notoriety when a police raid put an end to their "guerrilla training" in mountain camps, and when the Japanese police interrupted their plan to kidnap the then prime minister.

Thus, the hijackers chose to flee, in the hope that they might return on the glorious day of the Japanese Revolution, much like their idol Fidel Castro of Cuba once did. They initially contemplated an escape to Cuba, but later settled on North Korea as their destination. Of course, it was easier to travel to the North, and they needed to make a statement. Hijacking was as good a way to attract attention as any other.

The North Koreans accepted the hijackers. There was nothing unusual about that: in the days of the Cold War, hijackers from a hostile side were normally given protection — they were believed to be "freedom fighters," after all. North Koreans obviously wanted to use the youngsters in propaganda operations, and perhaps even shared their belief that the day of the Japanese Communist revolution would eventually arrive.

Thus, the Red Army Faction enthusiasts were feted by North Korean officialdom. Most of them were eventually settled in a specially designed walled compound, having no interaction with the outside world and under the close watch of North Korean security agents. However, the group was provided for according to the highest standards, could go for approved outings in specially designated Mercedes cars and were given generous living allowances.

In exchange, they were required to endure ideological sessions which lasted for many hours every day. Soon the hijackers made statements proclaiming their conversion to *Juche* and their willingness to carry the torch of the *Juche*-style revolution to the Japanese — who presumably eagerly awaited such happy news. Then the fugitives disappeared from public view for many years.

Some group members were taken away by their hosts, never to be seen again. But the majority remained in their golden cage. In 1975, the Yodo Group's leader reunited with his girlfriend, who had voluntarily made her way to North Korea. Obviously, the arrival of a young woman led to certain changes in the dynamic of the all-male group, and soon the North Korean hosts embarked on a new exercise: they went wife-hunting for their guests. Judging by the timing, this plan was approved at the very top level. I actually suspect that it was Kim Il Sung himself who ordered the provision of partners for the lonely Japanese males.

This was done with a good old Confucian disregard for such modernist and decadent niceties as the freedom of romantic choice. In this case, the old expression "wife-hunting" must be understood in the most literal way. The North Korean intelligence agencies began to look for Japanese women who could be kidnapped while traveling overseas and who were likely to be "redeemable"—that is, either apolitical or sympathetic to the Left. It is remarkable that Pyongyang apparently never considered marrying the Japanese defectors with Korean girls. Interracial and international marriages were (and are) a strict taboo in North Korea, where eulogies to the "nation's pure blood" have been the norm from the 1960s onwards.

Some of the would-be wives were lured to the North with the promise of study or an exotic trip. One unlucky girl was promised a trip to Mongolia, a country with which Japanese commonly share a fascination — and found herself trapped in Pyongyang instead.

The wife-hunting campaign was conducted with truly lighting speed and remarkable efficiency — yet another indirect confirmation of Kim Il Sung's personal involvement. By the spring of 1977, seven suitable Japanese women were located, kidnapped, subjected to a crash course in ideological re-education and delivered to their future husbands. In early May 1977, the Yodo hijackers received their wives, and soon Kim Il Sung himself arrived in person to congratulate the revolutionary fighters. The couples soon had children, born more or less simultaneously, and could enjoy their privileged, if sequestered and controlled, lives in the compound.

From the late 1970s or early 1980s, the Yodo Group won enough trust from their masters to be directly involved in North Korean secret operations overseas, from Europe to Japan and Thailand. So, their efforts paid off....

Death of a Runaway Prince

SOUTH KOREA IS SCARCELY NOTORIOUS for high rates of violent crime. So when, on February 15, 1996, the inhabitants of an apartment complex in Pundang, south of Seoul, discovered a bloodstained body in the stairwell, they were shocked. The victim, in his mid-30s, had suffered a gunshot wound to his head. He was still conscious when discovered and managed to blurt out "spies, spies!" He was rushed to hospital, only to be declared brain-dead on arrival.

The victim of this incident was 36-year-old Yi Han-yŏng; to date, he is the only known member of the North Korean ruling family to have defected to the South.

Yi Han-yŏng was born Yi Il-nam in 1960. His father, a promising scientist, was killed in a traffic accident when the boy was very young and Yi Han-yŏng was raised by his mother, a prominent writer and journalist. A leading role in the family was played by his grandmother Kim Won-ju. The old lady was once a star of Seoul's left-wing journalism world, but in the 1940s she defected to the North with her entire family. This "southern connection" rendered the family politically vulnerable and quite insecure, but they nevertheless remained members of the country's ruling elite. Yi Han-yŏng's aunt, Song Hye-rim, became a movie actress, arguably the most popular North Korean movie star of the 1960s.

It was Song Hye-rim whose fate changed the family's fortunes — for better or worse it is difficult to say. In the late 1960s the famous beauty attracted the attention of the young Kim Jong Il, and soon became his mistress. They had a son, Kim Chŏng-nam, who is now frequently seen as the would-be heir to Kim Jong Il. This union never won Kim Il Sung's approval, and eventually the lovers parted with Song Hye-rim sent to Moscow for psychiatric treatment. Nonetheless, the entire family came to enjoy the privileges and stresses of court life, which consisted of material comfort tempered with political instability.

In the late 1970s, Yi Han-yŏng went overseas to study in Moscow. This was a rare privilege: in those days North Korea was very wary of sending its youngsters even to supposedly "fraternal" Communist countries. Indeed, Moscow was a very liberal and free place when compared to Pyongyang, where a young North Korean aristocrat could enjoy freedoms unthinkable at home. It was possibly around this time that Yi Han-yŏng began to think of defection to the West.

An opportunity presented itself in 1982 when he was studying French in Geneva. He secretly contacted the South Korean Embassy in Switzerland,

and the diplomats there had him smuggled to the South. Seoul was happy to get hold of such a treasure trove of inside information about the North Korean leaders, but this defection was not used in the propaganda warfare. On the contrary, the defector was given a new identity: Yi Il-nam became Yi Han-yŏng. His defection remained a closely guarded secret. He even underwent plastic surgery which changed his looks.

However, Yi Han-yŏng soon learned that in the capitalist world prosperity was not for everybody. A spoiled brat is not prepared to work hard, and he can be easily misled due to his naiveté regarding the ways of the capitalist South. Thus, his 15 years in South Korea were a personal disaster — as he himself readily admitted in the last months of his life.

For a while, things went relatively well. In 1984 Yi Han-yŏng entered Hanyang University. After graduation from the university he married and had a daughter. Being a fluent Russian speaker, he briefly worked in the Russian Department of Radio Korea International (a branch of the KBS broadcasting corporation).

But then Yi Han-yŏng attempted to launch a business of his own. His company soon went bankrupt, and he was accused of embezzlement; he stood trial and received a three-year prison sentence. He was soon acquitted, but financially he was ruined nonetheless.

Then, in the mid–1990s he made what was to prove a fatal error: he decided to capitalize on his name and insider's knowledge of the North Korean elite. He broke his cover, and began to appear on talk shows and give interviews. He also published a book highly critical of the North Korean "royal family."

Perhaps it was this book that sealed his fate. Yi Han-yŏng understood the risks involved: after the book was published he formally divorced his wife, to ensure her safety, and went into semi-seclusion. But this did not help: the lonely amateur could not outsmart one of the world's best intelligence services. He was shot dead near the apartment he shared with his friend. His assassins were not apprehended, but some years later an arrested North Korean spy confirmed that the assassination was carried out by North Korean agents and was seen as a major coup in the North.

Leaving — With Much to Be Desired?

NOWADAYS, NORTH KOREAN DEFECTORS arrive in the South in ever-increasing numbers. However, one must wonder: what about defectors moving from the South to the North? Do such defections occur? The short answer is "yes" — even if we keep in mind that it is often difficult (indeed, impossible) to draw a clear line between defections and abductions.

Until the 1953 Armistice, large-scale migration was common in Korea. The leftists fled North while the rightists moved South in huge numbers. Nor did the end of the war mean the end of the movement. The total number of post-war defections to the North has never been made public by either side, but it appears that until the 1970s the number of defectors to the North roughly equaled that of those to the South.

In 1995 the armed forces made public the number of soldiers who defected to the North. Over the 1953–1969 period there were 391 reported defectors. In the 1970s, the number of defecting soldiers went down to 42, and in the 1980s it was a mere 17. Obviously, these figures reflect the general trend as well.

In the 1950s, North Korea was ahead of the South in both per capita industrial output and the rate of economic growth. The success in education, health care, science and technology, greatly and skillfully embellished by Pyongyang's propaganda, also made the North attractive to many South Koreans. It did not help that the South was an international basket case, an impoverished country run by an incompetent and corrupt government.

Most South Koreans were ready to accept this, not least because they had had the bitter experience of briefly living under the short but brutal Communist rule in the summer and autumn of 1950. But there were dissenters, and for some of them the North appeared a realistic and attractive alternative to the impoverished South. Apart from these misguided idealists, defectors included a number of people who had legal or psychiatric problems: in those days of the Cold War, a defector was a prize gift to either side.

Then, things began to change. The South did not become a democracy until the late 1980s, but its economy was developing with breathtaking speed while the North was first stagnating and then going downhill. In spite of all dictatorial tendencies, the South Korean strongmen were much softer on the population, too. Thus, the number of defections began to decline, and by the early 1980s only some starry-eyed leftist ideologues, remarkably oblivious to the obvious, could contemplate defection to the North (and there were such people, one has to admit).

To a large extent, the North treated defectors much in the same way as the South. They were given good houses, paid generous bonuses and encouraged to deliver important intelligence or military hardware. The question is, however, to what extent (and for how long) they could enjoy these privileges in the highly regimented North Korean society. "Adjustment shock," such a huge problem for defectors to the affluent and permissive South, took an even greater toll on those who went north, and a few incautious words could easily land them in prison. As of 1999, some 22 defectors were reported to be in prison camps — and the actual figure is likely to be higher.

However, such a fate is more likely to befall politically insignificant defectors — disgruntled soldiers, head-in-the-clouds university postgraduates or impoverished fishermen. Those who held prominent positions in the South have more chances of surviving and prospering in the North (once again, a clear parallel with the fate of North Korean defectors in Seoul). For example, Kang T'ae-mu, a Southern officer who defected with his unit shortly before the outbreak of the Korean War, is now a two-star general. Professor Yun No-bin from Pusan University, who defected as recently as 1983, is now employed as a journalist producing propaganda material targeting the South.

Perhaps the most prominent of all defectors was Ch'oe Tŏk-sin, the former South Korean minister for foreign affairs, who fled to the North in 1986 and died there in 1989. His defection became a major topic of the North's propaganda and even inspired a movie.

A large number of educated defectors work for the agencies responsible for psychological operations against the South. They are announcers, editors and writers in broadcast stations, and research fellows in the Institute of South Korean Studies and similar institutions.

PART 18

The Unnoticed Death
of North Korean Stalinism

The Failure of Juche *Agriculture*

FAMINES APPEAR A THING of the past — at least outside Africa. Indeed, modern technology makes it possible to feed crowded cities almost effortlessly. Thus, most famines are now the result of mismanagement and deliberate political decisions. The North Korean famine of 1996–2000 demonstrates this fact.

For decades, North Korea was probably the world's most perfect specimen of Stalinism, in many regards more representative than Stalin's Russia itself. Thus, its agricultural policy followed the old Soviet pattern, with the same sad results. Stalinist agriculture has never been very efficient. Lack of incentives usually makes it sluggish and wasteful. However, in some cases heavy investment in machinery and fertilizers has helped to overcome deficiencies created by the inept social system.

This was the case in North Korea. In the late 1950s, all North Korean farmers were herded into so-called agricultural co-operatives. While less restrictive than people's communes in Mao's China, they imposed harsher control than even Stalin's infamous kolkhozes.

However, in spite of all the pitfalls of collective farming, the North Korean government invested heavily in agriculture. Its efforts produced a remarkably energy-intensive agricultural system. Electric pumps ran huge irrigation projects and chemical fertilizers and tractors were used on a grand scale. In an attempt to reclaim arable land, steep hills were made into terrace fields. These fields, endorsed by Kim Il Sung himself, remained the poster image of North Korea's agriculture until the mid–1990s.

In the 1990s, all mechanization disappeared from North Korean fields. Photograph by Christopher Morris.

Initially these efforts seemingly paid off. In the 1980s North Korea produced some 5–6 million tons of grain (largely, rice and maize) every year. The population never enjoyed a real abundance of quality food: meat and fruit were rare delicacies, and fresh vegetables were largely consumed as kimch'i, Korea's spicy fermented cabbage. Nonetheless, the 6 million tons of grain was sufficient to meet the basic nutritional needs of the country, and provide the 20-odd million North Koreans with enough calories to go about their daily lives. All food was rationed, and depending on a person's position in the complicated hierarchy of social groups, the daily rations varied from 300 to 800 grams per adult, with 700 g being the most typical amount.

For decades, Pyongyang propaganda presented North Korea as the embodiment of economic self-sufficiency, completely independent from any other country. This image sold well, especially in the more credulous parts of the Third World and among the ever-credulous leftist academics. The real secret of its supposed self-sufficiency was simple: the country actually received large amounts of direct and indirect aid from the Soviet Union and China, but never admitted this in public. Though frequently annoyed by such "ingratitude," neither Moscow nor Beijing made much noise since both communist giants wished to maintain, at least superficially, friendly relations with this small yet capricious ally.

Bikes and people's backs are major means of transportation in the North Korean countryside. Photograph by Bernd Seiler.

But in 1991 the situation changed. The much-trumpeted "self-reliance" of North Korea proved to be a complete fake. The Soviet decision to discontinue sales of oil and other goods at hugely discounted prices to the North wrought havoc with the country's economy. Agriculture was especially vulnerable, since without a heavy input of energy and resources it stood no chance of survival. Tractors required diesel oil which was no longer in plentiful supply and electric pumps could not operate when power stations stood idle due to a shortage of spare parts.

In 1992-1993 the North Korean media began to argue that for better health one should have only two meals per day (the traditional three meals were seen as excessive and unhealthy). By 1994, people in some remote areas were not able to get food for days at a time. They were issued the usual ration coupons, but no foodstuff was available in the shops or distribution centers. The rations themselves were also reduced — this was a sign of things to come.

And then the real catastrophe struck. In July and August 1995, unusually heavy rains led to disastrous floods. The North Korean authorities placed all the blame for the subsequent developments on these floods. Pyongyang stated that some 5.4 million people had been displaced by the 1995 floods while a subsequent UN survey indicated that the actual figure was much smaller.

Politically, these statements were understandable: if the country had been hit by a natural disaster of unprecedented proportions, the authorities did not want to be held responsible.

There is, however, good reason to doubt their statements. Of course, the contribution of the flood to the disaster is undeniable. The already strained power grid was destroyed and the entire irrigation system was wiped out. Most of the terrace fields, the pride of "*Juche* agriculture," were simply washed away.

However, none of these can be seen as the major reason behind the 1996–1999 disaster. The crisis in North Korea's agriculture was evident at a much earlier date, and a possible solution was clearly demonstrated by China. In the 1970s, China was dealing with chronic food shortages. Just one decade later, its population was fed better than at any other time in its long history. And the reason? The switch from huge state-run and state-owned farms to individual household production. This switch was engineered by Deng Xiaoping in the late 1970s and within a few years completely changed the situation in Chinese agriculture. Similar reforms were implemented in Vietnam — and with equal success.

Why was this experience not applied then in North Korea? The North Korean leaders believed that only absolute control over the population would be conducive to the regime's survival. Independent farmers were seen as politically dangerous. Sure, this scheme worked well in other fellow Communist countries. But neither China nor Vietnam had a prosperous and democratic capitalist "other half." In other words, there is no South China whose existence could create problems for the Beijing leaders (Taiwan is far too small to be taken seriously).

Beijing could accommodate a little capitalism in its grand scheme, but in North Korea, similar reforms were likely to make people ask the simple question: "If the market economy is good, why is our system superior to that of the capitalist South?"

Thus, the decision was made in the final years of Kim Il Sung's long rule not to tamper with the system. No reforms were going to happen in the North. No dissent was going to be tolerated. This was seen as an essential condition of the regime's stability — and perhaps this indeed was the case. While other Communist governments went down one after the other, Pyongyang survived.

The policy was rational and efficient — as far as the regime's interests were concerned. But it had its price, and that price was paid by the commoners, by the untold numbers of people who perished in 1996–1999 to keep Kim Jong Il in power. The largest estimate of the victims' number is "over two millions," but perhaps the lowest figure of 600–900,000 "excessive deaths" (to use demographers' jargon) is closer to the truth. It is still a very large number — some 3–4% of the entire population.

The famine was a result of a political decision. This does not mean that the government wanted the famine to occur — it did not — but when it was faced with a choice between maintaining the status quo and running the risk of famine, or attempting reform and running the risk of revolution, it opted for the former.

Nonetheless, the famine initiated a raft of opportunities which in due course led to the dramatic transformation of North Korea. The North entered the 1990s as the world's last truly Stalinist society but by the early 21st century it had changed dramatically. The old system was dead, and a new system was emerging. The Stalinist dictatorship changed into a more conventional type of tyranny, even if some trappings of the old system and its rhetoric still remained in place.

North Korea Dances to a Southern Tune

IN EARLY 2005, I WAS TALKING to a Westerner who had been working in Pyongyang for a long time. Describing the recent changes, he commented: "Once upon a time, one had to return from an overseas trip carrying a trunk full of cigarettes. Now my North Korean colleagues want me to bring back movies, especially tapes of South Korean TV dramas." Indeed, North Korea is in the middle of a video revolution which is likely to have a deep impact on its future. The information blockade, which has been maintained for decades, is crumbling under the pressure of new technologies and increasing inefficiency in the old economy.

What did kill Soviet-style state socialism? In the final analysis, it was its innate economic inefficiency. The state is a bad entrepreneur, as the entire economic history of the 20th century bears witness. The capitalist West outproduced and outperformed the communist East, whose nations lagged behind in many respects, including the living standards of other peoples.

Thus, the Communist governments had to enforce strict control over information flows from overseas. There were manifold reasons for this, but largely it was done because the rulers did not want the commoners to learn how vastly more prosperous were the people of similar social standing in the supposedly "exploited" West. But people learned the truth eventually, and once that occurred, the fate of state socialism was sealed.

A South Korean manager and North Korean soldiers turned unskilled workers. Is it a sign of the future? Photograph by Byeon Young-wook.

In the USSR and other countries of the once Communist Eastern Europe, uncensored information was largely provided by the short-wave radio broadcast. BBC, Voice of America and Radio Liberty were especially popular. The USSR was a more liberal society than North Korea and Soviet citizens could easily buy radio sets in the shops. As far as I am aware, Moscow never considered a ban on short-wave radio sets in peacetime — perhaps because in such a vast country such a measure would cut off a large part of the population from any form of communication. The government occasionally resorted to jamming, but this was not always efficient, since it could work only near major cities.

The first breaches in the wall of isolation were unwittingly made by the North Korean official media itself. In the 1980s, North Korean TV briefly showed footage of the Kwangju uprising of 1980, and the great labor strikes of 1987-1988. These images perplexed North Koreans. The South Koreans did not appear to be starving, and they were not dressed in rags. Indeed, the attire of these "desperate struggling masses" was decisively better than that of the average North Korean, and none of them showed signs of malnutrition!

But the real collapse of the self-isolation began in the mid–1990s, when a large number of North Korean refugees moved across the border to find food and employment in northeast China. Many refugees eventually returned home, bringing new ideas, new information, and new tunes.

The Yanbian area in northeast China is home to two million ethnic Koreans, most of whom are Chinese citizens. When, in 1992, Beijing and Seoul established formal diplomatic relations, these areas also began to attract a growing number of South Koreans. Tourists, missionaries, educators, spies and, of course, businessmen rushed here and soon created an environment eerily reminiscent of the gold rush boom towns of the American West. Things South Korean were everywhere. The karaoke bars played the latest hits from Seoul, the Internet cafes provided access to South Korean websites, and Seoul periodicals — largely of the more salacious type, in tune with the tastes of the local lowbrow audience — were to be found everywhere.

Some half a million North Korean refugees have crossed into China between 1995 and 2005, and most of them eventually returned to North Korea bringing home stories of China's success and the almost unbelievable prosperity of South Korea. In a nutshell, they followed a pattern mentioned by one of the refugees: "China is a paradise when compared to our country, but the Chinese say that they are very poor when compared to South Korea!" Retelling these stories is dangerous, but it is done nonetheless.

South Korean pop songs began to spread throughout the North from the late 1980s, especially once tape recorders became commonplace in more affluent households. The Korean penchant for singing is well known, and the catchy tunes of the modern Seoul hits attracted a lot of attention in the North. For a while, the authorities tried to hold back the tide, and people were sometimes arrested for singing South Korean songs in public. These days the authorities prefer to turn a blind eye to such minor transgressions. South Korean pop songs are euphemistically called "Yanbian songs" as if they were created by the ethnic Koreans of China. Finally, in 2001, Pyongyang even included a few South Korean oldies on the list of songs officially approved by the authorities.

However, the real breakthrough came only recently, and largely thanks to videotape. If the Soviet Union was brought down by the short-wave radio, in North Korea a similar role is likely to be played by the VCR.

Just like many other great social changes, this one began from a minor technological revolution. DVD players have been around for quite a while, but around 2001 their price dropped dramatically. Northeast China was no exception. Local Chinese households began to purchase new DVD players, and this made their old VCRs obsolete. The Chinese market was instantly flooded with very cheap used VCRs which could be bought for $10 or $20. Many of these used machines were bought by smugglers who transport goods across the porous border between Korea and China. They were resold in North Korea at a huge premium, but still only cost some $40 to $60.

This made the VCR affordable to a large number of North Korean households. In the 1990s they would have had to pay some $200 for a VCR — a prohibitive sum in a country with an average monthly salary of $5. A $50 VCR is within the reach of many North Korean households, even if they have to save desperately to afford one. No reliable data are available, but according to recent estimates it seems that some 5–10% of all Pyongyang households have a VCR, and this is a political fact of great importance.

Against the dull background of the official arts, the VCR provides good entertainment. Needless to say, people do not buy these expensive machines to watch "Star of Korea," a lengthy biopic about the youth of the Great Leader! Since the world's only major producer of Korean-language shows is South Korea, it is only natural that most programs come from Seoul via China. The South Korean soaps are a major hit. In a sense, the much-talked-about *hanliu* or "Korean wave," a recent craze for Korean pop culture across East Asia, is a part of North Korean life as well. Young North Koreans enthusiastically imitate the fashion and idiom they see in South Korean movies. And this does not bode well for the regime's future.

The gap between the two Koreas and the corresponding difference in living standards is huge, far exceeding the difference which once existed between East and West Germany. The per capita GDP of the South is approximately U.S. $10,000, while in the North it is estimated to be between U.S $500 and U.S. $1,000. Obesity is a serious health problem in the South while in the North the ability to dine on rice every day is a sign of unusual affluence. South Korea, the world's fifth largest automobile manufacturer, has one car for every two adults, while in the North a private car is less accessible to the average citizen than a private jet would be to the average American. South Korea is the world's leader in broadband Internet access while in the North only major cities have automatic telephone exchanges and private phones are still a privilege reserved largely for cadres. This South Korean reality represents a remarkable difference from the North Korean propagandists' picture of long queues of exhausted people standing in front of employment offices in the vain hope of landing a job, or of innocent schoolchildren severely beaten because of their parents' inability to pay their tuition fees, or of crowds of women prostituting themselves to "sadistic Yankee soldiers."

The South Korean life of crowded streets, an occasional lunch in a street corner eatery, easily available cars and annual overseas vacations is reproduced in the serials quite faithfully.

Of course, the South Korean movie-makers did not deliberately pursue a political agenda, and their movies are usually melodramatic stories of love, family relations and escapist adventure. They are not produced with the North Korean audience in mind. But the movies reflect life in South Korea quite faithfully, and this image is vastly different from what the official North Korean media claims it to be.

I do not think that the North Koreans take what they see in the movies at face value. They know that their movies grossly exaggerate the living standards in their own country, so they would expect movie-makers from other countries, including South Korea, to do the same. Thus, they scarcely believe that in the South everybody can eat meat on a daily basis or that every Seoul household has a car. Such improbable affluence is beyond their wildest dreams. But there are things which cannot be faked — like Seoul's cityscape, dotted with high-rise buildings and impressive bridges.

Thus it is gradually dawning on the North Koreans that the South is not exactly the land of hunger and destitution depicted by their propaganda. This is certain to have political consequences in the not too distant future, since the myth of South Korean poverty has been fundamental to the survival of the North Korean state.

Pyongyang has always based its claims for legitimacy on being a better type of Korean government, supposedly delivering a quality of life that would be unavailable in the "exploited" and "impoverished" South. If the North Korean populace learns about South Korean prosperity, then the Pyongyang government is in deep trouble, as the fate of the much more successful East German government demonstrated: the economic gap between North and South Korea is much greater than was once the case in Germany. According to current estimates, the per capita gross national product (GNP) in the South is 10 to 20 times higher than in the North.

The video revolution is very important, but many more cracks are opening in the self-imposed information blockade so painstakingly constructed and maintained by Pyongyang for decades. This blockade has proven to be rather expensive to run and maintain, and the regime is short of money.

The radio sets sold inside Korea are still permanently altered and sealed, but that does not really matter since cheap transistor radios are now smuggled across the Chinese border. The North Koreans are widely listening to the Korean-language programs of Voice of America and Radio Free Asia as well as to the KBS programs which target the North Korean audience.

In 2003, a poll confirmed that 67% of defectors from North Korea had been listening to foreign and South Korean broadcasts before they fled. Of course, this is not very representative: the willingness to defect obviously makes a person more interested in listening to foreign broadcasts. Nonetheless, it is clear that information about the world beyond the Beloved Leader's tight embrace is spreading inside the North.

The daily controls are crumbling as well — and in the long run this is probably even more important. In earlier times, a worker had to spend several hours every day on ideological indoctrination sessions in which he or she was expected to memorize many speeches of both the Great Leader and his son, the Dear Leader. It is now becoming increasingly difficult to ensure that people attend these boring functions. The same is true with respect to many other public rituals which once defined the daily life of North Koreans, such as tributes to the portraits and statues of the Great Leader, mass rallies, and so on. The more privileged must still attend, since they have positions to lose and careers to make, but the North Koreans at the bottom of the official hierarchy, and those outside the hierarchy entirely, do not care any more.

Under these new circumstances, a worker from a long-defunct factory is aware that the state bureaucracy has neither the means to reward his "politically correct behavior," nor the means to punish his refusal to participate in a state ritual. If such a person survives economically, it is largely through his own small-scale business activities or handicraft. He or she is independent of the crumbling state-run economy and hence is immune to the subtle threats and incentives of promotion/demotion, increase/decrease in rations, etc., which had ensured daily compliance for decades. In this new situation, many minor transgressions are likely to remain unpunished and even go unnoticed or unheeded by authorities.

The newly emerging market vendors and other employees of the semi-legal private enterprises are especially independent from (or inured to) the subtle government pressures which had ensured compliance for decades. One cannot promote or demote a vendor, transfer him or her to a better or worse job, nor determine his or her type of residence (though admittedly, most people still live in the houses they received when the old system was still operating).

Will North Korea survive such a liberalization? It is commonly assumed that survival is possible — after all, post–Mao Zedong China survived and flourished. But there is a major difference: the Communist Party government of China did not have an affluent and democratic "other China" just across the border (except for Hong Kong and Taiwan, of course — but these two statelets were too small and weak). In the Korean case, the impoverished Northerners are likely to see unification with the South as an easy and quick fix to their manifold problems. Only their ignorance about South Korean prosperity, combined with the fear of persecution, keeps them from following the example of the East Germans. But what will happen when this ignorance and fear are gone? Will the government be able to find a substitute, or at least provide economic growth fast enough and on a sufficient scale to silence the voices of protest? It would appear to be highly unlikely.

To Market, to Market...

WHAT IS THE FOCAL POINT OF North Korean life — or, rather, what has become the focus since the mid–1990s? What is the single most important sector in North Korean cities? A majority of North Koreans would not have to think long and hard before answering the question — is it the city hall, the statue of the Great Leader or perhaps the metro? Given the opportunity, most North Koreans would probably answer: "The market, of course!" Indeed, the last decade has been a boom time for the markets of the North.

Relations between Communist states and markets have never been easy. The market by its very nature is the embodiment of grass-roots capitalism. It is not incidental that another (admittedly, more approving) name for the capitalist system is the "market economy." Nonetheless, few Communist regimes ever contemplated the abolition of markets. It was clear from the outset that the government-controlled distribution systems were inadequate, and thus markets must be tolerated, albeit subject to restrictions of all kinds.

Perhaps no other Communist state was so anti-market as the North Korea of the 1960s. In August 1958, soon after the abolition of private shops, Cabinet Decree #140 prescribed a complete change in the market system. Markets were allowed only three times a month, and cereals, including rice, could not be sold and bought in a market. The markets were also subjected to strict regulations of all kinds, and in general were looked upon with unease and contempt, as "relics of capitalism."

By this time all farmers had become state employees in all but name. They tilled land which belonged to the large state-managed cooperative farms and were required to sell their produce to the state at fixed prices. Nonetheless, farmers retained small private plots which could be used as gardens. The produce from these plots — largely vegetables and herbs — were permitted to be sold in the markets.

This system is more or less identical to that of other communist countries. What set North Korea apart was the dearth of privately produced food. The plots of North Korean farmers were much smaller than in other Communist countries — a mere 15–30 square meters per household. This was done on purpose. In many other Communist countries farmers had bigger plots — and made their living from them, safely ignoring their work obligations in the fields of the cooperative farm! However, without their own plots, farmers had no choice but to work more for the state.

In the 1960s, private markets almost disappeared from North Korean cities and were barely tolerated in the countryside. Economic reality, however, turned out to be stronger than the administrative bans. In 1969, Kim Il Sung

For most of these people the emerging market economy is the only way to survive and, with some luck, make money. Photograph by Byeon Young-wook.

himself admitted the failure of the anti-market policy and gave the market-places his stamp of approval. He also reluctantly admitted that state-run North Korean enterprises were unable to produce everything that the average North Korean really needed. In 1984, new regulations allowed an increase in the number of markets and allowed them to operate daily.

However, as recent as the late 1980s, markets were still seen as inappropriate for the capital of a "socialist paradise." They were something to be ashamed of and were thus pushed to the margins of the city. Until the early 1990s, most markets were located in places more or less hidden from view, inside residential blocks or on small side streets. In Pyongyang, the main city market was set up under a huge viaduct at the easternmost part of the North Korean capital, as far from the city center as was physically possible.

Until the early 1990s, North Korean markets were very small, surrounded by high walls and always crowded with people. Many items unavailable in shops could be easily found in these markets; however, the assortment of goods was not impressive. There was not much food for sale — just some apples, meat, ducks and chickens, soybeans, homemade sweets, and occasionally fish and potatoes. Neither rice nor grain could be sold (at least, not openly) in the markets until the 1990s.

And the market prices were exorbitant even well before the food crisis of the mid–1990s: a kilo of pork in 1985 cost some 20 *won*, or about a third of the then average monthly salary, while a chicken cost some 40 *won*. Obviously, food at such prices could be bought only by the few and only on special occasions.

From the early 1980s, the markets became major centers of trade in smuggled foreign goods and, sometimes, of goods stolen from government factories. The authorities knew this but could do little to halt the trade. In the 1980s, about two-thirds of the vendors at the average North Korean market were selling consumer goods: clothes, imported medicines, tobacco and so on.

But the slow-motion collapse of the Stalinist economy and public distribution system led to an explosive growth of these private markets. Nowadays, if we can believe a North Korean joke, one can buy "everything but cats' horns" at a North Korean market. Indeed, the last decade has been a boom time for the North Korean markets — despite the terrible state of the country's economy.

Around 1992, North Korea lost access to the subsidized commodities which it once purchased from the friendly Soviet Union and China. This led to a deep economic crisis. Soon famine struck the country as well, triggered by the floods of 1995 and 1996.

In 1995-96 the authorities came to realize that it would be impossible to keep the public distribution system working outside major cities. Food rations were not delivered in remote areas any more, and the inhabitants of small towns and villages were left to their own devices.

At the same time, the government relaxed the restrictions on domestic travel. Technically, every North Korean who ventures outside his native county must have a special "travel permit." However, in the mid–1990s, the authorities began to turn a blind eye to unauthorized travel.

The late 1990s will be remembered in Korean history not only as a time of great humanitarian disaster — a disaster which took between a half million and one million lives. The decade was also a time of unprecedented mobility when people left their native places in huge numbers. Many sought places where food was more readily available while others enthusiastically took up the barter trade.

Women were (and still are) especially prominent in this business. Many North Korean women were full-time housewives or, at the very least, held less demanding jobs. Their husbands continued to go to their factories, which had come to a standstill, and receive ration coupons which were hardly worth the paper on which they were printed. Meanwhile, their women embarked on a bout of frenetic business activity. Soon some of these women began to make sums which far exceeded their husbands' wages.

A private (or semi-private) food stall in Pyongyang. Photograph by Andrew Graham.

The markets became major centers for these deals. As of 1999, there were some 300–350 markets throughout the country. In addition, many railway stations became centers of large, if unrecognized, markets. This is understandable: the poor road network means that the railway remains the major means of transport in the North. It was estimated that in 1999, the average North Korean bought some 60% of his food on the free market. For consumption goods, the figure was even higher — more than 70%.

A large proportion of these goods is smuggled from overseas. In recent years, the markets have even been found conducting large-scale trade in South Korean goods, of which cosmetics are a particularly popular item. This is a significant departure from the recent past when the possession of a single South Korean item could easily land a person in jail.

Nor are markets simply a place for shopping. In recent years, private food stalls have begun to appear in large numbers on market squares. In spite of the food shortages, anyone with ready cash can enjoy a delicious — if not necessarily clean and safe — meal at such stalls.

South Koreans often compare the North Korean marketplaces with the Seoul markets of the 1950s, displaying the same raw energy, the adventurism, and the ever-present danger of violence. It might sound surprising, but a teenage defector remarked that the present-day South Korean markets, like

Tongdaemun or Namdaemun, failed to impress him: they did not look as lively as their North Korean counterparts! They say that you can now even buy pineapples and bananas at the markets — as long as you have the money.

But money is a problem. The market price has always been several times the price of the same product in government shops where these products could be obtained only with rationing coupons, if at all. The official price of rice has always been 0.08 *won* per kilo, while on the market it was sold in early 2002 at 40–50 *won* and after the "July reforms" this price increased even more. Only a minority of North Koreans can afford to buy anything but the most basic food, and many cannot afford even that.

Nevertheless, the sudden resurgence of markets has once again demonstrated the resilience of capitalism. Is this good or bad? Only time will tell....

The Nouveau Riche *of North Korea*

RECENTLY, FOREIGN NEWSPAPERS BEGAN publishing photos of North Koreans talking over mobile phones and driving luxury cars. Such scenes are correctly perceived as yet another confirmation of the serious changes which have taken place in the North over recent years. Mobile phones, classy private restaurants and advertising billboards for automobiles indicate that capitalism is quietly making inroads in what used to be the world's last Stalinist stronghold. But if there is capitalism, there must be capitalists. So who are these new rich in North Korea?

The last decade has turned out to be an era of the quiet collapse of Stalinism in North Korea. While the country's political structure still remains largely Stalinist, its economy has changed profoundly and perhaps irreversibly. This was not a result of some planned reforms; rather, North Korea's economic Stalinism died a natural death, being eaten away by the grass-root capitalism which began to grow around 1990. But can there be a capitalist economy without capitalists?

Of course the North Korea of the 1960s or 1980s also had its rich and poor. But the affluent were that way either because the party-state bureaucracy chose them (i.e., officials and individuals who were allowed to work overseas and were paid in hard currency) or at least allowed them to be affluent (this was the case for the repatriates from Japan who received hard-currency remittances). But this is not the case any more. People get rich, well, because they can get rich....

A street in Kaesong, the second largest city in the country. The economic crisis meant that traffic, never heavy, is almost non-existent outside Pyongyang. Photograph by Christopher Morris.

The private market trade began to grow explosively around 1990, and this was the time when North Korea's "black capitalism" was well and truly born. In order to succeed, one had to have a competitive edge, since the competition was tough. In the late 1990s, the North Koreans would say: "There are only three types of people in [North] Korea: those who starve, those who beg, and those who trade."

These early successful entrepreneurs usually had some background which gave them an advantage over others. Most of them were officials or managers of state-run enterprises who had manifold if not strictly legal ways to make an extra *won*. For example, in the 1990s a person who could command a truck easily made a fortune by moving merchandise around the country and taking advantage of the large differences in prices between the regions.

Managers of state enterprises often sold the product of their factories on the market. This was technically stealing, but in an increasingly corrupt and disorganized society, there was a fairly good chance of remaining uncaught. Retail personnel at all levels channeled the goods through the "back doors" of their shops, independent of the disintegrating public distribution system. The military and security personnel also had their advantages, since for decades they operated in what can be described as "states-within-a-state," beyond even the most nominal control of outsiders.

Finally, the "hard-currency earning" officials made a lot of money: they had been running quasi-market operations since the 1970s and had both the necessary expertise and the resources. After 1990, they began to use these resources for their own ends.

Even some humbler professions found themselves in a relatively better position, especially if they could exploit the huge differences in commodities' prices between various regions. Truck or car drivers, for example, could take money for moving passengers and merchandise — especially after the quiet breakdown of the travel restriction system around 1997. Train conductors augmented their salary by selling and buying goods themselves, and by taking bribes for allowing passengers into certain carriages. Of course, they had to share some of their profits with their supervisors....

We have seen similar developments in the former Soviet Union and China. However, in North Korea, it appears that the involvement of the party and state cadres in the new capitalist enterprise has remained relatively limited. Perhaps the government itself remains indecisive on whether to allow the officials to engage in private commerce on a large scale. Recent years have witnessed some experiments of this kind. But so far the major role in the emerging North Korean capitalism has been played by people who came from outside the state bureaucracy and, in many cases, from groups hitherto discriminated against.

Access to investment capital, however small, is a key to success in the post–Stalinist North Korea, and the country has three major groups who can boast this access: "Japanese Koreans," "Chinese Koreans" and "Korean Chinese." It is remarkable that for decades all these groups were seen as "suspicious" by Pyongyang's officials.

The Japanese Koreans are people who moved to the North from Japan in the 1960s (there were some 93,000 of these migrants). These people, their children and their spouses have relatives in Japan, and these relatives are usually willing to send some money to the hapless returnees who had come to the "socialist paradise" to discover that there was no way back.

Traditionally, the authorities looked on the Japanese Koreans with great suspicion, and these former repatriates were overrepresented among the inhabitants of prison camps. At the same time, money transfers from Japan have always been a major source of hard currency for Pyongyang, so the antics of the Japanese Koreans were often tolerated and this peculiar group even enjoyed some special rights, so that they were both privileged and discriminated against at the same time.

When the old system of state control and state distribution collapsed,

Japanese Koreans began to invest their money in a multitude of trade adventures. It did not hurt that many of them still had first-hand experience of living in a capitalist society.

Another group were people with relatives in China. The economic growth of China meant that the relatives there could also help their poor relations in North Korea. In most cases, this did not consist of money transfers, but assistance in business and trade.

The local ethnic Chinese, the only minority in North Korea, were in an even better position to exploit the new opportunities. After all, the Korean Chinese have been the only group of the country's inhabitants who could travel overseas as private citizens more or less at will. Even in earlier times, the ethnic Chinese used this unique position to earn extra money by moving merchandise across the border, albeit on a small scale. In the new climate of the 1990s, they simply switched to larger operations.

There is an irony in the sudden economic advance of these groups. For decades, their overseas connections have made them suspicious and led to systematic discrimination against them. In the 1990s, however, these very same connections became the source of their prosperity.

Fortunes are made in trade, but not in manufacturing, which remains controlled by the state. Money lending also provides good profit. In the 1990s the private lenders charged their borrowers a *monthly* interest of some 30–40%. The associated risks are high, too: these lenders had virtually no protection against the state, criminals or above all, bad debtors. They have to choose their clients carefully, largely from prominent officials who are engaged in private commerce.

Thus, by the late 1990s some businessmen (and, surprisingly, for such a patriarchal society, businesswomen) have amassed large fortunes, often reaching a hundred thousand U.S. dollars. This symbolically important mark seems to be the line between the rich and the filthy rich in the North. Thus a sudden turn of fate has made the pariahs of the past into the elite of the present.

But what about future? Does the future of North Korea belong to these new capitalists? I doubt it, frankly. If the North continues to exist as a separate entity, these market adventurers will eventually have to compete with the heavyweights from the state oligarchy who will sooner or later join the capitalist game (and some of them have probably done so already). If the entire state collapses, and the country is swiftly united with the South, most of them will be pushed aside by the capital from Seoul. In this regard, perhaps North Korea will be different from China or Russia.

Women's Market

A DEFECTOR FROM THE NORTH, a typical tough Korean auntie with trademark permed hair, smiled when asked about a "man's role" in North Korean families: "Well, in 1997-98 men became useless. They went to their workplaces, but there was nothing to be done there, so they came home. Meanwhile their wives traveled to distant places to trade and kept the families going."

Indeed, the sudden increase in the economic strength and status of women is one of the changes which have taken place in North Korea over the past decade. The old Stalinist society has died a slow but natural death and, despite Pyongyang's frequent and loud protestations to the contrary, capitalism has been reborn in North Korea.

But the new North Korean capitalism of dirty marketplaces, charcoal trucks and badly dressed vendors with huge sacks of merchandise on their backs displays one surprising feature: it has a distinctly female face. Women are overrepresented among the leaders of the growing post–Stalinist economy at least at the lower level, among the market traders and small-time entrepreneurs.

This partially reflects a growth pattern in North Korean neo-capitalism. Unlike the restoration of capitalism in the former Soviet Union or China, the "post-socialist capitalism" of North Korea is not an affair planned and encouraged by people from the top tiers of the late communist hierarchy. Rather, it is capitalism from below, which is growing despite the government's occasional attempts to reverse the process and turn the clock back.

Until around 1990, markets and private trade played a very moderate role in North Korean society. Most people were content with what they were officially allocated through the elaborate public distribution system, and did not care to look for any further opportunities. The government also did its best to suppress the capitalist spirit. The rations were not overly generous, but were still adequate for one's survival.

And then things began to fall apart. The collapse of the Soviet Union brought a sudden end to the flow of Soviet aid which was, incidentally, happily accepted but never publicly admitted by the North Korean side. This triggered an implosion of the North Korean economy, and in 1995-96 the public distribution system ceased to function in most parts of the country.

Like the authorities of most other Communist countries, the North Koreans expected that every able-bodied male would be employed by some state enterprise. It was illegal to remain unemployed — for males, that is. For married women, however, the approach was different. All Communist countries have admitted that a woman has the right to remain a full-time housewife, but this was not seen as a "socially healthy" or terribly responsible career choice. In the North, the number of stay-at-home housewives was unusually high. No precise data are available, but it appears that some 30% of the married women of working age stayed at home.

When the crisis began and the old system began to fall apart, the men still felt bound to their jobs by their obligations and rations which were distributed through their workplaces. The rations by this time were not forthcoming, but this did not matter. Accustomed to the stability of the previous decades, North Koreans saw the situation as merely a temporary crisis which would soon be overcome somehow. No doubt they reasoned that one day everything would return to the "normal" (that is, Stalinist) state of affairs. So men believed that it would be wise to keep their jobs in order to resume their careers after the eventual normalization of the situation. The ubiquitous "organizational life" also played its role: a North Korean adult was required to attend endless indoctrination sessions and meetings, and these requirements were more demanding on males than females.

Women enjoyed more freedom. Thus when the economic crisis began, women were first to engage in market activities of all kinds. It came very naturally. In some cases they began by selling those household items they could do without, or by selling homemade food. Eventually it developed into larger businesses. While the men continued to go to their plants, the women threw themselves into their market activities with gusto. In North Korea their trade involved long journeys in open trucks, and nights spent on concrete floors or under the open skies. They often bribed predatory local officials, and of course, women had the ability to move heavy material, with the vendor's back being her major mode of transport.

This tendency was especially pronounced among low- and middle-income families. The elite received rations even through the famine years of 1996–99, so the women of North Korea's top 5% on the whole continued with their old lifestyle. Nonetheless, some of them also began to use their abilities to acquire goods cheaply. Quite often, the wives of high-level cadres were and still are involved in the resale of merchandise which is first purchased from their husbands' factories at cheap official prices. It is remarkable that in North Korea such activities are carried out not so much by the cadres themselves, but by their wives. Cadres had to be careful, since it was not clear what the official approach might be to the nascent capitalism. Thus it was assumed that it would be safer for women to engage in such undertakings since they did not, nor do they still, quite belong to the official social hierarchy.

A typical story is that of Ms. Hwang, who has operated in the borderland area since the late 1990s. Many inhabitants of her native Yongch'on County still remember how in 1997, when the North Korean economy began to crumble and the public distribution system ceased to function, they received a special gift from the Dear Leader: everyone in the county was given a pair of nylon socks. Not luxurious goods, of course, but to get something in such trying circumstances was unusual. Few knew that these socks were not actually provided by the government, let alone the Dear Leader himself. The socks were donated by the above-mentioned Ms. Hwang.

Recently, Kwon Chong-hyon, an energetic China-based correspondent of the *Daily North Korean* paper, interviewed her and got her to relate her life story and exploits.

Ms. Hwang was born in China to a mixed marriage, her father being Han Chinese and her mother an ethnic Korean. Like many other China-based families of Korean origin they fled from Mao's "Cultural Revolution" in the 1960s and moved to North Korea. These days, when people are escaping from the North in their thousands, it is a little difficult to imagine that just a few decades earlier North Korea was often seen by the Chinese as a land of stability and affluence!

Like many other Koreans with "Chinese connections," Ms. Hwang began a cross-border trade business in the 1990s, when government control began to wane. Unlike many others, she had no need to resort to smuggling: having immediate relatives in China, she could travel there legally, and in recent years this has become a lot easier. Of course, getting a travel permit might be troublesome, but her money allows her to smooth over this procedure with a few judiciously placed inducements.

And naturally, her "Kim Jong Il's socks" publicity stunt also worked wonders. She bought 100,000 pairs of socks wholesale and presented them to the local government for distribution. In doing so the local authorities were able to win some praise from above and improve their political standing, and in return Ms. Hwang received powerful political support. And the common people got their socks!

Ms. Hwang frankly explained her survival strategy to Kwon Chong-hyon: "I know a lot of people in the foreign affairs department of the state security police in North Pyongan Province. Since I have a travel permit [to visit China], I can go there without trouble as long as I get it stamped by state security. If you have good relations with state security, it's easy to get travel permits; if you have good relations with police, it's easy to fight off the criminals; if you have good relations with the Party, it's easy to do trade."

Had the state given its formal approval to the nascent capitalism as had the still formally "communist" state of China, the men would have been far more active. But Pyongyang officialdom still seems to be uncertain what to do with the crumbling system, and it is afraid to give its unconditional approval to capitalism. Thus the men are left further and further behind and capitalism is left to the women.

This has led to a change in the gender roles inside families. On paper, communism appeared very feminist, but real life in the communist states was an altogether different matter, and among these communist states, North Korea was remarkable for the strength of its patriarchal stereotype. Men, especially in the more conservative northeastern part of the country, seldom did anything at home, with all household chores being exclusively the female domain.

But in the new situation, where men had little to do while their wives struggled to keep the family fed and clothed, many men changed their opinion about housework being something beneath their dignity — at least this is what recent research among the defectors seems to suggest. As one female defector put it, "When men had outside jobs and earned something, they were very boastful. But now they cannot boast and have become sort of useless, like a streetlight in the middle of the day. So a man now tries to help his wife in her work as best he can."

Recently, as it has become increasingly clear that the "old times" are not going to return, some men have been bold enough to risk breaking their ties with official employment. But they often enter the market not as businessmen in their own right but rather as aides to their wives who have amassed great experience over the past decade. Being newcomers, males are relegated to subordinate positions — at least temporarily — in fact, Ms. Hwang's husband also works as her assistant! Or alternatively, they are involved in more dangerous and stressful kinds of activity, such as smuggling goods across the badly protected border with China. As one woman defector noted: "Men usually do smuggling. Men are better at big things, you know."

Economic difficulties and the change in money-earning patterns as well as a new lifestyle and related opportunities in some cases have led to family breakdown. In South Korea the economic crisis of 1998 resulted in a mushrooming divorce rate. In the North, the almost simultaneous Great Famine had the same impact, even if in many cases the divorce was not officially recognized.

Of course we are talking about a great disaster here, and a large part of the estimated 600,000–900,000 people who perished in those years were women. And of the survivors, not all women became winners, bold entrepreneurs or successful managers: some were dragged into prostitution, which has made a powerful comeback recently, and many more have had to survive on whatever meager food was available. But still, it seems that for many women, the disaster of the 1990s has offered then an opportunity to display their strength, will and intelligence not just to survive, but also to succeed.

In Lieu of Conclusion:
With a Bang,
or with a Whimper?

By THE EARLY 1990s ALMOST EVERY expert around confidently predicted the imminent collapse of the inefficient, archaic, brutal and at times bizarre regime in North Korea. The policies of the great powers were based on the assumption that a North Korean collapse was imminent. It has been suggested that the U.S. signed the Agreed Framework of 1994 only because most people inside the Beltway believed this flawed agreement would not be carried through anyway. It was assumed that the North Korean regime would collapse well before the expected completion of the light water reactor project.

But this did not happen. Contrary to everyone's (well, almost everyone's) expectations the Kim dynasty has survived. Even the disaster of the Great Famine, arguably the worst famine Asia has seen since Mao's Great Leap Forward, was not enough to undermine its grip on power. No revolution occurred, and no army general drove his tanks into Pyongyang. Why?

One of the reasons is particularly disconcerting to idealists: as long as a modern government is determined to be cruel and is ready to shoot all troublemakers, it is pretty much invincible — at least, so long as it is not subjected to serious pressure from the outside. It has been long known that revolutions tend to erupt not in the worst times of tyranny but when a government wishes to liberalize itself. Bad governments are usually overthrown, not when they are at their most brutal, but when they try to become better. A government which does not play with the dangerous notions of "democracy" or "humanity" is in a much safer position than a government of soul-searching reformers.

In other words, the secret of Pyongyang's success in handling the situation is its remarkable indifference to the sufferings of the common people. The rulers were prepared to sacrifice as many lives as was necessary to ensure their survival. Had the DPRK government decided to disband the state-run agricultural cooperatives, the famine would not have occurred. But such an act would have brought on unacceptable weakening of central control and hence it was rejected. The death of some 600,000 people was the price that had to be paid, and the rulers couldn't have cared less.

Ermanno Furlanis, a famous Italian pizza chef, was invited to North Korea to cook for Kim Jong Il and his inner circle in 1997 when the famine reached its height, wiping out entire villages in the northern provinces. And what does the Italian maestro write about his own experience of this famine-smitten nation? "That evening, dinner — a feast worthy of Petronius' Satyricon — was served with an excellent Burgundy and delicacies from around the world. As an Italian I could not refrain from objecting [to the French wines], and three days later fresh from Italy a shipment of Barolo arrived." Or: "That evening we had a light dinner back at the base: a pair of lobsters, salad and French white wine." This is how servants (admittedly, very special servants) of the Dear Leader lived during those hard times. And what about the Great Man himself? "Every now and then a kind of courier would show up from some corner of the world. I saw him twice unloading two enormous boxes containing an assortment of 20 very costly French cheeses, and one box of prized French wines."

Does this mean that the Pyongyang rulers, the "top thousand," are cruel? Perhaps they are, but generally they are simply indifferent. Their behavior reminds me of the medieval European aristocracy. When the peasants were starving, the barons enjoyed their feasts, horses and castles without perceiving this behavior as shameful. They belonged to a different stratum, so the lavish feasts, the silk dresses and the occasional round of sex with a pretty maidservant was their birthright.

The North Korean elite has been hereditary since the late 1960s, if not earlier. And I do not mean the Kim clan alone. At the top levels of the state bureaucracy, many important positions are occupied by people who qualify for these posts largely as the sons or grandsons of guerrillas who fought in Manchuria in the 1930s or as descendants of some wartime hero. They have spent all their lives in the comfortable and sequestered environment of the privileged living quarters, special schools and hard-currency shops.

This also renders them less ready to defect. In the old Soviet Union or in China, the former Communist elite defected and transformed themselves overnight from party apparatchiks into capitalists. A similar strategy is unlikely to work in the North. In all probability, the collapse of the regime will lead to unification. And in a unified Korea, the former North Korean bureaucrats will have no chance: for better or worse, capitalism there will be built not by born-again apparatchiks, but by resident managers of Hyundai and Samsung. This means that the collapse of the system will mean the loss of a privileged life — and perhaps even persecution. The North Korean cadres know only too well how they would have treated the Seoul "reactionary puppets" had Pyongyang emerged victorious from the inter–Korean rivalry, and they do not see any reason why they would be treated any differently themselves. Thus they stick together, in the faint hope that they may survive.

And there is another reason as well: since 1990, the world has changed. North Korea is lucky in that it has not been subjected to any concerted attempt to take advantage of its severe economic crisis in order to bring down the regime. None of the countries involved have made a serious attempt to promote dissent within the DPRK.

This is very unlike, one suspects, what would have occurred in the 1970s or 1980s, when the Cold War was at its height and the crusade against the "Evil Empires" or "Evil Kingdoms" of world Communism was being waged. Today, in a less ideological age, North Korea's neighbors are wary of the inherent risks, troubles and costs associated with any collapse of the North Korean regime, and they are not too eager to hasten the process. An East German or Romania-style collapse of the Kim Jong Il government would undoubtedly lead to outflows of refugees which no neighboring country would be willing to deal with, to uncertain and potentially destabilizing changes in the local military balance, and to huge expenses which South Korea alone would be unable to sustain. Hence, instead of crusading for democracy, North Korea's neighbors are generally ready to tacitly support the Pyongyang leaders in their efforts to control the situation, and do not ask too many awkward questions about humanitarian or human rights problems resulting from these efforts.

And, of course, there is a nuclear program which is widely and skillfully used for blackmail: Pyongyang expected to be paid for not developing its nuclear weapons. The Geneva agreed framework of 1994 was a masterpiece of blackmail diplomacy, and North Korea received generous aid packages as a reward ... and then proceeded with a nuclear weapons program anyway.

Then, there was (and is) veiled but clearly evident rivalry between China and the USA. Beijing probably does not want a nuclear North Korea, but it is not happy about a unified country which could become — or rather remain — pro–American. It would also like a Communist regime or two hanging around to keep it company and help its current government survive. This means that China is willing to keep North Korea in operation by providing it with aid, especially with food aid.

Finally, there are South Korean phobias to exploit. In dealing with the broader public, nationalism is a favorite choice, but hard-nosed politicians are pressed to feed Pyongyang by a different set of considerations: the South is afraid of a democratic revolution in the North, politely known as an "implosion." A German-style unification is seen as a disaster since it would lead to a dramatic decline in the living standards of the South Koreans. This is a unique situation with few parallels in world history: a government feeding its enemy precisely to avoid its own swift victory!

All these things combined — the brutal rationalism of internal policies, the pragmatic cynicism of the post–Cold War world system and the admirable skill of the North Korean diplomats — have helped this, the world's most brutal regime, survive against all odds. It probably lives on borrowed time, but the very fact of its survival until 2006 is indeed an impressive achievement — for the pizza-munching, Burgundy-sipping patricians, that is.

But will this last forever? Probably not: the information is getting in, and this does not bode well for the regime. The gap with South Korea is too huge, and sooner or later the commoners will learn about this. Will they agree to remain poor in some slowly changing "kimilsungesque" state, or will they follow the example of East Germans and choose a seemingly faster solution? I believe that the second option is more likely, but only time can tell.

Further Reading

UNTIL THE MID–1990S, North Korea had been generally neglected in the English-language scholarship, but the recent decade produced a large number of publications dealing with North Korean issues. However, most of those books and articles deal with the international policy of North Korea and the nuclear crisis which has kept Pyongyang in the limelight for over a decade. The publications dealing with the history of the North and internal dynamics of this society, let alone with its daily life, are few and far between.

So far, the closest to our topic has been the work by Helen-Louise Hunter, who in the early 1990s analyzed the then rare testimonies of the defectors:

Helen-Louise Hunter, *Kim Il-song's North Korea* (Westport, CT: Praeger, 1999).

To some extent, the same approach is shared by Chris Springer's book, essentially an unofficial and informal guide to North Korean capital city:

Chris Springer, *Pyongyang: The Hidden History of the North Korean Capital* (Budapest: Entente Bt.; Gold River, CA: distributed by Saranda Books, 2003).

There are a number of books which can be recommended as primers for somebody who want to familiarize himself with North Korean history and politics. As introduction, I would recommend the following works:

Bradley K. Martin, *Under the Loving Care of the Fatherly Leader: North Korea and the Kim Dynasty* (New York: Thomas Dunne Books, 2004). A large compendium of information, based on interviews and numerous publications.

Kongdan Oh and Ralph Hassig, *North Korea through the Looking Glass* (Washington, D.C.: Brookings Institution Press, 2000). A review of North Korean society in the late 1990s. Perhaps the best general introduction to the country, its history and problems.

Don Oberdorfer, *The Two Koreas: A Contemporary History* (New York: Basic Books,

2001). An introduction to the relations between the two Korean states, beginning in the 1970s.

Adrian Buzo, *The Guerilla Dynasty: Politics and Leadership in North Korea* (Boulder, CO: Westview Press, 1999). A review of North Korean history, with special emphasis on the last 20–30 years.

It is also useful to read two quite old but still reliable works written by the founding fathers of North Korean studies in the West:

Suh Dae-suk, *Kim Il Sung: The North Korean Leader* (New York: Columbia University Press, 1988). A political biography of Kim Il Sung, but also a detailed history of North Korea from its inception to the mid–1980s.

Robert Scalapino and Chong-Sik Lee, *Communism in Korea* (Berkeley, Los Angeles, and London: University of California Press, 1972). A thorough description of North Korean society in the 1950s and 1960s, still very useful.

The travel accounts about North Korea are uncommon — not least because the country does not exactly welcome foreign visitors. As a rare example of such a travelogue, one should mention:

Nanchu with Xing Hang, *In North Korea: An American Travels Through an Imprisoned Nation* (Jefferson, NC: McFarland, 2003).

There are also notes of a Swedish diplomat who worked in North Korea in the 1970s and the 1980s:

Erik Cornell, *North Korea Under Communism: Report of an Envoy to Paradise* (New York: Routledge, 2002).

There are also two books written by people who lived in Pyongyang, being employed as editors of the North Korean propaganda publications (nearly the only positions available to the those citizens of the developed world who are willing to spend few years under close supervision in a remote and very lonely place):

Michael Harrold, *Comrades and Strangers* (Hoboken, NJ: Chichester, West Sussex, England: John Wiley & Sons, 2004).

Andrew Holloway, *A Year in Pyongyang.* The book has not been published on paper, but thanks to the efforts of Aidan Foster-Carter it is available online at: *http://www.aidanfc.net/a_year_in_pyongyang_1.html*

Finally, one should mention two English-language books describing the prison world of North Korea:

Kang Chol-Hwan and Pierre Rigoulot, *The Aquariums of Pyongyang: Ten Years in the North Korean Gulag* (New York: Basic Books, 2001). Memoirs of a former inmate in a North Korean prison camp.

David Hawk, *The Hidden Gulag: Exposing North Korea's Prison Camps* (Washington, D.C.: U.S. Committee for Human Rights in North Korea, 2003). A thorough research of the prison camp system, based on all available information.

Korean Works

The list of Korean-language publications in North Korea is remarkably longer, and these publications were extensively used for this book. Like English-language scholarship, the Korean literature also tends to dwell heavily on the political and security issues, but the social developments and daily life in North Korea are treated in much greater detail. North Korean studies are booming in recent years, even though the general interest in the "northern brethren" among the South Korean public is clearly small and declining. This academic boom produces literature of very uneven quality, but some of the publications are truly interesting and innovative.

First of all, it makes sense to mention a few books whose authors' approach was similar to mine: they wanted to use the available data (obtained largely, but not exclusively, via defectors) to reconstruct the daily life of North Koreans. Among such books, one should mention:

Chŏn Yŏng-sŏn, *Pukhan-ŭi sahoe-wa munhwa [Society and culture of North Korea]* (Seoul: Yŏkrak, 2005). The book pays much attention to daily life of North Koreans.
Kim Sŭng-ch'ŏl, *Pukhan tongp'o saenghwal yangsik-kwa majimak hŭimang [The life style of the North Koreans and [their] last hope]* (Seoul: Charyowon, 2000).
Pak Hyŏn-sŏn, *Hyŏndae Pikhan-ŭi sahoe-wa kajok [Contemporary North Korean society and family]* (Seoul: Hanul, 2004).
Pukhan chumin-ŭi ilsang saenghwal-kwa taejung munhwa [The daily life and mass culture of North Korean people] (Seoul: Orŭm, 2003). Collection of articles, with the title being largely self-explanatory.
Pukhan saramdŭl-i marhanŭn Pukhan iyagi [Stories about North Korea, as told by the North Koreans themselves] (Seoul: Chongt'o ch'ulp'an, 2000).
Pukhan-ŭi kajŏng saenghwal munhwa [Culture of family life in North Korea] (Seoul: Sŏul taehakkyo ch'ulp'anbu, 2001). Collection of articles.
Sŏ Tong-ik, *Inmin-i sanŭn mosup [How do people's masses live]* (Seoul: Charyowon, 1995). Large two-volume book, compiled by a person who had worked with defectors, based on his interviews and a vast array of published and unpublished material.
Yim Sun-hŭi, *Sikryangnan-kwa pukhan yŏsŏng-ŭi yŏhal mich' ŭisik pyŏnhwa [The food crisis and changes in the [social] roles and self-consciousness of North Korean women]* (Seoul: T'ongil yŏnguwon, 2004).

Puknyŏk' saram ŏttŏk'e salgo issŭlkka? [How do people of the North live] (Seoul: Sŏnin, 2004). The book is an oddity, but increasingly common these days: published by a left-nationalist magazine, it faithfully parrots Pyongyang propaganda, just slightly repackaged for the benefits of South Korean readers; while completely unreliable as a source of information, it gives a good idea of how North Koreans want to present their system to the world.

In the past, every defector who was able to express himself or herself in writing was nearly certain to produce memoirs. However, one must be somewhat careful with those defectors' writings published before 1990: the official anti–Communism and strict censorship, combined with defectors' own sincere animosity to Pyongyang regime, often led to distortions (not so much by direct lies, but rather through omissions, over- and understatements and unfounded generalizations). It did not help that the general tone of writing also was remarkably hysterical, and also that the South Korean intelligence censored the defectors' writings to make sure no secrets or sensitive information would be divulged. As examples of pre–1990 writings by defectors, one might cite:

Kim Pu-sŏng, *Nae-ga p'anŭn ttanggul* [*The tunnel I dug*] (Seoul: Kapja munhwa sa, 1976). Memoirs of a North Korean officer who was involved with operations against the South and defected in 1975.

Kong T'ak-ho, *Pukkwe kukka chŏngch'i powibu naemak* [*Behind the scene of the Northern devils' Ministry for the Political Protection of the State*] (Seoul: Hongwonsa, 1976). Heavily censored notes of a former North Korean secret police officer.

The situation changed after 1990, when anti–Communism waned in South Korea and establishment of a democratic regime brought an end to the censorship. The "new" defectors' writings are different from those of their predecessors: these texts are more neutral in tone, less critical of the North and far more informative. At the same time, only a few defectors write memoirs these days — and their books have to wait a long time before being published. The political changes in Seoul and general loss of interest in North Korea among the South Korean public have had their toll, so I am aware of a number of people who wrote their memoirs but have had a hard time finding a publisher. Among post–1995 writings, one should mention:

Ch'oe Chin-i, *Kukkyŏng-ŭl se pŏn kŏnnŏn yŏja* [*A woman who crossed the border three times*] (Seoul: Bookhouse, 2005). Memoirs of a North Korean poetess and feminist who fled the country during the famine and eventually arrived in the South.

Chu Sŏng-il, *DMZ-ŭi pom* [*Spring at the DMZ*] (Seoul: Sidae chŏngsin, 2004). Memoirs of a recently defected soldier, with special emphasis on the military.

Hŭin kŏs-to kŏmda [*White is black*] (Seoul: Nana ch'ulp'ansa, 1996). Collections of articles and short memoirs from various defectors.

Kang Ch'ŏl-hwan, *Suyongso-ŭi norae* [*Song of a prison camp*] (Seoul: Sidae chŏngsin, 2005). This book has been advertised as a Korean-language version of *The aquariums of Pyongyang*, but this is not really the case: the book describes the same events, but with greater detail, and addresses a Korean, rather than Western, reader).

Kang Myŏng-do, *Pyongyang-ŭn mangmyŏng-ŭl kkum kkunda* [*Pyongyang dreams of escape]* (Seoul: Chungang Ilbo, 1995). Memoirs of a former bureaucrat who felt out of grace.

Kim Chi-il, *Sarang-ŭl wihayŏ, chayu-rŭl wohayŏ [For the love, for the freedom]* (Seoul: Koryŏwon, 1992). Memoirs of a North Korean college student who defected to the South while studying in Russia.

Kim Chŏng-yŏn, *Pyŏngyang yŏja [A woman from Pyongyang]* (Seoul: Koryŏ sŏjŏk, 1995). Memoirs of a North Korean secret police officer, with good description of daily life in the 1960s and 1970s.

Ko Yŏng-hwan, *Pyŏngyang 25 si [25 hours of Pyongyang]* (Seoul: Koryŏwon, 1993). Notes of a North Korean diplomat, dealing with life of North Korean bureaucracy.

Kwon Hyŏk, *Konan-ŭi kanghaeng-gun [March of Hardship]* (Seoul: Chŏngt'o, 1999). A very realistic and thoughtful account of daily life in the countryside in the worst times of the famine, in 1998–99.

Sŏng Hye-rang, *Tŭngnamu chip [A house under wisteria tree]* (Seoul: Chisik nara, 2001). Memoirs of a daughter of South Korean left-wing activists, and eventually Kim Jong Il's sister-in-law, very well written.

Yi Yŏng-kuk, *Na-nŭn Kim Jŏng-il-ŭi kyŏnghowon-i yŏssta [I was Kim Jong Il's body-guard]* (Seoul: Sidae chŏngsin, 2004). The author indeed once served as Dear Leader's bodyguard, but the book's focus is much more on daily life and experiences of a North Korean of his generation.

Also, a number of defectors' stories, while never being published as a separate book, appeared in South Korean periodicals, both general and specialized (of which more later).

Among the general reference material dealing with North Korea, one should mention:

Pukhan ch'onglam, 1945–1982 [The general review of North Korea, 1945–1982] (Seoul: Pukhan yŏnguso, 1983); *Pukhan ch'onglam, 1983–1993 [The general review of North Korea, 1983–1993]* (Seoul: Pukhan yŏnguso, 1994). Both books are large volumes dealing with all aspects of North Korean life, and providing a wealth of data.

Pukhan ihae [Understanding North Korea] (Seoul: T'ongil kyoyukwon, 2000–2004). Annually republished reviews of changes in North Korean politics, economy and society.

Pukhan kaeyo [General review of North Korea] (Seoul: T'ongilbu, 2000–2004). Annual reviews of North Korea, prepared and published by the Ministry of Unification.

Pukhan kyŏngje ch'onglam 2004 [North Korean economic review 2004] (Seoul: Kukje chŏngbo yŏnguwon, 2004).

Pukhan ŏhwi sajŏn [Dictionary of North Korean expressions] (Seoul: Yonghap, 2002).

Pukhan yongŏ 400 sajŏn [Dictionary of 400 North Korean terms] (Seoul: Yonghap, 1999).

Yi Chong-sik, *Hyŏndae Pukhan-ŭi ihae [Understanding modern North Korea]* (Seoul, Yŏksa pip'yŏng sa, 2002).

Among the books dealing with the different aspects of North Korean life, I should probably mention the following books, with generally self-explanatory titles:

Ha Chong-p'il, *Pukhan-ŭi chonggyo munhwa [Religious culture of North Korea]* (Seoul: Sŏnin, 2005).

Pukhan tosi-ŭi hyŏngsŏng-gwa paljŏn [The formation and development of North Korean city] (Seoul: Hanul, 2004).

Pukhan-ŭi munhak-kwa munye iron [North Korean theory of arts and literature] (Seoul: Tongguk taehkkyo, 2003).

Yim Chae-uk, *Pukhan munhwa-ŭi ihae [Understanding North Korean culture]* (Seoul: Charywon, 2004).

Yu Ho-yŏl, *Pukhan-ŭi sahoejuŭi kŏnsŏl-gwa chwajŏl [The construction and disintegration of socialism in North Korea]* (Seoul: Saenggak-ŭi namu, 2004.)

In regard to prison camps, one should consider this important work of research:

Ichyŏjin irŭmdŭl [Forgotten names] (Seoul: Sidae chŏngsin, 2004). Biographical materials of all persons known to be in North Koreans camps, contains a lot of data on police control and daily life.

The life of the North Korean refugees hiding in China has been an object of many studies. Perhaps as an introduction one might use:

Tumanhang-ŭl kŏnnŏon saramdŭl [The people who crossed the Tumangang river] (Seoul: Chongt'o ch'ulp'an, 1999). A report about the situation of North Korean refugees in China, based on extensive field research.

By far the largest amount of material can be found in the South Korean press, in numerous dailies and weeklies. In this regard the *www.kinds.co.kr* website is of exceptional significance. This is a searchable database, supported by the Korean Press Institute, and it provides access to all materials published in major Korean dailies and weeklies from the early 1990s (alas, the only exception is *Joonang Ilbo,* which happens to publish the best articles on North Korean topics, but it can be searched separately on its own website).

Another important source of information are specialized journals dealing with North Korea and North Korean studies. Such periodicals are quite numerous, but most of them deal with "large" issues of international politics. Among the journals which regularly publish material on daily life and social problems of North Korea, one should mention *Pukhan (North Korea),* *T'ongil Hanguk (Unified Korea)* as well as the highly informative *DailyNK* online daily. Most of the material in the present book was drawn from these periodicals.

My talks to defectors provided a very large part of the material for this book, and my own trips to North Korea, including the most recent, in 2005, were useful as well.

Index

Pakkunton (Foreign Exchange Certificates) 222–224
PAL (TV standard) 58
Paris 82, 266
Party Foundation Day 119
Party Youth see *Saroch'ŏng*
PDS *see* rationing
People of Chagangdo (film) 65–66
People's Daily 55
People's groups *see Inminban*
Petersburg *see* Leningrad
Petronius 328
Pham Ngoc Cane 278, 280
photographing, restrictions of 242
Pirates of the 20th Century (film) 65
pizza 328, 330
playing cards 122
poaching 259
police, North Korean 50, 58, 99, 100, 104, 105, 112, 139, 142, 159, 175, 180–184, 215; raids and inspections 50, 58, 177–179; *see also* police informers; political police
police informers 140, 171–173
political police 99, 104, 105, 170–173, 177–178, 184–189, 191, 208, 210, 243, 251, 285, 290, 296
potatoes 102, 316
Pot'onggang Hotel 138
Pot'onggang river 91, 130
Pravda 54–55
prices: bikes 144; bus tickets 169; chicken 317; grain 227–228, 319; in hard-currency restaurants and shops 93, 104, 222; at markets 108; movie tickets 62; pork 317; refrigerators 250; TV sets 57
prisons and prison camps 30, 50, 144, 171–173, 184–187, 189, 230, 251, 285, 290, 296, 304
private economy *see* black market; merchants
privileges of the elite 69–72, 125, 129, 277, 296–297, 312, 327–330
prostitution 73, 137–140, 288, 326
Protestantism see Christianity
public distribution system *see* rationing
Pundang 301
purges 55, 66–67, 75, 171, 192, 206, 261; see also political police; prison camps
Pusan 164, 274, 304
P'yŏngsŏng 168
Pyongyang 12, 13, 24, 41, 56, 67, 71, 77–95, 98, 99, 101, 105, 109, 110, 112, 118, 121, 134, 146, 154–156, 176, 195, 207–208, 213, 220, 260, 263, 266, 269; bicycles in 141–144; dress 115–117; foreigners 93–94, 139–140, 192, 220–222, 241–246; geography of 93–94; history 44–45, 77–81; monuments of 17, 21, 23, 26, 45, 61, 81–87; privileges of residents 59, 69, 72, 103, 114, 138, 174, 180–183, 229–230, 285, 312; subway 160–164; traffic 112, 144, 151–152; trams 164–166; trolley-buses 166–169
Pyongyang liquor 101
Pyongyang-410 146

racism 278–279
Radio Liberty 49, 310
radio sets 49–50, 52–53, 178, 191, 310–311; fixed tuning 49–50, 52, 53, 191; *see also* broadcast
railroad 23–24, 26, 156–160, 181, 235; Kim Il Sung and Kim Jong Il's trips 60, 105–106; role in private trade 318, 321; workers' uniform 113–114
Rajin-Sonbong Special Economic Zone *see* Rason Special Economic Zone
Rakhmanin Oleg 246
Rakwon Department Store (hard currency) 103, 220–221
Rangoon incident 271–273
Rason Special Economic Zone 231–234
rationing 110, 125 137, 180, 193, 225–226, 227–231, 238, 277; collapse 102, 139, 229, 306–309; grain 14, 74, 175, 227–229, 251; liquor 102; tobacco 107
Red Army Faction, of Japan 299–300
Red Guards 34
Red won *see* Pakkunton
reforms, economic 62, 136, 144, 222, 225, 227, 319
refrigerators 109
refugees in China 262, 286–291; conversion to Christianity 204–205, 208, 290–291; deportation 204–205, 208, 290; impact on the situation in North Korea 310–311; marriage with Chinese 287–289; move to South Korea 289; punishment of 290–291; *see also* defectors
restaurants 62, 90–93, 138–139, 319; North Korean in Seoul 295–296; *see also* Ch'ŏngryugwan; Okryugwan
revolutionary operas 41–43
Rhee Syngman 238